Introduction
to Tourism

Thank you for choosing a SAGE product!
If you have any comment, observation or feedback,
I would like to personally hear from you.

Please write to me at **contactceo@sagepub.in**

Vivek Mehra, Managing Director and CEO, SAGE India.

Bulk Sales

SAGE India offers special discounts
for bulk institutional purchases.

For queries/orders/inspection copy requests,
write to **textbooksales@sagepub.in**

Publishing

Would you like to publish a textbook with SAGE?
Please send your proposal to **publishtextbook@sagepub.in**

Subscribe to our mailing list

Write to marketing@sagepub.in

This book is also available as an e-book.

Introduction to Tourism

Shailja Sharma

*Faculty, Indian Institute of Tourism and Travel Management,
Noida, Uttar Pradesh, India*

Los Angeles | London | New Delhi
Singapore | Washington DC | Melbourne

First published in 2021 by

⑤SAGE | TEXTS

SAGE Publications India Pvt Ltd
B1/I-1 Mohan Cooperative Industrial Area
Mathura Road, New Delhi 110 044, India
www.sagepub.in

SAGE Publications Inc
2455 Teller Road
Thousand Oaks, California 91320, USA

SAGE Publications Ltd
1 Oliver's Yard, 55 City Road
London EC1Y 1SP, United Kingdom

SAGE Publications Asia-Pacific Pte Ltd
18 Cross Street #10-10/11/12
China Square Central
Singapore 048423

Published by Vivek Mehra for SAGE Publications India Pvt Ltd. Typeset in 11/13 pt Garamond by Zaza Eunice, Hosur, Tamil Nadu, India.

Library of Congress Cataloging-in-Publication Data

Names: Sharma, Shailja, author.
Title: Introduction to tourism/Shailja Sharma.
Description: Thousand Oaks, California; New Delhi, India: SAGE Texts, an
    imprint of SAGE Publishing, 2020. | Includes bibliographical references
    and index.
Identifiers: LCCN 2020034940 | ISBN 9789353885106 (Paperback) | ISBN
    9789353885120 (ePub) | ISBN 9789353885113 (eBook)
Subjects: LCSH: Tourism.
Classification: LCC G155.A1 S474 2021 | DDC 338.4/791—dc23
LC record available at https://lccn.loc.gov/2020034940

ISBN: 978-93-5388-510-6 (PB)

SAGE Team: Amit Kumar, Indrani Dutta, Shruti Gupta, Aishna Bhatt and Rajinder Kaur

Contents

SECTION A: THE BUILDING BLOCKS OF TOURISM

SECTION B: LIFELINES OF TOURISM BUSINESS

DETAILED CONTENTS

SECTION A: THE BUILDING BLOCKS OF TOURISM

SECTION B: LIFELINES OF TOURISM BUSINESS

SECTION C: THE TRENDING HOLIDAYING

LIST OF ABBREVIATIONS

ADTOI	Adventure Tour Operators Association of India
AI	Artificial intelligence
AMEX	American Express
ASI	Archaeological Survey of India
ATOAI	Adventure Tour Operators Association of India
B&B	Bed and breakfast
B2B	Business-to-business
BTQ	Basic travel quota
CBD	Central Business District
CDC	Continuous Discharge Certificate
CFAR	Cancel for Any Reason
CPV	Consular Passport and Visa
CRS	Computer reservation systems
DMO	Destination management organizations
DNP	Department of National Parks
DSLR	Digital single-lens reflex
ETA	Electronic travel authorization
eTV	e-tourist visa
F&B	Food and beverage
FAITH	Federation of Associations in Indian Tourism and Hospitality
FDI	Foreign direct investment
FERA	Foreign Exchange Regulation Act
FHRAI	Federation of Hotel & Restaurant Associations of India
FIT	Free independent traveller
FRO	Foreigner's Registration Office
FRRO	Foreigners Regional Registration Office
FSCs	Full-service carriers
FTAs	Foreign tourist arrivals
GDP	Gross domestic product
GIT	Group inclusive travel
GPS	Global positioning system
HAI	Hotel Association of India

HOHO	Hop-on Hop-off
HRIDAY	Heritage City Development and Augmentation Yojana
IATA	International Air Transport Association
IATO	Indian Association of Tour Operators
ICAO	International Civil Aviation Organization
ICOMOS	International Council on Monuments and Sites
ICPB	India Convention Promotion Bureau
IHHA	Indian Heritage Hotels Association
IITTM	Indian Institute of Tourism and Travel Management
ILO	International Labour Organization
IMF	International Monetary Fund
INTACH	Indian National Trust for Art and Cultural Heritage
IOT	Internet of Things
IPL	Indian Premier League
IRCTC	Indian Railway Catering and Tourism Corporation
IT	Information technology
ITTA	Indian Tourist Transporters Association
J&K	Jammu and Kashmir
JKTDC	Jammu & Kashmir Tourism Development Corporation
KTDC	Kerala Tourism Development Corporation
LCCs	Low-cost carriers
LGBTQ	Lesbian, gay, bisexual, transgender and queer
LTPC	Le Passage to India
MEA	Ministry of the External Affairs
MICE	Meetings, incentives, conferences and exhibitions
MNCs	Multinational corporations
MOT	Ministry of Tourism
MPSTDC	Madhya Pradesh Tourism Development Corporation
MTR	Mass transit railway
NET	National Eligibility Test
NGOs	Non-governmental organizations
NTA	National tourism authority
NTOs	National tourism organizations
OTAs	Online travel agencies
PATA	Pacific Asia Travel Association
PPP	Public–private partnership
PRASHAD	Pilgrimage Rejuvenation and Spiritual, Heritage Augmentation Drive
PSDS	Public service delivery system
PTHPB	Punjab Tourism and Heritage Promotion Board
RBI	Reserve Bank of India
RPOs	Regional Passport Offices

RTOs	Regional tourism organizations
SDGs	Sustainable Development Goals
SIC	Seat-in-coach
SIT	Special interest travellers
SMEs	Small- and medium-sized enterprises
STDC	State tourism development corporations
TAAI	Travel Agents Association of India
TAFI	Travel Agents Federation of India
TCGL	Tourism Corporation of Gujarat Limited
TRT	Tax Refund for International Tourists
TVOA	Tourist visa on arrival
UGC	University Grants Commission
UN	United Nations
UNESCO	United Nations Educational, Scientific and Cultural Organization
UNWTO	United Nations World Tourism Organization
USP	Unique selling proposition
VFS	Visa Facilitation Services
VOA	Visa on arrival
WFTGA	World Federation of Tour Guides Association
WHO	World Health Organization
WTM	World Travel Mart/World Travel Market
WTO	World Trade Organization

LIST OF CASE STUDIES

PREFACE

We are living in an era of tourism. The new decade belongs to the new millennials for whom travelling is a way of life. As the appetite for travelling among young-sters is increasing day by day with travel becoming a way of life for many, the tourism industry has reached its zenith like never before.

The habits of new-age travellers, who are constantly travelling to add another feather to their travel hat, have changed evidently. These travellers are on a continuous journey of filling their bucket list with all the wonderful destinations of the world.

Tourism is increasingly being seen as the window to the world. It is all about building new human connections and newer perspectives. Tourism for the travellers is a way to explore the pristine corners of the world, experience rare encounters, create personalized itineraries, go for self-guided trips and create exclusive and lifetime memories.

The tourism industry is experiencing a massive transformation due to the increasing popu-lation of people choosing to travel due to an upsurge in the middle class with rising disposable incomes, more leisure time in hand, more interesting travel options at reasonable prices and more eased-out government regulations related to travel.

The travel and tourism industry has a significant role in the global economy and commu-nity. Tourism is seen as an important source of foreign exchange, which can turn around the economies of the world. Thus, many destinations of the world depend upon tourism for sustaining their economies.

In the world of cut-throat competition, where every destination is fighting for its lion share, the only way to woo the tourists is to have a clear differentiated offering by a country along with the positioning of the product in the right way using all the sources of media. A global traveller seeking a novel experience every time has pushed the buttons of the tourism industry service providers to add an experiential element to each tourism product being offered.

India has also joined the bandwagon of nations in increasing the influx of tourists in the nation. As India envisioned to increase its current share of 0.5 per cent international tourist arrivals in the world to 1 per cent in 2020 and to 2 per cent in 2025, with a target of having 20 million foreign tourist arrivals in 2020, the outbreak of the COVID-19 pandemic has adversely affected the tourist arrivals and now poses a major challenge not only to India but also the whole world. The current situation seems to be very grim at least for one more year till a vaccination for the pandemic is introduced that may spur the movement of tourists to normalcy again.

Some of the trending niche tourism products that India has in its basket to offer to the world include wellness tourism (Ayurveda, Yoga, Unani, siddha and naturopathy), medical tourism, MICE (meetings, incentives, conferences and exhibitions) tourism, adventure tourism, film tourism, rural tourism, ecotourism and cruise tourism. Along with the inbound tourism, there is a lot of focus on increasing the footfall of domestic tourists within the country. In fact, domestic tourism is thriving in the country, with travellers visiting destinations for pilgrimage, seeking adventure, visiting friends and relatives, doing business and so on.

Given the above facts, where tourism is seen as a torchbearer for the country's economy as well as its local communities, it is high time that we acknowledge and give due importance to this sector and create a pool of able and qualified human resources to plan and manage this tourism sector. Therefore, this book has been written to reinstate the importance of tourism in the student community and introduce this subject both as an academic discipline and as an industry option that can assure bright and promising career avenues for the students.

ACKNOWLEDGEMENTS

This book is very special to me as this subject is very close to my heart. It is an outcome of several personal travel experiences, my teaching experience and people who have come into my life to inspire me.

Over the years as I taught, I realized the dire need for an easy-to-understand text that would familiarize students and teachers with the evolving trends in the tourism industry. So if you aspire to make a career in tourism or are a teacher looking to deliver effective teaching in a more engaging and an informative way, this book is for you.

I would begin by thanking the one and only 'Almighty' who kindled in me the writing spirit and graced me with the gift of words. Thank you God for giving me the energy and discipline to accomplish this piece of work. I am eternally indebted to you.

Heartfelt thanks to my publisher, SAGE, for believing in my work. I am especially grateful to my editor Amit for his encouragement and guidance.

My sincere thanks to thousands of readers of my earlier book with SAGE—you enthused me to write this one.

My deepest gratitude to my husband Sorabh, who has been my rock and pillar, my constant in both travel and life. Travelling with him across the globe gave me tremendous exposure and useful insights into the exciting world of tourism. Each trip helped me add real-time experiences and examples that I am sure will speak to those reading the book.

Sorabh listened to my early drafts, pepped me along when I slackened and helped me in taking care of our little munchkin so I could devote my time to the book. My precious jewel and my lucky charm, my daughter Sayesha, came into my life while I was writing this book. Thank you, little one, for your patience even when you needed me to nurse and hold you.

My parents have bestowed on me the gift of their blessings, positivity and most importantly their invincible faith in me. Mom, your words of encouragement worked like capsules of energy that kept me going!

My sisters and my niece Atishaya, Atima and my nephew Vihaan—I am so fortunate to have your unconditional love.

I would also like to express my sincere gratitude towards my friend Shubra for continuously inspiring me and pushing me to write and nudging me to complete the book on time.

Last but not least, I would also like to thank my students, whose love and affection are my greatest treasure that I have earned over the years. It is their belief in me that motivates me to share what I know on these pages.

ABOUT THE AUTHOR

 **Shailja Sharma,** BBA (Management), MBA (Marketing), MTM, PhD, UGC (NET and JRF), is currently working as an Assistant Professor at the Indian Institute of Tourism and Travel Management (IITTM), an autonomous body under the Ministry of Tourism, Government of India. She has been the chairperson for the BBA (Tourism and Travel) programme for the Noida campus during 2015–2018 besides handling various other administrative assignments and portfolios since 2007.

She has a total of 15 years of experience with 13 years of experience in teaching and training in tourism and 2 years of corporate experience. She has extensively taught more than 3,000 students at IITTM, Delhi, and IITTM, Noida, in various programmes such as Postgraduate Diploma in Management (Tourism and Leisure), MBA (Tourism and Travel) and BBA (Tourism and Travel) besides being invited to deliver lectures in different universities of India. Her teaching interests include tourism concepts and practices, tour leadership management, tour guiding, marketing in tourism and human resource management in tourism. She has also been instrumental in introducing activity-oriented teaching pedagogy at IITTM, Noida.

She has trained over 1,500 tour guides and tour leaders. She is a qualified trainer of the World Federation of Tourist Guide Association from London. She has designed and delivered various tour leadership programmes for travel corporates along with various tour guiding and leadership programmes for various state governments. Besides these; she has designed and delivered more than 35 training programmes for a range of stakeholders in the tourism industry, which include tourist information officers, senior government officials posted in state tourism departments, cab drivers, travel agents, army personnel and so on. She has also been actively involved in community projects such as the Swachh Bharat Abhiyan.

She has a PhD in tour guiding and has published research papers in various reputed journals. She has also been associated with research projects with the Ministry of Tourism, Government of India, and Indian Council of Social Science Research. She has travelled extensively across 5 continents to 22 countries to gain an international experience and earn an insight into tourism management and its latest practices. In 2018, her co-authored title *Tour Leadership and Management* was published by SAGE, India. In 2014, she also co-authored the title *A Textbook of Travel and Tourism for Class IX* based on the guidelines given by National Vocational Education Qualification Framework and the syllabi prescribed by CBSE. She has also been actively involved in the making of 'Fundamental Glossary for Tourism' by the Commission of Scientific & Technical Terminology, Ministry of Human Resource Development, Government of India.

ABOUT THE BOOK

As tourism across the world is burgeoning like never before, the need for tourism professionals is ever increasing. Tourism is being increasingly seen as an important academic discipline where a strong need is felt to train the young aspirants who are well aware about the intricacies and the working of the travel trade. Thus, it becomes imperative for the tourism professionals to have a thorough understanding of the basic concepts and principles of tourism on which this industry operates. Generally, the leaders of the tourism industry complain that the textbooks on tourism do not address students from the industry's perspective and students thus lack the required knowledge expected of them to work in the industry. Thus, this book has been written keeping in mind the need for both theory from academic perspective and blending the theory with the practical aspects as expected by the industry leaders so that the students know and are well prepared to handle the dynamics of the industry before they start working for it. Thus, the author has tried to approach the book from a practical perspective in order to bridge the gap between the industry requirements and academic inputs. If the readers would thoroughly go through the content of the book, their understanding of tourism business would be quintessential.

Introduction to Tourism is a window to the world of tourism. It is a stepping stone for beginners who may be pursuing a postgraduation degree or undergraduation degree or diploma or certificate course in tourism or undergoing any kind of training in tourism. It has been conceived with a well-defined structure for anyone who aspires to make a career in the travel and tourism industry. This book has been written keeping in mind beginners who are new in the industry and have little or no knowledge about tourism. This book is also essential for thousands of those readers across the world who want to know more about the tourism sector.

This book will begin with building the basic concepts of the theory of tourism and applying the theory in the travel trade. It shall focus on the core aspects of tourism while also feeding the minds of readers from time to time about the emerging trends in tourism.

Various situational case studies have been introduced within the book to create awareness among the students about the kind of situations the tourists may face during travel while also encouraging the students to suggest ways to deal with those situations. Many successful destination cases have also been incorporated in the book to enlighten the readers about how the tourism boards of various countries are devising various marketing strategies to offset the competition posed by other destinations of the world. Also, various interesting facts about destinations and enticing tourism products from different parts of the world have been added in the book under various boxes, which would be small tourism capsules for sharpening the acumen of the students. All the real examples shared would add to the practicality of the book.

The book has been broadly divided into five sections. Each section has a well-defined plan and will gradually make a paradigm shift from basic concepts to more practical aspects of tourism. The first section of the book essentially deals with introducing the students to the basic concepts of tourism. The students will be introduced to the meaning of tourism along with some terms used in tourism as well as with the motivations for tourism, types of tourism, types of travellers, components of tourism, tourism resources, tourism products and a discussion on positive and negative impacts of tourism. The second section focuses on various components of tourism that are basically the 5 A's in the tourism industry, which include attractions, accessibility, accommodation (and alternative forms of accommodation), amenities and activities. This will be followed by the next section that primarily deals with trending holidaying. This section is more application-based and focuses on the practical aspect of tourism and the preparation required to visit a destination. It starts with a discussion on planning a vacation followed by travel stages, travel formalities, travel stress and pre-departure checklist. The fourth section gives useful insights into the experience facilitators of the tourism industry, who are necessarily involved in the delivery of tourism services to the tourists. This will start with a discussion on introducing the students to various touch points of the tourism industry, followed by an elaborate discussion on each role of the tourism service providers that may include the travel intermediaries, tour leaders, tour guides, cab drivers and role of government in promoting tourism. The last section of the book focuses on the challenges faced by the tourism industry and the opportunities that it holds for the future. It includes chapters on handling emergency situations, obstacles and threats in tourism, emerging trends in the tourism industry, career opportunities in tourism with the final discussion on overtourism and how to be a responsible tourist.

Overall, the book will bring fresh perspectives to the students and help them understand the significance of this discipline.

The book has been written in simple language which is easy to understand and has easy-to-digest content so that the readers can logically connect. This book would be a guiding light for all those who want to understand what this tourism industry is all about.

SECTION

THE BUILDING BLOCKS OF TOURISM

This section introduces readers to the basic concepts of the tourism industry. It focuses on introducing the learners to the meaning of tourism, the various terms commonly used in tourism and the facilitators that have led to the growth of tourism. It orients the learners on the reasons that motivate a person to travel. The section starts with a discussion about the types of tourism and various approaches towards tourism being currently practised. It also elucidates the various niche tourism products being offered by various destinations of the world. The readers are then introduced to the various components of tourism that are dependent on each other for the functioning of the tourism industry followed by defining tourism resources, and how they may be converted into a tourism product along with a discussion on the characteristics of tourism products. This is followed by a detailed discussion on the types of tourism markets that are emerging or being currently served by the tour operators, and a discussion on the new-age traveller and his/her characteristics that define him/her and differentiate him/her from the conventional traveller. The last two chapters in this section introduce the readers to both the positive and negative impacts of tourism. In short, the first section focuses on introducing the basic concepts of tourism to the readers.

At the end of each chapter, there are activities related to the chapter, which students may practise in their classrooms. Also, every chapter has interesting information for students to know, organized in boxes that the students are advised to read to increase their knowledge of tourism. After the completion of chapters in the section, there are certain case studies related to the section for the students to read, comprehend and analyse, followed by questions to be answered.

After going through the section, the students would know the following:

- What is tourism?
- What are the purposes of travelling to a destination?
- What are the various types of tourism and approaches to tourism?
- What are the emerging niche tourism products being offered by destinations?
- What are the various components of the tourism industry?
- What is a tourism resource, and how can it be converted into a tourism product?
- What are the types of travel markets served by the tourism industry?
- Who is a new-age traveller, and what are his/her characteristics?
- What are the positive and negative impacts of tourism?

So let us make a new beginning! Welcome to a new world of learning, dear learners. Let us start our journey, building our basic concepts about the tourism sector!
Happy learning!

What Is Tourism?

1

LEARNING OBJECTIVES

The given chapter shall clarify the following:

- What is tourism? What is the nature of tourism?
- What are the terms used in tourism, and what are its forms?
- What is tourism demand, and what are the factors that have led to the growth in tourism demand?
- What is the position of tourism in India?

FAROE ISLANDS! AN OUT-OF-THE-BOX TOURISM CAMPAIGN

- Do you want to control the moves of a Faroe Islander sitting on your chair at home?
- Welcome to one-of-its-own kind tourism campaign that allows you to be a virtual tourist! Using a mobile, personal computer or a tablet (used as joypads), you can interact with a local on a virtual exploratory tour from any part of the world.
- The remote island nation (18-island archipelago) between Iceland and Norway is a home to 80,000 sheep with only 53,000 inhabitants.
- For all those stuck in self-quarantine during the coronavirus epidemic, the Faroe Islands has launched this new tourism marketing campaign that offers the remote viewers to explore the island through the eyes of its locals.
- The virtual tourists may control the Faroe Islander to explore locations on foot or take helicopter rides.

- The virtual tour begins at new locations once in a day.
- Leading by example, the Faroe Islands shuts down once for the tourists every year. However, those who volunteer to clean the coastline are allowed to stay.

INTRODUCTION

Tourism and travel have become the buzzwords of the 21st century. Every individual seeks a change from his/her routine. Everyone is now gaga over vacationing and wants to experience travel. Everybody's idea of vacation may be different. Some may seek active vacations packed with activities, whereas some may seek passive vacations. Some may like lounging for days on a beach and thus may plan a beach holiday like visiting the *Mediterranean Coast* or *Caribbean Islands*, while some may think of going in for outdoor adventures like mountain *climbing in the Himalayas, surfing in Hawaii* or hiking around *Crater Lake National Park in Oregon* to witness one of the natural wonders of the world. Still, some may travel for rejuvenation of their mind and body like indulging in a massage in Kerala. Yet some may travel to learn *baking in Paris*, while some may wish to try the gastronomical delights of a destination, especially the local authentic delicacies, on a food tour like visiting *Chandni Chowk in Old Delhi, India*. While some may like to explore the heritage of a city on foot, some may travel in pursuit of excitement and entertainment. Some may travel to meet their friends and relatives, while some may travel out of culture curiosity to understand the cross-cultural differences between countries. Still, others may travel for business or medical reasons. Although the reasons for travel may have increased manifold, the fact that remains is that people are always on the move. Tourism activity is always pertinent.

UNDERSTANDING TOURISM

The concept of tourism has undergone massive transformation. It has constantly evolved over decades. From the basic need of a person to travel in order to survive so that he/she could fetch himself/herself food and shelter to travelling for doing business or for religious purpose, man has always been an inveterate traveller.

This industry has evolved faster than ever before. It has grown exponentially. Today, it is one of the most booming and the fastest growing service industries of the world. This fun activity is a great business opportunity today. The tourism industry has been recognized as one of the world's game changers of many economies due to the economic benefits that it accrues for the society as it brings a large amount of income and foreign exchange to the local economy of a nation. In other words, many economies of the world are driven by the tourism sector.

Realizing the importance of tourism for revenue generation and creation of job opportunities for the people of a country, countries are increasingly offering varied tourism products with *unique selling propositions (USPs)* to attract more and more tourists. They are exploring all kinds of possibilities to increase the footfall of tourists to a destination. Certain countries of the world that are rich in natural beauty such as *Scotland, New Zealand* and *Thailand* are using their natural resources to attract the tourists, whereas countries such as *Singapore* and *Dubai* that had no natural tourism resources but had a right orientation towards tourism have developed artificial tourism products like super structures such as the Burj Khalifa in Dubai and Marina Bay Sands in Singapore to attract tourists. Yet many high-income countries are promoting and positioning themselves in different ways as business tourism destinations or medical tourism destinations so as to woo tourists.

Given the massive impact that tourism has on a country's economy besides the sociocultural and environmental impacts, we need to understand in depth the meaning of tourism. So, what is tourism? Let us deliberate on the same.

The tourism industry may also be referred to as the travel industry. In simple words, tourism is travelling to another place for seeking pleasure during one's leisure time. It is about visiting a new destination to have fun. It involves the movement of people from one place to another along with the services they require during their travel.

In fact, now, tourism is not just confined to visiting and seeing a destination, but it is also about living the spirit of a destination. New tourism is all about cultural immersion. It is more about gaining first-hand authentic experience at a destination from a local's perspective. It may be in the form of experiencing local life at the destination by walking along streets, venturing into local markets, trying the regional cuisines, staying with the host community, cooking, singing and dancing with them, and participating in their local events and festivals. In short, tourism is one of the most interesting and exciting activities that lets people move out of their routine lives to experience something new.

The 4 Es of tourism, that is, it is ephemeral, existential, experimental and experiential, may essentially capture the essence of new tourism now. In other words, it is a multi-sensory, 360-degree experience for the travellers. It is a temporary phenomenon where a traveller wants to experiment and experience new things at a destination. It is important for his/her existence. The new age belongs to the 'experiential traveller' who wants to experience new things while travelling.

Although there are many definitions of tourism, one of the most universally accepted definitions has been given by the United Nations World Tourism Organization (UNWTO, a leading international body for tourism) that says:

Tourism comprises the activities of persons travelling to staying in places outside their usual environment for not more than one consecutive year for leisure, business and other purposes.

However, we may also study the following definition given by Mathieson and Wall in 1982 for the sake of more clarity:

Tourism is the temporary movement of people to destinations outside their normal places of work and residence, the activities undertaken during their stay in those destinations and the facilities created to cater to their needs.

Based on the above definitions of tourism, we may identify the following characteristics of tourism that have been discussed under the following heading.

NATURE OF TOURISM

- Tourism is a phenomenon of spending time away from one's home. It is a short-term movement of people to destinations away from one's residence. The idea is to move out of one's routine social environment.
- It is a temporary phenomenon. It cannot go on and on.
- Once leaving home, the person who wants to qualify as a tourist must have the intention of coming back home. He/she must not plan to settle in that destination permanently.
- Time is an important element to qualify as a tourist. The traveller must visit a place outside his/her domicile for not less than 24 hours and not more than a year.
- The main purpose of travel may be relaxation, recreation and pleasure besides travel for business or any other purpose that may include a visit to a destination for a medical treatment/to understand the ecosystems of a destination/for pilgrimage/ for watching sports/to offer voluntary services and so on.
- Tourism should be practised for non-financial purposes. Any person aiming to earn remuneration during his/her travel may not be qualified to be called a tourist.
- In the process of travelling, the tourist would make use of commercial tourism services. Thus, it involves the provision of services to the tourist by the tourism service providers.
- One may travel to either domestic or international locations.
- The idea is to keep the tourists happy and occupied during travel.

CONCEPTS AND TERMS

Before we proceed further, it is important for us to have an understanding of the basic aspects of tourism and the differences between the terms. Let us begin our discussion.

Traveller

All forms of tourism include travel, but every travel may not necessarily be considered tourism. In other words, travel is a significant component of tourism. But a person may not necessarily travel to experience tourism. He/she may travel in his/her city to go to work. Thus, to be a traveller, the only criterion is that one should be moving from one place to another that may range from a few kilometres to a few hundred kilometres.

Visitor

Any person who travels outside of his/her residence to another place with the intention of coming back home is referred to as a visitor. Further, visitors may be classified as tourists and excursionists.

Tourist

Any visitor who visits an area temporarily to stay there with the intention of coming back home, for at least 24 hours and not more than a year, for leisure, business or any other purpose may be referred to as a tourist. A tourist may visit a destination for fun and relaxation. Besides the above-mentioned reasons, many tourists visit a destination for business purposes or any other purpose such as medical reasons and playing sports.

Here, we may broadly classify the tourists into the following three types.

Leisure Tourists

Tourists who travel to have fun and relax at a destination are called leisure tourists. For example, a tourist visiting a destination for seeing an attraction such as the *Leaning Tower of Pisa* and *Colosseum in Italy*, indulging in a spa, visiting a beach, trying adventure sports/attending a music concert or a sports event and so on may be categorized as a leisure tourist.

Business Tourists

Tourists who visit a destination for attending a business meeting or go on an incentive trip to a destination or sometimes visit a destination to attend a conference or an exhibition are called business tourists.

The Leaning Tower of Pisa, Italy

The Colosseum, Rome, Italy

Bleisure Tourists

The new millennials or Generation Z are the new bleisure tourists. When business tourists combine their work with leisure travel, they may be referred to as bleisure tourists. Such tourists may like to extend their business trips to include more leisure time. They may like to explore the city being visited, enjoy the local food in the local restaurants there, discover new attractions or indulge in the activities that the destination may be famous for after they complete their work assignments.

Excursionists

A traveller who visits an area or a destination for less than 24 hours and comes back on the same day without staying there is referred to as an excursionist. For example, a person leaving from Delhi, India, in the morning for Agra, India, to see the Taj Mahal (one of the seven wonders of the world and the most iconic structure of the country) and comes back to Delhi on the same day in the evening may be referred to as an excursionist. If the same person makes an overnight stay in Agra and returns to Delhi on the next day, he/she may be qualified to be called a tourist. Excursionists may also be referred to as *day-trippers*.

Transient/Transit Visitor

A visitor who passes by a destination that may be a city or a country by virtue of his/her transportation connections or a layover without staying in that country or destination visited is referred to as a transit visitor. He/she may have to stay in that place for some hours to catch his/her next connecting means of transportation like a flight. However, to stay in a place in transit for more time and explore the country during transit, the traveller has to take a transit visa from the immigration authorities of that country.

FORMS OF TOURISM

There are different forms of tourism on the basis of which the tourists may be classified. Let us have a detailed discussion on each of the forms of tourism.

Outbound Tourism

The phenomenon of leaving one's own country to travel to another country is referred to as outbound tourism. For example, if Sayeesha, an Indian traveller, visits Switzerland to see the snow-capped Alps, she is an outbound tourist for India.

Inbound Tourism

The phenomenon of tourists coming from other countries to one's own country is referred to as inbound tourism for one's own country. For example, when Joe from the USA visits India, he is an inbound tourist for India.

Domestic Tourism

The phenomenon of tourists travelling within the geographical boundary of their home country is referred to as domestic tourism. For example, when Praveen Patel travels from Gujarat to Himachal Pradesh in India to experience snow in the winters, he is promoting domestic travel within the country.

Domestic tourism is seen as a yardstick for the developing nations as it supports opportunities by spreading development and regional economic benefits besides building national pride.

The above-mentioned classification further leads to the following concepts.

International Tourism

It refers to the tourism that includes both inbound and outbound tourism of a country at a given time. Tourism that emanates from the crossing of international borders may be referred to as international tourism.

National Tourism

It includes the movement or travel of nationals of a particular country. Thus, we may say that national tourism includes both outbound tourism (when the nationals travel abroad) and domestic tourism (when the nationals travel within their own country).

Internal Tourism

The phenomenon that includes travel within the geographical boundaries of a nation that may include both inbound tourism (foreign tourists visiting one's own country) and domestic tourism (nationals travelling within their own country) is referred to as internal tourism.

Inter-regional Tourism

UNWTO has divided the world into five regions that include Asia and the Pacific, Africa, America, Middle East and Europe. The phenomenon of travelling from one region to another region as specified by UNWTO is referred to as inter-regional tourism. For example, if a tourist is travelling from Spain to India (Europe region to the Asia region and the Pacific) or from the USA to South Africa (America region to Africa region), he/she is practising inter-regional tourism.

Intra-regional Tourism

When tourists travel to different nations within the same region as specified by UNWTO, the movement is referred to as intra-regional tourism. For example, a tourist travelling from Singapore (Asia region and the Pacific) to Indonesia (Asia region and the Pacific) or a tourist travelling from the Netherlands (Europe) to Italy (Europe) is practising intra-regional tourism as the movement is taking place in the same region as mentioned by UNWTO.

TOURISM DEMAND

Tourism demand is increasing day by day. People not just wish to travel but they are also ready to pay any amount to seek a novel travel experience. When travellers are willing to visit destinations and see the world by paying an amount for it, the phenomenon may be referred to as tourism demand.

FACILITATORS OF TOURISM DEMAND

There are many factors that have contributed to the growth of tourism demand. In other words, these may also be referred to as facilitators of travel. Now, let us have a detailed discussion on each of the following facilitators of travel that have given an impetus to the tourism industry across the world.

Easy Mobility

Travelling has become much easier now. With the advent of better and safer modes of transportation with wider options, better accessibility to destinations that may be via air, road or sea and with advancement of technology, distances have shortened now. Travel time has also reduced, making travel more convenient and faster for travellers.

Today's traveller has more transportation choices such as airlines, railways, buses, coaches, taxis, cruise liners, ferries, motor cars on rent and other means of public transportation that have made travelling much easier now.

Further, the construction of infrastructure such as roads, highways, airports, railway lines, railway stations and seaports in different destinations has facilitated better connectivity between the destinations. As a result, more and more people are travelling now.

For example, *Shirdi (the holy place of Lord Sai Baba) in Maharashtra, India,* attracts lakhs of devotees not only from India but also from other countries. However, accessibility to this town had always been difficult as there were no direct trains or any airport through which the tourists could directly reach this holy place. However, recently, in October 2017, the government opened an airport for passengers, which has made the accessibility of this place much easier now.

Affordability

Travel is more affordable now. With the proliferation of domestic airlines that are primarily *low-cost carriers* (LCCs that are budget airlines with no frills), flight rates have reduced drastically, making domestic travel more pocket-friendly for the tourists, thus making them travel more and more. In fact, many budgeted international airlines like *Air Asia* that offer lower fares for travelling abroad have also been introduced, which has further facilitated international travel on a massive scale. Many other international airlines have slashed their airfares to make air travel more accessible for travellers. Even many domestic airlines have started international operations that offer lower flight rates for various destinations.

Also, like never before, there are more variants of accommodation options available for all kinds of travellers, especially the budget travellers—homestays, apartments, couch surfing and work away—have made the stay of the tourists more affordable, leading to more travel and tourism. To encourage tourism by governments of different nations, many subsidies are being offered to the new accommodation set-ups that have led to the mushrooming of a number of hotels, hostels, guest houses and so on. The facility of **AirBnB** (explained in Chapter 29) has further made accommodation more widely available and more economical within almost every traveller's reach.

In fact, many travel companies are selling package tours with lucrative offers and schemes to attract different segments of tourists, which has made travel more affordable and easier for the tourists.

Even if one cannot afford to travel, the tourists can get their trips financed. Banks easily give personal loans to travellers for travelling abroad or within one's own country, facilitating travel for the tourists.

New Tourism Products

To cater to a broader segment of tourists, the tourism departments and boards, various tour operators and travel agencies keep identifying, innovating and developing new tourism products to quench the appetite of the hungry tourists. The government authorities are increasingly becoming conscious about the changing needs and preferences of the tourists and, thus, are adding unique and differentiated tourism offerings to the portfolio of destinations. New destinations are being identified, tourism circuits are being promoted and there is a lot of focus on developing infrastructure and superstructure for tourism. New attractions like artificial superstructures such as the *Miracle Garden in Dubai* and *the Statue of Unity and the Children Nutrition Park in Kevadia, Gujarat* are being developed to woo more tourists. In fact, many travel companies are coming up with cookie-cutter itineraries and new experiences to attract more tourists such as *Segway tours, ghost tours* and *literary tours*.

Effect of Media

The social media has created an aspirational lifestyle for travelling among youngsters in the world. As a result, the last decade has witnessed a phenomenal change in travel. Suddenly, travel and tourism has become a rage. People have become more enthusiastic about travel now. Awareness towards travel has increased among people, especially due to power of the Internet, social media and travel channels introduced on television. People are highly inspired by thrilling experiences and accounts of travellers on social media. As they say, 'seeing is believing'. Thus, when people see posts like pictures, videos or a travel blog of different places shared by their friends on Facebook or Instagram or view the videos of travellers on YouTube, they are also motivated to travel in expectation of a similar travel experience. Further, the various travel-related programmes broadcasted on travel channels and movies which show various international destinations in the backdrop also entice the potential travellers to visit those destinations. For example, *Croatia* and *North Ireland* became famous destinations after the television series *Game of Thrones* was shot there.

Use of Technology

Technology has absolutely revolutionized the tourism industry. The use of the Internet has revamped the tourism sector. *Smart tourism* is the new buzzword. It has deeply affected the psyche of the new-age travellers. Their travel needs and preferences are largely influenced by the world of the Internet, where everybody is sharing their travel stories. Tourism businesses are also to a larger extent driven by technology. The conventional 'mom and pop' travel agencies have been replaced by online travel portals. As the tourism business models have gone online, the customer has the ease of making his/her travel reservations at any point of time without anyone's intervention. In fact, many tourism businesses are well connected and integrated through this Internet technology. A number of tourism businesses such as hotels, transportation and travel agencies are increasingly using social media to market the various destinations and their services. In fact, every country has its own tourism website or travel app (application) to help the tourists plan their visit to the destination.

Flexible Government Policies

Most of the countries in the world have eased the barriers of documentation to increase the visits of tourists. The visa rules have been relaxed in many countries and further to encourage and boost more travel, the *visa on arrival (VOA)* facility has been introduced by many countries of the world. India has also introduced the VOA facility (with certain terms and conditions) for foreigners, making the travel procedures much easier, quicker and convenient for them. However, it is important to know that the rules for getting a VOA may vary from country to country.

Presence of Foreign Tourism Offices

The tourism authority of almost every country that wants to promote its tourism is opening its marketing offices in international markets which are a source of tourism for that country. For example, in India, many foreign tourism boards are opening up that are enticing Indians with various offers and incentives to encourage outbound tourism from India.

Strong Marketing Efforts by Tourism Service Providers

The dynamics of tourism marketing have changed now. Chasing the traveller with constant 'destination teasers' is the new trend. All service providers of the tourism industry, whether it is airlines, hotels, travel agents/tour operators, cultural and entertainment organizations or tourism authorities at local, regional and national levels, are aggressively finding creative ways to attract the tourist to their destination. These may include launching unique marketing campaigns; making a strong presence on print, electronic and social media; posting of testimonials by travelled passengers and opinion leaders on websites; using brand ambassadors to promote a destination; offering familiarization trips to media/tour operators; participating in international and national tourism events; organizing tourism events; bombarding the traveller with information on websites; or introducing travel apps.

The idea of destination marketers and other tourism service providers making consistent marketing efforts is to ultimately create a strong image of a destination in the mind of the prospective traveller. For example, *Turkey promotes itself as a thermal tourism destination, while New Zealand promotes itself as '100 per cent pure' and a destination for 'adventure seekers' and Bhutan sells happiness as its USP with its tagline 'happiness is a place'.*

Many websites of the destinations run by the tourism authorities or travel companies and review sites like *Tripadvisor* have every information for the discerning traveller that he/she may be looking for. They may give self-explanatory information about how to reach that destination, how to travel within, the famous itineraries that may be followed, the kind of accommodations to stay in, the must-visit restaurants to try food in and many other pieces of information that build the confidence of the traveller to travel to that destination. Thus, the websites act as a marketing tool in promoting a destination to the traveller.

Marketing may not only be done by the tourism authorities or the travel companies and other stakeholders of a destination but also by the already-travelled passengers themselves, sometimes knowingly and sometimes unknowingly. Sometimes, the tourism authorities or travel companies may ask such tourists to leave their testimonials (their travel experiences) on their websites in order to increase the popularity of their travel services among other travellers. Otherwise, many travellers may also leave their reviews on various review sites like Tripadvisor that may influence the destination and the tour operator choice of potential travellers. In an era of social networking, generally, travellers also keep posting their pictures/writing blogs/sharing their travel stories/ posting vlogs on YouTube with others, which act as a marketing tool for both the destination and the travel company (if the travelled passenger has taken a package tour). This further influences others to travel to the same destination and through the same travel company.

Thus, the combined marketing efforts by tourism service providers and the travelled passengers help in increasing the tourist traffic in a country.

Mushrooming of Tourism Businesses

With the growing interest of travellers to visit destinations, a number of tourism businesses, especially small- and medium-sized enterprises (SMEs), such as travel agents, tour operators and other service providers such as airlines, hotels, resorts and entertainment organizations like theme parks, have evolved that are aggressively offering lucrative travel packages and promoting various destinations using varied marketing strategies. Even the uneducated class of people who have money but no knowledge of travel procedures is comfortably travelling in numbers with the help of these travel intermediaries, who are assisting the travellers in facilitating the travel arrangements in every way. Thus, tourism is flourishing more and more in various parts of the world.

Use of Plastic Money

With the increasing usage of plastic money such as credit cards, debit cards and forex travel cards, almost in every part of the world, the hassle of carrying foreign currency in the form of cash has been reduced, making it easier for travellers to travel.

Availability of Food

Food is also an important add-on to the facilitators of travel. As travel has cut across geographical and political boundaries and people of different nationalities are travelling to every nook and corner of the world, many multi-cuisine restaurants have opened in countries to cater to the taste buds of the nationalities visiting a country. When food of one's own country is available in the country to be visited, the traveller is encouraged to travel to that destination. For example, many Indians who have conservative Indian food-eating habits, especially vegetarians and Jains (who eat neither onion nor garlic), may not consider visiting destinations that have hardly any Indian restaurants such as South Korea, Denmark and Japan as compared to visiting Dubai, the USA, Singapore and so on where ample Indian restaurants are available serving Indian vegetarian food.

Breaking of Language Barrier

The Internet has made such advancement that language is no more a barrier to travel. There are so many software and apps like Google Translate that one does not need any help in a foreign country to translate a language, and this further facilitates the movement of people to various destinations of the world.

More Per Capita Income

As the affluence of the middle class has grown in the past decade in the world and people have more per capita income, the standard of living of people has raised. Thus, globally, people are increasingly spending more on travelling after meeting day-to-day obligations. They now have more discretionary income at hand.

More Leisure Time

The leisure time has increased now as the working hours have reduced along with the concept of a weekend. As people have more time at their disposal, they tend to take short weekend breaks by vising different destinations of their choice. Further, the concept of compressed workweek which increases the leisure time to three days instead of two days has pushed people to travel more.

Paid Holidays

The concept of paid holidays has also given a push to tourism. Holiday entitlement which is paid allows the working professionals to leave their place and experience travel. Besides, government incentives like leave travel concession also lure the government employees to visit destinations outside their periphery area that in turn helps in promoting tourism.

Strong Networking of Travel Associations

Travel associations play a vital role in strengthening tourism in a country. Various travel associations at the international level such as the UNWTO, the World Tourism & Travel Council (WTTC), the Pacific Asia Travel Association (PATA), the United Federation of Travel Agents' Associations (UFTAA), the American Society of Travel Advisors (ASTA), the World Association of Travel Agencies (WATA) and International Air Transport Association (IATA) and Indian associations such as Federation of Associations in Indian Tourism and Hospitality (FAITH), Indian Association of Tour Operators (IATO), Travel Agents Association of India (TAAI), Travel Agents Federation of India (TAFI), Adventure Tour Operators Association of India (ATOAI), Outbound Tour Operators Association of India (OTOAI) and Tourist Guide Federation of India (TGFI) provide a platform to various tourism businesses to collaborate and network with the common objective of increasing the influx of tourists in a country or a region.

TOURISM IN INDIA

Tourism in India is growing fast. India was ranked 34 in the year 2019 in the Travel and Tourism Competitiveness Index of the World Economic Forum. Also, the number of foreign tourist arrivals (FTAs) was 10.8 million approximately in 2019 that was an increase of 3.1 per cent as compared to 2018.

The National Tourism Policy formulated in 2015 by the Ministry of Tourism (MOT), Government of India, not only envisions to encourage the Indian citizens to explore their own country and support the local economy but also positions India as a 'must-see' destination for the international travellers. Thus, the focus of the government has been to promote both domestic and inbound tourism within the country.

With a diverse portfolio of tourism products and 39 world heritage sites, India has a lot to offer to the world. Given the rich geographical and cultural diversity of the country, India is aggressively promoting its new products such as wellness tourism (Yoga, Ayurveda, siddha, Unani and naturopathy), medical tourism, adventure tourism, camping sites, MICE (meetings, incentives, conferences and exhibitions) tourism, rural tourism, ecotourism, film tourism and cruises to increase the influx of foreign tourists within the country. *As India is seen as the seat of spirituality,* this tourism product attracts not only Indians but also thousands of travellers from other parts of the world.

To increase tourism within the country, the government is actively engaging the private stakeholders and seeking community participation. Many tourism-related projects are working on the public–private partnership (PPP) business model. To facilitate foreign tourists, the government has eased the barriers of documentation by introducing VoA, providing facilities like sim card kits on their arrival, deputing tourist police at state levels for the safety of the tourists, launching tourist helplines, interactive travel planners and aggressively marketing the country by participating in every international/national event such as World Travel Mart (WTM) and South Asian Tourism and Travel Exchange (SATTE). These international events are an important tool for the travel trade partners to collaborate and connect with each other.

On similar lines, in order to increase domestic tourism, many schemes such as *Pilgrimage Rejuvenation and Spiritual, Heritage Augmentation Drive (PRASHAD)* and *Heritage City Development and Augmentation Yojana (HRIDAY)* have been launched by the Government of India to create a pool of required infrastructure and amenities at the pilgrimage and heritage destinations visited by the tourists in the country. Various funds have been channelized by the MOT, Government of India, to create the required infrastructure in the tourist destinations, sanction mega projects for the development of destinations and create new tourist circuits to attract more tourists. Although Indians always had a culture of summer getaway, now Indians are travelling more and more throughout the year as destinations are offering diverse tourism products throughout the year such as *monsoon tourism (promoted by Kerala and Goa), rural tourism, caravan tourism (promoted by Madhya Pradesh), fairs and festivals and wellness tourism including business travel.*

To promote domestic tourism amid the outbreak of coronavirus situation that has absolutely disrupted the travel activity within India, the MOT, Government of India, has launched a new initiative to engage the tourists virtually by launching a series of webinars called *Dekho Apna Desh* or 'see your country'. The webinars aim at enhancing the information of virtual tourists on various cities of India, which includes their rich heritage, culture, cuisines, folk arts, natural landscapes, festivals and so on. The virtual tourists may access the social media accounts of MOT such as Incredible !ndia Instagram and Incredible !ndia Facebook to know more about the destinations of India. The underlying objective of conducting the sessions of cities on webinars is to evoke the tourists to plan their travels in advance within India, once the situation of COVID-19 gets better.

Further, states of India have been advised to create a uniform protocol for interstate travel to make the domestic travel much easier while also creating short videos of new destinations within states as now the new domestic tourist wants to visit the less frequented new destinations. The government is also working on introducing System for Assessment, Awareness and Training for Hospitality Industry (SAATHI) to ensure safety norms for revival of tourism along with the creation of a National Integrated Database of Hospitality Industry (NIDHI), a scheme to develop a database of hospitality units. The Incredible India Tourist Facilitator (IITF) Certification Program has also been recently launched aiming at training tour facilitators/leaders of India.

As far as the Indian outbound tourism is concerned, it has seen a boom in the last decade. The frequency of international trips taken by Indian travellers has seen a phenomenal rise in the past decade. The growing middle class with adequate resources to travel, more affordable travel packages due to reduced fares of air travel and the proliferation of information on the Internet that has brought the destinations virtually on everyone's fingertips along with the aggressive marketing done by foreign tourism boards and travel agents/tour operators have created a strong desire within Indians to travel internationally. Visiting abroad is seen as a must-do activity by the Indian travellers. Although the seasoned travellers who have travelled before may think of visiting long-haul destinations such as Australia, New Zealand, the USA, Canada and Europe, the first-time Indian travellers generally prefer visiting Asian destinations such as Singapore, Malaysia, Indonesia, Bhutan and Nepal or Middle East countries such as Dubai and Abu Dhabi that are in close proximity to the country and less expensive to travel to.

THE WAY FORWARD

With a vision to increase its share of international tourist arrivals in the world to 1 per cent in 2020 and 2 per cent in 2025, India was aiming at a target of having 20 million FTAs in the year 2020, though the outbreak of the pandemic has severely affected the numbers now. The new draft of the national policy on tourism is likely to be introduced soon. The key thrust areas of the policy for India shall be employment generation, community participation, development of tourism in a sustainable and responsible way, creation of core infrastructure and tourism infrastructure and development of quality human resources in the tourism as well as hospitality sectors. It is expected that the sector will show the required resilience to bounce back from the pandemic shocks and once again benefit the people across the world.

SUMMARY

Tourism is considered an important sector of many economies of the world. There are different terms used in tourism such as traveller, visitor, tourists, excursionists and transients. There are different forms of tourism that include inbound tourism, outbound tourism, domestic tourism, national tourism, international tourism, internal tourism, intra-regional and inter-regional tourism. Tourism demand is incessantly increasing due to many facilitators of demand such as more income, more time, better mobility, affordability, more travel options, new tourism products, flexible government policies, effect of media, use of technology, use of plastic cards, mushrooming of tourism businesses, presence of foreign tourism offices, marketing by tourism service providers, paid holidays, strong networking of travel associations, availability of food and no language barriers. Indian tourism is also increasing and making a mark for itself in the world. The new tourism policy is in the pipeline, and Indian tourism aims to achieve strides in the tourism sector in the coming years.

ACTIVITIES

Activity 1: My City, My Story

Give 30–45 minutes to the class to think about the city they belong to and ask them to organize their thoughts about the following in a write-up:

- USP of the city (identify what the city is famous for and then introduce yourself first in an interesting way; for example, Hi, I am Shivaay from Amritsar, the city famous for the holy place of Sikhs, the Golden Temple, the mouth-watering Punjabi street food and the phulkari dupatta)
- The history of the city (how it got its name and any other historical significance, to be wrapped in four–five lines)
- How to reach the city (accessibility in terms of by air, road, rail or water)
- The tourist potential of the city (what kinds of tourists visit the place and why)
- The famous places to visit

Now, ask each student to come on the dais and speak on the above points without referring to the write-up for maximum five minutes. This activity may be extended to multiple classes. It is very important for public speaking, confidence building and increasing the knowledge of students about their own city along with teaching them the first lesson to see things from a tourist perspective.

Activity 2

Identify the top five tourist nationalities who are visiting your country along with their tourism statistics.

Activity 3

Now, ask each student to think about the challenges faced by the tourists that are impediments to the growth of tourism in their city/state/country. Ask them to discuss their views with the class.

BIBLIOGRAPHY

Mathieson, Alister, and Geoffrey Wall. 'Tourism: Economic, Physical and Social Impacts.' *Annals of Tourism Research* 6 (1982): 390–407.

United Nations. *Recommendations on Statistics of International Migration, Revision 1*. New York, NY: United Nations, 1998.

www.livemint.com (accessed on 20 July 2020).

www.tourism.gov.in (accessed on 20 July 2020).

www.outlookindia.com/outlooktraveller/travelnews/story/70208/india-tourism-ministry-launches-dekho-apna-desh-webinar-series (accessed on 24 April 2020).

https://www.instagram.com/incredibleindia/?hl=en (accessed on 24 April 2020).

https://www.instagram.com/incredibleindia/ (accessed on 24 April 20).

Motivations for Travelling

2

LEARNING OBJECTIVES

The given chapter shall clarify the following:

- What are the motivations that push a person to leave his place and travel?
- Apart from the traditional motivations, what are some of the unique triggers to travel?

Never get so busy making a living that you forget to make a life.

LAS VEGAS: A DESERT TURNED INTO A GOLDMINE!

- Welcome to the city of indulgence and a city that never sleeps! Famous for its nightlife and flashy neon lights, Las Vegas is also known as the 'entertainment capital' of the world. The city built on tourism offers unlimited world-class entertainment options such as interesting shows and performances, fine dining, electronic dance music, night clubs and so much more!
- Once a desert of the USA, Las Vegas is now pegged as the 'gambling capital' of the world, being home to world-class casinos in every hotel of the city.
- Nicknamed as the 'Sin City' of the world, gambling and drinking in public places are legal, which attracts a number of tourists to the city from all over the world. As also the famous saying goes, *What happens in Vegas stays in Vegas*.

- The most popular place in the city includes the Las Vegas Strip (known for a stretch filled with casinos and resorts) where every hotel is a tourism product in itself. Some of the famous hotels include Bellagio Hotel (known for its musical fountain shows), MGM Grand (largest hotel in the USA) and Flamingo Hotel.
- Many of the hotels in Las Vegas are known for their replica architecture such as Caesars Palace, Luxor, New York-New York, Paris Las Vegas and the Venetian. It is worth mentioning that the Venetian has an interior highlighting Venice, and it also offers the famous gondola ride on the canal built inside the hotel.
- Along with the Grand Canyon excursion, Las Vegas also offers amazing activities such as helicopter rides, deluxe bus tours of the city and the Hoover Dam tour.
- Rest easy business travellers! Las Vegas Convention and Visitors Authority is working hard to promote Las Vegas as a business destination by organizing meetings, conventions, exhibitions and so on.

INTRODUCTION

People leave their homes and voyage to destinations all over the globe for different reasons. These may be defined as motivations or 'triggers' that push a person to travel. Sometimes motivations may be intrinsic that force a person to experience travel from within, wanting to leave his/her present circumstances. It may be escapism from the routine drudgery or a journey to find oneself.

On the contrary, motivations may be extrinsic. Extrinsic motivation may be caused by exogenous (external) factors that create a desire within a person to travel. These may be due to the pull factors of a destination that attract the tourist to visit it. Some of the extrinsic motivational pull factors may be as follows:

- Offering of new tourism products by a destination (e.g., Wine Cruise Tours offered in Bordeaux, France)
- Building of new attractions at the destination (e.g., Dubai and Singapore, which have built attractions such as Burj Khalifa and Sentosa Island, respectively)
- More aggressive marketing by a destination to attract more tourists (e.g., Gujarat in India, which has used various marketing tools such as promoting its Rann of Kutch festival to showcase its rich heritage and culture, making Amitabh Bachchan the brand ambassador of Tourism Corporation of Gujarat Limited (TCGL) and using print, electronic and social media to attract more tourists to the state)
- Effect of social media such as pictures posted by travellers on Facebook and Instagram or writing of travel experiences by travel bloggers and posting of travel videos by vloggers that trigger a person to travel

Now, let us have a detailed discussion on each of the intrinsic and extrinsic motivations that make a person leave his/her routine and make him/her travel.

TO SEE ATTRACTIONS

This is the most basic objective of tourists visiting a destination. Tourists may have a bucket list of attractions and destinations for which they may be ready to travel miles to tick off their chosen destinations. Some may wish to see the *Dead Sea in Israel*, while some may travel to see the *Grand Canyon or Antelope Canyon in the USA*. While some may wish to see the *Bora Bora Island in French Polynesia*, others may wish to see the *Machu Picchu in Peru*. While some may wish to see *Venice* before they die, others may wish to see the *Pamukkale in Turkey*. The list of attractions can be endless for the globetrotters.

FOR A SLOWER AND RELAXING PACE OF LIFE

Life in cities can be very strenuous and difficult. Generally, people are caught in the vicious cycle of minting money that they have no time for themselves. In the fast pace of life and in the rat race of trying to catch up with the daily pressures, people forget to lead a normal life that brings peace to them. Thus, for many travellers, travelling is a way of experiencing a slower and relaxing pace of life. They may be seeking a change from the urban life that surrounds them and thus, travel to destinations in search of tranquillity and to experience a slower pace of life.

WANDERLUST AND EXPLORATION

Many people have gypsy souls who want to travel as much as they can. The travel bug inside them makes them travel. Such travellers may be maniacs for travelling as for them travelling is a necessary part of their lifestyles. Such travellers may be referred to as vagabonds who have consistent travel goals. For them, exploring, seeing and experiencing new places is food for their soul. They may keep travelling to different places and add to their kitty of lifetime travel experiences. Such travellers may not have any fixed itineraries. Even if they have, they may be ready to face any kind of hardships during the trip. They are thrill-seekers and adventurers by nature.

TO VISIT FRIENDS AND RELATIVES

One of the main reasons for travelling to destinations is to meet one's friends or relatives. Some family members or friends may have settled in different parts of the world. It may be one's urge to spend quality time with family or friends to renew one's bond and further strengthen one's relationships. Staying with relatives/friends or the families at the place being visited allows oneself to explore the local culture at the destination more closely and get an insider's view from the friends/relatives who have spent a reasonable time at that destination. This kind of travel develops social cohesion and leaves the traveller more refreshed and emotionally charged.

TO SOCIALIZE

As tourism is a perfect opportunity to socialize, many tourists may just visit destinations to meet new people from different cultures and from different backgrounds, interact with them and then make new friends both at the destination and en route their journey.

TO BE CLOSE TO NATURE

Some tourists just want to be in the vicinity of nature. They may want to enjoy the simple bounties of nature like seeing the sunset, being in the mountains, relaxing amidst the flora or just sitting and admiring the nature while travelling to natural areas like a biosphere reserve or a hill station so as to be at peace with nature. Sometimes, just enjoying the rain droplets falling from the trees in the hills or relaxing on a beach chair watching the sea waves or just sipping a cup of coffee sitting by the side of the river can be some unique ways of being in the company of nature for which a traveller may travel miles.

CHANGE OF WEATHER

Travellers sometimes visit destinations just for a change of weather. For those experiencing scorching heat, travel to hill stations may be the only antidote to experience a change of weather. On the contrary, for the travellers who experience extremely cold temperatures, travelling to destinations with warm temperatures may be an ideal choice. They may race to experience sunshine so as to tan their bodies and thus may opt for beach destinations. Many Europeans staying in Scandinavian countries with extremely cold temperatures prefer to visit Mediterranean destinations to experience comparatively warm temperatures.

Yet some may just travel to experience snowfall. For example, many travellers in India during the New Year time, with the beginning of snow time, travel to hilly areas such as Manali in Himachal Pradesh and Ranikhet and Almora in Uttarakhand to experience snowfall.

TO ENSURE ONE'S WELL-BEING

Travelling brings joy to a person by reducing his/her levels of stress. It heals him/her physically and emotionally. Travellers may visit destinations for medical care to get rid of diseases and pains. They may also travel to seek wellness treatments to various destinations in order to relax, destress and unwind. Wellness may connote different meanings for different people and there may be different ways of seeking wellness treatments for everyone. Some of the popular well-being treatments among tourists are taking spas, mud therapy, thalassotherapy, massages, detox, rejuvenation, organic diets, learning Yoga and meditation in Yoga retreats, taking Ayurveda treatments and many more to become physically fit.

For example, many travellers visit the *Dead Sea in Israel for thalassotherapy to cure their health problems*. Thalassotherapy refers to therapeutic treatment of one's skin diseases through seawater, algae, seaweed, mud, sand and other sea products. Besides the Dead Sea, popular destinations for this kind of treatment are France, Greece, Great Britain and so on. Likewise, foreigners visit Kerala in India, 'the land of Ayurveda', for Ayurvedic treatments, especially Ayurvedic massages such as Panchakarma and Shirodhara.

FOR BUSINESS AND PROFESSION

Travelling for business is a big travel business today. Some tourists travel to destinations by virtue of their profession or business. They may visit destinations to attend meetings, conferences, exhibitions, trade fairs and so on related to their business. Such travellers may be classified as business tourists. Yet many business travellers may visit a destination to enjoy an incentive tour like a dealers' meet that is sponsored by their company. Such travellers in the travel trade parlance may be called as corporate incentive groups as they travel in groups. Setting official contacts and networking at another destination are also the reasons why business tourists travel to other destinations.

EDUCATIONAL OR STUDY PURPOSE

Some travellers may visit a destination to undergo a particular training at an institute/college/university or to pursue a short-term course at a destination. Some others may travel to a destination as a part of a study tour of the academic programme that they may be pursuing. While studying is the main objective, travellers may explore the destination, stay in hotels, do shopping, eat at local eateries and therefore, may spend time as a tourist. For example, many students pursuing tourism courses travel to destinations as a part of their course curriculum. Students studying adventure travel may go to an adventure destination to gain first-hand knowledge about adventure. Thus, education in this case becomes a prime motivation.

TO EXPERIENCE CULTURES

Tourists may travel to see the lifestyle of locals living at a destination. They may participate in their local festivals, eat their local food, live in homestays and so on to understand and assimilate the local's culture within. Thus, experiencing the local's culture becomes a prime motivation for many travellers to visit a destination.

TO CELEBRATE EVENTS

Travellers may visit destinations to attend the local events and festivals in order to understand the local culture closely such as the *Lohri festival of Punjab* and *La Tomatina festival of Spain*. They may also travel to attend personal events that may include attending a reunion of old friends, a wedding festivity, a baby shower celebration, arrival of a baby, a graduation ceremony or any other special family get-together like a birthday or an anniversary celebration.

FOR FOOD

Many foodies visit destinations to pamper their taste buds. They may travel to far-flung destinations around the globe to taste the local cuisines and to savour the flavours of the world. Such travellers may also participate in food festivals and go for food walks to taste the authentic regional cuisines.

FOR SHOPPING

Shopping activity has been seen as a major influence on tourism trends globally. Some shopaholic travellers may visit destinations primarily for doing shopping. They may visit local streets, shopping malls, shopping emporiums, haats, duty-free shops at airports and so on of a destination with a shopping list in hand. Some tourists may prefer buying local souvenirs of destinations that they may carry as mementos for their loved ones on returning from their destination. Such local shopping of souvenirs supports the local artisans of a destination by bringing economic benefits to the local community besides keeping their tradition and heritage alive.

To capitalize upon shopping as an opportunity for tourists, destinations must offer authentic and quality certified products, accept as many forms of payments as possible, give tax refunds to international tourists on things purchased, organize shopping festivals and shopping incentives like sale bonanzas, create brand awareness and integrate the shopping tourism as a product in their marketing campaigns. Few countries promoting shopping tourism are Dubai, Thailand, South Korea, Hong Kong and India.

HONEYMOON

Honeymoon is a special once-in-a-lifetime experience for the newly-wed couples and a big reason to travel. It is a universal ritual for couples when they get tied in wedlock to travel to a new destination to spend quality time with each other and celebrate their moments of togetherness. Beach destinations, islands and hill stations are the most preferred destinations for honeymooners when they plan their holidays.

BABYMOON

It is a new concept in the tourism industry that celebrates the arrival of the little one in the womb of a mother by travelling to a destination. Here, the expecting mothers travel to destinations to seek a change, refresh their minds and celebrate their motherhood with their partners, generally in the second trimester of their pregnancy that is comparatively safer for travelling as compared to other two trimesters of pregnancy. Thus, many destinations are promoting this kind of travel for expecting mothers and now, babymoon is a big motivation to travel for expecting mothers.

SEEKING ADVENTURE

Surfing in Amusement Park, Gold Coast, Australia

Doing a particular kind of adventure brings a sense of accomplishment within many people. Thus, adventure enthusiasts may opt for land-, water- or air-based adventure as per their personal choice. Thus, all those who like thrill and excitement with a certain amount of risk visit destinations primarily with the objective of indulging in adventure activities.

FOR PILGRIMAGE

Many travellers visit destinations to seek the blessings of God or to offer obeisance. They may also visit a place to make *mannats* (to make a wish), to become pure and get rid of their sins or to attain salvation. Yet some religious people may travel to attend religious festivals like the *Kumbh Mela, the largest conglomeration of pilgrims in the world*. In all cases, pilgrimage travel is the main motivation while visiting a pilgrimage destination.

TO SEE WILDLIFE

Feeding Kangaroos in Philip Island, Australia

Nature is endowed with a variety of wildlife that cohabit this planet. Many wildlife enthusiasts wish to experience this wildlife from close proximity and appreciate this creation of nature. For this, they may visit destinations that are a haven for these exotic species. It may not be less than adventure for them to visit biosphere reserves, national parks, forests and wildlife sanctuaries so as to witness the wildlife with their naked eye. They may walk the nature trails, take pictures of the fauna, enjoy safaris while viewing the wildlife and doing bird watching. Thus, seeing the wildlife in their natural haven is a motivation for many travellers to travel to a destination.

FOR TRANSIT

Many travellers visit destinations by virtue of their flight connections. When travellers take connecting flights, they may halt at a destination for some time due to the transit there and wait for the next connecting flight to catch up. Hence, such travellers may be called transit passengers who may stop at the airports, spend their time shopping at the airport, eat in the restaurants and so on. Sometimes, if the halt is quite long, then such travellers may take a transit visa at the airport and may explore the destination as per the transit visa rules of the country being visited. For example, a traveller transiting through Dubai and wanting to explore the city may get the transit visa on the condition that his minimum transit time in the city is eight hours and he/she should be carrying his/her onward ticket with him/her. However, a transit visa is valid for a very short term that the immigration authorities of a country may be issuing to the transit tourists and the transit visa rules vary from country to country.

LOTTERY

Some people may just travel if they are lucky enough. They may win a lottery or a lucky draw by virtue of which they may travel. In such cases, all their travel arrangements are financed by the sponsoring companies.

TO ENGAGE IN NICHE TOURISM PRODUCTS/PURSUE SPECIAL INTERESTS

Some travellers may be looking for particular niche tourism experiences that match their interests. For example, they may visit a destination to learn how wine is made, learn an art, learn cooking, play golf, attend a concert, volunteer at destinations, learn scuba diving, go on a biking tour, visit literary trails and so on. The special interest tours are generally customized according to the need of the tourists.

OTHER TRIGGERS FOR TRAVELLING

Many travellers may visit destinations for personal reasons. Some of these intrinsic motivations are as follows.

Spending Time with Oneself

Travelling provides space and time for oneself. Travelling on one's own is an ideal time to reflect upon oneself and one's life. It gives the desired space and time to know one's own strengths and weaknesses and discover new facets of one's own self. Sometimes, it clears the mist of uncertainties and doubts that one may be surrounded by.

Getaway

Sometimes, there is a need to disconnect with the present circumstances and the pressures that one is surrounded by and escape from one's routine in search of a restful vacation to renew oneself. Travelling allows people to move out of the shackles of their family life, workplace and the society that creates continuous pressure on them. It gives them an opportunity to feel free by being away from the daily life chores. It gives them the independence to do whatever they want to do that can be personally very gratifying and liberating for one's soul. Rest refreshes a person and brings lots of positive energy to him. A change of weather and being close to nature or going for a wellness retreat may be a better way of rejuvenating oneself on a vacation. Travelling reboots one's mind and body and changes one's outlook towards life. It recharges one's batteries to cope up with the daily stress.

To Get Out of Comfort Zone

Staying in one's routine keeps a person in a safe zone. Going to the same office/college every day, meeting the same people, sleeping on the same bed and following the same routine can make the traveller feel very comfortable. Thus, many travellers travel to destinations to challenge their own comfort, see whether they are fit enough to face the hardships of life and push themselves beyond limits. It builds in them a sense of confidence when they travel to new places, meet new people and try new activities like engaging in adventure. Overcoming challenges makes one personally stronger and makes him/her feel more worthy and confident.

To Gain More Exposure

Travelling has the magic of changing people's perspective about things. When people travel to destinations, the stereotypes they might hold about a particular nationality, community or a religion break as people meet new people from different parts of the world. It simply opens their mind and broadens their perspective to new ways of life. Thus, travelling helps them gain more exposure to people and the world.

The different settings in which people live in different parts of the world make one realize that people can coexist in different ways that one may have never imagined. It helps people consider fresh ideas and helps in developing a wider world perspective. Such people become well-rounded global citizens as they become more tolerant of different beliefs and ways of life, thus coming home with broader notions and possibilities.

To Educate Oneself

Travel is the best teacher. For many travellers, tourism is a great way to educate themselves. The process of real learning starts when one moves to an unfamiliar environment. Travelling is real education as one becomes more enriched and wiser when one travels the world and discovers new ways of life. Seeking new experiences, visiting new attractions, meeting new people and so on add on to one's experiences. Each destination teaches a traveller new lessons. Thus, travelling may add more enriching experiences and learning to one's existing knowledge.

To Learn a Particular Skill

Every destination has something unique to offer to a visitor. Some travellers may travel to learn a specific skill at a particular destination with the objective of enriching one's skills. For example, people may travel to learn a folk art, a folk dance, a new language, a traditional cuisine and so on in order to deepen one's sense of the local culture of a destination.

To Elevate One's Mood

Sometimes, distractions work wonders. Many travellers visit destinations to deal with a major loss. It could be loss of a loved one like the death of a near one or break-up with the loved one, divorce or miscarriage that leaves one emotionally shattered. Sometimes it could be loss of a job, financial crisis, major health issue and so on that may cause a lot of stress and anxiety to a person. In such cases, travelling is a great respite. Travelling to new places, meeting new people and seeking new experiences is a great way to heal from the pain and be at peace with oneself.

To Impress Others

Travelling now has become a symbol of status for many. Many people undertake travel under social pressure to show off among their friends or flaunt their status that they are no less from them. Travelling to destinations, especially to international destinations, has become a ritual to impress others. It is a way to elevate one's ego by sharing and boasting one's travel stories with friends and relatives and feeling more worthy among others. It has become a fad now to post things on social media such as Facebook and Instagram. This has in turn become a strong motivation for many people to travel.

For Self-actualization

Some travellers visit destinations to test themselves by immersing in difficult or offbeat experiences that are not regularly practised by them such as trying extreme adventure activities or doing a meditation course, etc. This can personally be very gratifying for a person as it helps him/her realize his/her own potential by experiencing the unknown, thus leading him/her to experience self-actualization in many ways.

SUMMARY

Travel is the best experience that one can have. To live a life without regrets, one must make time to appreciate life and thus not leave anything undone on his/her bucket list. Travelling is more than just seeing places. It is a change that goes on deep and permanent in the way of one's living. The motivations for travelling may vary from person to person. Tourism professionals must know how to tap these motivations and offer tourism products according to the motivations, tastes and preferences of the tourists.

ACTIVITIES

Activity 1

Visit any famous attraction in your area and interview any five foreign tourists. Ask them their motivations for travelling in your country. You may prepare a questionnaire for interviewing the foreigners, which may include their basic profile such as nationality, age, profession, gender and duration of their stay in the country. A detailed response may be elicited regarding their motivations, their good experiences in the country, the challenges that they faced, if any, and any suggestions that they may like to give to the government of the country. Students may also make a video of the interviews of the foreigners besides documenting their experiences in a questionnaire. After preparing the questionnaire, ask the students to submit a report on this and share their experience with the class by giving a PowerPoint presentation.

Activity 2

Enlist any two dream destinations you wish to travel to along with the motivational factors that trigger you to travel to those destinations.

Types of Tourism

3

LEARNING OBJECTIVES

The given chapter shall clarify the following:

- What are the various types of tourism?
- What are the approaches to tourism?

WELCOME TO THE CYCLING CAPITAL OF THE WORLD!

- Also synonymous with 'tulips' and called the 'Venice of the North' and 'a city of canals', Amsterdam (capital of the Netherlands) is a city known for its tulip flowers, windmills, canals, pebbled streets and nightlife.
- It is also known as the 'city of sins' for its drug freedom and red-light areas.
- The best way to explore Amsterdam is either by walking or by riding a bicycle. The city is known as the 'cycling capital of the world' as it has over 32,000 km of bicycle paths.
- This city attracts more tourists than residents. Thus, to avoid over-tourism, the Tourism Department of Amsterdam has initiated several campaigns to promote local beauty and sustainability such as 'marry an Amsterdammer for a day' and 'slow tourism'.
- Typical day tours in Amsterdam include visits to the Wooden Shoe Factory, the cheese factory, Madurodam amusement park in the Hague, windmill bus tours and so much more!
- Want to indulge in Dutch traditions? Do visit the villages such as Zaanse Schans and Haarlem to experience the authentic way of living. You can see many windmills, wooden Dutch houses, chocolate making and the exciting northern city at its fullest.

- Ever seen 30,000 kg or 2,200 whole cheese at one place? Go to the Alkmaar Cheese Market to soak in the traditional way of cheese trading.
- Witness the Dutch tradition at *Royal FloraHolland* (world's biggest flower auction house) that sells over 20 million flowers and plants every day!
- One of the largest flower gardens in the world known for its tulips, *Keukenhof Tulip Garden* is home to more than 7 million flower bulbs and plants.
- So much at one place, come and explore this city!

INTRODUCTION

As the tourism industry is growing, there are many types in which tourism can be classified. For the sake of our clarity, we may divide types of tourism into two categories. First is the conventional category of different types of tourism that are being promoted for a long time. Second is the other category of tourism products which are specialized tourism products meant for specific tourist segments. We shall have a detailed discussion regarding the category of specialized tourism products in the next chapter.

In the given chapter, we shall try to assimilate the generic conventional forms of tourism that are being offered by various destinations of the world followed by approaches to tourism. Let us begin with the discussion now.

LEISURE TOURISM

This is the most basic form of tourism in which travellers visit destinations just to rest, relax and rejuvenate their mind, body and soul. The idea of relaxation may vary from person to person. Some may like to spend their leisure time at a destination while doing nothing, whereas others may want to relax at a beach or be close to nature such as being at a hill station just resting and recharging. However, some may believe in having fun while visiting attractions, taking sightseeing tours, making new friends and seeking recreation in different ways. Thus, such travellers who travel with the sole purpose of having a good time at a destination without any pressure of work may be termed as leisure tourists.

BUSINESS TOURISM

Travelling to destinations for the purpose of doing business, visiting other destinations for attending meetings, conferences or exhibitions, or corporate incentive travel is called business tourism. It may also be referred to as *MICE tourism or corporate travel.* Business tourism also involves travelling for trading goods, networking and setting contacts, selecting a site, conducting business transactions and so on. Thousands of travellers also visit foreign countries to attend the trade fairs in order to network with people from the same trade. Many top- and middle-management representatives such as CEOs, MDs, GMs and middle managers also travel across the world to do business deals or to work on a particular project.

Business tourism is seen as a more perennial source of income for travel companies as compared to leisure tourism as the corporate movement takes place throughout the year unlike leisure tourism that is driven by seasons. Business travel is also more lucrative as most of the business tourists' trips are sponsored by the companies, and business tourists spend more as compared to leisure travellers.

The *India Convention Promotion Bureau (ICPB)* is responsible for promoting India as a MICE destination.

MASS TOURISM

When travellers visit destinations, in large numbers, that are highly popular or being heavily commercialized, the phenomenon is called mass tourism. The travel is further pushed by cheap package deals that spur the movement of travellers to the same destination. This kind of tourism though in the short term may benefit the local economy, in the long term it has far-reaching deeper negative impacts on the environment and the society that outweigh all the positives. It is an unsustainable approach towards tourism. For example, due to the mass movement of Indian travellers visiting hill stations every summer to escape the scorching heat of plains, the hill stations are under a great threat, as it has led to increasing negative environmental effects for the hill stations such as deforestation, climate change, water scarcity and traffic jams which have directly affected the local communities staying in the hill stations. Many destinations in Europe have also promoted mass tourism such as France, Spain and Italy, which has now backfired on the local communities of these countries.

CULTURAL TOURISM

Visiting destinations of the world with the sole objective of understanding the different cultures and lifestyles of locals of a destination is called cultural tourism. This kind of tourism involves interacting with the host community, sometimes also staying with them (homestays), learning their different languages and art, exploring their religion and food habits, preparing meals with them, participating in their local festivals and so on. For example, many foreign travellers visit India for its rich culture and traditions. They may visit South India (*Dakshin Bharat*) known for its rich culture, rituals, temples, traditional festivals and so on. Likewise, the tourists in order to understand the Punjabi culture may visit Punjab and visit the mustard fields, go for tractor rides, eat *sarson ka saag* and *makki ki roti* (the famous local cuisine of Punjab), visit gurudwaras and taste the *langars*, buy *phulkari dupatta* and Punjabi *jutti* (footwear), participate in local festivals like Lohri and so on.

ETHNIC TOURISM

Visiting destinations to connect with one's original roots where one's ancestors used to live for the purpose of ethnic reunion is called as ethnic tourism. Even though migration may have moved the tourist to another country, they may travel back to their own country with the desire to reconnect with their families. They may want to get back to their roots to develop a deeper understanding of their own culture and to acquaint their younger generations with their forefathers and their roots. Such travellers may be motivated by the desire to search for their identities, preserving the culture of their minority and endangered ethnic groups, bringing back a sense of ethnic pride and strengthening their own communities.

Many North Americans in order to trace their ancestry visit parts of the UK such as Scotland and Ireland as their history is that of migration. Likewise, many Punjabi NRI families settled abroad in countries like Canada visit with their children to villages of Punjab in India to show them the traces of where and how their forefathers lived. The contacts with the indigenous culture are found to be more authentic and intimate in ethnic tourism.

It may include cultural, heritage, village, tribal and other similar kinds of tourism.

HERITAGE TOURISM

This kind of tourism is practised by tourists who have a keen interest in the history of a destination. Heritage may be in both tangible and intangible forms. Such travellers may visit monuments, important historical sites, forts, palaces, castles, museums and so on that give them a wealth of information about the heritage of a destination. India, having been ruled by different empires from time to time, has a rich cultural heritage which has an international appeal for the foreign tourists. To promote heritage sites and spread awareness among the people, the *International Council on Monuments and Sites (ICOMOS) observes 18 April as the World Heritage Day or the International Day for Monuments and Sites* every year. India has a total of *39 world heritage sites declared by United Nations Educational, Scientific and Cultural Organization (UNESCO)* including the latest Kumbh Mela (the largest religious festival of India) declared as the Intangible Cultural Heritage of Humanity in 2017. These sites are a treat for the tourists, especially for historians, researchers, students of history, anthropologists, archaeologists and so on. In fact, many cities of the world such as *Ahmedabad and Jaipur in India, Melaka in Malaysia, Bath in England* and many more have been declared as world heritage cities that are a must-visit destination in the bucket list of heritage lovers. To promote the holistic development of heritage destinations and facilitate the tourists, the Government of India has launched HRIDAY scheme in 2015.

PILGRIMAGE TOURISM

This kind of tourism is driven by the staunch faith of people in religion who travel to religious destinations for different reasons. It is also called as religious tourism or faith tourism.

Visiting sacred destinations may be for the following reasons:

- To offer prayers to God
- To obtain salvation
- To offer obeisance and seek blessings of God
- To get rid of sins
- To perform any religious rituals (e.g., many Hindus visit Haridwar or Varanasi to perform last rites of their loved ones after their death)
- To participate in important religious events (such as Kumbh Mela and Guru Poornima)
- To get spiritual enlightenment and spiritual elevation

India, being the birthplace of many religions, has a lot of pilgrimage sites for people with different faiths. Pilgrimage tourism is quite popular in India, especially among the senior citizens of the country. Some of the popular pilgrimage sites of India for different religions are Char Dham (Badrinath, Jagannath Puri, Dwarkadeesh and Rameshwaram), Vaishno Devi, Tirupati, Shirdi, Mathura, Vrindavan, Haridwar, Allahabad, Varanasi, Pushkar, Nashik and so on for Hindus, Golden Temple,

The Golden Temple, Amritsar, India

Hemkund Sahib and so on for Sikhs, Ajmer Sharif and Mecca and Medina for Muslims, St. Basilica Church and Jerusalem for Christians, Bodh Gaya, Sarnath and so on for Buddhists and many other similar popular religious sites for people of other religions.

To encourage pilgrimage tourism in India, the Indian Railways wing, *Indian Railway Catering and Tourism Corporation (IRCTC)*, has launched many special trains that run on pilgrimage circuits such as *Sri Ramayana Express* (covering destinations associated with the life of Lord Shri Ram worshipped by Hindus) and *Mahaparinirvan Express* (train running on Buddhist circuit). Besides these trains, IRCTC also offers special pilgrimage tour packages for pilgrims.

To further spur the pilgrimage tourism in India, the government has also introduced the PRASHAD scheme in order to create adequate infrastructure in the pilgrimage destinations in the country so as to facilitate the pilgrims visiting these destinations.

MEDICAL TOURISM

Health is very precious to every human being. No one can take chances with one's health. To save one's health, people can travel across international boundaries to ensure their well-being.

Thus, another very upcoming segment of tourists across the world is that of medical tourists. When people travel to a destination to seek treatment for a particular disease/health check-up/surgery/any particular treatment such as for infertility and so on, this phenomenon is called medical tourism. Medical tourism is also called health tourism.

The reason for travelling to another destination to seek medical treatment may be availability of better medical facilities such as good hospitals and medical expertise as compared to one's place. Another major reason for seeking medical treatment at another place is that cost of treatment at the medical destination may be significantly less even after including the cost of travelling and stay as compared to the treatment cost in one's own country. In India, one can save up to 65–90 per cent as compared to taking the same treatment in a country like the USA. Even the waiting time for getting the treatment may be too long in one's own country and the patient may not be able to wait too long for the treatment or surgery for which he/she may choose to travel to another destination.

Thus, many destinations across the world are marketing and positioning themselves as medical tourism destinations. The hospitals in such destinations highly specialize in different medical treatments with able teams of doctors and nurses speaking fluent English due to which language is not a barrier for the patients visiting from another destination for treatment. In fact, many hospitals have separate packages for different treatments where the medical tourist can choose according to his/her requirement and budget. It comprises all the medical facilities and travel arrangements including transportation and accommodation.

India has come up in a big way as a medical tourist destination with lots of tourists coming from all parts of the world for medical treatment, especially from Middle East and Africa. India also boasts of having the expertise of qualified doctors who are trained in the USA, Europe and so on, and Indian nurses who are fluent in English, besides having world-class medical facilities and equipment. As per the international standards, some of our best hospitals include AIIMS, PGI, Medanta, Apollo, Ganga Ram, Max and Fortis. Chennai is considered the health capital of the country. India has also introduced a separate visa for medical tourists called *'M' visa* and *'MX' visa* for attendants coming with the patient.

Various tourists come to India for medical treatments such as knee replacements, hip replacement surgery, cardiac surgery, cosmetic surgery and organ transplants. Some of the famous destinations offering world-class medical facilities besides India are Thailand, Singapore, Malaysia, *South Korea (world capital of plastic surgery)*, Costa Rica, Brazil, Mexico and so on.

DENTAL TOURISM

Another niche product of medical tourism is dental tourism. The practice of visiting destinations including any international destination for seeking a dental treatment by combining one's vacation is called dental tourism. People travel internationally for this treatment so as to save upon a good deal of money as the dental treatment in their country may cost them a fortune. Even if a tourist spends on his/her travel ticket and stay, it would cost him/her less than taking a dental treatment in his/her own country. Some of the countries specializing in dental tourism are:

- India
- Costa Rica
- Hungary
- Mexico
- Thailand

WILLIFE TOURISM

Jurong Bird Park, Singapore

Watching the wildlife in its natural habitat closely is a thrill for many tourists. Many destinations of the world are popular for their natural reserves, forests, national parks and wildlife sanctuaries. Tourists may visit these wildlife havens to do wildlife photography, go on jungle safaris, feed the animals or just see them with their naked eye. Out of the innumerable wildlife treasures of the world, a few are listed below:

- Masai Mara National Reserve, Kenya
- Serengeti National Park, Tanzania
- Glacier Bay National Park and Preserve, Alaska
- Cairngorms National Park, Scotland
- Galapágos Islands, Ecuador
- The Amazon Basin, Brazil
- Yellowstone National Park, USA
- Kruger National Park, South Africa
- Jim Corbett National Park, Uttarakhand, India
- Ranthambhore National Park, Rajasthan, India

ECOTOURISM

According to The International Ecotourism Society, 1990, ecotourism is 'responsible travel to natural areas that conserves the environment and improves the well-being of people'. Visiting natural areas where one can find flora and fauna in an untouched environment such as mangroves, wetlands, coral reefs, mountains, hills, deserts and biosphere reserves is referred to as ecotourism. Ecotourists may stay in eco-friendly destinations offering ecotourism products such as stays in eco-lodges and eco-friendly souvenirs ensuring not to harm the natural environment where the tourists visit. *Costa Rica is one of the world's most eco-friendly destinations. Likewise, in India, Kerala is the most eco-friendly destination.* The Ecotourism Society of India (a non-profit organization and a national body for promoting responsible tourism in India) ensures to promote the concept of environmentally responsible and sustainable tourism practices to the tour operators, hoteliers, tourists and others while allowing local communities to live at peace with nature. The state of *Kerala in India* has been on the forefront to promote ecotourism in the country.

URBAN TOURISM

Also referred to as city tourism, urban tourism connotes the phenomenon of travelling by people staying in the countryside to see the city life of people living in metropolitans and cosmopolitans. The urban landscapes, the skyscrapers and the fast pace of life are all an attraction for the tourists staying in villages who have not seen and experienced this aspect of life.

RURAL TOURISM

Visiting the countryside away from the bustling noisy urban life for temporary escapism is a wish of many travellers. Rural tourism is the practice of visiting rural areas or villages. Tourists basically travel to enjoy rural areas, rural communities and gain rural experiences in order to learn, understand and appreciate the life of rural people. It gives pleasure to experience the simplicity of life and enjoy the slow pace of life that is absent in the city life. In rural tourism, experiencing the lifestyle of rural people is the main attraction for urban tourists. Visitors thus visit villages, learn local arts, do various activities such as bird watching and photography, eat their local organic food, visit the fields, go for tractor rides, pick fresh vegetables and fruits, participate in the local traditions and festivals, buy local village products and so on to learn and understand more about the rural culture. The socio-economic benefits accruing to the rural community is the major objective for encouraging this kind of tourism in rural areas.

To promote rural tourism in India, MOT, Government of India, has created *'Explore Rural India', a sub-brand under the Incredible!ndia brand, where the ministry has identified 153 rural tourism sites (36 sites are the United Nations Development Programme supported project for capacity building)* that are rich in culture, handicrafts, handlooms, textiles, heritage, crafts and arts. Some of the famous rural sites of India are *Mawlynnong (Asia's cleanest village) in Meghalaya, Chitrakote in Chhattisgarh, Raghurajpur and Pipili in Odisha, Jyotisar in Haryana, Lachung and Lachen in Sikkim, Bishnoi villages in Rajasthan, Hodka in Gujarat* and many more. Rural tourism is also popular in other parts of the world, especially in Europe such as *Romania, Italy, Croatia, Portugal and Poland.*

ADVENTURE TOURISM

Adventure today has become a rage, especially for the new young travellers. Anything that moves the travellers out of their comfort zone, involves risks and creates an adrenaline rush due to the nature of the activity that one is performing is called adventure tourism. 'Expect the unexpected' is the mantra for such adventurous travellers. The different forms of adventure that adventure lovers can practise are land-, water- and aerial-based adventures. Adventure tourists may choose travelling to those destinations that specialize in offering certain kinds of adventure under trained supervision. Some of the adventure activities may include trekking, mountaineering, rock climbing, mountain biking, bungee jumping, parasailing, snorkelling, scuba diving, white water rafting, hot air ballooning, paragliding, skydiving and so on. Some of the adventure-based destinations in India are Ladakh, Uttarakhand, Himachal Pradesh, Goa, Andaman and Nicobar Islands and so on. A few world-class adventure destinations of the world are as follows:

- Queenstown, New Zealand
- Cape Town, South Africa
- Vancouver, Canada
- Kathmandu, Nepal (for mountaineering)
- Las Vegas, USA
- Machu Picchu, Peru

New Zealand is considered the 'adventure capital' of the world. In order to promote adventure tourism in India, the government has opened more than 120 peaks for trekking and mountaineering for the adventure enthusiasts in 2019.

EXTREME TOURISM

Popular in countries such as Russia, Ukraine and Azerbaijan, and some South American countries such as Peru, Chile and Argentina, this kind of tourism involves travelling to places associated with danger and participating in dangerous activities there. Dangerous places may include jungles, caves, mountains and so on. This kind of tourism may also be referred to as *shock tourism.*

SPORTS TOURISM

Watching the sports events live is a delight for the sports aficionados. Many travellers plan their visit to destinations during a sports event taking place there. Therefore, visiting destinations to see sports events or participation in sports events is referred to as sports tourism.

International sports events such as Olympic Games, Commonwealth Games, Asian Games, FIFA World Cup, Boxing World Championships, ICC World Cup and Indian Premier League (IPL) attract thousands of tourists all over the world to cheer their favourite players and teams to the destination hosting sports events. Niche products of sports tourism include golf tourism and polo tourism which are discussed in detail in the next chapter under the heading 'Niche Tourism Products'.

CRUISE TOURISM

Holidaying on a cruise is a lifetime experience as travelling by sea has a different charm attached to it when the ship rolls through the rough blue waves. A cruise ship or a cruise liner is a passenger ship which is primarily used for leisure voyages. Many tourists prefer to spend their vacations in a lavish and an extravagant way in these floating hotels. Guests get spoilt for choices onboard. All kinds of facilities that a traveller can think of while on a holiday, for example, enjoying in swimming pools, dining in multi-cuisine restaurants, seeking experiences in spas, ice rinks, gyms, golf course, badminton court and so on can be found at cruises. The travellers may join the ship at the port and then go for *shore excursions* during the day.

Cruises are quite popular among North Americans and Europeans who have a lot of love for waters.

The leading destinations of the world for cruises are as follows:

- The Caribbean
- The Mediterranean
- Northern Europe
- Australia/New Zealand
- Alaska
- Asia

The leading cruise companies of the world are as follows:

- Royal Caribbean International
- Norwegian Cruise Line
- Disney Cruise Line
- Princess Cruises
- Cunard
- Viking Ocean Cruises
- Star Cruises

India with its long coastline is also becoming an upcoming attractive cruise destination as the government is taking steps to utilize its potential and launch cruises in the coming times.

BEACH TOURISM

Travelling for sun, sea and sand is a charm for many travellers. Visiting destinations known for their exotic beaches is a dream for beach bums. Beach vacations are a must for those travellers who have a love for the blue seas. They may just throng the destinations to just relax and spend their idle time watching the sea, swimming in the waters, reading a book on the beach loungers and getting their bodies tanned, taking beach Yoga classes or just gazing the stars in the night lying on the beach or engaging in water-based activities at the sea such as surfing, parasailing, jet-skiing, snorkelling, scuba diving and finding the hidden treasures of marine life. There are many countries in the world that are thriving their economies on beach tourism. *Some of the world-famous beach destinations are Mauritius, Maldives, Hawaii, Miami, Fiji Islands, the Bahamas, Curacao in the Caribbean Islands, Thailand, Gold Coast in Barbados, Goa and the Andaman and Nicobar Islands in India and so on.*

ISLAND TOURISM

For the discerning travellers who want to experience tranquillity and exclusivity and a break from the social life while staying in remote locations with waters all around, islands are the best place to spend one's vacation. Tourists visit islands to escape from the rat race for relaxing and gazing at the serene blue seas or indulging in various water activities. Some islands may feature coral reefs, luxuriant jungles or lofty peaks. Travellers, thus, may travel to these islands for their exotic beaches, unique local cultural experiences, stunning topography and the beautiful marine life.

Many islands like the Andaman and Nicobar Islands in India organize 'island tourism festival' annually to promote these islands in order to increase the footfall of tourists in the islands. However, as islands have a fragile ecology and a limited carrying capacity, it is imperative to keep a check on the number of visitors visiting the islands. Some of the famous islands of the world are *Maldives, Seychelles, Santorini in Greece, Bali in Indonesia, the Cook Islands in New Zealand, Boracay in the Philippines, Phi Phi Islands in Thailand, Faroe Islands, Fiji Islands, the Bahamas, the Caribbean Islands, Lakshadweep Islands in India* and so on. The *world's largest river island is Majuli, Assam, in India in the Brahmaputra river* which is becoming a popular island destination among tourists to visit.

SHOPPING TOURISM

Generally, shopping is one of the activities clubbed with sightseeing while visiting a destination. However, for those going for shopping tourism, travel for shopping is the main purpose with some sightseeing and leisure activities as a top-up. Thus, for shopaholics travelling to destinations with the intention of shopping is called shopping tourism. Shoppers may travel to buy local specialities of a destination while making a visit to the famous local streets, local markets, haats, exhibitions, shopping emporiums and shopping malls.

Many destinations of the world position themselves as shopper's paradise such as *Dubai, Singapore, and Kuala Lumpur and Jakarta in Malaysia.* The Dubai Shopping Festival is quite popular among the tourists. Some of the famous shopping areas of the world are as follows:

- Janpath, New Delhi, India
- Bloemenmarkt, Amsterdam (iconic floating market of flowers)
- Nanjing Road, Shanghai, China
- The Grand Bazaar, Istanbul, Turkey
- Deira Gold Souk, Dubai (world's renowned largest gold bazaar in the world)
- Deira Spice Souk, Dubai
- Chandni Chowk, Old Delhi, India
- Khari Baoli for spices, Chandni Chowk, New Delhi
- Flea market at Anjuna Beach on Wednesdays in Goa
- Dandenong market, Melbourne, Australia
- Harrods Mall, London
- China shopping tour for women in Guangzhou and Shenzhen
- Ibn Battuta Mall, Mall of the Emirates and Dubai Mall at Dubai
- Orchard Road, Singapore (Asia's famous shopping street)

CULINARY TOURISM

This kind of tourism may also be called *food tourism or gastronomical tourism.* Food can also be a major pull factor for attracting tourists to any destination. It forms the part of the rich heritage and culture of a destination. Thus, it may be considered as a subset of cultural tourism.

A destination may be very famous for its street food such as Amritsar and Chandni Chowk in India. Regional cuisines that offer diversity across different states of India may also woo the tourists such as the *Wazwan of Kashmir, Thali of Gujarat* and *Chettinad delicacies of South India.* To promote culinary tourism, destinations may promote food tours, food walks, food festivals and so on. In 2012, MOT, Government of India, had also launched 'Incredible Tiffin' campaign to showcase the regional delicacies of the country.

APPROACHES TO TOURISM

These are approaches to organizing tourism and related activities. Some of the popular variants of approaches towards tourism are as follows.

Sustainable Tourism

We need to understand that environment is very fragile as natural resources are limited. The environment has a limited capacity according to which it can accommodate tourists which is called the carrying capacity of the environment. When tourists visit a destination, they consume resources during their visits that create pressures of consumption at any destination. Any kind of tourism activity beyond the carrying capacity of the environment will negatively impact the environment and thus the society.

Therefore, sustainability in tourism is an approach which addresses social, economic and ecological sustainability of a place. Sustainable tourism ensures the use of natural resources in such a way that not only the needs of present generations are addressed but also the resources are kept intact and available for the future generations. Sustainable tourism advocates for judicious use of resources in a sustainable way without harming the environment by trying to mitigate the negative impacts of tourism. *The beginning of 2020 is a decade of action— another 10 years to achieve the 17 Sustainable Development Goals (SDGs) as defined by UNWTO. Destinations like Tromso in Norway are promoting sustainable travel.*

Green Tourism

Green tourism aims to be committed to the idea of sustainability with minimum impacts on the environment. Green tourism is a responsible and sustainable approach towards tourism that encourages the stakeholders and various tourism businesses such as airlines, hotels, bed and breakfast inns and attractions to promote environment-friendly tourism. It is an ideal way of being close to nature without harming it. It may involve activities such as simple walks in the woods, bird watching, cycling and berry picking.

Slow Tourism

Tourism at a relaxed pace keeping in mind the principle of rest for oneself is called slow tourism. It focuses on the quality and not the quantity of experiences. Therefore, the tourist is not in a rush to do everything. In fact, it allows him/her to rediscover himself/herself by spending time with himself/herself and letting go of stress. It emphasizes reducing the pace of doing too many touristic activities that keep a traveller preoccupied and he/she is not able to have time for himself/herself to reflect. It aims at enjoying in a calm and relaxed way that allows the tourist to spend time with the new environment and the people or the host community of a destination. Slow tourism activities may include activities where visitors can be in sync with the natural rhythm of the destination. *Some of the activities in slow tourism are hiking, bicycling, meditating, cross-country ski running, taking pleasure trips, rowing, doing water sports, visiting protected areas, discovering caves and so on. Many destinations like Turkey are promoting slow tourism.*

Accessible Tourism

Accessible tourism aims to make tourism accessible for all. It focuses on people with special abilities who have physical limitations and disabilities, senior citizens and expecting mothers for whom mobility is an issue. This segment of travellers is quite huge and thus, cannot be ignored.

Many destinations have become barrier-free now with the attractions, hotels, airports, railway stations and so on becoming barrier-free and the professional staff trained primarily to meet the needs of these people. Besides, many facilities and equipment such as wheelchairs, hearing aids, lifts, escalators, ramps, golf carts and accessible washrooms have been introduced in various tourist spots to make them accessible for such tourists. *Many tour operators such as Planet Abled, UMOJA and Girls on the Go Travel Club are promoting tour packages to people with limitations and disabilities in order to make the travel accessible for all.*

Pro-poor Tourism

Pro-poor tourism is an approach to tourism that helps in the eradication of poverty. Here, the ultimate objective of any kind of tourism activity is benefiting the poor people. Tourism being a labour-intensive industry involves the local people in tourism development and thus helps in reducing the poverty to an extent.

Community-based Tourism

The host community forms the focal point for development of any tourism activity at a destination. Their acceptance of the tourism phenomenon is very important. The community must be educated about the advantages of tourism. This can happen by designing tourism in such a way that the benefits accruing from tourism go back to the community. In community tourism, the community takes the ownership of tourism activities and is also involved in delivering tourism services that create opportunities for the community to be deeply engaged with the tourism phenomenon that encourages the community to boost tourism. For example, Sikkim, the first organic state of India, promotes community-based tourism by involving its local community in various tourism activities like encouraging them to offer homestays for the tourists, training the locals to be tour guides and involving them in many other similar tourist activities.

Safe and Honourable Tourism

A code of conduct was adopted in the year 2010 by MOT, Government of India, to promote safe and honourable tourism in the country by all the service providers of the tourism industry that included the travel agents, tour operators, transporters, hoteliers, tour guides, entertainment organizations and so on. This tourism approach ensures the safety and well-being of the tourists as well as the local community at the destination keeping in mind the *suraksha* (safety), one of the important seven pillars of National Tourism Policy, 2002. It advocates for zero tolerance for the exploitation of women and children in any form. It also issues strong guidelines for all the stakeholders not to cheat the tourists that build an element of mistrust among them that may eventually tarnish the image of our country. It also advocates for the prevention of activities like drug abuse, giving wrong information or any other similar wrongdoings to the tourists that bring the country to bad limelight.

SUMMARY

It is important for learners to have an understanding of different types of tourism existing in the tourism markets. Although the new tourism products may keep evolving, these basic tourism products will be evergreen products forever. There will always be reasonable markets to buy these products. We also need to learn and appreciate the importance of approaches towards tourism and ensure their proper implementation at the grassroots level to minimize the negative impacts of tourism on environment and society. The above-mentioned types of tourism were just an illustrative list and not an exhaustive approach.

ACTIVITIES

Activity 1

Pick up any five states of your country that are famous tourism destinations. Now identify their tourism authority/tourism board/tourism department that is responsible for promoting tourism in the state. Also, discuss the tag line given by the state for promoting tourism in the state along with the types of tourism promoted by them.

Activity 2

Name the top five international business tourism destinations of the world. Discuss their reasons for being the famous business destinations.

Activity 3

Discuss in detail the role and functions of ICPB in promoting business events in India.

Activity 4

Think of any destination that has immense potential to be promoted as a tourism destination but is lacking in its marketing efforts. Now share your views with the class about the various ways in which you would initiate to market the destination to the tourist. For this, create a detailed marketing plan for the destination with the existing tourism products that it has that may be offered to tourists, the kind of tourism markets that must be tapped by the destination, USP that it can use to market itself and the brand ambassador that you would use to promote the destination. Also, create a logo and a tag line for the destination to promote it to the tourists.

Niche Tourism Products

4

THE ROMAN BATHS: AN ANCIENT SPA!

The Roman Baths, England

- The Roman Baths is one of the most iconic well-preserved thermae in the city of Bath in England (Bath, declared as a world heritage city in 1987 by UNESCO).
- The Roman Baths is one of the historic sites in the world which dates back 2,000 years. It is a beautiful historical heritage, constructed around 70 AD as a grand bathing and socializing complex.
- This is one of the most-visited attractions of the UK as more than one million tourists throng this place annually.
- The tourists may spend around two hours in the historical place by either opting for an audio guide in one of the 12 languages or take a guided tour, according to their requirement.
- The Roman Baths has been made more accessible and comfortable for people as they have added facilities which help people with sensory impairment. The facilities include

audio guide, sign language guide, fully descriptive tours and enabling touchable site tours for blind visitors to give them a full experience.

- The Roman Baths also has a description site for people with autism so that they know what to expect in the tour.
- If you want to take a sip of spa water with curative properties, then visit the pump room. The water is said to contain 43 minerals, which attracts many people from all over the world.

INTRODUCTION

With tourism becoming an integral part of everyone's life and the tourism industry seeing phenomenal growth in the last decade, the tourism service providers are continuously innovating new tourism products to cater to the changing needs and preferences of the travellers. Tourists are looking for offbeat experiences rather than just experiencing regular kind of tourism products. There is a lot of focus on adding the 'experiential element' while developing new products for the new segments that are emerging. Many niche tourism products are being marketed by various destinations across the world to woo particular segments of markets in order to increase the visits of tourists in their destinations.

Niche tourism products may be referred to as specific products that are meant for specific segments of markets that suit their needs and desires. These segments may not be very large; however, they are quite profitable. Destinations promoting niche tourism products are referred to as niche tourism destinations.

Now let us have a detailed discussion on the emerging niche tourism products being marketed by destinations.

WELLNESS TOURISM

This kind of tourism is very popular among those tourists who are very health-conscious and for whom physical and mental well-being is very important. It is one's personal interest in maintaining and enhancing his/her personal health that he/she opts for wellness tourism. Basically, the idea is to improve one's well-being, maintain health and aim at a better quality of life. One learns to take better care of oneself in all aspects, that is, physically, psychologically as well as spiritually.

Thus, wellness tourism involves travelling to those destinations that help in the holistic rejuvenation of one's body and mind. It involves participating in various health and wellness programmes to detox oneself such as taking healthy nutritious diets, participating in weight loss programmes, following an exercise regime, taking Yoga classes, going for spa treatments, de-stress and rejuvenation treatments and massage treatments. For some tourists, it may be through spiritual healing like going for meditation for finding inner peace of mind.

Thus, such travellers may visit various spas, ashrams, wellness centres/retreats, Yoga schools and healing centres for seeking wellness treatments. Many hotels have special wellness rooms and suites to keep up with the healthy lifestyle of travellers. Most of the hotels today also have dedicated wellness professionals to advise the guests on matters of wellness.

India is promoting wellness tourism in a big way. India has contributed to wellness tourism in a unique way by giving the gifts of Yoga and Ayurveda (a 5,000-year-old science of healing that heals with natural herbs, oils and massages, diet and lifestyle) to the world. Thousands of tourists from the USA, the UK, Australia, the UAE and so on visit India to take alternative medicinal treatments to heal naturally. The *Ministry of AYUSH* in India is aggressively promoting the concept of wellness in India. The acronym AYUSH refers to *Ayurveda, Yoga and Naturopathy, Unani, Siddha and Homeopathy,* which are alternate medical treatments. Some of the wellness destinations in India are as follows:

- Kerala (known for its Ayurveda, especially the Panchakarma and Shirodhara treatment)
- Ananda Spa in the Himalayas, Rishikesh
- Kayakalp in Himachal Pradesh
- Bengaluru for Ayurvedagram Heritage Wellness Centre, Atmayaan

Some popular international destinations of the world for wellness tourism are Italy, Austria, Turkey, Japan, Bali, Thailand, Japan, Australia, New Zealand and Costa Rica.

THERMAL TOURISM

As old as the history of humanity goes, man has known the curative properties of thermal and mineral waters for relaxation, releasing stress and other health purposes like curing skin diseases. The modern tourists plan to spend healthy vacations by taking care of their bodies and overall health. Thus, *spas are the tourism of the new millennium.*

Thermal tourism is a part of health or wellness tourism that involves taking care of one's health through indulging oneself in thermal spas and hot water springs that contain minerals. Various kinds of wellness tourism packages have been introduced that include various therapies like spa treatments such as 'cure with water', hot water baths, mineral springs, steam bath applications, exercise, beauty and body care, hot tubs, thalassotherapy, massage therapies, diet and nutrition, aromatherapy, anti-stress and anti-ageing therapies, mud therapy and hot stone massage that are used for healing bodies. *Soaking in hot springs is called balneotherapy* that reduces stress and promotes sleep.

One of the leading tourism destinations for thermal tourism or wellness tourism in Europe is Turkey. *Turkey is known to have natural thermal springs.* Many Europeans visit Turkey for hot spring treatments in Turkish baths called *hammams.* The two cities, *Izmir* and *Anatolia* (a geothermal belt with around 1,300 geothermal resources), are very popular destinations among tourists for seeking thermal therapies that are known to cure skin diseases, gastrointestinal diseases, kidney and urinary tract diseases, various allergies and so on.

Likewise, another destination famous for its natural thermal springs rich in natural healing elements is *Tuscany in Italy*. It has a turnaround of more than two million tourists who throng this destination annually in various seaside resorts to relax or for prevention and treatment of many pathologies.

Similarly, *Japan* is very famous for its *onsens* (hot springs) that have curative properties due to the presence of various minerals such as potassium, calcium and silica in them that supply more oxygen to the body and thus, help in reducing stress and improving sleep.

Besides Turkey, Japan and Italy, other countries that promote thermal tourism are Germany, France, Greece, Switzerland, Russia, Hungary and Czech Republic.

WINE TOURISM

Wine tourism may also be referred to as *enotourism, oenotourism* or *vinitourism*. Many wine enthusiasts have an interest in visiting the wine-producing regions of the world. Watching how wine is made is a treat for wine enthusiasts. Such wine lovers may plan 'wine getaways' to visit the wineries (companies manufacturing wine) and vineyards (plantation of grape-bearing vines) for understanding the process of how wine is produced. Some tourists may also visit restaurants known to serve unique vintages. They may taste it, purchase it or consume it. Wineries organize wine tours for the wine lovers to watch how different kinds of wines are made. Tourists may also enjoy food pairing and wine tasting sessions and grape stomping besides taking wine spa treatments to relax and rejuvenate their skin.

As wine tourism brings economic benefits for the host destination, many wine festivals and wine exhibitions are organized by wine companies and hotels to promote wine tourism in the country. The major 'Old World' wine-producing countries of the world are *Duero River Valley in Spain and Portugal, Bordeaux in France, Tuscany in Italy, Hungary, the Aegean Islands in Greece, Portugal, Austria and Germany*. The 'New World' wine regions of the world are *Australia, New Zealand, Argentina, Chile, Mexico, South Africa, Napa Valley in the USA* and *Okanagan Valley in Canada*. The *Bordeaux wine getaway in France* is popular among the tourists for its Instagrammable images and offers a 'wine tasting river cruise' in the Garonne river.

India has also joined the League of Nations promoting wine tourism by increasing wine production in the country and organizing wine tours and wine festivals. The major wine-producing states in the country are Maharashtra and Karnataka. One of the famous wine tourism destinations in India is *Nashik in Maharashtra also called the 'wine capital' of the country*. *Sula Vineyards* is the most popular haven for wine lovers in Nashik, Maharashtra. With their first wine resort in the country that promotes wine tourism, Sula Vineyards continues to create an awareness of wine culture among the tourists in the country.

TEA TOURISM

It involves visit of tea connoisseurs to destinations famous for cultivating tea where they visit the tea plantations and tea factories to learn about the processes of how tea is made. The tourists may stay in the colonial era bungalows to get a taste of British architecture and the lush green gardens of the tea estate. They may enjoy the process from plucking of tea leaves to their withering, rolling, oxidation, drying and then finally the most interesting part of the tea-making process, the tea tasting where they can taste different kinds of teas from black tea to green tea to white tea.

India, being one of the largest producers of tea in the world, is fast positioning itself as a tea tourism destination for tea lovers on similar lines of wine tourism in Europe. Destinations in India promoting tea tourism are Assam, Darjeeling, Munnar in Kerala, Nilgiris district in Tamil Nadu and Palampur in Himachal Pradesh. Besides India, China, Sri Lanka, Vietnam and Kenya are the other major tea-producing countries in the world.

DARK TOURISM

Dark tourism may also be referred to as *black tourism, grief tourism, graveyard tourism or thanatourism*. It involves travel to destinations or tourist attractions/sites that are associated with death and sufferings. It may include visit to locations like disaster sites that may be man-made or natural, battlefields, dungeons or any other site where people were killed or given endless suffering that brings a feeling of remorse and pain in the hearts of the tourists. As many people may have died at a site, visitors may visit to pay tribute to the people who suffered there. Sometimes, they may also visit graveyards to pay homage to their ancestors. Many tourist sites/attractions may recreate such painful experiences by constructing a museum or an exhibition to educate the tourists about the incident that took place there. For example, The Titanic Museum in Belfast, North Ireland, is a recreation of the drowning sailing vessel Titanic

Tea Tasting in a Tea Estate, Darjeeling, India

Miniature of the Titanic, Titanic Museum, Belfast, North Ireland

where thousands of passengers died onboard meeting an accident with the iceberg in the year 1912 in her maiden voyage. The museum has nine galleries that have a display of pictures of the ship and the letters that the passengers had sent to their families before the incident happened. They have also replicated the linen and crockery that was used in the ship along with the different kinds of cabins that were constructed in the ship for the different class of passengers. At one point in the gallery, one can also hear the echoes of the drowning passengers that have been virtually rec-

Replica of a Cabin in the Titanic, Titanic Museum, Belfast

reated for the tourists to experience and connect with the whole incident. While moving through the different zones of the museum, one may actually feel the sufferings, pain and fear of the drowning passengers that is a very sorrowful experience for the tourists.

Some other similar sites for dark tourism are as follows:

- Jallianwala Bagh, Amritsar, India
- The Cellular Jail, Andaman and Nicobar Islands, India
- Union Carbide Gas Tragedy, Bhopal, India
- Yad Vashem, Jerusalem (World Holocaust Remembrance Center)
- Pripyat in Ukraine (known for its Chernobyl Disaster, 1986)
- Fukushima, Japan (the world's worst nuclear accident in 2011 where 1,600 people were killed in the accident as the nuclear power plant was hit by tsunami)
- Nazi extermination camps in Germany and Poland
- Ground Zero in New York, USA

EVENT TOURISM

Events are a major crowd puller for many tourists. These may include fairs, festivals, sports events and so on. Tourists may sometimes plan their vacation around the time of an event taking place at a destination. Thus, lots of destination marketers intelligently market these events to attract the tourists to a destination. These events act as a branding tool for increasing the footfall of tourists to a destination.

For example, *Gujarat tourism promotes Kutch as a tourism destination in a big way.* The 'Rann Utsav' that was initially designed and introduced to market Kutch and the Gujarati culture is now a magnet that attracts a large number of tourists to experience the cultural vibes of the state in this white desert. Tourists stay at tented accommodations, attend cultural Gujarati performances, enjoy the various Gujarati cuisines, while also enjoying the white desert in the full moon night view.

Similarly, many destinations holding sports events such as IPL, FIFA and Cricket World Cup also promote themselves aggressively during sporting events to attract the sports lovers in the hosting destination.

As India is often described as a 'land of festivals and festivities', some of the popular events that attract many foreign tourists are as follows:

- International Yoga Festival, Rishikesh
- Holi, Barsana, Uttar Pradesh
- Pushkar fair of Rajasthan
- International Kite Festival of Gujarat
- Bikaner Camel Festival, Rajasthan
- Desert Festival, Jaisalmer
- Goa Carnival, Goa
- Nehru Trophy Boat Race of Kerala
- Taj Mahotsav, Agra
- Hornbill Festival, Nagaland

Likewise, there are many international events that attract many tourists. *One such festival worth mentioning here is 'the Oktoberfest', the largest beer festival in the world.* It is held annually for 16–18 days in Munich, Bavaria, Germany. With more than six million visitors coming together from all walks of life to attend the festival, it is considered as *the largest folk festival in the world.* The activities here include dancing, singing, drinking beer, eating the traditional food such as pork sausages, roasted chicken and pretzel, enjoying the colourful parades and a variety of fairground rides.

Some other famous worth attending lifetime international festivals that are opportunities for tourists to pack their bags and attend the festival as well as explore the country are as follows:

- Cherry blossom festivals, Japan
- Harbin International Ice and Snow winter festival, Harbin, China
- Winter Carnival, Patnitop, Jammu and Kashmir (J&K), India
- Burning Man, Nevada, USA
- La Tomatina festival, Spain
- Rio De Janeiro Carnival, Brazil
- Running of the Bulls, Spain
- Cooper's Hill Cheese Rolling festival, England
- Songkran water festival, Chiang Mai, Thailand
- Gay Pride Parade, San Francisco
- Boryeong Mud Festival, South Korea
- The Edinburgh Festival Fringe, Scotland (world's largest art festival)

AGRITOURISM

It involves the visit of tourists to an agriculture farm or a ranch, especially those tourists who have a keen interest in how food is produced. Tourists while visiting these farms can actually learn how their food that they get on their tables is made in the fields, what efforts go in nurturing the seeds into a crop and finally seeing how it is harvested and stored right so that it can reach the final consumer. This kind of tourism builds an appreciation for farmers in the minds of the tourists who are educated and told about the food production process by their continuous interactions with the farmers and the processors where they actually see the source of their food in the fields.

It is a niche tourism product that is growing in countries including Canada, Australia, the USA and so on, though it is quite popular in countries such as Italy and Latvia. It involves farm stays (stays of tourists at bed and breakfast (B&B) on farms), engaging in activities such as cheese-making, cow milking, feeding animals, riding horses, picking fruits and vegetables directly from the trees and the farms, shopping the local produce of farms and learning about the farming processes and farm products besides getting an opportunity to see the lifestyles of farmers and realizing the advantages of staying in the countryside.

FARM TOURISM

Farm tourism has become very popular among the urban population who visit nearby farm-houses and stay there for weekend getaways. In India, the state of *Haryana* pioneered in initi-ating the concept of farmhouses and farm stays. Being away from the hustle and bustle of urban life and escaping to find tranquillity are the main mottos of such tourists who visit farms and stay in farmhouses. Participating in farm activities such as engaging in plucking orchids, taking cattle rides, mud bathing, tasting honey, horseback riding, taking bullock cart rides or tractor rides, feeding cattle, going for herbal excursions, participation in organic farm-ing and growing crops are some of the activities that the tourists may look forward to while staying in the farmhouses. Besides these activities, the tourists may practise Yoga and medita-tion, take pottery or cooking classes, enjoy a bonfire at night with barbeque dinners and local dance performances and engage in much more similar activities during their stay at the farm-houses. Few other states such as Punjab, Maharashtra and Kerala in India too are taking steps to encourage the concept of farmhouses. Some of the examples where travellers may stay in farmhouses are as follows:

- The Surjivan Farm, Haryana
- Citrus County, Punjab

MUSIC TOURISM

Lovers of music travel to any part of the world to attend international events like to see the rock band performances or to listen to their favourite singer. Thus, the practice of travelling to des-tinations for attending or participating in music festivals and musical concerts is called music tourism. Some of the must-attend music festivals for music lovers are as follows:

- Tomorrowland Music Festival, Belgium
- The Glastonbury Festival, England
- Edinburgh Jazz & Blues Festival, Scotland
- The Sunburn Festival, India
- The Ziro Music Festival, Arunachal Pradesh, India
- The Tansen Music Festival, Gwalior, India
- Montreal International Jazz Festival, Canada

LITERARY TOURISM

Many literature enthusiasts who have a keen interest in literature and are inspired by an author's environs may wish to take literary tours that involve travelling to those places which are related to the famous authors or novelists who have lived there, or whose fictional characters in the novels have lived there. It could involve visiting the house of a poet/an author/a novelist, following the route of a fictional character and so on. To promote literary tourism, many literary tours are organized by various travel companies. The United Kingdom has many literary trails where travellers may go to visit the birthplace, homes, museums, burial sites and other related attractions of authors or their created characters on these trails. *London is supposed to be 'world's literature centre'* as it has been the place of famous authors such as Charles Dickens, H. G. Wells and Sir Arthur Conan Doyle (who created the famous Sherlock Holmes character). Several destinations in order to promote literary tourism also organize literary festivals. *Jaipur Literature Festival in India is quite popular.*

Some of the world-famous literary destinations are as follows:

- Stratford-upon-Avon, UK (home of the famous playwright William Shakespeare)
- Edinburgh, Scotland (declared as the first UNESCO city of literature and famous for the Writers' Museum)
- Dublin, Ireland (famous for Dublin Literary Pub Crawl)
- Melbourne, Australia
- St. Petersburg, Russia
- New York and San Francisco, USA

SPACE TOURISM

Travelling on space to experience weightlessness and incredible views of the earth from is a dream for many. For those tourists who dare to go on space and experience a lifetime event in their lives, space tourism is the right answer. Although to book one's tour to space, one really needs to be fully geared up both physically and mentally and take adequate training to learn to live in a small spacecraft, to gain this experience one must be able to afford it enough as it is a very expensive tourism product. The first tourist to go in space was Dennis Tito from the USA in 2001.

POP CULTURE TOURISM

Many tourism authorities leverage on the popularity of the films to showcase their destinations in order to promote destinations. Placing beautiful destinations at the backdrop of the movies is the most effective medium to get the travellers attracted to a destination. When tourists are motivated by different forms of entertainment like movies, magazines, radio or any other form of entertainment that features different spectacular locations that push a tourist to actually travel to that destination, the phenomenon is called pop culture tourism. For example, when the movie *Zindagi Na Milegi Dobara* was featured in Spain, many Indians planned their holidays in Spain to experience the local festival La Tomatina that was featured in the movie and also witness the scenic locations of the country. Likewise, *Dilwale Dulhania Le Jayenge* increased the Indian footfall to Switzerland that featured in it. Few shots that were taken for *Game of Thrones at Dark Hedges, Belfast, North Ireland* increased the tourist footfall to the given location. In short, we may say that pop culture can highly influence and boost tourism in destinations.

GOLF TOURISM

Golf tourism is a niche tourism product of sports tourism. Destinations such as India and Scotland are a paradise for golf lovers. Travelling to a destination on a holiday with the prime objective of playing golf at the destination is called golf tourism. Since golf is a very expensive game and needs a well-maintained world-class infrastructure, many countries may not promote it. Only those countries that have world-class golf courses offer golf tour packages to woo the golf lovers across the world.

In fact, India is being preferred as a golfing destination by international tourists. India has world-class golf courses in the country where golf enthusiasts eagerly look forward to attending golf events in the country. *India also boasts of having the highest golf course in the world in Gulmarg, Kashmir.* Established in 1829, the oldest golf course of the country is the Royal Calcutta Golf Club in Kolkata. Besides these, some of the finest luxury golf destinations for golfers in the world are in North America, Spain, Portugal, the UK and so on.

POLO TOURISM

Polo is a popular game among many sports enthusiasts. Many destinations of the world are promoting polo as a tourism product to tourists to come and play polo in their country as it offers economic benefits to the host destination. Polo, being the heritage sport of India, some of the states in the country are aggressively promoting polo to woo tourists. The state of Manipur in India is considered home to polo. India also has the oldest polo club in the world, Calcutta Polo Club, which is approximately 150 years old.

SLUM TOURISM

Slum tourism or ghetto tourism, though criticized for different reasons, is still a reason for many travellers to visit destinations that are inhabited by slums. Many foreign tourists visit the slums to view the marginalized and impoverished communities. Seeing how people manage to live in the poverty in utter bad conditions in slums is a subject of interest for such travellers who may have never experienced poverty or seen such kind of life. Rich people gawking at the underprivileged people of the society making mockery of their poverty can get very discomforting for these people also for whom they are objects of interest. *Slum tours may also be referred to as reality tours or poverty tours.* Many travel companies such as *Salaam Baalak Trust in Delhi* and *Reality Tours & Travel in Mumbai* organize slum tours for the travellers. Slum tours are becoming popular in the following places:

- Street life of New Delhi, India
- Slums of Manila, Philippines
- Dharavi slum tours, Mumbai, India
- Kibera slums in Kenya
- Hutongs in Beijing and other Chinese larger cities
- Favelas in Brazil

HIGHWAY TOURISM

Travelling by road is a charm for many. However, this is only possible if there is a good network and infrastructure of roadways and highways. Highway tourism, thus, focuses on building a good network of highways that facilitates road travel for the tourists. It also focuses on creating wayside amenities for the tourists to take stopovers such as cafes, restaurants, public conveniences and motels. The first state to pioneer the concept of highway tourism in India was *Haryana* with an idea to increase road travel within the state. Many food lovers, who enjoy eating the roadside food like in dhabas, travel on these highways to take a stopover at the dhaba and relish its food. For example, many foodies from Delhi specially visit *Murthal*, a small village in Haryana, that is famous for its roadside dhabas selling paranthas with butter.

WEDDING TOURISM

Wedding is always a special occasion in one's life to celebrate. Many people wish to double this joy by celebrating this lifetime event in a special and unique way at a destination that may be famous for holding weddings. This may be referred to as wedding tourism. Destination weddings are a popular choice for many as these days, many tourists want to experience their marriage according to the detailed rituals and customs of the famous wedding destination and make it a larger than life celebration. As a Hindu wedding is very elaborate full of rituals and ceremonies, it attracts many foreign tourists to come and get married in India. Some destinations in India such as *Udaipur*, 'the city of lakes', and *Jodhpur* in Rajasthan are increasingly being positioned and marketed as an ideal place for 'destination weddings' where tourists can celebrate the grandeur of Indian weddings in forts and palaces in the most exuberant and royal style. *The Oberoi Udaivilas, the Leela Palace Udaipur, Taj Lake Palace, Jagmandir Island Palace, the Lalit Laxmi Niwas Palace, City Palace* and so on are some of the costliest and famous places to have a lavish wedding ceremony.

Visitors may like to get married in forts and palaces in different styles. However, many tourists may also like to get married in a simple style in India in temples and ashrams for which they may prefer to visit South India. For destination weddings, many tourists hire wedding planners who make all wedding-related arrangements including travel and stay.

ELECTION TOURISM

With the first of its kind in the world, election tourism is a niche tourism product, especially in India. Lots of people from other parts of the world who take a keen interest in politics are interested to see and understand the polling and election system of the largest democracy in the world, India. They may also keep a keen watch or sometimes even participate in various political rallies and festivities before and after elections. The first state to pioneer the initiative of promoting elections as a tourism product in the country was *Gujarat*.

SPECIAL INTEREST TOURISM

When tourists travel for pursuing special interests at specific destinations to learn various arts or pursue a particular hobby, it may be called special interest tourism. These tours are customized to the needs of the travellers.

Cookery tours, travelling to do photography, painting, learning different local art forms of the country, bird watching, bicycling tours and so on may be classified under special interest tourism.

HALAL TOURISM

It involves travel of Muslim families to Muslim-friendly destinations that respect their religious values and sentiments. The idea is to make the travel of Islamic community comfortable so that the tourist footfall increases at the destinations. *Malaysia, Turkey, Abu Dhabi, Morocco* and so on are few of the destinations that are promoting halal tourism for attracting the Muslim travellers.

Halal tourism advocates the restaurants that are halal certified and only serve halal meat. Keeping in consonance with the value system of Islam, the airline service providers also have segregated seats for men and women and have pocket-friendly Qurans and in-flight entertainment loaded with Muslim prayers. These Muslim-friendly airlines do not serve alcohol and ensure that the meat served is halal certified. The hotels also have separate swimming pools for men and women and serve halal meat and do not serve pork and alcohol. They also provide translation services and any other services wanted by these tourists like making announcements for prayers during their prayer time. Tour operators also take care in devising itineraries that have in-built breaks for five daily calls to prayer as per the Islam religious practices.

BIRTH TOURISM

Many tourists visit destinations to give birth to babies at a new destination more specifically a country. The idea is to use the baby as an anchor to get permanent residentship in a country. They may also want to avail better facilities for their child such as free education and medical facilities. Especially, this practice is more predominant among people of upper-middle income countries who want their children to become citizens of high-income countries by taking birth there so that eventually they can also enjoy the benefits of becoming a permanent citizen of the country by virtue of being a parent. Although people travel to countries such as Canada, the USA and the UK for birth tourism, this practice is not much encouraged by many countries of the world and the laws are also becoming stringent day by day in few countries discouraging this kind of practice.

NAUTICAL TOURISM

This term is interchangeably used with the maritime tourism. This kind of tourism is focused on spending a vacation during summer while sailing and boating in the waters as the main attraction. The waters may include sea, lakes, rivers, canals and so on. Such nautical tourists may sail in cruises, boats, yachts or any other sailing vessels. Travellers may enjoy various water activities such as diving, surfing, rafting, fishing, rowing and visiting lighthouses. Therefore, the purpose of nautical tourism is recreation, sports, entertainment and so on. Nautical tourism has lots of economic benefits for a country. Tourists may sail during the day and stay near the shores at the overnight accommodation. Nautical tourism is quite popular in Europe, South America, the USA and the Pacific Rim.

VIRTUAL TOURISM

Technology has made travel easy as with the use of the Internet, travellers can visit places virtually. It cannot be equated with the real-time travel experience where the traveller travels physically and experiences a change of place. Here, the travellers take a virtual tour of the destination on their smartphones or computers with the Internet by using images, image-based models and videos along with sound effects, music and narration that make them travel in an electronic environment. However, the advantage of this kind of tourism is that it saves one's time and money besides creating a thought in the mind of the person to actually travel to a destination.

Many destinations of the world are actively promoting virtual tourism such as Faroe Islands especially during the time of COVID-19 to induce travel after restrictions to travel are uplifted once normalcy prevails.

WAR TOURISM

This kind of tourism involves visiting sites of armed forces such as war zones, war memorials, war museums and military sites and hence may be called military tourism.

For example, many tourists while visiting New Delhi, India, may visit the *National War Memorial at India Gate* for paying tribute to the 25,942 Indian soldiers who had laid down their lives for the country since Independence. The names of those soldiers who sacrificed their lives for the country have been etched in the stones forever. While visiting the memorial, one may also visit the Obelisk and the Veerta Chakra with six bronze murals depicting different battles at the site along with the visit to Param Yodha Sthal where one can pay tribute to the busts of 21 Param Vir Chakra awardees, the highest military honour of the country. A war museum is also being constructed on the same site.

Many destinations like *Kosovo, South Korea* and *Israel* are promoting war tourism taking advantage of the growing interest of travellers in conflict zones.

COPYCAT TOURISM

This kind of tourism involves travel to replicas of famous tourist attractions without actually visiting the destinations that are famous for these attractions. Many destinations in order to increase the tourist footfall have superficially created artificial structures that are replicas of famous attractions. This kind of tourism satisfies the desire of those travellers who cannot actually afford to travel to those destinations due to the paucity of time and money. Hence, it saves the precious time and money of the travellers along with the hassle required to travel to different destinations. Few destinations for copycat tourism are as follows:

- China
- Seven Wonders Park, Kota, Rajasthan, India
- Waste to Wonder Park, New Delhi, India

DISASTER TOURISM

Travelling to destinations where a disaster has occurred that may be a natural calamity or man-made is called disaster tourism. For many travellers, visiting the site to see how the disaster took place, asking people what must have happened and how they are leading their lives after the disaster are an area of interest. Visiting places that have been struck by earthquakes, flash floods, tsunami and so on are a few examples of disaster tourism. However, this kind of tourism is criticized as it can hurt the sentiments of local people as for tourists, they are mere objects who may narrate the painful stories.

LGBTQ TOURISM

The term LGBTQ stands for lesbian, gay, bisexual, transgender and queer. The movement of LGBTQ to different destinations is also called as *gay tourism*. It has been under criticism as many destinations still do not support this kind of open culture. However, realizing the growing need of these segments that bring *pink dollars/pounds* to the economy, many travel companies are offering special packages for such travellers. However, while planning packages for such travellers, the travel companies must be sensitive towards the needs of such travellers and offer only those destinations where they find a supportive environment to conduct themselves. Some famous destinations of this segment of the market are *Brighton in England, Prague in the Czech Republic, Tel Aviv in Israel, Puerto Vallarta in Mexico* and so on.

SUICIDE TOURISM

People who suffer from dreaded diseases that are incurable and for whom natural death is desirable, but death seems to be a distant dream and these people die every day of pain and suffering, death is the only solution. However, in some countries committing suicide to get rid of dreaded pain and suffering is illegal. Thus, such travellers visit those countries where euthanasia is legal to help the patient get rid of all the pains and sufferings. This is called suicide tourism. In countries such as the Netherlands and Belgium, this kind of tourism is legal.

DRUG TOURISM

Visiting destinations to buy and consume drugs that may be illegal in one's own country or destination is called drug tourism. This kind of tourism has many legal implications. However, in many destinations of the world, this drug culture is legal that makes travellers visit these places to get the forbidden substances. Amsterdam in the Netherlands is an example of a destination where drug tourism is legal.

GARDEN TOURISM

The concept of garden tourism began in England and Germany. Travellers who are nature lovers like to visit gardens that may be a collection of different kinds of flora. They may visit the botanical gardens, public parks and some scenic parks that blossom with flowers where they can take local tours and learn about the different kinds of flora grown in the gardens. Few gardens may be opened for some seasons when the flowers blossom and it is worth visiting them at that time. *Many festivals are also organized to promote gardens to increase the visits of tourists such as the Garden Tourism Festival that takes place in the Garden of Five Senses, New Delhi.* Some famous gardens of the world worth visiting for the tourists are as follows:

- The Mughal Gardens, New Delhi
- The Keukenhof Tulip Gardens, Amsterdam
- Dubai Miracle Garden, Dubai
- The Gardens by the Bay, Singapore
- The Royal Botanical Gardens, Australia
- The Tulip Garden, J&K, India

Gardens by the Bay, Singapore

RAIL TOURISM

This kind of tourism promotes travel through railway network. As India has a huge network of railways across the length and breadth of the country, IRCTC has introduced many rail packages where destinations are clubbed together on various circuits to encourage the travellers to travel by rail. Packages may be offered with itineraries covering the heritage circuits, pilgrimage circuits and so on. Tourists may travel on *luxury trains such as Palace on Wheels, Golden Chariot, Deccan Odyssey, Maharajas' Express* and *Royal Rajasthan on Wheels.* Pilgrim tourists may travel on *Mahaparinirvan Express* covering Buddhist circuit, *Punj Takht Express* covering Sikh community pilgrim points and many other similar pilgrimage trains. Some other tourist trains are *Bharat Darshan, toy trains* and *steam trains.*

DOOM TOURISM

It is an emerging trend in the tourism industry that urges travellers to visit those destinations/sites that are deteriorating. These sites are either threatened by environmental or human threat. Thus, it is a last chance for travellers to visit the sites before they dwindle. Hence, doom tourism may also be referred to as last chance tourism. Mount Kilimanjaro region in Tanzania, Amalia Glacier in South Patagonia and Chile are being promoted as doom tourist destinations.

SUMMARY

In an increasingly competitive environment, offering niche tourism products by a destination is a unique way to position itself as a brand and establish itself as a niche tourism destination. It also helps in differentiating oneself from other destinations and creates a clear-cut strategy for marketers to project the niche tourism products in such a way that they evoke strong images of the destination in the minds of the tourists. It also clears the clutter that may be created in the mind of a tourist due to the offering of too many tourism products by a destination. It is a product-led approach that focuses on appealing to certain segments of markets with a particular product offering.

ACTIVITIES

Activity 1: Roleplay

Divide the class into different groups. Now ask each group to take any type of tourism that they may like to enact in the class such as dark tourism, cruise tourism, wellness tourism, tea tourism and wildlife tourism. Give sufficient time to the class to prepare their roleplay. The students may be allowed to use props, videos, audios and so on so as to make their roleplay more real and interesting. The students may organize a roleplay, talk show, puppet show or an exhibition regarding the kind of tourism given to them. Let the excitement roll!

Activity 2

Identify the names of cities by what they are famous for.

1. City of sins
2. International Yoga capital of the world
3. Spa capital of the world
4. Entertainment capital of the world
5. City of lakes
6. City of temples
7. City of lights

Components of Tourism Industry

LEARNING OBJECTIVES

The given chapter shall clarify the following:

- What are the various components of the tourism industry?
- Who are the major service providers in the tourism industry?
- What are the 5 A's of tourism industry?

SANTORINI: TRULY A GREEK PARADISE!

- Santorini, a volcanic island in Greece, is an ideal romantic destination famous for destination weddings, along with picturesque sunsets and pearly white-washed buildings with blue windows and unique stairways and windmills.
- The precious gem of the Aegean Sea, also famous for its own active volcano, is a home to some of the best attractions that include the Fira (the capital of Santorini) famous for its cafes, souvenir shops, bars with patio/balconies, Oia for its incredible sunsets, Caldera, Akrotiri archaeological site, Red Beach, White Beach, Black Beach and many historical monuments like blue-domed churches.
- Tourists may soak themselves in activities such as sunset viewing, cruising on catamarans, water sports, wine tasting, sailing and taking walking tours, biking tours, photo tours, village tours, hiking tours, sunset boat tours, yacht tours, cultural tours and volcano tours.
- The island is truly a culinary delight for the gourmets, where they may try the sumptuous local dishes such as fava, cherry tomatoes, white aubergines (eggplant) with goat cheese, Greek salads and much more!

INTRODUCTION

The tourism industry is a service industry as all the industries that come together to create a tourism product are primarily service industries. As the new-age travellers are increasingly becoming more demanding and want to be pampered at every step during their vacation, it is equally more important for the service providers also to become competitive and dynamic in nature like never before in order to match the rising aspirations of the new-age travellers. Any flaw at any level by any service provider in the delivery of a seamless service can totally mar the experience of a traveller, making him/her neither travel to the same destination again nor with the same travel company/service provider again.

The tourism industry does not exist as a stand-alone industry. In fact, it has strong linkages with other industries. It is a composition of sub-industries that combine to deliver a pleasant experience to the traveller. It is a meta-market where other industries are complementary and supplementary to each other that function in coordination with each other to facilitate an overall pleasant experience for tourists during their holiday.

Every industry that contributes to serving and facilitating the tourists is a component of the tourism industry. These may also be referred to as the supply chain of the tourism industry, who are involved in the delivery of services. The stronger the intra- and interlinkages among the various service providers, the better would be the experience of a tourist.

The tourism industry is a combination of a wide range of industries that include transportation, accommodation, food and beverage (F&B), retail, culture, sports and recreation. The primary customers of this industry are the international tourists, domestic tourists, leisure tourists and business tourists.

Each component of the tourism industry has been discussed in detail as a separate chapter under Section B of the book as 5 A's of tourism. The readers are advised to go through the content of each chapter covering each component for their better understanding. In the given chapter, let us get an overview of the overall components of the tourism industry. For the sake of our clarity, we have divided the components into two parts:

- Core components
- Service providers

Now, let us discuss each of these in detail.

CORE COMPONENTS

These form the base of the tourism industry around which all the arrangements are aimed at. Let us have a detailed discussion on each of these.

Destination

The whole tourism activity takes place at a destination. It forms the core of the tourism phenomenon. A destination is basically a place that may refer to a city, town, village, state, region or a country. For tourism to develop at a destination, it must synchronize the efforts of various service providers and create infrastructure along with adequate facilities to bring the tourists to a destination. A destination must build its image among the prospective tourists by offering interesting and engaging tourism products and experiences. It must entice travellers in unique ways to capture the attention of travellers. Thus, it must focus on its USP along with the segments to be targeted. It must continuously evolve its offerings according to the changing needs of the travellers and must bridge the gap between their expectations and the kinds of experiences being offered. It must develop a competitive advantage over other destinations.

Attractions

The main component of tourism around which the whole tourism activity revolves is attraction. Attraction is the main starting point and a pull factor that motivates a traveller to visit a destination. Attractions may be classified as follows:

- **Natural attractions** such as beaches, lakes, hill stations, national parks, deserts, mountains and natural landforms such as volcanoes and gorges.
- **Man-made attractions** such as historical sites, archaeological sites, palaces, forts, museums, art galleries, artificial structures such as skyscrapers, amusement parks, theme parks and casinos.
- **Cultural attractions** such as folklore, dances, festivals and regional cuisines.
- **Social attractions,** that is, the host community of a destination.

It is important to manage the tourist attractions well so as to increase the visits of tourists at a destination as the attractions are the primary driving force for bringing the tourist to a destination.

Infrastructure and Superstructure

For any destination to attract the tourists, it must have the required infrastructure to support the tourists and make their stay comfortable at the destination. Infrastructure refers to the basic facilities extended to the residents of a destination that are also used by tourists in order to facilitate their visit and stay. It may include transportation facilities, accommodation, Internet services, telecommunication systems, continuous supply of electricity and water, proper drainage and sanitation systems and so on.

Besides the basic facilities, a destination must create a huge superstructure to increase the influx of tourists at a destination. Many destinations of the world that did not have natural attractions have created landmark superstructures to attract tourists. Some of these superstructures are tourism products in them-selves. Superstructure in tourism may refer to major buildings and facilities that include air-ports, terminals, luxury hotels, F&B outlets, restaurants, souvenir shops, amusement parks, theme parks, shopping malls, shopping empori-ums, convention centres, museums, archaeologi-cal sites, botanical gardens, business centres and so on. Dubai and Singapore are two destinations that have phenomenal superstructures where the tourists come from every nook and corner of the world to appreciate. Likewise, the Statue of Unity in India, the Statue of Liberty in the USA, Atomium in Belgium, Madurodam in Holland, Genting Highlands in Malaysia and so on are some other superstructures that have been created in the world to attract tourists.

The Statue of Liberty, New York

Tourists

They are the seekers of tourism experience. As also discussed earlier, a tourist is a person who is travelling to another destination for leisure, recreation, business or any other purpose for more than 24 hours and less than a year with an intention to come back home.

The main fulcrum of tourism industry is the tourists at whom all the marketing activities are targeted by the destination authorities and tourism service providers. The tourist is the king/queen of the tourism industry who must be pampered by all service providers offering a tourism product at every step of the service given to him. Every destination aims at increas-ing the repeat visits of tourists at a destination.

A tourist may have spent a fortune of money to make his dream come true of visiting a destination. He/she may have been planning and thinking for years about being at a place and exploring it fully. Thus, his/her expectations must be met in the first place through the coor-dination of all service providers who must ensure to deliver an impeccable service. In the second place, the service providers must go an extra mile in their service that exceeds expecta-tions of the tourist so that the he/she is delighted and spellbound. The jaw-dropping moments and experiences may lead to his/her repeat visits to the same destination. Besides, he/she may share his/her pleasant moments and travel experiences with his/her family and friends that can further lead to more tourists turning around at the same destination.

Hosts

Hosts are an important component of the tourism industry. Hosts refer to the local commu-nity or local population of a destination where the tourists visit. Sometimes, hosts are a tourism product in themselves as tourists may plan to visit a destination with the sole objective of interacting with the host community and understanding their culture. Hosts may be the cynosure of their whole tourism experience where the tourists may want to immerse in their culture, especially those wanting to indulge in cultural tourism.

The behaviour of the host community towards the tourists is a deciding factor for many tourists while planning a visit to a destination and whether they would want to return again to the same destination in the future. Some destinations are very tourist-friendly like Dublin, one of the friendliest destinations of Europe, where the tourists feel welcomed and wanted by the host community. The tourists feel so comfortable and at home at such places that they want to retire to the same destination again and again due to the warmth and affection showed by the host community towards them. For this, the host community of a destination must be made aware of the economic benefits along with other social and cultural benefits brought by the tourists to a destination. Similarly, the tourists must also be educated to behave responsibly and to respect the local sensitivities of the local communities while visiting a destination.

SERVICE PROVIDERS

These may be referred to as givers or suppliers of a travel experience. These stakeholders have an important role in creating the positive 'moments of truth' for the tourists. Now let us have a discussion on each of these service providers.

Accessibility (Transportation Industry)

One of the most important pillars of tourism is the transportation industry. Journey from one's place of residence to a destination that holds an attraction is only possible through a means of transportation. Thus, the means which helps the travellers to reach their intended holiday destination and getting around after they reach or arrive at that destination is called transportation. This may also be referred to as accessibility of a destination. If a destination is not directly accessible by a mode of transportation, it may not be the first choice for a visitor. The transportation basically includes the civil aviation industry, road transportation industry, railways and water transportation industry. The tourists may choose the transportation vehicle depending upon their personal choice, time and money in hand, distances, level of comfort and convenience and so on. Civil aviation includes travel by scheduled airline carriers, charter flights and so on. People who want to save on time for longer distances may prefer to travel by air. LCCs are popular choices for tourists travelling on domestic routes. Airlines such as GoAir, IndiGo, SpiceJet and JetLite are domestic LCCs for travellers planning to travel within India. However, full-service carriers (FSCs) may also be the choice for many travellers. The tourists may also cover certain destinations through helicopter services. However, road transportation is also a very popular mode of transportation. People who like to enjoy the sceneries or drive through places may prefer road transportation. Tourists may travel to destinations or go for internal sightseeing within a destination by coaches, car rentals, private cabs such as Uber and OLA, bus services and so on. These coaches may be owned and operated by the government like the Road Transportation Corporation in India or private transport operators such as Volvo and Mercedes-Benz. Many people who prefer to discover the countryside and have the convenience of travelling longer distances in lesser time as compared to travelling by road or by water may prefer to travel by rail. National railway networks of the world such as the Indian Railways, Eurail, BritRail and Amtrak facilitate interstate and intercity travel. Water transportation is one of the most exciting modes of transportation for many tourists. Tourists may travel by luxury cruise liners that are floating hotels with the best amenities one can even think of. Besides cruises, some other popular modes of transportation in water bodies are ferries, boats, yachts, water taxis and so on.

For further detailed information on transportation you may refer to the chapter on 'Accessibility'.

Accommodation Industry

Accommodation is a very important part of the tourism industry. According to the definition of tourism, it involves an element of stay as a tourist visits a destination for more than 24 hours. The stay of tourists at an accommodation plays an important role in his/her overall tourism experience. Tourists may stay in a hotel, motel, B&B, homestays, guest houses, youth hostels, self-catering apartments and so on. Some popular hotel chains of India are Taj Group, Oberoi Group, ITC Group, India Tourism Development Corporation and so on. A detailed description on the accommodation sector and its types has been given in Chapters 12 and 13.

F&B Industry

Food is not only a basic requirement for a traveller but also an attraction for him/her. This sector ensures that tourists are provided with meals and refreshments at all stages of their travel. This may include essential food arrangements during one's travel to a destination, meal arrangements at the holiday destination while staying and exploring the destination and arrangement of meals while coming back to one's own residence. Dining together is also one of the best ways for the tourists to socialize on their travels. Various fast-food restaurants such as McDonald's and KFC, family restaurants such as Haldiram's and Bikaner, fine dining restaurants, cafes, pubs, bars, coffee shops, local eateries and so on are in the business of F&B industry.

It is important that the restaurants must promote the local cuisines and local drinks of their region to share the cultural flavours of a destination. However, the restaurants should not only serve their local cuisine but also serve international cuisines catering to the different taste buds of different nationalities visiting a country.

It is important for the F&B industry to provide good quality of food to the tourists who are away on a vacation for a long time. The way the food is served, its hygiene and its presentation along with the right blends of spices and flavours all add to the experience of a tourist. Since F&B is a service industry, the people involved in serving the food must have the right spirit of service.

Besides, catering is also an important part of F&B. Catering, that is, provision of food outside is equally important for the tourists during their journey on modes of transportation such as trains, flights and cruise ships besides attractions and entertainment centres.

Entertainment and Recreational Organizations

When tourists visit a destination, they want entertainment. They want to have fun and enjoyment there. In fact, some travel in pursuit of entertainment only that they may not find in their own city or town. Thus, entertainment at the holiday destination becomes the main attraction for the travellers. Many destinations are known for offering entertainment to tourists. For example, *Las Vegas in the USA is known as the 'entertainment capital of the world' that offers*

Boat Ride in a Lake, Victoria, Australia

nightlife, casinos and so on. Similarly, destinations such as Mumbai, Hong Kong, Bangkok, Amsterdam and Tel Aviv are famous for their nightlife. These destinations have multiple options for entertainment of the tourists. However, many destinations create entertainment options in order to capitalize on the existing tourism in that country or to attract more tourists. They may create artificial structures such as amusement parks, amphitheatres, bowling alleys and gaming zones to attract the tourists. For example, *the world's biggest amusement park, that is, Ferrari World in Abu Dhabi has been created to attract the tourist to Abu Dhabi.*

Entertainment may include watching shows (e.g., the Lido show of Paris, France, the Zangoora show of the Kingdom of Dreams in Gurugram, Haryana, India, musical fountain show of Dubai and so on), playing local games, gambling in casinos, taking a spa, participating or watching the performing arts, watching comedy performances, watching theatre (e.g., Prithvi Theatre in Mumbai, Piccadilly Circus in London and so on), operas, concerts, circus, dance performances, taking rides and watching shows in amusement parks and theme parks, attending events such as cultural festivals and local fairs and so on.

Thus, it is imperative that destinations promoting tourism must also ensure that there are enough entertainment options available for tourists. There must be dedicated cultural and entertainment organizations engaged in the business of entertaining tourists. These may be government owned or privately owned. In India, the *Indian National Trust for Art and Cultural Heritage (INTACH)* is an important non-profit organization responsible for promoting the culture and heritage in the country. It promotes heritage walks for tourists in various parts of Delhi such as Chandni Chowk and Mehrauli Archaeological Park. Many other recreational and sports organizations may also be involved in providing entertainment to tourists. These may include organizations running night clubs, spas, casinos, amusement parks, theme parks, shopping malls, theatres, music venues, pleasure boats, bikes, motor bikes, canoes, go-karting, golf courses, fitness centres, bowling alley and so on.

Travel Intermediaries

Disneyland, Los Angeles

While travelling to a destination, the traveller has two choices. He/she may either book his/her tour online or may take a ready-made or a tailor-made package from an agent who has an expertise in combining the various components of tourism together and presenting them as one package for the convenience of the traveller. Such agents are called tour operators who are primarily travel companies engaged in providing tourism services to facilitate the tourists visiting a destination. These companies are responsible for making all the necessary travel arrangements for tourists along with giving them advice on travel, if they require. However, the travel agents may sell individual components of a tour such as transportation and hotel on a commission basis that they may charge from the suppliers. These days, most of the travel organizers conduct their business online and hence may be called *online travel portals* or *online travel agencies (OTAs)*. Some of these may be *Expedia, Travelocity, MakeMyTrip, Goibibo* and so on. Here, the customers have the option of buying travel packages online.

The travel agents/tour operators also have tie-ups with the tour guides and tour leaders who may be arranged to facilitate the package tour of the tourists or if personally requested by the traveller on their customized tours. Many travel agents and tour operators may also form associations to raise their issues on a common platform. In India, some famous travel trade associations are FAITH, IATO, TAAI, TAFI, Association of Domestic Tour Operators of India (ADTOI), ATOAI and so on.

Some of the famous tour operators of India are Thomas Cook India Ltd, Cox & Kings, Kuoni and so on.

Government

The government plays a very important role in identifying the tourism resources that can be converted into tourism products, investing the funds in developing infrastructure that can support the tourists and then marketing the tourism products and the destinations to the prospective tourists in order to increase their footfall at a destination. The government is also responsible for the launching of various schemes that aid in the overall development of a destination or a region. For example, in India, many schemes have been launched by the government such as HRIDAY and PRASHAD, which are helping to rejuvenate the heritage and pilgrimage destinations of India. It also helps in launching various schemes for capacity building of service providers who are associated with the tourism industry. These may be the hoteliers, travel agents, tour guides, cab drivers, transfer assistants and so on who must be trained how to deal professionally with the tourists. The government also ensures to bridge the gap among the stakeholders of the tourism industry and to integrate their efforts towards creating delightful experiences for the tourists. It also plays a regulatory role in managing the dynamics of the tourism industry. It is responsible for developing and implementing tourism policies and tourism plans for various destinations as well as the country. The *national tourism organizations (NTOs)* and *regional tourism organizations (RTOs)* are generally the government bodies responsible for promoting tourism in the countries and states. However, this may depend from country to country. In India, NTO, which is the apex body of the government at the national level, is MOT. The regional tourist organizations are the various tourism departments and state tourism development corporations that are responsible for developing tourism within the states.

Ancillary Service Organizations

The extra services that may be required by the tourists to facilitate their travel at a destination are called ancillary services. The organizations offering the ancillary services required by the tourists are called ancillary service organizations. It may include assistance required for travel documentation which may include getting a passport and visa services, airport parking services, travel insurance, foreign exchange services, luggage transportation services, arrangements of tickets for watching theatrical performances and so on.

Other Service Providers

The other service providers involved in the delivery of services are the tour guides, tour leaders, cab drivers, immigration officers, tourist information officers, airline staff, hotel staff and many more. A detailed discussion on each of these service providers has been given in Chapter 23, 'The Touch Points of Tourism Industry'.

5 A's OF TOURISM

Another way of looking at tourism is by understanding its 5 A's that give an overall holistic picture of the tourism industry. These 5 A's form the pillars of the tourism industry and are a must for any destination to qualify as a tourist destination. These are important cornerstones for repeating the visits of tourists at a destination. Lack of any of these 5 A's may hinder the tourists from visiting that destination. Let us just enlist the 5 A's for our clarity:

- Accessibility
- Attractions
- Accommodation
- Amenities
- Activities

A detailed discussion of each of these has been given in subsequent chapters.

SUMMARY

Tourism calls for the collaboration of various industries that work in tandem to give pleasant moments and memories to the tourists. Each industry within the tourism industry is both independent and dependent in different ways for the creation of an overall experience of a tourist. The transportation industry, hotel industry, F&B industry, travel intermediaries, recreational organizations, government, host community, ancillary service organizations and attraction authorities must all come together to create happy moments for the tourists and give them the best-ever holiday experience of their lifetime.

ACTIVITIES

Activity 1

Identify the various entertainment and recreational organizations in your city. Now, suggest which entertainment organization that has not been much commercialized would you like to introduce in order to increase the influx of tourists in your destination.

Activity 2: Talk Show

Divide the class into different groups and ask each group to choose a city of their choice. Now ask each group to organize a talk show for their city. To conduct the talk show, prepare a detailed inventory of 5 A's of your own city and share your 'city's insider view' with the class. A group may comprise an anchor who would host the talk show, two tourists, a tour operator, a tour guide, a representative from the local community, a representative of the tourism department from the government and a person from media who could be a travel blogger, a travel journalist and so on. However, the composition may vary depending upon the strength of the group. Also, more characters may be added depending upon the need of the presentation. Now present your city in the best possible way. Start with the history, 5 A's, SWOT analysis of the city, challenges faced by the tourists in your city, any suggestions and so on. You may seek the help of a presentation at the background. Now let the anchor initiate the discussion and let every member play their designated roles. The show may be made more interesting by taking commercial ad breaks in between. Finally, the show may be closed with a question–answer session with the audience.

Tourism Resources to Tourism Products

LEARNING OBJECTIVES

The given chapter shall clarify the following:

- What are tourism resources and tourism products?
- What are the characteristics of tourism products?
- What is the classification of tourism resources and products?

AUSTRALIA: A NATURE'S WONDERLAND!

- One of the world's natural wonders is in Western Australia, near Esperance. Lake Hillier (also known as Australia's pink lake) attracts tourists from all over the world.
- Shaped like a footprint, the lake is vibrant pink in colour due to the presence of salt-loving algae and pink-coloured bacteria known as halobacteria.
- The most exciting part is that the bubblegum colour of water does not alter when taken in a container.
- A perfect way to enjoy the spectacular view of the lake is by air as many travel service agencies provide scenic flight tours for tourists.
- Want to witness the world's most famous colour-changing rock? Visit Australia's most famous site Uluru-Kata Tjuta National Park (UNESCO world heritage site).
- Home to an extraordinary landscape with amazing deserts, mountains and gorges, people from all over the world visit this national park to see Uluru (Ayers Rock) changing its shade from orange, red, purple and back!
- Did you know that Uluru Rock is higher than the Eiffel Tower with the height of 348 metres?

- Take a scenic helicopter ride to indulge in the spectacular view of Uluru/Ayers Rock and the amazing desert surroundings.

INTRODUCTION

Tourism is more about experiential travel now. People travel to places to get novel experiences to feed their minds and souls. The whole tourism phenomenon revolves around tourism products. The tourism industry is heavily dependent on resources for its existence. These resources may be natural or man-made. Some tourism products may be created from tourism resources.

Resources may be defined as a type of supply or sources that offer benefits to the end user. They are vital to the existence of a community. In fact, these may be defined as the tangible and intangible assets of a community. For the tourism industry to exist, it is important to harness the existing resources. Any resource can become a tourism product if it is packaged with services and then managed well. Adding experience to a resource can convert it into a tourism product. Thus, collective resources of a community which include hills, beaches, culture, heritage, traditions and so on are assets that can become tourism products when we add value to them.

In the case of tourism, the whole experience of a tourist from the time he/she leaves his/her home until the time he/she is back falls within the ambit of tourism products. Now, let us have a discussion on the different types of resources that have been harnessed for the development of the tourism industry.

NATURAL RESOURCES TO NATURAL TOURISM PRODUCTS

Nature has always been bountiful for mankind. The world is bestowed with a number of natural resources and man has been intelligent enough to make use of them. These resources are related to nature and the environment. These may include climate, deserts, hills and mountains, forests, flora and fauna, beaches, islands, countryside, rivers, lakes and waterfalls and other natural landforms. These resources either attract nature lovers or adventure lovers.

Augmenting the natural resources with facilities and services for the consumption of tourists and selling them as a tourist attraction make them a nature-based tourism product. *Las Vegas is an excellent example of how a destination that was only a desert transformed itself into the 'entertainment capital' of the world.* The long strip of flashy hotels known for their artificial structures, shows and, of course, the casinos are pulling tourists world over.

This can be a successful case study for many destinations that may not have much to offer but with careful planning and a progressive approach towards tourism development, it is possible to channelize a resource to be a tourism product. The point to discuss here is that the facilities and services have to be created and an active involvement of both the government and the local community is required to drive any tourism development around the natural resources to convert them into a tourism product. It is important for the community leadership to take the lead and decide the natural forms that can be used to attract visitors.

Hotel in Las Vegas

Another example of natural tourism product in India are the Himalayas. People who have a love for mountains visit India from different corners of the world to see the Himalayas and experience the life there. While some tourists visit the Himalayas to explore the wildlife there, the adventurers find it a haven for adventure activities and expeditions. While some may retire to the Himalayas to interact with the local communities and learn about their culture, some visit to meditate here in the monasteries and forests. Yet some may travel to indulge in spa treatment in Ananda Spa in Rishikesh, others may visit the hill stations in the Himalayas to elope the scorching heat of summers. The Himalayas also attract the pilgrims as they are also considered to be the spiritual abode for the travellers being a home to many pilgrimage destinations of India.

Likewise, some travellers may visit the islands to enjoy the solace and tranquillity. Travellers visiting India may go to the Andaman and Nicobar Islands or Lakshadweep to engage in water activities such as snorkelling, scuba diving and parasailing; watching the marine life like coral reefs and so on or just basking in the pristine beaches and enjoying the sunshine. *Yet many travellers may visit Niagara Falls in the USA and Canada to watch one of the most scenic waterfalls of the world and enjoy the 'Maid of the Mist tour' to view the waterfalls from a close.*

Niagara Falls, USA

Deserts, when channelized, can be offered as an exciting tourism product. Visitors visiting Dubai may try the Camel safaris, sand dune bashing along with camping in the deserts and relishing the local dinners along with belly dancing by the locals. Likewise, the 'white desert' of India, 'the Rann of Kutch' or the 'cold desert' of India 'Ladakh' are increasingly being commercialized as tourism products. Ladakh, also known as the 'rooftop of the world', is a travellers' paradise famous for its breathtaking landscapes such as *Pangong Tso Lake, the Himalayas, Khardung La, ancient Buddhist culture, monasteries* and *rich Ladakhi culture.*

The major caretakers of natural tourism products are generally the government and regulatory bodies. Sometimes, there may be private players too.

HISTORICAL RESOURCES TO HISTORICAL TOURISM PRODUCTS

Any destination, site or an event that has some connect with the past and carries historical importance is called a historical resource. A site may be constructed to connote the importance of that place in remembrance of a person/event that may draw the visitors to visit these historical tourism products. The site may relate to any of the following: (a) an event, massacre or a war that might have happened there; (b) residence of the royal families such as forts, palaces and castles; (c) a place of mythological importance like the Stonehenge in England; and (d) a monument that might be created to commemorate someone like Taj Mahal in India. These resources eventually may be converted to historical tourism products.

The Glamis Castle, Scotland

Various historic and archaeological sites such as monuments, forts, palaces, castles, museums and art galleries are the structures created through the ages that are archaeological or heritage assets of the country.

Now these historical resources sold as tourism products attract a number of tourists. Many destinations of India such as Delhi, Jaipur, Agra and Ahmedabad are home to many historic monuments of the world that attract tourists from different corners of the globe.

Other man-made structures are the religious shrines that attract a patronage of tourists who have strong belief systems in particular sects such as the *Akshardham Temple of New Delhi, the Ranakpur Jain Temple, Rajasthan, the St. Peter's Basilica Church in the Vatican, the Lotus Temple, Delhi* and the *Golden Temple of Amritsar*.

Some of the important historic tourism products where the tourists visit in large numbers are as follows:

- Hampi, Karnataka, India (declared as a world heritage site by UNESCO)
- The Khajuraho Group of Monuments, Madhya Pradesh (declared as a world heritage site)
- The Lothal site, Gujarat
- The Lincoln Memorial, Washington DC
- Chittor Fort, Rajasthan (declared as a world heritage site by UNESCO)
- The Buckingham Palace, the UK
- Roman Baths, England

In India, the *Archaeological Survey of India (ASI)* is responsible for the protection and maintenance of historical monuments.

CULTURAL RESOURCES TO CULTURAL TOURISM PRODUCTS

Anything which is related to the culture of a place that includes the lifestyles of locals such as their beliefs, traditions, customs, food habits, folk dresses, handicrafts, folk dances, folk music, art, heritage and local fairs and festivals is referred to as a cultural resource. Every destination will have its own cultural resources. When these cultural resources are preserved and showcased for the consumption of tourists, they may be referred to as cultural tourism products.

Cultural tourism products are a major attraction for many tourists while visiting a destination. These community-owned assets have a huge potential for increasing the footfalls of tourists at a destination. Cultural tourism products may be experienced by visiting locals, living with them, interacting with them and learning about their lifestyles, participating in their local festivals, visiting art galleries and museums, visiting local markets, visiting local exhibitions and so on.

However, while promoting the cultural tourism resources, the consent of local community is very important. Generally, there is a wider acceptance for promoting cultural resources as cultural products by a community as it accrues sufficient economic benefits such as generation of employment and increase in income of the locals, thereby giving a boost to their economy besides giving an impetus to reviving their culture and instilling a sense of pride within them.

These cultural assets may be promoted as festivals that are the best way to showcase their local traditions, local folklore, local handicrafts and local cuisine of the destination. Some popular festivals such as *Pushkar Camel Fair of Rajasthan, the Rann Utsav of Gujarat* and the *Hornbill Festival of Nagaland* are successful examples of how these destinations have used these cultural resources and converted them to tourism products to attract the tourists to their destinations. Many museums in India such as the *Crafts Museum in New Delhi, Calico Museum of Textiles in Ahmedabad* and *Jawahar Toy Museum in Pondicherry* are a great way to see and appreciate the cultural resources of a destination and learn the keen difference among the varied cultures prevailing in different parts of the country.

MAN-MADE RESOURCES TO MAN-MADE TOURISM PRODUCTS

Sources that are created by human beings for their own utilization are called man-made resources. These might be the activities, entertainment and events created by man and may be created as a means of entertainment for the local community. These may include artificial structures, amusement parks, sports events and so on. When these man-made resources are promoted as assets to tourists for their utilization, they are called man-made tourist products and may also be referred to as man-made tourist attractions.

Many structures are created for the entertainment of tourists. These may be artificially created islands (e.g., Palm Jumeirah in Dubai), amusement parks, theme parks, casinos, artificial structures like skyscrapers, gardens, aquariums, shopping malls, haats and activities such as nightlife and gambling and so on for promoting tourism at a destination. For example, *Dilli Haat* is a man-made tourism product that showcases the handicrafts and handlooms of India in a traditional setting in New Delhi. The concept of local open markets called 'haats' has been recreated here bringing all the artisans of India a step closer to the tourists under one roof. Likewise, *Chokhi Dhani of Jaipur, Sadda Pind of Amritsar, Kingdom of Dreams in Gurugram, Haryana, Sentosa Island in Singapore, Children Nutrition Park in Kevadia, Gujarat* and so on are all theme-based man-made tourism products to engage the tourists at a destination.

SYMBIOTIC TOURISM RESOURCES TO TOURISM PRODUCTS

The products which are given by nature but require the monitoring and management by man to be used for tourism purposes as a tourism product may be referred to as symbiotic tourism products. National parks and wildlife sanctuaries may be classified under symbiotic tourism products. Some examples may be Gir National Park in Gujarat, Bharatpur Bird Sanctuary in Rajasthan, Jim Corbett National Park in Uttarakhand and so on.

Adventure activities that may be aerial, water-based and land-based may also be classified as symbiotic tourism products. Adventure symbiotic products may include parasailing, scuba diving, mountaineering, trekking, hot air ballooning, sky diving, white water rafting, windsurfing, rock climbing and so on.

EVENT-BASED RESOURCES TO EVENT-BASED TOURISM PRODUCTS

Events are a major attraction for tourists. Many local events at destinations that may be local fairs or festivals are packaged as tourism products to increase the visits of tourists to a destination. Many tourists plan their vacations during the time of events so as to be able to witness the culture of a destination closely. Events may be the fairs and festivals, sports events and so on. As India is a cultural hub, being home to 'fairs and festivals' round the year, it is one of the chosen destinations, especially by foreign tourists to experience the local culture, dances, folk songs, local cuisines and local life closely during the time of the festival. *The International Kite Festival of Gujarat, the Ziro Festival of Arunachal Pradesh, the Surajkund Crafts Mela of Haryana, the Dance Festival of Khajuraho and the Tansen Music Festival of Gwalior are some local festivals that are showcased as local tourism products.* These play an important role in bringing tourists to a destination. Likewise, sports events such as FIFA World Cup, Commonwealth Games and IPL are also promoted as tourism products to bring tourists to a destination.

'OTHER COMPONENTS' AS TOURISM PRODUCTS

'Other components' of the tourism industry may also be repositioned as tourism products/ attractions for tourist.

Transportation

Adding experience and facilities to a mode of transportation such as trains and cycle rickshaws can position a transportation system to a tourism product. Travelling on heritage trains, toy trains, taking helicopter rides and so on are all experiential tourism products within themselves.

Accommodation

Staying in tree houses, glasshouses, underwater hotels and so on can be the most exciting experiences of a lifetime. Such accommodation operators convert a simple accommodation to an attractive tourism product by adding value and facilities with unique experiences to it, which becomes a unique tourism product in itself.

UNDERSTANDING TOURISM PRODUCTS' CHARACTERISTICS

A tourism product is basically one or more attractions at a destination packaged with other services such as transportation, accommodation and basic amenities at the destination. We need to understand here that the tourism product may not always be a stand-alone product. It may be a combination of offerings that may complement one another at a destination. The various attractions and facilities created around the attractions make a tourism product. There may be a high level of interdependence of tourism products on each other. The objective is to create a memorable destination experience for visitors.

Hitting the right 'triggers' to ensure that the customer is convinced to buy the tourism product is a challenge for tourism marketers. Travel companies and tourism boards must do enough research, identify the need of the traveller and then create such tourism offerings that will satisfy his/her need. Having an understanding of what the customer wants should be the first point of consideration for the tour operators. Now, let us discuss the characteristics of tourism products that differentiate them from other products.

Intangibility

Tourism is different from other products. It is not any 'physical product' but an 'ephemeral experience' that is being sold. Tourists do not carry any physical product with them when they buy it or consume it. They only take away the experiences and memories with them. It is a service with few components that are tangible in nature such as a hotel room, a coach and an aircraft seat.

Since there is nothing tangible as it is a service, the risk on the part of the consumer increases as he/she cannot test it before the actual consumption. Suppose a travel company offers a travel package of Switzerland that includes the complete travel arrangements from the time the traveller leaves his/her home to the time he/she is back home, the traveller cannot test the package unless and until he/she actually visits Switzerland through the company. There is always an element of perceived risk by the traveller. He can only rely on the past testimonials and reviews of the travelled passengers to get an idea about the services offered by the company. As these products cannot be touched or tested before they are bought and consumed, it gets challenging to sell a product to the customer. This may be referred to as intangibility.

Let us take another example of air travel. Here, the airlines promise the travellers a safe and a comfortable travel that includes comfortable seats in the aircraft, decent in-flight services, professional staff to assist, facilities such as in-flight entertainment, Wi-Fi, on-time arrival and sometimes the facility of airport transfers too. The quality of all these individual components determines the overall experience of a traveller. So here the tangible product is the aircraft with its good quality seats, the kind of meals that are served to the passengers, the entertainment services, the kind of vehicle given during the airport transfers and so on, whereas the professional attitude of the staff, the on-time arrival of the flight, on-time airport transfer with a professional chauffeur are the services extended by the airline which are intangible in nature.

Thus, tourism product is a combination of both products and services that are largely intangible in nature.

Inseparability

The tourist and the service provider in the tourism industry cannot be separated from each other. In other words, the production and consumption of services take place at the same time. For example, to enjoy the services of a tour guide at a monument or to enjoy a train ride, the tourists have to be physically present at the point of service being given. Thus, the service providers in the tourism industry must focus on creating pleasant interactions and experiences among the travellers. Here, the 'moment of truth' is very crucial that takes place between the service providers and the tourists. This aspect of the service provider and the tourists together who are inseparable from each other in order to consume services may be referred to as inseparability.

Heterogeneity

Since the services given by the service providers in tourism industry heavily entail an element of human involvement, there are maximum chances of errors as there cannot be any set standardization as human behaviour is highly unpredictable subject to a number of circumstances. A good quality service given by a service provider may not be the same next time if the service provider is not comfortable or in a good mood. This can be very challenging for the service providers as the tourists may be expecting a very high standard of service every time that may not be delivered at the end of the service provider. This may disappoint the tourists.

For example, a traveller may have visited with an 'X' company on a Europe tour on a particular package. His/her personal experience may have been very pleasant. He/she may recommend travelling with the same 'X' company for visiting Europe to his/her close friends and family. On the recommendation of the traveller, a friend may plan to avail the services of 'X' company to travel to Europe on the same package taken by the traveller. However, his/her experience with the company may not be very pleasant that may highly disappoint him/her. Thus, we see the variability in services offered by the same company. This may in turn depend upon the kind of services offered at that point of time and the personal expectations of a traveller. In the latter case, he/she may complain about the unprofessional approach of the company staff, the not-so-knowledgeable tour leader and so on. Thus, consistent delivery of high standards of services is imperative to ensure an uninterrupted flow of business in tourism and customer satisfaction along with the setting up of standing operational procedures to avoid any difference in the services. Understanding the expectations of the customers and then matching the services with his/her expectations are challenges for the tourism business. This is called variability or heterogeneity.

Perishability

Tourism services cannot be stored for sales in the future. If the services are not consumed on the same day, the revenue is lost forever. As the tourism industry is primarily a seasonal industry, the consumption of services becomes a matter of concern. It becomes difficult to match demand and supply. For example, if the occupancy of the hotel on a particular night was only 60 per cent, the revenue of the 40 per cent rooms has been lost forever. It cannot be carried forward for the next night. Likewise, if the airlines did not fly with all seats full, the empty seats are lost forever. This may hold true for any tourism product like a visit to a sightseeing attraction or a restaurant. This characteristic of services that cannot be stored may be referred to as perishability.

Lack of Ownership

In tourism industry, there is no title transfer of services unlike buying a product. Tourists can only use a product for a limited span of time, but he/she cannot own the product. For example, a tourist may buy a seat with an airline for travelling to a destination for a limited span of time until he/she flies. However, he/she cannot own the airline. Likewise, he/she may use an accommodation for a limited time, but cannot own it.

PRESERVING THE TOURISM RESOURCES AND PRODUCTS

It is important for the stakeholders of the tourism industry to take collective responsibility to preserve these tourist resources and products. It may be the private players of the tourism industry (travel agents/tour operators, transporters, hoteliers, guides), the government, the tourists and even the host community which should come forward to protect the tourism products.

The whole responsibility cannot be fixed on the government. Tourists can play a major role in protecting the tourism resources and products by using them judiciously and not overusing them. For example, tourists must be educated that when they visit a beach, they must not throw bottles, polythene bags and so on around the beach which spoil the look of the beach. Also, tourists must be told how to conduct themselves when they visit national parks and wildlife sanctuaries so as to not disturb the fauna in their natural settings. Demonstrating responsible behaviour by tourists can help in increasing the longevity of tourism resources and tourism products. A code of conduct must be issued for the tourists as well as the stakeholders to be followed while visiting tourism resources.

Various approaches such as sustainable tourism, green tourism, slow tourism, responsible tourism, ecotourism, pro-poor tourism and community-based tourism must be considered while developing tourism resources to tourism products. Tourism resources must be developed at a destination but within the limited carrying capacity of the environment.

SUMMARY

It is imperative to tap the tourism resources that may be converted into tourism products for bringing the tourists to a destination. Tourism products may be natural, historical, cultural, man-made, symbiotic or event-based. Other tourism components when showcased as attractions like transportation or accommodation may also be marketed as tourism products. Tourism products may be differentiated from other products on the basis of their characteristics of intangibility, inseparability, heterogeneity, lack of ownership and so on. We also need to protect and preserve the tourism resources and products for future generations.

ACTIVITIES

Activity 1

Visit your city and prepare an inventory of resources that have untapped potential and can be converted into a tourism product. Discuss your thoughts with the class.

Activity 2

Pick up any local festival of the world of your choice which is a successful tourism product. Now discuss with the class in detail its history, its significance, the way it is conducted, the tourist footfall during the festival and so on.

Types of Tourism Markets

ADVENTUROUS TROMSØ: A GATEWAY FOR NORTHERN LIGHTS!

- Tromsø is the largest city in Northern Norway and is located at 350 km above the Arctic Circle.
- The city is ranked among the best places on earth to observe the incredible Northern Lights at night as the city is set right in the middle of the 'aurora zone'.
- The best time to witness the beautiful lights up in the sky is during polar nights. Each year between late November and late January, Tromsø is jam-packed with tourists. There are countless Northern Lights-oriented activities such as dogsledding, snowmobiling, camping and boat trips.
- From 20 May to 22 July, Tromsø blesses people with midnight sun—a natural phenomenon where people experience sun for 24 hours.

- Tromsø has emerged as the best destination in Northern Europe for marine wildlife expeditions and fun activities such as whale safaris, kayaking, hiking and fishing.
- The *Film Festival* and the *Northern Light Festival* organized in Tromsø are major crowd pullers, attracting hundreds of tourists from all over the world.
- Tromsø has become a sustainable destination as it promotes green travel by reducing environmental footprints and only certifying those businesses and tour operators who meet the best practices of sustainable standards.
- Tromsø is now a part of 'Visit Norway Green Travel Standards'—a scheme for sustainable destination.

INTRODUCTION

The travel market is very volatile and dynamic. With changing times, the travellers' preferences are continuously changing and getting more complex, which is pushing the buttons of the tourism industry. There are different sections of travellers that the tourism industry needs to cater to. Every traveller exhibits some typical characteristics that every service provider in the tourism industry needs to understand. By understanding the needs of these travellers, the tourism industry service providers can create such tourism products that can effectively meet their needs and requirements that can in turn generate revenue for the tourism suppliers.

As tourism is being considered an important economic driver, many destinations and tourism industry service providers feel the need to learn about the kind of travellers visiting the destinations. The service providers now acknowledge and appreciate the differences in the travellers who may vary in terms of their preference for travel, experiences, privacy requirements and so on.

Thus, tourism markets refer to various travellers being catered to by tourism industry service providers. As the tourism markets evolve, the tourism industry must also be aware of the evolving segments that it has to cater to. Knowledge of the tourism markets may help the tourism industry to strategize and be better prepared to serve the current markets in a more efficient and effective way. Similar marketing mix can be devised according to the needs and preferences of the evolving travellers who have similar kinds of needs and wants with greater chances of offering a tourism product that may satisfy their needs and wants.

For example, keeping in mind the types of tourism segments visiting Singapore, the Singapore Tourism Board has clearly differentiated the tourism product offerings according to the special interest travellers (SIT) such as foodies, collectors, explorers, action seekers, culture seekers and socializers.

Placed below is a detailed discussion on the kind of travellers who visit a destination. For the sake of clarity, we have tried to categorize the travellers according to the typical traits that they exhibit. Let us discuss them one by one.

ON THE BASIS OF THE NUMBER OF TRAVELLERS ACCOMPANYING THE TRAVELLER

While choosing to travel to a destination, the traveller has two choices. Either he/she travels alone or goes in group package tours that have fixed departures. Thus, such travellers may be classified on the basis of the number of travellers accompanying them. Let us discuss them in detail now.

Individual Travellers

As per the tourism industry standards, these travellers may be referred to as *FIT that connotes free independent traveller*. These travellers may prefer to travel on their own with their friends or family. They may not prefer travelling and mingling with members of an unknown group as they may feel that it affects their privacy. Such travellers may either make the travel arrangements on their own searching on the websites for different travel options. On the contrary, some individual travellers may prefer to make their arrangements through a travel company. In such a case, they may get a tailor-made package from a tour operator customized to their own set of requirements.

However, in both cases, these individual or independent travellers may prefer to be on their own as they would have a self-decided itinerary, though they may take the opinion of the tour operator. By and large, they are independent travellers.

Group Travellers

Many tourists, across the world, especially families, first-time travellers and old-aged tourists may prefer to travel in group package tours and not on their own. The composition of a group may vary with respect to the group members. The kind of travellers may vary in a group from youngsters to senior citizens, from passive sightseeing travellers to adventure seekers. As per industry standards, they may be referred to as GIT that connotes Group Inclusive Travel where tourists prefer to travel in groups through the travel company's regular marketed brochure tourist packages that have fixed departure dates and a fixed pre-decided itinerary set by the travel company.

There are many reasons for going on package tours. One of the significant advantages of going in groups is that these trips are financially more economical as there are special group deals for the tourists. Also, with more people around, the tourist feels more safe and secure. Many first-time travellers who may have a hitch to travel alone prefer to go in groups as they may feel more secure in the presence of others. Another significant advantage of going in group packages is that the guests do not have to waste their time in planning their trip and then to struggle to make travel arrangement at every point. Group departures are hassle-free for the tourists as everything from preparation to execution is the headache of the travel company. Camaraderie may also be another reason for going in groups as for many travelling is an opportunity for socialization. Sometimes, moving in group packages also gives lifetime friends. Besides the above-cited reasons, the primary reason for travelling on group package tours is getting the complimentary services of a person who can make a lot of difference to a trip with his/her presence. This key person is the tour leader.

ON THE BASIS OF BUDGET

Other criteria for classifying the travellers may be on the basis of their capacity to spend on a holiday. Such travellers may be as follows.

Backpackers

This is an important segment of travellers who have a passion for travelling. In other words, these travellers are wanderlust travellers who are generally low-budget class travellers. Such travellers visit destinations generally for a longer duration. They may stay in youth hostels, B&B inns or dormitories to maintain their budget. They primarily visit a destination with the objective of exploring it fully. They are rough and tough travellers who may not be looking for amenities while visiting a destination. They are happy facing hardships as long as they get to taste the authentic experiences at a destination. For them, visiting every nook and corner of a city, interacting with locals and learning about their cultures are the major mottos of their travelling. Such travellers may prefer travelling alone or in closed groups with the idea of seeking adventure at every step. Such travellers may surf the Internet, go to Visitor Information Centres to seek information about a destination or may follow the guidebooks like *the Lonely Planet* to extensively explore the destination that they plan to visit.

Luxury Travellers

Luxury is the new trend. Such travellers believe in visiting exotic locations and getting the most luxurious experiences while on a holiday. They may not ready to compromise on the quality of the services during their holiday. They may lavishly spend on their transportation, on their stays and so on. They may prefer to travel only by private cars which are luxury cars, stay only in luxurious properties of a destination like private villas with own swimming pools, Jacuzzis and so on, and sometimes they may hire a charter, yachts and so on to have a luxurious holiday of its own kind. Such travellers can spend a good amount to experience the best on their holiday.

ON THE BASIS OF FREQUENCY OF TRAVEL

Travellers may be classified on the basis of frequency of their travel. This may be as follows.

First-time Travellers

Such travellers may be travelling for the first time internationally or within their own country to a destination and thus may be apprehensive of travelling. Such travellers may not be aware of the travel procedures/formalities, especially required to visit an overseas destination. Few things that may worry him/her may be as follows:

- Language barriers
- The airport handling procedures
- The fear of travelling by air
- Visa formalities
- Immigration procedures
- The fear of being in an unknown destination

In the absence of an experienced traveller accompanying the first-time traveller, he/she may feel lost and uneasy in a new country.

Weekenders

Many travellers, especially working professionals, may not be able to spare enough time to travel. Taking holidays from the job is not always easy. Therefore, such travellers may plan their travel on weekends, especially to nearby destinations that are in proximity to their area of residence. Sometimes, they may think of going to little distant destinations if it happens to be a long weekend. Therefore, many destinations may package themselves as 'weekend getaway' destinations to cater to the holiday need of such working professional travellers. Such travellers may just escape to nearby farmhouses or cottages during weekends to get a break from the hustle and bustle of the city. The idea is to get a break from a similar environment and come back rejuvenated and refreshed.

Long-duration Travellers

Many travellers visit destinations for a long time. The idea is to get immersed in the new experiences. They want to live in the city and not just see it from a distance wearing an artificial lens and come back. They believe in getting an insider's view. Thus, such travellers may visit destinations for a longer duration to understand the local culture of the host community and have maximum interaction with them to know about their lifestyle. Sometimes, they may also travel to the destination with the purpose of serving the local community voluntarily.

Globetrotters

These travellers are mature world-class travellers. With their evolving experiences and the passage of time, they become seasoned travellers. They are confident about travelling in any part of the world, and they know which travel mistakes they need to avoid. Such kinds of travellers believe in seeing maximum countries of the world in their lifetime. They generally do not like to repeat their destinations as they want to explore as much as possible in their lives. Being seasoned travellers, they have well-researched on reasonable transportation means, good accommodation choices, places to see and so on.

They may like to make their bookings on their own based on their own preferences, though at times, they may take day tours from local tour operator or a coach operator. However, some travellers may also choose to make arrangements through travel agents/tour operators to avoid any hassles.

Being frequent travellers, they may evolve and know their exact requirements with each experience they may have.

ON THE BASIS OF ACTIVITY

Travellers may further be divided on the basis of the nature of the holiday that they may be looking for. Some travellers may just be looking for an action-packed holiday, while others may be looking for relaxation. Accordingly, they may be divided into the following categories.

Active Travellers

Such travellers have a list of to-do things when they travel. Thus, they believe in having an action-packed itinerary where they get an opportunity to explore the destination to its fullest. They may desire to utilize every second of their holiday time engaging in various activities such as going for walking tours, engaging in adventure activities, participating in local events and festivals, meeting new people and so on so as to get the actual feel of a destination. Such travellers are very high on energy who believe in seeking authentic local experiences at a destination. They focus on experimenting and experiencing new things during travel. They may continuously engage themselves in activities from the dawn of the day until the time they are completely tired.

Passive Travellers

Many travellers may visit a destination just to enjoy the sightseeing. They may not indulge in activities. Their idea of vacation may just be to relax and rejuvenate at a slow pace. They may avoid action-packed itineraries where there is no respite for oneself. For example, some travellers may just travel to a destination to stay at a resort and spend their maximum time staying at the resort and relaxing there. They may practise slow tourism as for them seeking a slow pace of life with quality experiences is most essential as compared to seeking quantity experiences.

ON THE BASIS OF PURPOSE OF TRAVEL

Travellers may be classified on the basis of their purpose of travel. The classification is as follows.

Leisure Markets

This is an important market for tourism service providers. These may be referred to as holidaymakers who necessarily travel to destinations with the sole idea of relaxing and chilling at a destination. Such travellers may travel to destinations for:

- Taking a spa
- Relaxing in the beaches
- Exploring the destinations
- Change of place
- Better weather

Business Markets

A business market refers to travellers visiting a destination for attending a meeting, conference, exhibition or availing an incentive trip sponsored by the company. These are the major markets for the tourism industry as they are the perennial source of income for them. The business markets as compared to leisure markets are not bound by seasons. Due to the nature of their work or to attend meetings, business travellers may have to travel round the year. Business travellers also spend more as compared to leisure travellers as their trips are sponsored by the companies that they travel on behalf of. Many travel agencies/tour operators specialize their businesses in dealing with MICE/business segments only as these are mass tourists' movements that are a promising lucrative business opportunity for the tourism industry service providers.

Student Markets

Students are another important segment of the market for the tour companies. Many school children and college-going students may travel on educational tours as a part of their course curriculum. Taking students on tours requires a lot of preparation and a lot of consideration on the part of tour operators. Safety and security of students is the most important priority of tour operators. These are generally group tours where students visit a destination in numbers. The idea of students travelling to destinations may be to educate them on history, culture and architecture of a destination. Some courses may have specific requirements for students to travel. For example, students doing a course in tourism studies may travel to an adventure destination to purse an adventure course related to tourism. Likewise, many school students are sent for astronomical tours to destinations where they can clearly see the skies and do star gazing and learn about the galaxies and the planets.

Thrill Seekers

Many travellers seek excitement and something offbeat while visiting a destination. Such travellers are motivated to travel to destinations where they can experiment with different adventures and involve themselves in extreme kinds of adventure activities. They do not believe in seeking regular travel experiences but believe in doing something that may be quite challenging and risky for a common traveller, which gives them an extra kick. Some activities that such travellers may engage in are as follows:

- Caving
- Bungee jumping
- Skydiving
- Volcano boarding
- Downhill mountain biking

Medical Tourist Markets

Many travellers visit destinations as they require special medical attention and intervention by expert medical doctors. These travellers may be bound to travel to destinations due to either of the two factors, that is, there is no proper medical facility in their city or the medical treatment is too expensive in their country. Such travellers visit destinations for a better medical aid that may cure them of a disease or any other health issue. For example, many travellers travel to Thailand and India for their medical treatments related to surgeries, transplants, dental treatments, infertility treatments, cosmetic surgeries and so on.

Wellness Tourist Markets

Many travellers may visit destinations to cure and enhance their physical and mental well-being. They may travel to detoxify their bodies, lose weight, beautify themselves, increase their physical strength or just improve their mental health. They may take alternative medicine treatments such as Ayurveda, Unani, siddha and homeopathy. They may also visit ashrams or attend Yoga and meditation camps to improve their overall well-being.

Event Travellers

Sometimes, many travellers visit destinations to attend events. The events may be local festivals at the destination such as the *Rann of Kutch Festival in Gujarat, India, the Tomorrowland music festival in Belgium* and *Rio Carnival in Brazil* or a destination wedding of a friend/relative, a sports event and so on.

Pilgrims

Many travellers visit sacred places to pay homage to God. Such travellers are driven by staunch faith in God that makes them travel to destinations. They may visit pilgrimage destinations according to their faith and beliefs. They may travel to seek blessings of God, pay gratitude to Him for fulfilling their wishes, attend a religious festival/a special religious eve or just travel to these religious places as prescribed in their religion to attain salvation or to get rid of their sins.

Special Interest Travellers

This is another important segment of travellers who travel to destinations with a specific purpose. Such travellers are looking for non-mainstream experiences or offbeat experiences. They may be travelling for seeking adventure or pursuing a particular passion. For example, a group of friends may visit the famous *Chadar trek on Zanskar river in Ladakh in winters*, while some wildlife enthusiast may travel to destinations for seeing the wildlife in Kenya. Similarly, SIT also includes ecotourists who visit wetlands or mangroves; photographers who are looking for breathtaking views of a destination to capture in their camera lens; food lovers who are looking for gastronomical treats on food tours; tourists visiting destinations to learn a particular art, pottery, local cooking and so on. Such SIT visit with the intention of seeking novel experiences at a destination that makes them richer in travel experiences.

SIT may further be divided into the following categories.

Researchers

Many researchers may travel to destinations in search of something new. For example, students studying agriculture may visit agri-farm tourism destinations, while researchers of geology may visit destinations to study rocks.

Foodies

Some travellers may travel to destinations in search of food that may satisfy their souls. They may go on gourmet expeditions to satisfy their taste buds. For example, Amritsar in Punjab is quite famous for its street food.

Nature Lovers

Many tourists have an affinity for nature. They love travelling to be around nature. Travellers may travel to mountains, water bodies and forests to be around with nature.

Culture Seekers

The world is a repository of cultures. Many travellers travel to destinations to immerse themselves in the local's culture. They travel to destinations to embrace and discover others' cultures. They may stay with the locals, eat with them, celebrate their festivals and understand their cultures. Fusion of cultures here can be quite interesting.

Photographers

Many passionate photographers especially go on tours to capture the images of spectacular sites in their lens. Sometimes, they may have a theme in mind on which they would like to cover particular destinations. For example, a travel photographer may like to capture the colours of Holi in his/her lens. Thus, he/she may travel to *Barsana town near Mathura*, the only town in the country to have a temple, that is, the Radha Rani Temple dedicated to Radha (the lover of Lord Krishna). The same town is also famous for its Lathmar Holi that attracts photographers from all over the world to capture the colourful images of the festival in their camera. The beautiful scene of men from Nandgaon village coming to play Holi with women from Barsana only to be greeted with sticks from women is worth a shot.

Likewise, a photographer may like to visit *Tromsø, the gateway to the Arctic and a city in Northern Norway* to capture a panoramic view of the colourful Northern Lights with auroras that fill the sky with green light. He/she may also visit Tromsø for attending a night photography workshop before going on Northern Lights adventure.

Art Lovers

Some travellers may visit a destination to appreciate its art. For example, a group of art lovers may visit the *Louvre Museum in Paris* to appreciate the Mona Lisa painting there. Likewise, a traveller may visit *Khajuraho temples of India* or temples of South India to appreciate the architecture there.

Shoppers

Many shopaholic set of travellers may visit destinations like Dubai with the sole purpose of shopping at a destination. They may travel to explore the local markets or visit luxurious shopping arcades and malls to buy imported stuff from another country.

ON THE BASIS OF STAGES IN FAMILY LIFE CYCLE

Another classification of travellers may be on the basis of stages in the family life cycle that they are in. This may help the travel companies aim at specific markets with the appropriate marketing mix that may help them to capitalize and use this as an opportunity for business.

Bachelors

At this stage of life cycle, a bachelor who is unmarried has least responsibilities. He may have enough money to spend on his vacations. Such travellers may travel in groups with their friends of the same age to explore a new destination so that they can party and enjoy. They may prefer visiting adventurous destinations, beach destinations and so on. However, many may opt for solo travelling too. For example, a bride getting married soon may plan to celebrate her bachelorette party with her friends in *Las Vegas by hitting the pool parties, enjoying a limousine ride there, watching spectacular shows, doing bar crawling, visiting night clubs, taking a relaxing spa and many more fun activities in the sin city.*

Couples

This is the stage of the family life cycle when one gets married. Many couples who enjoy travelling together may have travelling goal that binds them together. The main motto may be to give time to each other and spend quality time away from the routine, thereby strengthening one's bond. They may also just escape away to save themselves from the social obligation that might always surround them in their daily lives. Especially for a dual-career couple where both are working professionals, it might be a good change besides a bonding exercise.

They may prefer privacy during their travel and may just desire to explore the destination, its culture, local cuisine, local pubs, discotheques and gain novel experiences on their own. They may visit destinations just to relax may be on the beaches or to indulge in an adventure activity if they both have a penchant towards adventure activities. Countries, especially islands such as *Seychelles, Maldives* and *Mauritius,* may be ideal destinations for them.

However, from the tourism industry perspective, couples may also refer to gay couples or lesbian couples who are an important segment and bring pink dollars/pounds to the tourism businesses. They must also be treated with equal respect while travelling to a destination. Travel companies must be sensitive towards the needs of such travellers and must promote only those destinations to such travellers that show acceptance and respect towards them.

Families

This is the family life stage when couples have children. For many families, taking holidays annually is a ritual. It is seen as a family reuniting and bonding exercise. Families may plan to visit destinations that are family-friendly wherein everyone can find something for themselves of interest to enjoy. Families may vary from nuclear families to joint families where the grandparents and siblings may also join in for the vacation.

In families, sometimes, children may drive the decisions of the family. They may prefer those destinations where their children can find good travel options and they can also have a good vacation time. For example, a family may think of travelling with their children to Disney World in the USA/Disneyland in Hong Kong, Sentosa island in Singapore and so on.

Senior Citizens

This is the empty nest stage of a person where his/her children leave their home and are settled in their own lives. At this stage, the responsibilities of parents are over and since most of them retire from work, they may have enough time to travel. Although for them mobility may be a challenge, for those whose health permits to travel and those who have enough savings, they would like to travel.

Therefore, senior citizens are also a very important segment of tourism markets who are heavy travellers. However, their needs and requirements may be different. They may require wheelchairs, golf carts, ramps, hearing aids and so on while they travel. They may also prefer to travel in groups as they may have the services of a knowledgeable tour leader who can take care of them during the tour and look into their specific needs and requirements. Also, their purpose of travel may be different depending upon which place they originate from.

EMERGING TYPES OF TRAVELLERS

With the changing times, many other travellers are evolving. Some of them are as follows:

- Women solo travellers
- Expecting mothers
- People with special abilities
- Travel bloggers

A detailed discussion on each of these has also been given in Chapter 31, 'Emerging Trends in Tourism'. Now, let us discuss these emerging sections of travellers in brief.

Women Solo Travellers

Of late, the segment of women travellers travelling solo is emerging. These are bold confident women ready to face any challenges during the travel and do not conform to the conventional approach of only travelling with family, relatives or known friends. Solo travelling has become a fad now with women travellers seeking solo travel more actively with the idea of exploring themselves while they travel. Such travellers believe in travelling alone with the idea of enriching themselves with lifetime experiences they may encounter while travelling. Many women travel in search of their own identity and feeling that travel will change them and make them more confident. They become more decisive while making confident decisions at every point and with the kind of situations they may have to deal with. They may sometimes travel in groups to make new friends during the journey and make their travel more interesting.

However, it is important for tourism industry service providers to know the requirements of women and accordingly offer interesting packages for the women that may appeal to them.

Many hotels in order to cater to women solo travellers offer dedicated floors, housekeeping female staff, rooms with feminine interiors and decor and so on to specifically cater to their requirements.

It is important to mention here that the top priority for women solo travellers is safety and security. Therefore, destinations must be prepared to welcome women travellers with adequate safety measures in place for them. Women tourist police, emergency helplines and so on must be in place that may increase the confidence of such travellers.

Expecting Mothers

Due to the trending concept of babymoon, many expecting mothers are happy travelling during their pregnancy. It is a ritual for them to plan their travel during their second trimester of pregnancy and visit destinations that can give them comfort and relaxation.

People with Special Abilities

This is another class of travellers that instead of living with their limited abilities choose to travel to destinations. However, such kind of travellers may be accompanied by family or friends or they may travel in groups. Many destinations cater to such kind of travellers who have special requirements. These are destinations that have developed accessible infrastructure so that they can cater to travellers with disabilities. Such destinations must have accessible public transportation, footpaths, sidewalks, ramps, toilets, attractions, assistance for disabled at airports, adapted hotel rooms, wheelchairs, golf cart facility, hearing aids and so on so as to promote accessible tourism for people with special abilities. In fact, many tour operators promote and specialize in accessible travel by catering only to this segment of the market.

Travel Bloggers

Another emerging section of travellers is the travel bloggers who travel to destinations to get a first-hand information about a destination. Such travellers through their travel experiences at destinations get food for their blogs. Thus, when they come back, they may post their travel experiences on their travel blogs on the Internet. Many travel companies and hospitality organizations are focusing on this budding segment of writers who write good content for their companies or their destinations that help them to market their destination and tourism products to the followers following their travel blogs.

SUMMARY

For many travellers, travelling satisfies their insatiable need for the exotic and thrilling experiences of a lifetime. Travelling for them is an emotional recharge that connects them with their own self. The ubiquitous travel images on social media, the growth of the middle class, a surge in affordable travel options and rising government support have altogether accelerated the growth of the tourism industry. The service providers of the tourism industry need to understand that it is not enough to serve the conventional trip category. They must be prepared to also serve that emerging segment of travellers who are looking for novel experiences.

ACTIVITIES

Activity 1

Based on the discussion above, identify yourself with the type of traveller that you are. Justify your type with valid reasons.

Activity 2

Identify at least five travel companies that sell tour packages and cater to a specific segment of the market. Now make a chart presentation of these companies, elaborating on the kind of travellers that they cater to. Now do a comparative analysis and present it to the class.

Activity 3

Think of yourself as a travel start-up. Now you want to launch yourself as a unique travel brand. Which segment of travellers would you like to sell the tour packages to and why? Justify your answer with a relevant argument.

The New-age Traveller

8

TURKEY: A HONEYMOON DESTINATION!

- Did you know that Istanbul is a city in Turkey which is built on two continents, Asia and Europe?
- According to International Congress and Convention Association, Turkey is listed among the world's top 10 meeting and congress destinations.
- Turkey is also promoting wellness tourism which is famous for traditional Turkish baths (also called hammam) and thermal hot springs.
- Turkey is also a perfect paradise for adventure lovers and sports enthusiasts as it offers activities such as canyoning, golfing, trekking and winter sports.
- Turkey is being positioned as a perfect honeymoon destination by the Tourism Ministry of Turkey as it is home to spectacular coastlines, magnificent landscapes and exotic cities.
- The four famous seas around Turkey are the Mediterranean Sea, the Sea of Marmara, the Black Sea and the Aegean Sea.

- The Turquoise Riviera is a beautiful coastal stretch in Turkey famous for the butterfly valley where people can take a boat tour to see hundreds of gorgeous species of butterflies.
- Some other highlights for a honeymoon couple include the following:
  o A romantic dinner on cruise on the Bosphorus.
  o Shopping for antiques in one of the largest and oldest markets, *Grand Bazaar*, in Istanbul.
  o If you have a sweet tooth, you must taste the most famous sweet in Turkish cuisine called *baklava*.
  o *Hot-air ballooning in Cappadocia*. Also, do not miss the chance to experience various boat tours, volcano and hot spring tours, catamaran cruise tours and so on.
- Turkey is an official member of the Cittaslow movement which initiates improving the quality of life in towns by slowing down the fast city pace. It promotes slow tourism, which gives you a chance to relax and enjoy the peaceful atmosphere.

INTRODUCTION

With the changing times, as the tourism industry evolves, the traveller is also evolving. There is an essential paradigm shift that has taken place from the conventional traveller to the new-age traveller. At this juncture, it is important for the service providers of the tourism industry to be aware of the preferences and needs of the new-age traveller so that they can offer those tourism products for the tourists that may match with the travel expectations of the tourists.

The new-age traveller is different from the conventional traveller in terms of his/her choices, expectations from the trip and the behaviour that he/she exhibits during the trip. His/her needs and preferences are continuously evolving. We have the new-age traveller now who is more confident about the travel choices that he/she makes and who has a greater exposure of travelling. The new-age traveller today is more demanding, well informed and restless. His/her quest for tourism needs to be instantly gratified. Today's traveller wants to have a positive impact on the communities and environment of a destination that he/she is visiting. We have the new-age experiential travellers who want more local interactions.

Now let us have a detailed discussion on the preferences and choices of the new-age traveller.

AWARENESS OF SELF

The new-age traveller is more mature. He/she is more sorted and clear about his/her travel preferences. He/she seeks a destination at his/her own pace. He/she knows exactly what he/she wants from a holiday. He/she lives with no excuses and travels with no regrets.

MORE INFORMED

The new-age traveller is more informed now. He/she has access to unlimited information today that he/she may use for his/her travel. With the proliferation of the Internet and the easily available information at one's fingertips, the new-age traveller is more aware and knowledgeable today. He/she has well researched the information beforehand about the destinations and the attractions that he/she plans to visit for his/her vacation. The new-age traveller has an opportunity to go through the travel information posted on the websites, travel blogs, vlogs, social media and so on to form an opinion about a destination. In other words, while planning to travel, the traveller has all the means by which he/she can gather maximum information about a destination before he/she actually visits it. Being knowledgeable about the things that can happen with him/her on the tour due to the overflowing information available on the Internet, he/she may be more prepared and in a better situation to handle the unforeseen circumstances during the tour. In short, he/she knows it all when he/she travels as compared to the conventional traveller who hardly knew anything about what to expect from the holiday destination before his/her actual travel due to less information available at those times.

EDUCATED AND LEARNED

Today's traveller is more educated and learned in terms of his/her formal education. Due to his/her formal education background, he/she is more aware of the travelling benefits. He/she knows that travelling widens one's perspective.

TRAVEL BUFF

For the new-age traveller, travelling is a way of life. The travel adventures define his/her life. He/she loves to travel. For him/her travelling to destinations is a ritual that satisfies his/her soul. He/she wants to venture to new unknown destinations as he/she may have constant travel goals.

ACTIVE

The new-age traveller is more active. The new-age travellers are engaging participants, not mere spectators. Unlike the earlier traveller who was a passive traveller only visiting destinations with the primary objective of sightseeing, the new-age traveller is more action-oriented. The new-age traveller wants an activity-based holiday. He/she wants an action-packed holiday full of local activities that he/she can try hands on at the holiday destination. However, this may again vary depending upon one's purpose of travel, the age factor and one's personal interest.

MORE ADVENTUROUS AND RISK-TAKING

The new-age traveller is more willing to take risks and to experiment as he/she wants to indulge in extreme adventure and sports. He/she is more adventurous in his/her travel habits. He/she wants to push himself/herself beyond limits and do things that he/she may have never tried before. He/she wants to try different adventure experiences every time he/she travels such as visiting mountain expeditions, skydiving, bungee jumping, caving and similar other adventure activities. He/she may dream of *rafting in Rotorua rapids, ice cycling in Mongolia, cruising in Antarctica, terrain hikes in Argentina, trekking on Chadar Trek at Zanskar river in Ladakh* and so on.

SPONTANEOUS

The new-age traveller is more volatile about his/her travel choices. He/she is more impulsive. He/she may plan his/her holiday in a wink of an eye. Sometimes he/she may not even plan his/her holiday and spontaneously make his/her travel decisions or make spontaneous travel bookings and reservations as and when required during travel. He/she may choose to go with the flow taking things as they come to him/her on a holiday. Spontaneous travellers are generally more flexible to changes if things do not work out according to their laid itinerary since they do not believe in advanced planning. They are more adaptable and ready to 'expect the unexpected' during their travel.

MORE TECH-SAVVY

Today's traveller not only knows the importance of technology but also knows how to use it to its maximum advantage. Many travellers prefer to make their own travel arrangements with the assistance of phenomenal information available on the Internet. The new-age traveller may visit the Internet for gaining knowledge about the destination, learning about the various ways to explore a destination, read the reviews of travelled passengers on the websites, consult various travel apps, do a comparative analysis of the websites, then finally make the bookings of his/her travel on the websites and travel apps and then eventually travel as per the planned bookings. Even if he/she does not make the bookings through the online portals himself/herself, he/she may go through all the information posted on these sites. Further making use of the technology post travel or even during his/her travel, he/she may broadcast his/her trips on social media by posting his/her experiences and pictures on the social networking sites such as Facebook and Instagram. In this process of sharing his/her travel experiences, he/she may inspire his/her friends and family to travel to the same destinations through his/her interesting posts.

DIFFERENT BOOKING BEHAVIOUR

The new-age traveller has a changed booking behaviour. He/she is more spontaneous and believes in booking at the last moment. He/she is more self-reliant now as compared to earlier travellers who used to be heavily dependent on travel agents for making their travel arrangements. These travellers are more dependent on technology and can, thus, make online travel bookings on their own without consulting or taking the expertise of a tour operator.

INDEPENDENT

Today's traveller has a more independent approach towards travel due to the easy access of travel information available at his/her disposal. Being able to gather all the information from the Internet and make his/her travel bookings on his/her own, the new-age traveller feels more in charge of his/her holiday vacation. Since he/she is not dependent on the travel agents/tour operators who can make travel arrangements for him/her, he/she feels more confident and more independent as a result of choices that he/she can make on his/her own. On the other hand, through his/her own comparisons, on the contrary, he/she may give information to the tour operators as to what exactly he/she is looking for, in case he/she is planning to book any travel arrangements through them.

EMPOWERED

The new-age traveller is more aware of his/her rights today as compared to the earlier traveller. He/she is more vocal about his/her opinions than ever before. He/she has access to various public platforms now on which he/she can raise his/her voice today, especially the social media where his/her one negative feedback about the service provider can badly affect the service provider's credibility and bring him/her to negative limelight in public space. Also, he/she has a number of travel choices to choose from while planning to visit a destination. Thus, the power of having access to being heard and the various travel options at his/her discretion make the new-age traveller feel more empowered.

MORE EXPERIENTIAL IN NATURE

The new-age traveller prefers authentic travel experiences. He/she does not want to just visit a destination, but now wants more to live the life of a local at a destination. He/she wants to immerse himself/herself in the local experiences and get the 'local feel' of a destination. He/she wants to interact with the local community in their natural locale, eat their local food served in local style, dance to the local tunes of the folk music of the destination and sometimes even stay with them. In short, he/she wants to live like a local and not as a tourist who is just happy gazing the lifestyles of locals from a distance. He/she wants to experience authenticity by living with locals like a local.

NOVEL TOURISM EXPERIENCES

The new-age traveller is more experimentative in nature seeking newer epic experiences. He/she wants experience-based travel. The new-age traveller does not believe in the conventional experi-

A Swiss Localite Playing Folk Music using Alphorn for the Tourists

ences. He/she wants an offbeat experience. He/she wants to travel to new destinations and does not want to repeat them.

The new-age traveller wants to try niche tourism products such as cruises, golf tourism and wellness tourism. He/she may want to travel and stay in caravans, heritage trains, try out the local food of a place, visit unexplored destinations, try different kinds of adventure, meet people from different cultures or explore the cities on foot, Segways or bikes. He/she wants to experience something different as compared to the regular experiences experienced by the mass tourists.

PURSUES SPECIAL INTERESTS

The new-age traveller has defined special interests and particular preferences and choices that must be addressed while travelling to a destination. For example, he/she may like to visit Italy and *Spain* to learn about wineries, India to play golf or he/she may travel to *Kenya* for a jungle safari. He/she may visit *France* to take baking classes or visit China to learn about different types of tea.

FREQUENCY OF TRAVEL IS MORE

The new-age traveller travels often. He/she wants short breaks at multiple intervals to experience quick getaways. Even the weekends are a good time for holiday lovers to spend their time relaxing and rejuvenating at a destination. Thus, many tour operators commercialize many destinations as weekend getaways for the new-age travellers. For example, from Delhi, many tour operators such as *WanderOn* and *Just Travel* organize weekend getaways for the tourists. Some of the popular destinations for weekenders from Delhi that they may visit are as follows:

- Bir Billing, *the paragliding capital of India* in the state of Himachal Pradesh (famous for paragliding, mountain biking, trekking and camping besides experiencing the Buddhist culture as it is a Buddhist town)
- Auli, the *skiing capital of India* in the state of Uttarakhand
- Rishikesh, the *Yoga capital of the world* in the state of Uttarakhand
- McLeod Ganj, the little Lhasa in the state of Himachal Pradesh
- Kasauli, Lansdowne, Nainital, Shimla, Dhanaulti, Mukteshwar and so on are scenic hill stations in Himachal Pradesh and Uttarakhand
- Jim Corbett National Park in Uttarakhand
- Jaipur, the Pink City and the Neemrana town famous for Neemrana Fort Palace in Rajasthan

WELL-TRAVELLED

The new-age traveller is no more restricted by geographical and political boundaries. His/her new bucket list is no more confined to domestic destinations, but he/she is seeking to travel internationally and see the world. Today's traveller is well travelled and, thus, has more exposure to things. As they may be globetrotters, they know how to travel, when to travel and the various nitty-gritty that are involved in the travel. Since they know the various procedures involved in travel, they are more confident and aware.

MORE DEMANDING

The more travelled the tourists, the more set of expectations they have from the service providers. Such travellers are quite aware of exactly what they are looking for on their holiday. Due to greater exposure to travelling, they know what to demand and expect from the travel organizers who facilitate arrangements for them. The new-age traveller expects efficient services at the wink of his/her eye. As a result, it becomes quite challenging to please such travellers who are highly demanding in nature.

QUALITY CONSCIOUS

The new-age traveller is more conscious of the quality of travel services now as compared to the earlier traveller. Since many of the new-age travellers may have already travelled a lot, they know the world-class standard of services provided by the tourism and hospitality service organizations. They expect the same quality of services to be maintained every time they travel. However, the issue of quality is quite relative that may vary from person to person and from destination to destination. In remote destinations, one may not expect a very high quality of services. Thus, for a positive experience, tourists must moderate their expectations according to the kind of destination being visited.

RESPONSIBLE TRAVELLER

Today's traveller is more aware of his/her carbon footprints when he/she travels around. Thus, he/she is more conscious and sensitive towards the nearby surroundings and the environment. While visiting a destination and its attractions, he/she ensures that he/she does not litter around, abide by the dos and don'ts at the attractions and take care of the flora and fauna around while visiting national parks, wildlife sanctuaries and various treks. He/she is also more respectful of local cultures. He/she believes in taking care of the local sensitivities when he/she travels on a holiday. In short, he/she is a responsible tourist now who is mindful of his/her behaviour when he/she visits a destination.

SUMMARY

The new-age traveller is a smart traveller today as he/she knows how to use technology and, thus, he/she is more aware and well informed. He/she understands the importance of travelling and what travelling does to him/her. The new-age traveller prefers independence and wants to be in charge of his/her holiday plans when he/she travels. He/she wants to experience new things, has high expectations from the tour as he/she is more travelled and is more educated too. He/she is more confident about his/her choices and is well aware and more sorted in his/her choices.

ACTIVITIES

Activity 1

Enlist the new ways that travel companies are adopting to woo the new-age traveller.

Activity 2

'The new-age traveller is defining new industry standards'. Discuss and debate.

Activity 3

Based on the discussion above, do you think that you qualify as a new-age traveller? If yes, prepare an inventory of the characteristics that define you as a new-age traveller.

Positive Impacts of Tourism

'LONG LIVE THE GORILLAS'

- Gorilla trekking expedition and gorilla safaris are a major highlight for wildlife adventure enthusiasts. The tourists specially throng regions of Uganda and Rwanda in Africa to see this nature's creation.
- Due to over tourism, the mountain gorilla species have been declared as critically endangered by the International Union for Conservation of the Nature Red List.
- In order to conserve the mountain gorillas and stabilize the population of these endangered species, tourism boards and wildlife conservation authorities have initiated controlled tourism by limiting human footfall in the regions by taking the following steps:
    o The wildlife authority of regions with gorilla-trekking tours has ensured to limit the number of people in group tours and increase the gorilla-trekking fees.
    o The development boards have also limited the permit access for a day and made the permits expensive. By doing this, limited people are visiting these endangered species, which has resulted in peaceful habitation for mountain gorillas.

> o The conservation authorities have also introduced park guards, veterinary care, community support projects and so on in the region to help the constant efforts in saving mountain gorillas and their habitat.
> - Generally, gorilla permits can only be attained six months prior to the trip due to high demand.

INTRODUCTION

Tourism is considered as one of the world's largest economic sectors. It is one of the main pillars and an economic driver of many countries of the world. It plays a significant role in the social and financial development of a country. The importance of tourism to economies of countries cannot be ignored. Seeing the advantages accruing from the tourism activity, governments of big and small countries, at central, regional and local levels, are apparently considering the tourism sector as an important contributor to their economies. Tourism today is increasingly being recognized as an instrument of socio-economic development for the communities of a country.

Back in the 1980s also, tourism gained impetus when the emphasis was given on its importance in the Manila Declaration on Tourism stating, *'tourism is an activity essential to the life of nations because of its direct effects on the social, cultural, educational and economic sectors of national societies and on their international relations'*.

Based on the above definition, we may conclude the following:

- It is considered as an important activity for the countries of the world.
- It impacts the society of a nation in different ways that may include the economic, social, cultural and educational impacts besides the political impacts.
- It may be considered as an 'image builder' of a nation or a 'passport to peace' as it helps in improving the relations between nations.

In other words, tourism is a tool for development and sustainability, respecting the environment and different cultures and practising solidarity and care for each other while creating new opportunities for everyone.

Now, let us have a detailed discussion on the positive impacts of the tourism sector on the countries of the world.

For the sake of our clarity, we shall try to address this chapter by discussing the positive impacts of tourism from two perspectives:

1. Country's perspective
2. Tourist's perspective

FROM A COUNTRY'S PERSPECTIVE

Now, let us initiate the discussion first from a country's perspective. For further clarity, we have addressed the positive impacts of tourism from a country's perspective at three levels, that is, positive economic impacts, positive sociocultural impacts and positive environmental impacts.

Positive Economic Impacts

The benefits and the impacts that accrue to the economy of a country by virtue of the tourism sector are called economic impacts of tourism. Tourism is the backbone of many economies of the world. Countries such as Thailand, Singapore, Malaysia, Switzerland, Mauritius, Aruba, Seychelles, Bahamas, Fiji Islands, Macau, Curacao, Barbados, Cambodia, Maldives, Malta, British Virgin Islands and many more are highly dependent on tourism. A significant proportion of their country's gross domestic product (GDP) is contributed by the tourism sector. A fair chunk of their economy is driven by the tourism sector. Tourism has a significant economic importance as it provides an opportunity to inject wealth in the local community when the tourists spend their money in multiple ways that increases the purchasing power of the locals in turn boosting the local economy. Some of the economic benefits to a country are as follows.

Increases the National Income of the Country

Domestic tourism is a big contributor to the tourism industry. Especially for India, it is the backbone of Indian tourism. When we talk in the context of India, domestic tourists may be motivated to travel within the country especially to socialize and see their family and friends, visit pilgrimage places within the country, travel for health and medical purpose or any other purpose such as leisure, business, education and training, and shopping.

When the domestic tourists travel within the country, they spend money on different travel arrangements. They may spend money on local transportation, accommodation, eating at local restaurants, doing shopping, visiting sightseeing places and engaging in all sorts of entertainment. As they spend money in local businesses, the money multiplies. The local businesses in turn spend on their requirements. Thus, money starts percolating within the economy, leading to increasing the national income of the country. Therefore, tourism acts as a tool for bringing wealth to the local communities of a destination.

Increases Spending of Local Community

The tourism industry is predominantly run by small businesses and micro operators. Thus, every dollar that a foreign tourist spends at a destination is easily felt by the people in the tourism business who in turn boost the local economy by spending money on things of daily usage. Thus, the money spent by the tourists at the local destination is reinjected into the local economy. Thus, tourism revenues create a 'multiplier effect' as the dollar that the tourist spends, a large percentage of it is reintroduced in local economy again and again by the local's spending and thus the money keeps multiplying. The more dollars are spent by the tourists, the more benefits accrue to the local community. This is called the *multiplier effect*. Thus, it raises the standard of living of the local community.

Brings Foreign Exchange

Tourism is also called the 'golden goose' that brings in foreign exchange within a country. Inbound tourism contributes to invisible exports to a country as the foreign tourists bring foreign exchange to a country without exporting anything to a foreign country. It is often referred to as an invisible export as the foreign tourists spend their currency in exchange for a 'touristic experience' of a country that is largely intangible. Tourists visiting a foreign country buy local things of a country in their local currency in exchange for their own country's currency. Thus, they invest their local currency in a country bringing foreign exchange to a country. However, foreign exchange has more value if the denomination of a foreign currency is higher than the host country's own local currency. Increase in international tourism leads to a favourable effect on the balance of payments of a country. It, thus, improves the value of currency of a country where tourists visit.

Tourism also leads to multinational corporations (MNCs) investing in tourism-related projects like the construction of airports and hotels which leads to foreign direct investment (FDI) in a country.

Generates Employment

Tourism is a source of bread and butter for many people. This sector supports 1 in every 10 jobs on the planet and, thus, is seen as a dynamic engine for employment opportunities, especially supporting the marginalized people of the society like artisans. It is a labour-intensive industry. Many people across the world are directly or indirectly employed through the tourism industry. Various people working for airlines, hotels, restaurants, travel agencies/tour operators, online travel portals, local transporters, entertainment organizations, sightseeing attractions and others such as souvenir merchandisers, local artisans, local shopkeepers, local guides, drivers and photographers earn their living through tourism. Tourism not only provides direct employment to people working for it, but it also benefits the supporting industries such as food production and retail. Many local businesses too are supported by the tourism industry. It also encourages the local community to become entrepreneurs and start up their own local businesses such as restaurants, local eateries, hotels and B&B that are opportunities for the local community to establish new services and facilities that further benefit the local community too.

For example, the complete economy of pilgrimage destinations runs on the pilgrimage tourists visiting a destination. *Let us take the example of Shirdi here which is a holy place of Lord Sai Baba.* Thousands of people, in fact almost the whole town, is involved in earning their income either directly or indirectly through pilgrimage tourism. Not only the local travel agents, local transporters or hotels and other supplementary accommodation providers (e.g., dharmshalas, guest houses and so on) earn their living through tourism but also the local businesses that include the local restaurateurs, the shopkeepers selling souvenirs, *prasad* (offering to God) and flowers, local photographers and so on earn their bread and butter through tourism. Thus, thousands of people of the local host community thrive on tourism for their sustenance. Tourism, thus, affects all walks of life and generates employment for everyone.

Diversification

Tourism allows an economy to develop an additional source of income. By banking on the tourism industry, the economies of the countries can diversify, which just rely on a single industry for their growth. Tourism becomes an additional source of income for the economy of a country that can also support the traditional industries of a country. The tourism sector allows an opportunity to a community to diversify their sources of income, thereby reducing their dependence on a single industry that could be a risky proposition to bank upon. It, thus, acts as a cushion against any financial crisis that a destination may face in the future.

Positive Sociocultural Impacts

These are the positive impacts of tourism which affect the society and life at a destination by virtue of tourists visiting that destination. Some of the sociocultural impacts on a destination are as follows.

Creation of Urban Infrastructure and Public Services

The Skyline, New York

For tourism to flourish at a destination, it must have the required infrastructure and superstructure to support the tourists and make their stay comfortable and hassle-free at a destination. Therefore, destinations that attract tourists focus on developing infrastructure and superstructure for the tourists that in turn becomes an asset for the host community living at the destination.

The revenues that come into the community through tourists' footfall allow many public projects to be launched by the local councils or governments. As a result, infrastructure improves that brings in more visitors supporting the economic development even further.

Development of superstructure for the tourists such as airports, runways, terminals, roads and highways, public transportation systems, hotels, restaurants, attractions, public parks, business convention centres, recreational centres, amusement parks, shopping malls and hospitals is useful for the host community as well. Tourism, thus, creates and facilitates opportunities for entertainment and recreation for the local community.

Protects Culture

Culture is the tourism product for many tourists. When tourists visit destinations, they interact with the locals and sometimes even stay with them. Many of the tourists are inquisitive to learn various aspects of the locals' culture such as their customs, traditions, languages, local cuisines, art, and folk songs and dances. In fact, through experiencing tourism activity, the tourists get an opportunity to gain a glimpse of locals' lifestyle.

In this process of showcasing their culture to tourists, the locals realize the importance of their own culture which is a heritage passed to them by their ancestors and needs to be preserved and nurtured. The coming of tourists to a destination and taking interest in the host community's culture creates a sense of pride within the locals that further strengthens their belief in their community identity and re-instills a sense of pride within them towards their own culture. This helps in the preservation of culture of a destination.

Preserves National Heritage

When travellers visit places, they want to understand the tangible and intangible heritage of a place. They may visit museums that are repositories of ancestral heritage or may visit heritage sites and archaeological sites that have a historical significance. These sites are a primary attraction and a must-see site for the tourists on their itineraries as these showcase the traditions and heritage of a country. Thus, tourism acts as a tool for restoring the heritage and dying culture of cities of the world.

This is the advantage of tourism activity that has saved many local heritage sites from destruction. National heritage and culture that may be at risk of being lost are being preserved through the tool of tourism.

Many government bodies/non-governmental organizations (NGOs) and sometimes even the private bodies are primarily responsible for the conservation and maintenance of these monuments that are major tourism products for a destination. Many attractions and cities have also been declared as world heritage cities and sites by UNESCO, which have a significant heritage value of national importance. *Some of the world heritage cities recognized by UNESCO are Ahmedabad and Jaipur in India, Melaka in Malaysia, Bath in England and many more.* To further increase the importance of heritage, raise awareness of the cultural monuments and sites and understand the importance of preserving the world's cultures, the World Heritage Day is celebrated on 18 April annually, initiated by ICOMOS. To mark the international observance of the day, people visit monuments and heritage sites, give write-ups and articles in newspapers and magazines, organize round table conferences, workshops and so on to sensitize both the locals and the tourists towards the idea of heritage preservation.

Creates a Conductive Environment

Tourism is often said to be the passport of peace that connects people together. It provides cultural exchange opportunities. When people from two different cultures and ideologies meet, they tend to develop an understanding for each other. They start respecting each other's culture and develop a tolerance for each other. It breaks the conventional stereotypes that a person may be holding about the other's culture, religion, nationality and so on. Travelling brings him/her closer to reality, opens his/her horizons to the newer perspectives as he/she interacts with new people from new cultures, thereby fostering new friendships. It bridges the gap between the nations and creates an atmosphere of peace.

Keeps the Country Clean

When tourists visit a destination, they expect it to be spick and span. Hygiene of a destination is considered to be a qualifying factor while choosing a destination to visit. Thus, destinations in order to attract the tourists start focusing on their sanitation standards by educating the local communities to keep their city clean. This in turn reinforces the tourists to keep the destination clean when they visit there.

Positive Environmental Impacts

Tourism and environment share a close association with each other as tourism is highly dependent on environment. Equally, tourism is a tool for environmental conservation. Now let us have a discussion on the impacts of tourism on the environment.

Conserves Environment

Many tourism products that are created revolve around the natural environment resources. These may be mountains, hills, deserts, islands, water bodies, biosphere reserves, national parks, wildlife sanctuaries, forests and so on. The tourism industry channelizes these natural resources endowed from the environment (like the Giant's Causeway in North Ireland) to create an experiential product for the tourists. Some tourists are always looking for nature-based tourism products to experience being close to nature. Thus, the tourism industry in order to attract the tourists to the areas of natural settings helps in maintenance and conservation of the environment by keeping their beauty intact. However, to maintain the sanctity of the environment and minimize the negative impacts of tourism on environment, tourism must be promoted with a balanced approach keeping in mind the carrying capacity of a destination. In the process of conservation of environment, tourists too can share their responsibility by conducting themselves as responsible tourists.

The Giant Causeway, North Ireland

Conserves Endangered Species

Viewing the wildlife and watching the birds is of interest to many wildlife enthusiasts and bird watchers. Thus, in order to promote wildlife tourism, many national parks and wildlife sanctuaries that are a haven of endangered species are conserved to showcase the wildlife to the tourists. Thus, tourism acts as a tool for conservation of endangered species.

Creates Environmental Awareness

Tourism in many ways teaches the importance of the environment to the tourists. By visiting nature-based tourism products, tourists realize the vital role that the environment plays in increasing the number of tourists to a destination. As they travel more and confront with the environment, they learn to appreciate the role of the environment in creating a positive experience for the tourists. They become more sensitive to their roles that can help in keeping the environment pristine and unspoilt. Their environmental awareness becomes more heightened and thus, they contribute more to the environment by behaving as responsible tourists.

Even many tour operators contributing towards sustainability are offering eco-friendly packages that promote nature-based tours and help in the conservation of the environment. They also create environmental awareness among the tourists who travel with them by sharing the code of conduct to be followed by them at a destination to support the cause of conservation of the local area and its communities. The tour operators may suggest the tourist to eat local food, buy local souvenirs, not to do anything that deteriorates the environment further, participate in local activities, stay at the community-owned establishments and support the cultural diversity of the place by being sensitive to the needs of the local community. The tourists are advised to act responsibly, who through their visit add value to the local community.

Generates Revenue

Managing environmental resources is a big task. It requires large funds and investments to keep the nature-based tourism resources clean and in a usable form not only for the present but also for the future generations. Thus, while visiting national parks, wildlife sanctuaries or other tourism-based resources that are nature-based, tourists are charged with an entry fee that may be quite nominal by the government authorities. This revenue earned through the entry fees paid by the tourists may further be used towards the conservation of the environment. Besides the above-mentioned entry fees, funds may also be raised from tourist taxes, user fees, rents on recreational equipment that may be eventually used to manage the environmental resources.

FROM A TOURIST'S PERSPECTIVE

Tourism has a deeper impact on a person. It is the best teacher. The most intense form of learning is only possible through travelling. Travelling changes you as a person. Many virtues and values of life can be imbibed through travel. As one travels more, he/she becomes wiser. There are many advantages of travelling. Let us have a discussion on each of these.

Emotional Recharge

Travel is a great healer. Travelling allows us an opportunity to emotionally reconnect with our own selves. It gives a person the 'me time' where one may get an opportunity to establish a deeper connect with oneself. It allows oneself time and space to think about oneself and emotionally recharge oneself to take up future challenges.

Well-being

Tourism is a key to happiness for many. It makes one happier. As a person takes out time for his/her own physical and emotional health, it improves his/her overall well-being.

Improves the Quality of Work Life

Doing away with the work pressure for some time and taking a good holiday break actually recharges one's battery and energizes the person to take up future assignments with more effectiveness and productivity. Thus, travelling is known to improve the quality of work life.

Facilitates Bonding

Travelling strengthens one's family ties and friendships. The shared experience of travelling together brings everyone together and develops tolerance for each other. It is a perfect opportunity to connect with each other.

Couples travelling together get good quality time with each other away from the worries of home and job that brings them together. A family getaway with grandparents, parents and children is the time to spend together and renew bonds. Likewise, spending time with parents, siblings and relatives helps discover new bonds and new qualities about each other. Similarly, travelling with school-time friends or college mates is an experience of its own kind that deepens friendships.

Travelling with colleagues in business or profession is also an opportunity to bind together and even smooth over grudges, if any, that they might hold against each other.

Travelling is also a great opportunity to socialize with fellow travellers and locals to foster new friendships with them. Certain friendships become valuable friendships that are an asset for a lifetime.

You Become Stronger

Travel may not always be a cakewalk. It may sometimes be full of scary and crazy experiences. Things may not always work out as initially planned. One may lose his/her passport, luggage or may miss a train by a few minutes or may find it difficult to communicate with the locals due to the language barrier that may make travel more difficult for a person. However, such unexpected situations test one's patience. They make one emerge as a stronger person when one faces such difficulties during travel.

Discovery of One's Talent

Travelling inspires people to accomplish things that they never thought they could. It may spur the inner artist within a person while seeing the art galleries, museums and other incredible pieces of art around the world. Sometimes, it may introduce an adventure enthusiast within him/her.

A well-travelled person may also become a better storyteller. As one travels more, he/she has more stories to tell. It helps the traveller to move out of his/her bubble and push himself/herself beyond memories.

Changes Perspectives

Travelling makes a person see the bigger picture of the world that alters his/her perception of life. Meeting new people, listening to their stories and understanding their world view make the problems of the travellers appear so small and things do not seem the same anymore. Therefore, travelling makes people look at issues with a fresh perspective. It opens their horizons and breaks their stereotypes.

Educative Value

Travelling teaches you at every step. It adds to one's existing knowledge. Various experiences of travelling such as knowledge about destinations after visiting them, interacting with locals and learning about their cultures, and any challenge that you might have to face during travelling make you more knowledgeable and educated.

Increases Tolerance

While exploring the rich diversity, the tourist may undergo cultural shock as his/her culture may be totally different from the culture at the destination that he/she has visited.

Seeing the different parts of the world and knowing that people can coexist in different ways make the travellers respect the differences and become more tolerant of each other.

Improves Communication

Travelling is known to improve the communication and social skills of a traveller. As tourists travel to different parts of the world where people may speak different languages, communicating with the locals and the tourism service providers becomes important at every step of travelling. However, it can be a great challenge too. One has to be extrovert, more expressive and conversant to communicate his/her point. Thus, travelling teaches the traveller to learn a new language, to be more expressive and state one's own ideas with conviction to others, which improve one's confidence and interpersonal skills.

Improves Life Skills

Travelling teaches life skills. It teaches you the way of life. One may learn:

- Social skills
- Language skills
- Hiking, swimming, surfing and so on

Appreciating One's Own Life

As one travels and sees the other parts of the world, one may feel luckier and appreciable of how he/she is leading his/her own life. He/she is in a better situation to assess and compare his/her city and country with other places that he/she has visited. It gives a traveller a fresh perspective of his/her own hometown and his/her real life as he/she might have lost sight of being in the same place and following the same routine always. After returning from a holiday, he/she may begin to appreciate and value more his/her own lifestyle, city and country.

SUMMARY

The tourism industry is flourishing day by day. Many countries of the world which are realizing its potential and tapping tourists are benefitting to a great extent. In a competitive global market, the tourists visiting a country are making an impact never seen before. It is bringing prosperity to the economies of the country, raising the profile of destinations in the world by giving them a chance to showcase themselves and is also serving as an important tool to preserve the environment. Tourism is now not only considered as an engine of economic development but is also considered as a vehicle for sharing cultures and developing mutual understanding. Thus, its importance and contribution to the countries of the world cannot be undermined. With the right approach, the governments must include it in a business strategy and pave the way for the success of various economies of the world.

ACTIVITIES

Activity 1

Have you ever travelled to a city/state/country that has changed your perspective about things? If yes, share your travel story.

Activity 2

Discuss in detail any five cities/states in your country that have benefitted from tourism. Share your views with the class.

Activity 3

Identify the capitals of the following countries:

- Austria
- Germany
- Malaysia
- Australia
- Singapore
- Turkey
- Hungary
- Finland

Negative Impacts of Tourism

LEARNING OBJECTIVES

The given chapter shall clarify the following:

- How is tourism a source of destruction for the environment?
- How does tourism affect the social fabric of the society?

INTRODUCTION

Kayaking in River Liffey, Dublin

Tourism, to a larger extent, is driven by the natural resources of a destination. It flourishes in areas where environmental attractions and natural resources are abundant. Since nature offers various resources such as landscapes, mountains, water, snow, forests and deserts, the phenomena of tourism utilizes the tourism potential of a place by creating tourist products based on the natural resources of a destination. The countries with such natural gifts capitalize on their resources by developing tourism products such as nature-based tours, wildlife sanctuaries, national parks, beach resorts, hill stations and adventure activities such as sky diving and paragliding. Destinations such as *Uttarakhand, Central Vermont, Switzerland* and *Canada* are thriving on the activities such as snowboarding, snow bikes, skiing and trekking expeditions. Similarly, islands such as

Mauritius, Bali and Fiji are featuring water-sports activities such as kayaking, jet skiing and scuba diving. Amazing resorts are built on the beaches of Goa, Miami, Australia and Dubai to attract the tourists.

People from different corners of the world travel a great distance to visit these beautiful places which offer countryside atmosphere, adventure activities, lush greenery, hill stations and natural resources such as waterfalls, volcanoes, cliffs and beaches. For example, nowadays, people are increasingly indulging in adventure and wildlife tourism by going on *treks in Uttarakhand, road trip until Ladakh, wakeboarding in Goa beaches, snowboarding on mountains in Hokkaido in Japan* and *visiting Africa to see the wildlife.*

Seeing the potential of tourism as an important source of driving an economy, many investors, be it the government or the private players, have started exploiting the potential of a destination by building resorts, hotels, parks, zoos, adventure sports centres, spas and so much more to attract more tourists. This puts a lot of pressure on the environment and its natural resources. When people cross the line by visiting a destination beyond its carrying capacity, the environment starts to suffer.

Now let us discuss in detail the negative impacts of tourism. For the sake of our clarity, we have divided the negative impacts into environmental impacts, social impacts and economic impacts.

NEGATIVE ENVIRONMENTAL IMPACTS

Let us now discuss the negative impacts of tourism on the environment. We have further divided the negative environmental impacts of tourism on the basis of land, water and air.

Amazon Wildfire 2019

Spanning 1.7 billion acres, the Amazon rainforest is widely regarded as 'the lungs of the world'.

Thousands of acres of land have been destroyed.

Deforestation is the major cause of the fire.

Negative Impacts of Tourism on Land

Infrastructural Development

A destination that has a tourism potential eventually becomes a magnet for various investors of tourism industry who may like to build roads, airports, lodges, hotels, amusement parks and the other required infrastructure and superstructure to attract tourists. Thus, clearing the forests or deforestation begins at the destination that creates adverse effects for the

> ### Landslide in Uttarakhand
>
> On 28 August 2018, heavy rains triggering landslides killed three people in Tehri district.
>   Scientist state that the causes are geological vulnerabilities and anthropogenic pressures such as overcrowding and demands for fuel.

environment such as soil erosion, loss of natural habitat for animals, desertification and climate change leading to natural calamities such as forest fire, landslides, flash floods, earthquakes, tsunami and cyclones.

Littering

As more people visit a destination, they bring their annoying habits with them such as littering and trashing. This causes a chain reaction because when the next visitor notices the pile of garbage in an area, he/she throws the trash in the same area. Such land pollution is causing deaths of wild animals and birds in the area and groundwater pollution. *The famous Mount Everest, world's highest peak is now the world's highest garbage dump with rubbish left by tourists on these mountains such as oxygen cylinders, food wrappers, climbing gears and beer cans.*

Trampling

When tourists visit a particular destination and use the same trail over and over again, it tramples the natural vegetation of that place. This happens especially when tourists visit mountains for trekking expeditions.

Sewage Problem

The construction dump, industrial waste and other garbage of hotels and resorts get released in the sewage system. These sewage lines are connected to the water bodies causing a large amount of dirty and hazardous waste to get mixed with water.

Wildlife Tourism Activities

National parks, wildlife sanctuaries, biosphere reserves, mangroves, wetlands, aquariums and so on are a haven of flora and fauna including the endangered species and are an important attraction for the wildlife enthusiasts. To attract such tourists, they offer various expeditions such as wildlife safaris, hikes, tours and animal rides. Such activities cause disturbance in the vegetation and expose the biodiversity to poachers who hunt animals for trophy and selling, thereby posing a threat to the biodiversity. Constant viewing of the wildlife puts a strain on them.

Australia's Bush Fire

- An unprecedented outbreak of bushfire destroying approximately 18 million hectares of land started from June 2019 that ended in March 2020. It was declared as the Black Summer of Australia.
- Spread across many other states of Australia, the most affected state was New South Wales.
- Killed more than 1 billion animals including more than 5,000 koalas.
- Many people died while thousands have been rendered homeless.
- More than 3,000 homes were destroyed.
- Australia has experienced one of its worst droughts in decades caused by a combination of record-breaking heat and high wind conditions.

Animal Shows

Many amusement parks/bird parks and so on, in order to attract tourists, organize various animal shows. The animals are trained and programmed to act in a certain way that stresses them. A few shows that take place in different countries of the world are as follows:

- The Tiger Show in Dreamworld, Gold Coast, Australia
- The Shamu Show, SeaWorld, San Diego, USA
- The Sea Lion Show, SeaWorld, San Diego, USA
- The Dolphin Show, SeaWorld, Jakarta, Indonesia
- The Bird Show, Jurong Bird Park, Singapore

Pet's Rule Show, SeaWorld, San Diego

Tiger Show, Dreamworld, Gold Coast

Negative Impact of Tourism on Water Resources

For promoting tourism of a place, the destination uses water as a tourism product so that more tourists are attracted. Using this as a tool, tourism has offered many

> ### Water Crises in Bali, Indonesia
>
> - In Bali, Indonesia, 65 per cent of the island's groundwater is poured into the tourism industry, drying up 260 out of more than 400 Balinese rivers.
> - Groundwater over-extraction has lowered the island's water table by some 60 per cent, risking irreversible saltwater intrusion.

activities by using water resources to increase the tourism potential of a destination. However, any kind of tourism product that makes use of water such as cruise, water activities and rides causes water contamination and, thus, is a threat to marine life. Let us have a discussion on a few of the different sources of water pollution.

Cruises

Cruises are an important experiential tourism product. This industry is growing day by day as a number of tourists are choosing cruises as their vacation spot. However, cruises are a major source of water pollution. These cruises often dump the waste of thousands of people in the waters creating a dump yard underwater, thereby polluting the water and affecting the marine life.

Water Activities

When tourists visit places such as Goa, Maldives, Bali and Australia, they indulge in activities such as jet skiing and motor boating. Such tourism products contaminate the water as they release harmful oils and chemicals. Similarly, activities such as scuba diving, under-water diving, parasailing and other water activities disturb the fragile marine ecology.

> ### Coral Reef Bleaching
>
> The Great Barrier Reef, located off the northeast coast of Queensland, Australia, is the largest coral reef system in the world.
>
> Rising ocean temperatures have caused coral bleaching in vast portions—a condition in which the coral turns white.
>
> Until now, half of the reefs have died from bleaching.

Water Rides

- The boats and jets often scrape at places when in the water. The metal pieces and particles are causing a high number of deaths in marine wildlife because these particles are swallowed by the marine creatures.
- Rust, zinc and chemicals present on these water rides mix with the water causing disastrous effect on marine life such as their ability to thrive and survive, their life span, mutation and death.

Marina Development

Major destruction of coral habitat is because of marina development. Overtourism and activities on the waters such as jet skiing, motor boating, scuba diving and other water sports, construction of the beach resorts, ship groundings, creating passageways connecting to the island, overfishing and over sewage flow are becoming the reason for the deaths of coral reefs in the world.

Shimla Water Crises, 2018

- In May 2018, Shimla, a city in Himachal Pradesh, India, faced major water shortage as its residents went through dry water taps for more than eight days.
- Tourists were told not to visit Shimla during this water crises.

Water Scarcity

Water is a major natural resource of the environment and a big victim of tourism, especially freshwater. Every day, the tourism industry is overusing water for pleasing the tourists by providing amenities such as 24/7 running water, washing of linens every day, laundry service, maintaining of swimming pools, water rides in resorts and maintaining golf courses. Such activities are causing water scarcity in many destinations, especially such places where water is already in a limited supply.

Negative Impacts of Tourism on Air

Air Pollution

As the number of tourists is increasing, the use of transportation services such as aeroplanes, railways, automobiles and ships is also increasing. These heavy mechanisms not only require a ton of energy to operate but also emit dangerous gases into the atmosphere which cause air pollution.

Noise Pollution

Heavy vehicles such as planes and ships and every transportation service cause noise pollution in the local areas. Services created for the tourists such as Jet Skis and snowmobiles cause disturbances in the wildlife due to which animals change their natural pattern because of the noise pollution caused by people in that area. Tourism is also highly associated with noise pollution caused during events and festivals. Another type of pollution which is associated with noise is when engines used in water rides create harsh sound waves which affect marine life, especially dolphins.

Global Warming

Due to constant deforestation and increase in the use of tourism products, the surface temperature of the earth is rising to the point of threat to everyone on this planet. This is not only melting the glaciers and stripping the homes of polar bears, penguins and other animals in the cold region but also causing wildfires across the globe which has killed millions of animals and trees.

Climate Change

As discussed before, when natural vegetation is compromised by construction of resorts, hotels and other infrastructure, the climate starts to change. As a result, many destinations are experiencing unseasonal heavy rains, harmful hailstorms, heavy snowstorms, extreme hot weather and drought. For example, *major hill stations in Uttarakhand in India witnessed heavy snowfall in winters in 2019, which highly affected the normal life to a large extent.* Major roads on those hill stations were blocked due to the snow.

Depletion of Ozone Layer by Chlorofluorocarbons

The ozone layer has reached alarming levels of depletion due to tourism activity. When tourists visit a destination, they often choose to stay in resorts or hotels. These tourism products often try to please tourists by meeting their high expectations such as providing hot water and electricity 24/7. The air conditioners, refrigerators, Jacuzzi system and so on used in the hotels, resorts and restaurants release chlorofluorocarbons in the atmosphere, which is further leading to depletion in the ozone layer.

NEGATIVE SOCIAL IMPACTS

The tourism phenomenon involves an interactive relationship between the host community and the tourists. When tourists visit a destination, majority of the time, the host communities feel joyful and welcoming towards them. However, when the tourists or tourism overstep their boundaries, there are certain changes in the feelings of hosts towards the tourists. Overtourism diminishes the life of local residents and creates a negative experience for the visitors. Now, let us discuss in detail about the negative impact of tourism on society.

Depletion of the Local Resources

When tourists visit a destination, they are bound to use the resources such as water, food, fuel and electricity. The problem arises when there is already a scarcity of such resources in an area and locals have to suffer from power outage and water scarcity as the limited resources have now to be shared with the tourists also.

Displacement and Destruction of Local Charm

For the development of tourism, a large area of land is required. To do so, industries cut down the natural vegetation of a place and build infrastructure such as resorts, malls, hotels, spas, sports centres and tourist attractions. Such actions create a negative emotion within the locals as their home which once was a beautiful paradise has now been ruined because of tourism. For example, *Cinque Terre in Italy is famous for its beautiful bright houses on the cliffside of the Italian Riviera.* Due to overtourism, the land capacity of that place is deteriorating and the infrastructure has taken a toll causing occasional landslides. To avoid this, the government had to initiate a few steps to combat overtourism such as increasing the visa fees, refusing to issue permits and sometimes closing the entire destination, especially islands.

Acculturation

Every destination has its own culture, ethics, social values and religion. When people from a different culture travel to a place, the possibility is that the hosts or the tourists are influenced by the new cultural environment. This sometimes brings a change in their social values, perspective, attitude, ethics and behaviour. Such a process is termed as acculturation which is very common in the tourism industry. *In other words, it refers to a phenomenon in which two cultures when they meet each other, they tend to learn from each other.* Acculturation is not a bad effect if it does not cause a threat to the emotions and integrity of the social environment in a locality. However, sometimes the hosts start emulating the culture and lifestyles of the tourists without realizing the reason to adopt it. This is referred to as the *demonstration effect*.

The youth are an easy target for acculturation as they fall prey to the demonstration effect as they start opting for the new or different culture at the cost of their own culture that starts causing harm to their local social values and ethics. Due to the heavy influx of tourists in Nepal, the youth of Nepal are known to be affected by the tourists as they have adapted the new cultural trends such as abandoning their own cultural attire, disrespecting their elders, and using slangs and abusive language.

Traffic Jams

Due to the overcrowding of tourists in a destination, the number of transportation vehicles used for travel increases that causes major traffic jams and inconvenience for the locals of a destination. Recently, in 2019, tourists themselves became the victims of traffic jams while visiting hill stations from Delhi to escape from the scorching heat. It was reported that due to the increased road trips taken by people from larger metropolitan cities, there were such agonizing traffic jams in places such as *Shimla* and *Mussoorie* that led to many people spending their night sleeping in the cars. Another incident was of the 4-km stretch of traffic jam on Manali–Leh highway. This clogging of people in hill stations and in many tourist areas of the world has led to massive traffic jams, thereby disrupting the lives of locals living in these places.

Privacy Intrusion and Trespassing

Not only that, tourists have the habit of stopping anywhere and clicking photos, be it a vintage-looking house. Sometimes, they even take the pictures of the locals without their permission. This leads to invading the privacy of the householders and trespassing on their block.

Harm to the Historical and Archaeological Sites

A destination which has intriguing history and monuments and was built decades ago attracts lots of tourists. Majority of the visitors treat such places as a public property without caring for these tangible heritage assets of a nation. When they visit these attractions, they litter around and write on the walls of these historically significant monuments and the archaeological venues and harm them. *Because of the constant flocking of tourists, the Spanish steps in Rome are now decorated with wine stains and lumps of chewing gum that have spoilt the beauty of the place. The government has now made it illegal to sit on those 15 stairs and restored it multiple times.*

Increase in the Crime

Tourism has become a source of many crimes. Following are the sources.

Drug Tourism

Some people, especially drug addicts, travel to a destination for just obtaining drugs which are illegal or non-existent in their area or country. This is another reason for overtourism as drug users are travelling in bulk for a drug-induced holiday to places like *Amsterdam as it is tolerant of drug use and prostitution*. Drug tourism has become a menace worldwide as tourists are even smuggling drugs across countries for selling them. This causes damage to the social norms and public health of a destination and to the locals as well.

Sex Tourism and Women Trafficking

Generally, tourists travel to a place to enjoy the natural beauty and man-made attractions of a destination. But unfortunately, many tourists are motivated to travel to destinations to indulge in unethical practices such as sex tourism and prostitution. *Millions of people visit red-light areas in several destinations such as Bangkok, Amsterdam and Las Vegas.* The prostitution industry understands the market for it and thus, makes various efforts to increase the tourist traffic of a destination by hiring more woman who are in desperate need of resources such as shelter, food, money and medical care. When visitors visit such a destination, they ask for prostitution services and pay big bucks to indulge in such activities which is why this market is becoming fearless and ever-growing.

Thus, the growth in the market encourages the businesses to do woman trafficking which is a huge crime. As a result, millions of lives are ruined because of the demands of tourists for sex workers under the garb of tourism.

Paedophilia

People have the habit of making unethical and atrocious demands and they like travelling too. When they visit places where the environment is little tolerant, they feel a certain freedom in doing criminal actions like sexually harassing children which is a very big crime in society.

Gambling

Tourism offers many activities to the tourists but sometimes those activities cause a huge negative impact on the local communities. Some destinations such as *Las Vegas and Macau are recognized as a hub of gambling*. Millions and millions of bucks are invested in this industry every year. At times when people gamble, they tend to win more than they invested but the majority of the time they lose everything they own. The hunger to win a large amount of money drives many tourists to a destination that offers such activities. This triggers a harmful greed in the locals too when they witness tourists winning large lump sum.

Alcohol-related Crime among Holidaymakers

Every tourist visits a destination to have a relaxing holiday and spend time enjoying every minute. Many times, these tourists intake alcohol without any control or limit. In doing so, they tend to forget the ethics and cultural dignity of that destination and misbehave under influence. This not only disturbs the peace of the locality but also creates a threat to the locals who cross path with such tourists. For example, *Goa is packed with tourists every day and a majority of them enjoy their times with alcohol in their system.* During the peak season, such tourists cross the boundary of alcohol limit and behave unethically which scares the locals. The locals cannot even visit their local areas like beaches at night because of such tourists. Similar is the case with Amsterdam and Venice where tourists behave in an unruly manner affecting the local lives of the people.

Breaking of Rules by Tourists

There are a certain set of rules and regulations established by the government of every destination for the tourist to follow. Any rule breaking by the tourists causes disturbance in the local environment and the host communities start having a negative attitude towards the tourism industry.

Threat to Privacy

In Kumbh mela, a religious gathering in India, tourists even take photos of naked sadhus and saints without seeking their permission for their own amusement. This is a huge slap to the privacy and insult to the religious values of the saints.

Other Crimes against the Tourists

When 'strangers' are introduced to the local communities, the offenders target them the most and tourists become victim to the local crimes such as scamming, pickpocketing, thievery, rape and harassment. The high number of tourists in a destination encourages such offenders because for them there is more fish in the sea. Thus, such situations increase the crime rate at a destination.

Commercialization of Culture

When people from different places visit a destination, they are often intrigued by the beauty of the place, especially the local culture and atmosphere. Tourists always love to take a souvenir from such places which will remind them about the cultural experience they had at a destination. The tourism market and private sectors commercialize on such opportunities and needs by making souvenirs and offering cultural experiences via local tours to cultural icons and religious places, thereby increasingly leading to commercialization of culture of a country.

Local Accommodation Problems

Accommodation services like AirBnB that offers a temporary homestay for tourists at a destination are increasingly trending. Thus, when tourists stay in these local properties, some tourists are reported to misbehave in the homes of the host communities by breaking certain rules of the house such as drinking in the house, creating noise late at nights, breaking of the property and belongings of the owners and even sometimes stealing things of the hosts. Thus, such behaviour has given another reason to the host communities to have a hostile attitude towards tourists and tourism.

Also, the locals are now increasingly using this opportunity to make maximum money out of the accommodation requirement of the tourists as what they pay is more than what a local is willing to pay which is why the accommodation providers have set soaring rents for their places. This service is nowadays reserved just for tourists, not the locals which is causing a huge social gap between the communities and values are turned into commercial agenda.

NEGATIVE ECONOMIC IMPACTS

Overdependence on Tourism

Many economies of the world such as Mauritius, Maldives and so on are dependent on tourism. The mainstay of their economies is tourism. However, this overdependence may turn out to be fatal sometimes as in the case of uncertainties such as the outbreak of a disease or a pandemic like coronavirus, natural calamities such as earthquakes, tsunamis and so on, the economies are worst hit. The tourism service providers and the working tourism professionals lose their source of earning during such unavoidable situations. Thus, it is always good not to put all the eggs in one basket. In other words, the governments of countries must follow a balanced and diversified approach to offset the risk of dependence on tourism. They must simultaneously focus on other industries too.

Price Inflation

Tourism is a commercial industry. When a destination has the potential for attracting traffic, the private sector immediately seeks benefits by establishing several activities for a charge. The tourists usually do not mind paying what the seller asks for which encourages the local vendors and businesses to increase the value of their goods and services. It is a known fact that the tourists have a high spending power when they visit destinations as compared to being in their own native place. The locals suffer through such inflation as even they have to pay the high prices for the stuff they need. Even restaurants increase their prices as tourists have a higher capacity to spend money.

SUMMARY

As every coin has two sides, the tourism industry also has its darker side. When tourism exceeds the carrying capacity of a destination, it affects the environment and the local communities negatively. Tourism causes land pollution, air pollution and water pollution besides negative impacts on wildlife and the climate of a destination. When two cultures meet, they learn from each other, which is called the acculturation model. When tourists visit a destination, they carry their own values and customs along with them that sometimes the locals may try to imitate. This is called the demonstration effect. Tourism leads to depletion of local resources; privacy intrusion and trespassing; traffic jams; harming of archaeological sites when tourists do not respect them; crimes such as drugs consumption, gambling, alcohol-related crimes, prostitution and women trafficking, and paedophilia; local accommodation problems; law-breaking by tourists; commercialization of culture; and price inflation.

ACTIVITIES

Activity 1

Is tourism a necessary evil? Debate.

Activity 2

Tourists and host communities are becoming commercial in nature. Comment.

BIBLIOGRAPHY

www.amp.cnn.com

Case Studies

A.1. DUBAI: A CITY OF WONDERS

Introduction

Positioning itself as the first-choice destination for international leisure travellers as well as business travellers, Dubai Tourism is a successful story to be shared with the world.

Situated on the Persian Gulf coast of the UAE, Dubai city is full of beautiful man-made attractions and extraordinary deserts. People from faraway lands visit this city to indulge in amazing activities it offers. Known as the 'city of gold', Dubai was once a city with nothing but oil to survive. The government knew that one day, this oil would run out, and the country's survival had to be planned.

With brilliant tourism marketing and branding strategies, Dubai has successfully overcome the challenges of tourism. Apart from the beautiful deserts and waters, everything attractive about Dubai is man-made which is very impressive. This Middle East city attracts approximately 10–15 million tourists every year. In 2019, Dubai attracted approximately 16.73 million tourists. Dubai Tourism and the Government of Dubai have made high efforts and spent a huge amount of money to make that city what it is today. Creating outstanding marketing and tourism campaigns, Dubai Tourism has elected the Bollywood celebrity Shah Rukh Khan as their brand ambassador and has created various short films using his public reach, especially to attract the Indian tourists, which is a big market for the city. Dubai attracts a lot of first-time Indian travellers because of its close proximity to India.

Smart Dubai 2021

- Smart Dubai envisions a city where all its resources are optimized for maximum efficiency, and services are integrated seamlessly into daily life.

دبــي الذكية **2021**
SMART DUBAI

- The roadmap defines ambitious targets across three impact axes: customer happiness, economic growth and resource and infrastructure resilience.
- Smart Dubai 2021 has established six strategic objectives: smart liveable and resilient city, globally competitive economy powered by disruptive technologies, an interconnected society with easily accessible social services, smooth transport-driven by autonomous and shared mobility solutions, clean environment enabled by cutting-edge ICT innovations and digital, lean and connected government.

Source: https://2021.smartdubai.ae/ (accessed on 31 July 2020).

Building world-famous attractions and creating fun activities by making use of limited natural resources such as deserts and seashores, Dubai's tourism is now blooming with happy tourists. Let us discuss why!

Background

Trading and marketing of oil was Dubai's major way of generating income for the country. The Sheikhs and the government were well aware that oil will someday run out, and the country would need revenue. The government estimated that the last remaining oil deposits would run out in 2029–2030. Given the deadline, the Government of Dubai started taking some important measures to make the country free from this pressure by making tourism the centre of attention. They realized that even if the oil runs out, Dubai can still earn 90 per cent of its income by making 100 per cent use of their tourism. With extraordinary planning and hard work, the Dubai Tourism, Government of Dubai (the principal authority for planning, developing and marketing of the tourism sector in Dubai), strategized and started introducing various amazing tourism products to the people. With the mission of making Dubai the world's leading tourism destination and a commercial hub, the Dubai Tourism, Government of Dubai, has been making relentless efforts through introducing new innovative tourism products and activities, making new artificial superstructures and aggressive marketing to bring Dubai on the world tourism map. Their products have not only improved the financial stability of Dubai but today Dubai stands tall with the most successful tourism backbone.

Dubai, which was once and still known as the trading hub, has also become a travel destination among the travellers. This city has not only attracted tourists for leisure from different parts of the world, but it has also become an international hub for business travellers as many companies nowadays are offering a visit to Dubai as a corporate incentive destination and business gathering destination.

Below are a few tourism products which are worth mentioning in making Dubai what it is today.

Dubai Tourism Initiative

Dubai tourism envisions to make Dubai the most visited destination with more than 23 million visitors by 2025.

This entails a stronger and even more urgent agenda to synchronize efforts in the delivery of five strategic pillars:

1. Increase leadership across core and diversified markets
2. Offer end-to-end and 'Only-in-Dubai' experiences
3. Communicate the Dubai offering through personalized and data-driven marketing
4. Further enhance our attractiveness as a business destination
5. Deliver as one agile tourism ecosystem

Tourism Products Introduced by Dubai Tourism

Some of the tourism products introduced by Dubai Tourism are as follows.

Airlines

The UAE has widened its reach by expanding its airline networks of Emirates and Etihad airlines. By providing the best customer services and luxury choices, the airlines of Dubai have become one of the best airline services in the world.

Shopping

Dubai is famously known as the 'Shopping capital of the Middle East' where many people from various countries visit Dubai just with a shopping agenda. People love travelling to this destination as it offers a variety of choices for all kinds of products. From luxury cars in malls to rare automobile parts in the market streets, it is a 'shoppers' paradise'.

Souk

Souk is an Arabic word for a marketplace where all kinds of goods are sold and exchanged. Many people visit Dubai to soak in the traditional souk culture where they can enjoy special shopping experience. Tourists are intrigued with many different and unique types of souks scattered throughout the city, each specializing in goods that represent the traditional Emirate culture. Souk is located in Deira, along the Dubai creeks where visitors can experience a unique market atmosphere. Every street is named after the goods sold in bulk. For example, Al Khor street in Deira is known as gold souk where tourists can find all kinds of precious metal and gems, jewellery made by people who are trained in designing and crafting special

Arabic style ornaments and so much more! This marketplace offers various souks such as textile, perfume, spice and sculptures.

Malls

The city of Dubai has around 96 shopping malls with an array of products for the shopaholics. One of the largest malls in the world, The Dubai Mall in Downtown Dubai, offers exclusive products, services and activities to the visitors. It not only has outlets of all the famous brands such as Zara, Dior and Bloomingdale's but also offers an Olympic-sized ice-skating rink, Dubai Aquarium and Underwater Zoo, virtual reality (VR) park, haunted house known as Hysteria and so much more! The best among 96 malls are the City Mall in the Dubai creek, City walk in Al Safa street, Ibn Battuta Mall, which is among the world's largest theme malls, and WAFI mall near Dubai creek.

Beaches

Tourists have the time of their lives along the shorelines of Dubai. Clear blue water, sandy beaches and fun water sports, Dubai's beaches have it all!

- Jumeirah Beach Park is one of the most famous beaches in Dubai, offering beautiful golden sands, palm trees and grassy areas. This beach has been rewarded with the Blue Flag certification for adhering to strict international standards.
- Umm Suqeim Beach is famous for its stunning view of Burj Khalifa. This beach is filled with beautiful white sand, and kite surfers have a blast every day here.
- Kite Beach (Wollongong Beach) is favourite among tourists as it offers kite surfing, kayaking, volleyball and soccer activities.

Events

Dubai keeps organizing events and festivals to attract tourists to the city. As events are a tool for branding the tourism of a destination, Dubai uses festivals to increase the influx of tourists in the destination. The shopping festival is a big hit across the world. On a similar line, they have also initiated the Dubai Food Festival which is a magnet for food lovers. This festival offers various food-related activities, events, promotions, musical performances and of course, mouth-watering and world-class taste of Dubai's best dishes. A two and a half week-long celebration gives tourists a chance to explore the city and indulge in food, from street stalls to fine dining experiences.

Dubai Shopping Festival

- Initiated by the Tourism of Dubai, the Dubai Shopping Festival is a month-long annual festival put together by the Dubai Festivals and Retail Establishment.

- The idea for the festival was first created by Sheikh Mohammad Bin Rashid Al Maktoum, and the first festival was held on 16 February 1996.
- This mega event showcases the best of what Dubai has to offer. People can enjoy extravagant shopping experiences, contests, amazing dining experiences, attractive discount offers and sales, mind-blowing events and mesmerizing fireworks.
- Dubai Shopping Festival allures over three million tourists from around the globe in a single year.

Man-made Attractions

- **Burj Khalifa:** Offering the most beautiful panoramic view of the city skyline from the observation deck on the 124th floor, Burj Khalifa is the tallest skyscraper in the world! Opened in 2010, this building is the most famous landmark in the UAE. The entire building is known to light up on special occasions and honours. This amazing sky-scraper is home to many apartments, restaurants, hotels, parking spaces and so much more!
- **Burj Al Arab:** An iconic Arabian luxury, Burj Al Arab is among one of the tallest five-star hotels in the world. With the complex and unique architectural design, this luxurious hotel sits on a man-made island, just 280 metres off the shore of Dubai. This hotel has a private man-made beach on the terrace, dramatic helipad, luxurious interior made with gold and Swarovski crystals and world-class highly-trained chefs. This spectacular hotel also owns a Rolls Royce chauffeur-driven fleet. Along with that, it also has many other luxury cars parked outside for shuttle service.
- **Dubai Miracle Garden:** Located in the district of Dubailand, this garden is a beautiful artificially created flower garden which occupies 72,000 square metres and filled with 150 million flowers arranged in colourful arches, patterns and unique shapes. The garden is worth visiting during mid-November to mid-May when the entire area blooms into a beautiful and magical landscape.
- **The Palm Jumeirah:** In the shape of a palm tree, Palm Jumeirah is amongst the best man-made creations in Dubai. This artificial island is home to luxury hotels, top-notch residential towers, amazing malls, world-class restaurants and so much more. The palm island is a dreamland for every tourist who visits Dubai.
- **Global Village:** Combining 90 countries and their culture in one place, the Global Village is a multicultural amusement park and the region's first destination for culture, shopping and entertainment. It has hundreds of shops, more than 50 amusement rides and mind-blowing performances at nights. It is a perfect spot to enjoy with your family, friends and kids.
- **The Dubai Fountain:** Outside of the Burj Khalifa, The Dubai Fountain is another one of tourist's favourite attractions. People enjoy the illuminated and choreographed water dance in this fountain show which looks mystical especially at night. People can also enjoy Ziplining over the fountain, even when it is dancing!

- **Dubai Marina:** Dubai Marina, an artificially created canal city, is home to Jumeirah Beach Residence, amazing cruises waiting for a fun tour, the Dubai Marina Mall, the beach and so much more. People can take a stroll on Dubai Marina walk where they can shop, eat and enjoy the city lights and a cool breeze.

Amusement Parks

- In order to position Dubai as a kid-friendly destination, Dubai has many jaw-dropping amusement parks. Located in Abu Dhabi, a city which is one and half hour's drive from Dubai is the famous amusement park 'Ferrari World', which is a must on the itineraries of the tourists visiting Dubai. It is the world's first Ferrari-branded theme park with home to world's fastest roller coaster along with some other amazing thrill rides.
- Not to forget the amazing Wild Wadi Waterpark, situated right in front of the five-star hotel, Burj Al Arab. This park offers 30 rides and attractions for everyone and is kids friendly. Wild Wadi is themed around the tale of Juha, a known character from the Arabian tales.

Activities in Dubai

Besides doing the sightseeing and shopping, the following activities may be tried by the tourists:

- **Desert safari and desert camping:** Dubai Tourism offers desert expeditions like desert safari packages which include camel riding, jeep safari and also camping. Setting up a tent under a thousand stars and lighting up a bonfire in the middle of a desert is a must-do for those who visit Dubai.
- **Cruising:** Dubai offers a wonderful opportunity for people who love water activities. Dhow Cruise is an Arabic sailboat in which tourists can enjoy a tour of Dubai's creek, ride across illuminated palaces and souks and also an exceptional feast with traditional belly dancing performances.
- **Seaplane flight tour:** A flying experience like never before, Dubai's seaplane flight offers the most adventurous tour for thrill-seekers. A mesmerizing plane tour where tourists get to see scenic attractions of Dubai, finest city view and classic deserts of Dubai.
- **Camel polo:** A Middle East travel management company launched a distinctive Dubai version of the traditional polo game played with camels. This activity has attracted a huge number of travel enthusiasts and gave Dubai a unique touch.
- **Ski Dubai:** Ever heard skiing in the desert? a Ski Dubai is an indoor ski resort where you can ski any day of the year. It is a part of the Mall of the Emirates, one of the largest shopping malls in the world, located in Dubai, UAE.

- **Fly boarding:** For water lover and thrill-seekers, Dubai offers flyboarding over the Persian Gulf which is a perfect activity for those who want adventure.
- **Hot-Air ballooning:** Dubai Desert Conservation Reserve offers a spectacular hot air balloon rides to the people where they can fly high above the deserts and enjoy the epic view.
- **Dune buggy ride:** Tourists get picked up from their hotels in four-wheel-drive vehicles and are given an exhilarating ride on dune buggies across the beautiful deserts of Dubai.

Dos and Don'ts for Tourists

As tourists, it is very important to learn and respect the ethics, culture and customs of a destination. Dubai is an Islamic country and as a foreigner in Dubai, having some knowledge of Islam would be very useful. Nonetheless, Dubai is a city with religious freedom and no restrictions are present regarding any culture and ethnicity. While visiting Dubai, some of the considerations that tourists need to adhere to are as follows:

- Tourists are not allowed to consume alcohol in public places except licenced venues such as restaurants, bars and private homes.
- For non-Islamic tourists, it is important to know that eating or drinking in a public place at daytime during Ramadan fasting is restricted.
- Dubai is a cosmopolitan city where all kinds of clothing can be seen but it is considered respectful and important to dress modestly in places such as malls, business centres and religious areas, especially for women.
- It is very important to respect the religion and its practices by all as apostasy is a major crime which is punishable by death in the UAE.
- Gentle handshakes are considered as a respectful way of greeting between Arab men. Handshake initiated by women is also considered as a sign of respect. Also, the public display of affection (PDA) is advised to be kept minimum.

Keeping the above in mind, Dubai is a city waiting to be explored as the tourism of the UAE is taking extra measures to pull the tourists towards the city of gold and wonders.

Conclusion

Dubai tourism has ensured to keep the GDP and revenue generation for the UAE intact and evergreen via introducing amazing tourism activities and products in this Emirates city for people. The government has taken creative initiation and invested a large amount in developing the tourism of Dubai by building extraordinary infrastructure and many man-made attractions. These attractions continue to bring the flow of tourists in the city and keep the tourism industry growing day by day.

Learning Outcomes

- Dubai Tourism has shown that regardless of limited resources, proper planning and strategizing can revive the revenue system and tourism of a country. A successful tourism establishment requires a definite game plan. The initiation taken by the Government of UAE is outstanding as they built Dubai as it is today from scratch by tapping the right nerve of the tourism industry. As Dubai has limited access to natural resources, almost every part of the city which attracts millions of tourists every year is largely man-made.
- More than half the percentage of revenue is generated by the tourism sector. To keep the flow steady and ever-growing, new initiations are introduced by the tourism of Dubai from time to time without harping upon their existing infrastructure.

Points for Discussion

- As the world's leading tourism industry, Dubai has outdone itself by introducing extraordinary tourism products. Discuss the possible strategies to enhance the tourism sector even more.
- Have you ever been to Dubai? Discuss your point of view as a tourist.
- Is there any downfall to the tourism products offered by Dubai? Research and discuss in detail

Bibliography

https://www.visitdubai.com/en (accessed on 31 July 2020).

A.2. ISRAEL

Israel is eager to invite tourists from different parts of the world. In fact, recently over the years with the consistent and aggressive marketing efforts by MOT, Israel, with its tagline 'The Land of Creation', the tourism in the country has seen unprecedented growth with around 3–4 million tourists visiting the country every year. Israel is being positioned as a destination for all and for every reason. Be it promoting it as a cultural destination for its age-old traditions or beach tourism that attracts millions of tourists, be it a paradise for shoppers with world-famous renowned markets such as Carmel Market (Shuk HaCarmel) in Tel Aviv and Machane Yehuda in Jerusalem or a destination for pilgrims of different faiths, a destination known for its natural landforms such as deserts and sea or a wellness destination offering spas and mud therapies in the Dead Sea, a dark tourism destination with Yad Vashem (National Holocaust Memorial in memory of six million people murdered by Nazis and their allies) or an action-packed adventure for the adventure enthusiasts, the country has a pot-pourri of diverse tourist products that can satisfy the appetite of any kind of tourists visiting the country. The country is one of the world's best culinary destinations that attracts food lovers from different corners of the world. The Israeli breakfast is a must-have for the tourists! Wine connoisseurs must visit this country known for its wine.

The country is accessible for people with special abilities as well as for senior citizens. Although Hebrew and Arabic are the formal spoken languages here, English is the mode of communication which makes this country a tourist-friendly destination for the visitors.

The country is home to world-famous destinations. One of the most popular vacation destinations of the world, famous for its history (almost 5,000-year-old city), architecture and its holy sites such as Western Wall and Jerusalem Church, is Jerusalem. Jerusalem is the largest city of Israel and also the designated capital of Israel. Religious tourism is the main tourism product here as it is the holy place of Jews, Christians and Muslims. The city is also famous for its festivals such as the Wine Festival, Beer Festival, Film Festival, Jerusalem Marathon, Farmer's market and summer parties.

Do you want to reduce the carbon-foot prints while visiting Israel? Be ready to bike or ride a Segway on the trendiest and most luxurious cosmopolitan destination of the world, Tel Aviv, that has 100 km of dedicated bike lanes. With 9 miles of beaches, Tel Aviv is a major Mediterranean beach resort in the world. The city, known for its amazing beaches and electrifying nightlife with world-class night clubs and dance clubs, is a must-visit for the youngsters. It is a city that never sleeps! Known for its Israeli party culture, Tel Aviv is also called as the cultural and entertainment capital of Israel.

The city also offers free Wi-Fi services at around 80 different public locations that make it more tourist-friendly. Known as the ultra-luxury city and a hub for gourmet dining, the city offers award-winning chef restaurants serving Mediterranean feast and many vegan-friendly options as the city is vegan-friendly. Some good news for the LGBTQ community! Tel Aviv is also an LGBTQ-friendly city. The White City of Tel Aviv with Bauhaus architecture is a world heritage site declared by UNESCO. The southern and oldest part of Tel Aviv, the city of Jaffa is in stark contrast of other parts of Tel Aviv that still retains its old-world charm. It is one of the world's most ancient port city (as early as 7500 BC) and home to many historical sites and art galleries, that is certainly not to be missed. CNN travel has referred to it as a must-visit destination in 2019. The colourful bazaars, flea markets and artisanal boutiques are a treat to one's eyes.

The Mediterranean coastline along the west of the country is known for its spectacular beaches with golden sands. Do not forget to carry your bathing suit, beach shoes, sun-glasses, sunscreen and a sun-hat while visiting Israel.

The Sea of Galilee, the Dead Sea and the city of Eilat offer exciting beach activities for tourists. Known for its action-packed adventure or a romantic getaway, Eilat is the destination waiting to be explored. It is also a 'shoppers paradise' as shopping is tax-free here. Also, recognized as the world-famous scuba-diving destination, the city of Eilat is most famous for its Red Sea, that attracts a number of tourists to the city. It is a paradise for beach bummers and sports enthusiasts who may enjoy activities such as windsurfing, stand-up paddle boarding and kitesurfing on the beaches of Red Sea along swimming with the dolphins. The tourists may also camp out, barbeque, dine in the beach bars and restaurants or just relax in the golden sands by the beach. Tourists may also visit the famous Dolphin Reef and the coral beach besides Red Canyon while enjoying the evening in Eilat Promenade famous for the market and restaurants.

Another one of the most visited places of Israel is the Dead Sea. Known as the oldest natural spa in the world and the largest open-air spa for its natural hot sulphurous hot springs, the Dead Sea is a Salt Lake in Israel that is a magnet for the tourists. Due to the high level of salt in the water, one may enjoy floating in this wonder of nature. The waters will not let you sink! Wellness lovers from different parts of the world throng this destination and stay in the health resorts seeking spas and black mud treatments on their bodies that are used for healing many skin diseases. One may enjoy getting muddy on this lowest place on Earth. One may also explore the Qumran Caves near the lake or go on hiking trails in the Wadi valley.

For all those, who wish to explore the desert side of Israel, a visit to Negev Desert is a must which is loaded with activities for tourists. One may experience the Bedouin (a group of nomadic tribes) hospitality and soak in the cultural experiences staying in traditional Bedouin tents with traditional Bedouin dinner along with camel rides. A visit to Masada, a world heritage site declared by UNESCO, is a must. Taking a Kibbutz experience, while staying with this local community based on agriculture is an experience of its own kind.

Another not to be missed in the itinerary of Israel is the city of Nazareth, also known as 'the Cradle of Christianity'. It is one of the most important pilgrimage sites for Christians around the world. Tourists must also visit Bethlehem and pay a visit to the Church of Nativity where Jesus Christ was born.

Conclusion

Israel is truly a blend of divinity and modernity. The country is not only a confluence of strong religions as it is considered a biblical holy land, but it also boasts of beautiful landscapes, cultures, culinary delights, modernity and unlimited adventures. The country of Israel is truly a treat to one's senses!

Learning Outcomes

- For tourism to flourish in any destination, it is important to identify its natural as well as cultural resources.
- The tourism potential of each destination should be identified, and then efforts should be made to create different tourism products from the existing ones.
- It is equally important for the government of a country to have the right approach towards the development of tourism. In the given case, the marketing efforts made by MOT, Israel, towards the promotion of tourism in the country are commendable.

Points for Discussion

- Identify the gastronomical delights of Israel. Now create a food walk for the travellers in the city of your choice.
- Prepare an itinerary for a honeymoon couple who wants to visit Israel from India for 12 days. Suggest the airlines by which they may travel along with the places that you would suggest for them. Chalk out a detailed tour programme day wise.

Bibliography

www.goisrael.in (31 July 2020).

A.3. SINGAPORE: THE LION CITY

This is an amazing story about the successful tourism establishment of a city which lacked in natural tourism resources. With the right orientation towards tourism by Singapore Tourism Board, the city is now thriving with happy tourists. As the official tagline says, 'Passion Made Possible', Singapore has passionately built the city's tourism from scratch.

Introduction

'Lion City', 'City of Gardens', 'Smart City', 'Safe City', Singapore has been given many names, and each stands tall with its own identity provided by the constant efforts and innovations made by the tourism board of Singapore and government bodies. Known for its iconic waterfront attractions, world-class theme parks, lush greenery and the world's first night safari, Singapore is overqualified as one of the most alluring leisure destinations of the world. It is a perfect one-stop shop for nature lovers, discoverers, history buffs, trekkers, backpackers, city trippers, shopaholics, foodies, party lovers and many more!

Being a hub for global transportation, trade and finance, Singapore Exhibition and Convention Bureau (SCEB) works diligently to make the city a perfect MICE destination for the world by organizing business events with the best professional facilities and services. This city not only focuses on entertainment and leisure but takes care of business travellers too.

Not only that, the Tourism Board and Government of Singapore are also promoting eco-tourism by focusing on establishing sustainable travel, water resource management, waste management, incorporating eco-friendly technology and conservation of natural reserves.

Background

Singapore is an island city-state (located in Southeast Asia) which is filled with amazing tourism products and attractions. It has become an ultimate magnet for tourists from all over the world due to its strategic location and some of the best man-made world-class attractions. In January 2020, Singapore had about 1,687,344 visitor arrivals from all over the world. The reason for such footfall of tourists in Singapore is because of what the city offers. Singapore is thriving because of its culture, traditions, activities, cuisines and it also offers the tourists with so much more to explore! Here are a few highlights of Singapore Tourism products which have made the city an alluring tourist destination.

Tourism Products of Singapore

Singapore Airlines

Providing amazing customer aviation services, Singapore International Airlines focuses on providing nothing but the best customer experience to the traveller, the moment he boards the flight for Singapore. It provides the 'wow moments' to the travellers focusing on its 'experiential travel'.

Singapore Changi Airport

The Changi Airport is a major tourism product in itself that draws tourists from all parts of the world. Changi Airport's focal point is its jewel hub which is a combination of nature, art and mind-blowing architecture. It is a lifestyle destination in itself. Below are a few attractions at the airport.

- The airport has a rain vortex which is a 40-metre-high waterfall surrounded with over 2,000 trees and tropical plants indoors.
- Butterfly garden, cactus garden and sunflower garden in different terminals.

- Singapore's tallest slide in Terminal 3.
- It also has playgrounds, family zone, swimming pool, spas, shopping centres, restaurants, entertainment corner, hotels and so on.

Man-made Attractions

- **Gardens by the Bay:** The most famous tourist spot in Singapore, Gardens by the Bay is a natural place filled with attractions such as the Cloud Forest, Floral Dome, OCBC Skyway and Supertree, art sculptures and so on.
- **Singapore Botanical Gardens:** Listed by UNESCO as Singapore's first World Heritage Site, this amazing garden is home to national orchid garden, ginger garden, tropical rain forest with 314 species of plants and so much more!
- **Esplanade—Theatre on the Bay:** The most famous performing arts theatre in Singapore offers visual art displays, musical shows, world-class performances, entertainments, cultural walkthrough, leisure spots and so much more!
- **Merlion park:** The iconic landmark in Singapore and most-recognized symbol of Singapore is the Merlion Statue. Many tourists from all over the world are intrigued by the tale of Merlion as its head represents the former name of Singapore—'The Lion City'.

Merlion Statue, Singapore

- **Marina Bay Sands:** Singapore's most luxurious and versatile attraction, Marina Bay Sands, is an iconic luxury resort/hotel offering an elegant experience to the tourists along with entertainment, mouth-watering cuisine and not to forget, the infinity pool at the top!
- **Robertson Quay and Boat Quay:** Robertson Quay offers a variety of spots to enjoy like amazing restaurants, shops, cafes, art houses, wine bars, high-class condominiums, malls, museums, theatre and so much more! While you are there, do not forget to visit the famous Boat Quay nearby!
- **Sentosa island:** The most happening island of Singapore, Sentosa, is thriving with amazing resorts, artificial beaches, theme parks, restaurants, bars, adventure activities and so much more! It is home to Adventure Cove Waterpark, Dolphin Island, S.E.A. Aquarium and Universal Studios.
- Visitors who are seeking sites which are abundant in culture, heritage, art, murals, boutiques and so on, Little India and Chinatown are the places to go.

- **Tours:** There are many ways to explore the city. Some of the best ways are Trishaw Tour (bicycle with a side car), Historical Bicycle Tour, Electric Scooter Tours and so on.

Festivals and Events

Singapore is home to unlimited festivals that add vibrancy and cultural richness to the country. Some of the major festivals include:

- Singapore Food Festival
- Marina Bay Countdown (city's largest celebration)
- Chinese New Year (enjoy the Chingay Parade with displays of giant floats, dancing dragons, stilt walkers and so much more!)

Activities

Singapore is filled with thrills and adventures. It offers many interesting activities, suitable as per one's choice, to the tourists. Some of the activities include:

- Shopping at the Orchid Street and local markets
- Enjoying night life, beach parties and partying in the night clubs, dance pubs and bars
- Night Safari Park (world's first nocturnal park/zoo) which included over 2,000 animals
- Watching shows at Sentosa Island and Gardens by the Bay
- Adventure rides and water rides (try them in the famous Universal Studios Theme Park and Wild Wet Water Park)
- Jet blading (available at Ola Beach Club)
- Bird watching in Jurong Bird Park (Asia's largest bird park)
- Cruising in the Singapore river
- Segway tours in Sentosa
- Experience the steepest and longest zipline in Mega Adventure Theme Park

Amenities of Smart Singapore

- Singapore has taken the initiative to make the city smart by establishing a digital marketplace for all sectors. The initiative called 'Smart Nation' which not only made the city technologically innovative, but also provided smart solutions to problems such as traffic, economy, transit, government, safety and so on, has three main pillars known as digital economy, digital government and digital society. Free Wi-Fi in majority of public places, portable Wi-Fi or pocket Wi-Fi for rent at tourist places and so on, are some of the things which make an easy travel experience for tourists.

- Singapore Tourism and the government has introduced amazing essentials for people to make their travel, stay and visit convenient and easy. A few of the innovations include smart applications which help users in getting around the city, transportation availability, train maps, travel guides and so on. Some of the apps include GoThere, Grab, MyTransport, Visit Singapore Travel Guide and so on.
- Singapore Tourism Website is by far the most convenient travel guide created by Singapore Tourism Board. The information feed and alignment are based on types of tourism markets and customer preferences. For example, there is an individual segment reserved for foodies, another box dedicated for festivities lover, collectors and so on.

Eco-friendly Malls in Singapore

- Singapore has taken sustainability and eco-management seriously.
- A few places in the city have turned themselves into environment-friendly shopping destinations.
- Reduced air conditioning unless required, eco-friendly waste management system, energy-efficient architecture and technology and so on, are some of the environment-friendly techniques used by some shopping spots.

Singapore Local Rules and Law Every Traveller Should Know

- Chewing gum is illegal. Proper prescription is needed to carry more than two packets of chewing gums with you.
- Littering is strictly prohibited. Use of waste bins is heavily recommended unless you want to suffer heavy fine.
- One must always respect the 'No Jaywalking Sign'. Random crossing earn penalties by police.
- Singapore has serious laws against carrying and consuming drugs. Random drug tests are also conducted of both locals and foreigners.
- Not flushing the toilet and urinating in elevators is not just an indecent act, but also a crime in Singapore.

Conclusion

Singapore's tourism is built on innovation, man-made attractions and smart utilization of the city's land mass. Tourism Board of Singapore and the government of the city made reliable efforts to tap into the market and recognize the requirements of a tourist. Singapore is not only a place for entertainment and leisure, it is also being promoted as a business destination. This ensures that there is a continuous flow of inbound tourists and the economic stability is remained intact.

Learning Outcomes

- A destination's reputation is based on the tourism products it offers. For establishing a good image in the tourism industry, the tourism authorities and government of a destination must have out-of-the-box strategies and innovative ideas.
- Lack of natural resources does not stop a destination from becoming tourist-preferred place. Right tourism products and marketing strategies can increase tourist footfall in a destination.
- Tourism authorities and the government must take collective measures to make a destination safe, clean and convenient for the tourists as well as the locals.

Points for Discussion

- Converting a city into MICE destination is helping the economy and tourism of that country. Discuss how?
- What are common mistakes made by tourists which lead to law enforcement upon them?

Bibliography

https://www.stb.gov.sg/content/dam/stb/documents/statistics-marketing-insights/Quarterly-Tourism-Performance-Report/STB-Q3-2019-Tourism-Performance-report-FINAL.pdf (accessed on 04 July 2020).

https://www.visitsingapore.com/ (accessed on 04 July 2020).

https://mobility.here.com/singapore-smart-city-holistic-transformation (accessed on 04 July 2020).

https://www.budgetdirect.com.sg/travel-insurance/research/singapore-tourism-statistics (accessed on 04 July 2020).

https://www.tablebuilder.singstat.gov.sg/publicfacing/createDataTable.action?refId=1991 (accessed on 04 July 2020).

A.4. GOING OFF-TRAIL

About a few years ago, a group of allocentric travellers had an unforgettable experience when they decided to visit Kharghar Hills and trekked till the Pandavkada Waterfalls after their college hours. Kharghar Hills are very famous for their scenic waterfalls, lush greenery and dense forests up the hill. It is also a well-known tourist spot in the region, and many people enjoy their time at those hills every day.

The group reunited after the last lecture and purchased a few essentials such as water, some snacks and plastic bags. Within half an hour, they reached the start of the trail and began their trek. The group was very familiar with the route as this was not their first visit to the Kharghar Hills.

The plan was very simple and usual—stay on the track, be careful along the stream and rocks, reach the falls, relax for a while and return. After 15 minutes of trekking, the group came across two paths. One was leading towards the falls, and the other was still unknown to them. Because they had visited this place many times, they felt maybe it was the time for something different. Everyone in the group was pretty excited about the change of paths and agreed to the new plan. The other route was more of a hike between giant rocks and thick trees. As they ascended, the surrounding started to become denser. Beautiful but unknown territory gave them a rush of adrenaline. Some of the friends started getting antsy as the hike became difficult because of the odd growth of the trees, but none suggested to turn back. They came across a small stream covered with thick branches of giant trees, dense with dark green leaves. They rested there for a bit.

Everyone was so quiet because all they could hear was the flow of water as it hit the branches, sound of the birds somewhere distant and sound of the rustling of tree leaves. No one dared to speak a word and break the peaceful silence. After a few minutes, they started to move forward carefully as the difficulty was increasing with every step they took. Everyone was aware of the risks for their action and informed their family and friends before they lost the network. Soon they realized that there was no sign of any human activity like litter on the lands, which was very common around the area. After good two hours, they finally reached a comfortable, walkable land filled with lush green grass, tall trees with dense canopy but each tree within a safe distance from each other creating a clear view of the entire area. All they could see was greenery everywhere. It was almost too good to be true.

Suddenly, everyone heard a whisper of their friend calling them towards a small little opening, more like a natural cave formed because of the unusual growth of the trees and a small creek with water flowing peacefully beneath. That moment changed everything. In front of them was a big swarm of orange butterflies, hundreds of them just flying in that spot. Nobody moved a single muscle as they had never witnessed these many butterflies at one place. It was almost like no human ever touched that side of the mountain—small yellow flowers on the fresh green grass and hundreds of beautiful butterflies. They thanked the Lord for this amazing view and also themselves because if they did not choose to go off track, they would have never witnessed something so surreal.

In the state of awe, the group of adventurers returned to their homes happily. They decided to never disclose that spot as it would be a tragic event if anything were to happen to that beautiful place. It was too precious to get littered by humans.

Conclusion

This case study shares an experience of allocentric travellers who choose to go off track on their expedition and discover something mystical. Sometimes, if your instincts are telling you to explore a new path, chances are you might stumble upon something greater. The group would not have experienced such beauty if they chose to walk on the regular path toward the waterfalls. Thankfully, everyone is a nature lover, so they treasured the place by keeping it a secret as they are aware of the local people's behaviour and their careless habits.

Learning Outcomes

- Trekking and hiking are not everyone's cup of tea as it involves various risks. One must always weigh the pros and cons before choosing an unknown path.
- People who like experimenting and trying new roads would always learn something out of the usual. Allocentric tourists have a different set of decision-making instincts, and they choose what is out of the box.
- Nature has gifted humankind with many wonders. It is vital that we treasure such gifts and respect nature.
- Tourists should act more responsibly and must have a sustainable approach towards every destination. They must ensure not to throw litter while visiting any tourist attraction so that the next visitor or generation can enjoy the destination's beauty as it is.

Points for Discussion

- The group has never witnessed something so surreal. Share any of your similar experience while travelling.
- The group decided to respect the privacy of that place. Did they make the right decision, or should they have shared it with others to attract tourists?
- There are three types of travellers—allocentric, mid-centric and psychocentric. Which one are you?
- Going off-trail on a hike can be exciting as well as extremely dangerous. Did the group make the right decision by changing their paths?

SECTION

LIFELINES OF TOURISM BUSINESS

The given section is about introducing the readers to the five A's of the tourism industry. It shall make an attempt to delve deep into how the five A's are important in increasing the influx of tourists at a destination and thus may be defined as the lifelines of the tourism industry. As the whole tourism industry is driven by attractions, the readers would first be introduced to the attractions that are the very reason as to why tourists travel throughout the world. To reach the attractions, travellers need transportation systems in place. The destination must be easily accessible by air, road, rail or water. Thus, in this section, the readers would be made to understand the importance of accessibility. When a tourist visits a destination, he/she also stays there. He/she needs an accommodation to stay. Thus, the readers would be introduced to the basic concept of accommodation, the factors that the travellers consider while choosing an accommodation and the most used form of accommodation, that is, hotels. This would be followed by a detailed discussion on the alternative forms of accommodation such as youth hostels, guest houses and lodges that travellers may also use instead of hotels along with a discussion on the emerging trends in the hospitality sector. Thereafter, the students would be introduced to the amenities at a destination which are important to make a destination tourist friendly. The last chapter would be an attempt by the author to create a possible inventory of maximum activities offered by destinations to attract tourists.

At the end of each chapter, there are activities related to each chapter, which students may practise in their classrooms. Also, every chapter has interesting information for students to know, organized in the boxes that the students are advised to read to increase their knowledge of tourism. After the completion of chapters in the section, there are certain case studies related to the section for the students to read, comprehend and analyse followed by questions to be answered. Thus, after going through Section B, the learners would know the following:

- What is an attraction? What are the various types of attraction? What are things to be considered while visiting an attraction?
- What is the importance of accessibility in a destination? How can accessibility be improved in a destination?
- What is an accommodation? What are the factors that a traveller considers before choosing an accommodation? What is a hotel, and what are its types? What are the types of rooms in a hotel?
- What are the alternative forms of accommodation?
- What are the amenities required for a destination to make it tourist friendly?
- What are the activities that tourists pursue when they visit a destination?

So let us keep building our concepts of tourism and know the importance of the five As of tourism that are essential components of the tourism industry.

Stay on this journey of wisdom! Happy learning, dear readers!

11

Attractions

LEARNING OBJECTIVES

The given chapter shall clarify the following:

- What is an attraction? What are the different kinds of attractions?
- What are the different means of exploring an attraction?
- What are the various facilities available at an attraction?
- What are the things to know before visiting an attraction?
- What are the ideal ways of managing an attraction?

THE LOUVRE MUSEUM: AN ART LOVER'S HEAVEN!

- The Louvre Museum in Paris is among the most-visited places and one of the top attractions in the world. It is also listed as one of the world's largest art museums.
- It is heaven for art lovers and a must-visit for tourists in Paris.
- It is home to the most-celebrated work of art—the painting of Mona Lisa made by Leonardo da Vinci.
- To make the museum more interactive, it is equipped with guided tours, audio guides, educators and a fully detailed website which also provides thematic trails. It also offers visitors with touch gallery experience, shops, restaurants and bookstores within the museum.
- In 2017, Emirates leaders in Abu Dhabi decided to do a cultural collaboration between two countries (the UAE and France) and launched the development of the universal art museum—The Louvre Abu Dhabi.

Sightseeing is an integral part of a travellers' experience. One of the most important motivations or the pull factors is the attractions at a destination that push a tourist to leave his/her domicile and travel to another place. Attractions are the fulcrum around which the whole of the tourism industry revolves. Tourists travel miles to witness the attractions with their naked eyes.

The destinations across the world are bountiful with a myriad of attractions. Some destinations may be bestowed with natural attractions such as mountains, valleys, beaches, deserts, hot springs and other natural views for which the tourists visit these destinations. However, many destinations of the world where nature is not bountiful such as Singapore and Dubai have created man-made attractions to attract tourists from different corners of the world.

INTRODUCTION

A tourist attraction may refer to a place of interest where tourists visit typically for its inherent or exhibited natural or cultural value, historical significance, built beauty, offered leisure, adventure and amusement. Tourist attractions may be of different types. These may be *natural attractions* or *man-made attractions*. Natural attractions are the gifts of nature. These may include mountains, hills, deserts, beaches, national parks, forests, water bodies or any other natural landscapes or scenic viewpoints. Man-made attractions are created by man. These may further be categorized into *heritage attractions* that have been constructed to commemorate the history or culture of a place. These may include monuments such as forts, castles, palaces, museums, art galleries, ancient worship structures, historical trains and ships. However, some artificial structures may just be created to add entertainment value to a destination such as theme parks, shopping malls and landmark attractions such as skyscrapers, bridges and botanical gardens. These may also be called *purpose-built attractions*. *Events* such as fairs and festivals, and cultural events may also be classified as attractions of a destination.

For the sake of our clarity, the different gamut of attractions that tourists generally visit may be broadly divided under the following categories along with their suitable examples.

- **Monuments and historical places**
  o The Colosseum, Italy
  o The Taj Mahal, Agra, India
  o The Great Pyramid of Giza, Egypt
  o Acropolis of Athens, Greece
  o Machu Picchu, Peru, South America

Stonehenge, England

o Stonehenge, England

o The Cellular Jail, Andaman and Nicobar Islands, India

o Ground Zero, New York, USA

Opera House, Sydney

- **Forts, palaces and castles**

o The Palace of Versailles, Paris, France

o Schönbrunn Palace, Vienna, Austria

o The Buckingham Palace, London, UK

o The Red Fort, Delhi, India

o The City Palace, Udaipur, India

o The Glamis Castle, Scotland

o The Edinburgh Castle, Edinburgh, Scotland

o The Windsor Castle, England

o The Forbidden City, Beijing

- **Iconic artificial structures and buildings**

o The Statue of Unity, Gujarat, India (world's tallest statue with a height of 597 ft)

o Zhangjiajie Glass Bridge, Hunan, China (world's tallest skywalk bridge)

o The Great Wall of China

o The Madurodam, Holland

o The Burj Khalifa, Dubai

o The Eiffel Tower, Paris, France

o The London Eye, London, UK

o The Sydney Opera House, Sydney, Australia

o The Golden Gate Bridge, San Francisco, USA

o Chinese Fishing Nets, Kerala

The London Eye, London

- **Botanical gardens and parks**

o The Central Park, New York, USA

o The Keukenhof Tulip and Flower Gardens, Holland

o The Gardens by the Bay, Singapore

o The Miracle Garden, Dubai

o The Hyde Park, London

o The Mughal Gardens, New Delhi, India

o The Royal Botanic Gardens, Victoria, Melbourne, Australia

- **Museums**

o The Louvre Museum, Paris, France

o The Boston Tea Party Ships & Museums, Boston, USA

o The Metropolitan Museum of Art in New York City, USA

o The Polar Museum, Tromsø, Norway

  o   The Corning Museum of Glass, New York, USA
  o   The Madame Tussauds Museum, London, UK
  o   Van Gogh Museum, Amsterdam
  o   The Digital Museum, Amritsar, India
  o   The Swarovski Crystal World, Austria
  o   The Natural History Museum, London
  o   The Teddy Bear Museum, Pattaya, Thailand
  o   The Sulabh International Museum of Toilets, New Delhi, India
- **Art galleries**
  o   The Metropolitan Museum of Art, New York, USA
  o   The National Gallery, London, UK
  o   The National Gallery of Modern Art, New Delhi, India
  o   The National Gallery of Art, Washington
- **Religious shrines**
  o   Vaishno Devi, J&K, India
  o   The Sun Temple, Konark, India
  o   The Ajmer Sharif Dargah, Ajmer, India
  o   The Golden Temple, Amritsar, India
  o   The Thiksey Monastery, Ladakh, India
  o   Notre-Dame Cathedral, Paris
  o   The St. Peter's Basilica Church, Vatican
  o   The Blue Mosque, Turkey
  o   The Western Wall, Jerusalem
  o   Angkor Wat Temple, Cambodia
  o   Mecca and Medina
- **National parks, wildlife sanctuaries, zoos and aquariums**
  o   The Yosemite National Park, USA
  o   Great Smoky Mountains National Park, North Carolina and Tennessee, USA
  o   Death Valley National Park, USA
  o   The Serengeti National Park, Tanzania
  o   The Melbourne Zoo, Australia
  o   The Sea Life Aquarium, Sydney, Australia
  o   Ranthambore National Park, Sawai Madhopur, Rajasthan, India
- **Amusement parks and theme parks**
  o   The Disney World's Magic Kingdom, Orlando, Florida, USA (the most magical place on earth)
  o   The Ferrari World, Abu Dhabi, UAE
  o   Genting Highlands, Malaysia
  o   Sentosa Islands, Singapore
  o   Disneyland Paris, Paris, France
  o   The Dreamworld, Gold Coast, Australia
  o   Universal Studios, Osaka, Japan

- o The Universal Studios, Los Angeles, USA
- o The Chokhi Dhani, Jaipur, India
- o Sadda Pind, Amritsar, Punjab, India
- **Natural sites such as mountains, hills, caves and deserts**
  - o Batu Caves, Malaysia
  - o Mt Titlis, Lucerne, Switzerland
  - o The Grand Canyon, Arizona, USA
  - o The Trou aux Cerfs Volcano, Mauritius
  - o The Great Barrier Reef, Australia
  - o The Thar Desert, Jaisalmer
  - o The Cold Desert, Ladakh, India
- **Water bodies (lakes, waterfalls, beaches, rivers)**
  - o The Dead Sea, Israel
  - o Lake Michigan, USA
  - o The Loch Ness Lake, Scotland
  - o Navy Pier, Chicago
  - o The Pangong Tso Lake, Ladakh
  - o The Manly Beach, Sydney
  - o The Rhine Falls, Europe
  - o The Niagara Falls, USA and Canada
  - o The Ganges River in Haridwar and Varanasi, India

- **Famous shows**
  - o The Acrobatic Show, Shanghai, China
  - o The Lido Show, Paris, France
  - o The KÀ show in Las Vegas, USA
  - o The Garden Rhapsody Show, Gardens by the Bay, Singapore
  - o The Water Show, Akshardham Temple, New Delhi, India

The Sound and Light Show in the Gardens by the Bay, Singapore

- **Events such as fairs, festivals and sports**
  - o Tomorrowland, Belgium
  - o Pushkar Fair, Rajasthan, India
  - o La Tomatina Festival, Spain
  - o IPL, India
- **Famous local markets**
  - o Grand Bazaar, Istanbul, Turkey
  - o Faneuil Hall Marketplace, Boston
  - o Floating Market, Pattaya, Thailand
  - o Camden Market, England

- o   Tsukiji Fish Market, Japan
- o   Janpath, New Delhi, India
- **Special rides**
  - o   Cable Car Ride at Mt. Titlis, Switzerland
  - o   Gondola Ride, Venice, Italy
  - o   Canal Boat Tour, Amsterdam
  - o   Camel Safari, Jaisalmer, India
  - o   Yak Safari and Double Hump Camel Ride, Nubra Valley, Ladakh, India
  - o   Elephant Safari, Kerala
- **Study tours and factory visits**
  - o   Visit to the Cheese and Shoe Factory, Amsterdam, Holland, for watching cheese-making
  - o   Murano Glass Factory, Venice, Italy for viewing glass manufacturing
  - o   Cuckoo Clock Demonstration, Black forest, Germany for seeing the demonstration of cuckoo clocks
  - o   Sula Vineyards, Nashik, India/Napa Valley Vineyards, San Francisco, USA, for understanding how wine is manufactured
  - o   Glenburn Tea Estate, Darjeeling, India for learning how tea is made
- **Special ceremonies**
  - o   The Changing of the Guard, the Buckingham Palace, London, UK
  - o   The Change of Guard, Wagah Border, Amritsar, India
  - o   The Palki Sahib ceremony at Golden Temple, Amritsar, India
  - o   The Ganga aarti ceremony at Ganga Ghat, Varanasi, India
- **Special walks (walking tours, heritage walks)**
  - o   Heritage walk and food walks in Chandni Chowk, New Delhi, India
  - o   Walking tours in Philadelphia, USA, and Rome, Italy
  - o   Skywalk in Grand Canyon, USA
  - o   Hollywood Walk of Fame, Hollywood, CA
- **Ethnic communities**
  - o   Chinatowns in the USA

The Cheese and Shoe Factory, Amsterdam, Holland

The Palki Sahib Ceremony at the Golden Temple, Amritsar

    o Black British Neighbourhood of Brixton, London, England
    o The Gond tribe of Central India
    o Bhutia tribe of Sikkim, India
- **Famous city squares**
    o Times Square, New York, USA
    o Trafalgar Square, London
    o Tiananmen Square, Beijing, China
    o Saint Peter's Square, Vatican City, Rome
    o Plaza Mayor, Madrid, Spain
    o The Grand Place, Brussels, Belgium
    o Red Square, Moscow

MEANS OF EXPLORING AN ATTRACTION

There are many ways of visiting an attraction. Tourists might travel to an attraction on their own or may book a package tour through a travel agent/tour operator who may facilitate their visit to these attractions.

Some of the ways followed by tourists to these attractions are as follows.

Self-exploration

Many tourists visit a destination on their own. They may read about the attractions through the Internet or seek information from the Visitor Information Centres/through their friends and relatives/read in the travel guides or travel magazines and then visit on their own to explore these attractions. They may also make use of audio-guided devices if they do not wish to hire the services of a tour guide at the attraction. Such tourists prefer to be on an auto mode where they enjoy exploring a destination on their own with least intervention of others.

Hiring a Local Guide

Sometimes, tourists who are on their own still may feel that a better way of exploring an attraction is through taking guided tours where they may seek the services of a local guide or a site-specific guide. They may take guides so as to be able to make more sense of the place and enjoy the pleasure of being taken care of.

For example, many tourists who wish to explore *Lutyen's Delhi in India* in an adventurous way take a guided Segway tour riding on a Segway. Another example of a guided tour can be of a *guided walking tour in Florence, Italy,* to explore the city at its best with the help of a tour guide.

Hop-on Hop-off Buses

Another way for visitors to explore the attractions of a city on their own is to take a 'city tour' on hop-on hop-off (HOHO) buses. These buses stop at important tourist attractions where the driver acts as a driver-cum guide and gives commentary while passing through the specific tourist points. Tourists may get down at points wherever they want to and then go and see a particular attraction. After having visited the attraction, they may board another HOHO bus service to see the other tourist attractions. These buses operate on fixed itinerary routes and have a very frequent bus service. Generally, one may avail deals on buying different combination passes depending upon the number of days that one has for sightseeing and the number of passengers who are travelling together.

Package Tours

On package tours, the mechanism is different. Many travel agents/tour operators and coach operators (e.g., Cosmos and Globus) package multiple attractions as sightseeing tours for the tourists. Some sightseeing tours may be for a half-day duration, while some may be for a full day covering the overall attractions of a destination. If a destination has a number of attractions, then the sightseeing tour may be for multiple days. In package tours, sometimes, half of the day may be on own/at leisure for the tourists to explore the destination or shop at the destination on their own.

The tourists are taken on a coach where it may operate according to the itinerary laid out by the tour operator. They may be led by tour leaders on such attractions. The tour leader may sometimes act as a spokesperson for the attraction who introduces the guests to an attraction. However, generally, the tour leader would avail the services of a local tour guide who due to his/her specialized knowledge is well versed with the sites. In the presence of a tour leader and a tour guide, the tourists can gain a better perspective of the attractions.

Panoramic Coach Tours

In some cases, the groups of tourists are taken on panoramic coach tours where they are shown the important landmark attractions of a destination on a coach from a distance. This may generally happen if the duration of stay at the destination is short and there are many other activities or places to be covered. Such tours may be operated by tour operators or coach operators such as Cosmos and Globus who are global players in coach tours. In such cases, either the driver acts as a tour guide or there may be a hired tour guide who may travel with the guests on a coach explaining about important city attractions. However, the tour guide or the driver may occasionally give a photography opportunity to the guests, wherever possible. He/She may allow an opportunity to his/her guests to click pictures by asking his/her guests to get down of the coach for 10–15 minutes duration to capture the attractions in their camera lens and then depart for the next attraction.

FACILITIES AT AN ATTRACTION

It is important for the tourism authorities of a destination to understand that the attractions must be tourist-friendly. Although the duration of stay of guests at an attraction is generally very less, however, the services and facilities available at an attraction create an overall image of the attraction and, more particularly, affect the image of a destination. The presence of facilities at an attraction makes the overall experience of the tourists more comfortable and hassle-free. Some of the facilities available at an attraction are as follows.

Wi-Fi Facility

To qualify as a tourist-friendly attraction, a tourist attraction must offer free Wi-Fi facilities for the tourists to get connected with the Internet. On registering oneself with one's email id account or a Facebook account, one may be authorized to use free Internet services.

This helps the visitors at an attraction to share their updates/upload their pictures and share their live statuses at the attraction (sometimes while also attending some important events/concerts) on the social networking sites with their family and friends. This indirectly helps in promoting an attraction. If the tourists are on their own, they may also read additional information about the attraction using Wi-Fi services.

Lockers

Attractions must have locker facilities for the tourists. In many attractions, certain items are restricted. For example, while visiting *Akshardham Temple in New Delhi, India, the tourists are not allowed to carry any leather items such as purses, belts and other items like mobile phones inside the holy temple.* In such cases, the tourists before entering the holy shrine may keep their belongings within the locker to keep them safe and intact. Similarly, in cases of *Disneyworld, selfie sticks are not allowed for safety reasons.* Therefore, in case the tourists are carrying the selfie sticks, they may submit the same inside the locker. The idea of having lockers inside the attractions is to give space to the tourists to keep their personal belongings in case they are forbidden from carrying the items inside or they do not want to carry the burden of their personal baggage inside the attraction.

Public Conveniences

The attractions must have public conveniences for the guests to use. Proper restrooms must be available for both males and females with proper signage. They must be kept tidy and hygienic for guests to use.

Garbage Cans

There must be garbage cans placed at even points at an attraction. This may help the guests to keep the attraction clean as they can throw the trash in the garbage cans, in case if they have any.

Bistros

Many attractions have bistros, cafes and restaurants as a facility for satisfying the hunger of the tourists. This facility is especially available in those attractions that are large enough area wise and may take a long time to move around to properly explore the attraction. For example, in *Glamis Castle, Scotland,* which is the childhood home of Queen Elizabeth, there is a Victorian Kitchen Restaurant that serves different varieties of English light snacks for the tourists. Besides the snacks, tourists in advance may make the reservation for the very famous English afternoon tea that is served there.

Parking Lots

An attraction must have designated parking spaces for the tourists to park their vehicles. The parking spaces should be large enough to accommodate big tourist coaches that may come in numbers during the season time of a destination.

Signage

Every attraction must have proper signage pointing out to the important points of interest and the important facilities available for the tourists. This helps in the easy navigation of the attraction, thereby making it more possible for the tourists to be on an auto mode.

Maps

Many attractions have signage of maps, interactive maps and printed maps that are placed for the facilitation of the tourists. It is important to share the layout of the attraction at the entry point of an attraction, especially for those attractions that are large enough. This helps the tourists to easily navigate through the attraction and figure out exactly where the public conveniences, drinking water facilities, merchandise stores, restaurants and bistros and so on are located. For example, the detailed map of *Disneyland theme park in Los Angeles, USA,* is available at the information counters at the entry point which may be collected by the tourists for their usage. The map contains the following information for the visitors:

- Layout of the Disneyland
- Information about amusement rides, that is, their timings and the venue
- Information about restaurants and eating outlets
- Information about shopping arcades
- Other facilities available such as washrooms and lockers along with their locations
- Show timings

This may be useful for the tourists to plan their stops during their visit to the park accordingly and thus, utilize their limited time at the attraction in the most productive way.

Souvenir Shops

Many attractions have souvenir shops that are a storehouse of the items related to an attraction. The idea is to encourage the tourists to buy the local stuff of the attraction and thus increase the merchandise of the store as many attractions use this money for maintaining the attractions. *Generally, the souvenir shops are intelligently placed at the exit points of the attractions.* As after visiting the attraction, the tourists may be fascinated by the various aspects of an attraction, they may be evoked to buy the souvenir items related to the attraction.

For example, while exiting the *Sea World at Jakarta, Indonesia,* there is a souvenir shop at the exit point where the tourist may buy stuff toys, key chains, clothing and so on in the form of different sea animals as a souvenir for their families and friends. Likewise, there are souvenir shops at *Gardens by the Bay, Singapore, exit point* and *Titanic museum in Belfast* selling related articles of the displays inside these attractions.

Information Kiosks

Many attractions have their own information centres/kiosks within the attraction. The staff at the information centre may assist the tourists with the following kinds of information:

- Important points of interest or must-visit points inside the attractions (e.g., inside the Central Park, that stretches across approximately 843 acres in prime Manhattan, New York City, the tourists are advised to visit the strawberry fields, Central Park Zoo and so on)
- Any activities that may be tried (within the Central Park, one may go for walking, jogging, cycling, gazing around the skyscrapers, watching concerts and shows, ice skating, doing Yoga and so on)
- Facilities available at the attraction

- Any conducted tours at the attraction (many tours are conducted at the Central park), these may include the following:
  o Bike tours
  o Horse and carriage tours
  o Pedicab tours
  o Photo tours
  o Walking tours
  o Running tours

Thus, the vital information provided by these kiosks assists the tourist to explore the attraction fully and utilize their time in the most effective way.

Exhibition Centres

Many attractions may also have exhibition centres to showcase the significance and evolution of an attraction. The idea of exhibition centres is to help tourists appreciate the importance of an attraction.

For example, *the world's leading Titanic visitor experience awaits in Belfast in the Titanic Museum, North Ireland.* Here, one may visit the exhibition centre that exhibits the various important literature and artefacts related to the sinking of the ship.

Tour Guide Services

Many attraction authorities may have deputed authorized trained tour guides who may be adept in different foreign languages. The tourists may avail the services of a tour guide, if they wish to at an attraction. With the help of a tour guide, one can learn about the important facets of an attraction in the most engaging way.

Audio-guided Devices

Many tourists may not be comfortable hiring the services of a local tour guide as they may prefer to be on their own. Such guests in order to make sense of the attraction may use the audio-guided devices at an attraction. Thus, many attractions offer the facility of audio-guided devices for tourists.

Audio-guided devices have pre-recorded commentaries of the important points of an attraction. At reaching every significant point of the attraction, the sensors get activated and the pre-recorded commentary begins. Audio-guided devices may be available in different languages that may be chosen according to the language choice of the traveller. Use of audio-guided devices makes the navigation of travellers easier and allows them to be on an auto mode. Some of the examples of attractions where tourist may find audio-guided devices are *The Roman Baths in England, St Basicilica Church in Vatican city, Virasat-e-Khalsa in Anandpur Sahib* and many more.

Lost and Found Box

Many attractions have a lost and found box. The idea is that in case the tourist has left any of his/her belongings at the attraction by mistake, the same may be collected by the attraction authorities and submitted in the lost and found box to be collected by the tourist later.

First-aid Facility

Attractions must have a first-aid facility for the tourists. In case, any tourist meets an accident or hurts himself/herself, he/she may be provided with the first-aid assistance at the attraction by the trained professionals.

Shuttle Services

The Giant Causeway, Northern Ireland

Many attraction authorities may provide shuttle services within an attraction to facilitate the movement of tourists within an attraction, especially for those travellers for whom mobility is an issue, for example, aged travellers, travellers with health issues, expecting mothers, parents with young toddlers, people with special abilities and so on. This shuttle service can be a great assistance. For example, *while visiting the UNESCO world heritage site in Northern Ireland, 'the Giant's Causeway', the tourists have to park their vehicles/coaches in a designated place.* After the vehicle has been parked, then the tourists have an option either to walk the long distance to reach the attraction or to board the coach provided by the attraction authorities to reach that point. Even inside the Disneyworld, the attraction authorities provide toy trains and golf carts to navigate through the place. Also, at *Amber Fort, Jaipur,* to reach a particular point, one may hire the Jeeps to cover a sufficient distance. Beyond that point, one has to walk down until the Amber Fort.

Accessible

Many attractions to be accessible for people with special abilities offer wheelchair services, hearing aids, ramps, accessible toilets, golf carts and so on to facilitate tourists and increase their visits. Even the senior citizens or anyone who is uncomfortable walking due to a health issue may also avail these services.

THINGS TO KNOW BEFORE VISITING AN ATTRACTION

A tourist must be aware of certain facets of an attraction before arriving at an attraction. He/She must acquire all the following necessary information before he/she departs for an attraction.

Visiting Hours of the Attraction

Every attraction has fixed hours of visits. A tourist must be aware of the visiting hours so that he/she may plan his/her itinerary according to hours of visits so that he/she may not miss on the attraction.

Days Closed for the Attraction

Some attractions may be closed on particular days and on public holidays. For example, *most of the museums in India are closed on Mondays. Likewise, the famous Taj Mahal in India is closed on Fridays.* It can be very disappointing for the tourists if their visits have been planned on the closing days of an attraction.

An attraction may also be closed on account of security reasons due to some event taking place in that attraction on the day of the tour. For example, *on the eve of Queen Elizabeth's birthday in London, many attractions like the Buckingham Palace and*

The Changing Guards Ceremony, Buckingham Palace, London

nearby monuments and streets may be sealed for security reasons. Also, during the 'Changing of Guards Ceremony' near Buckingham Palace, there may be limited access for the public, and the timings of the ceremony may also be revamped accordingly. Also, at times of strikes or a procession taking place, an attraction may be closed. Thus, the tourists must keep himself/herself updated with such information before planning his/her visit to an attraction.

Best Time to Visit

Many attractions may be closed for particular periods. For example, many national parks and wildlife sanctuaries may be closed for specific time zones. Thus, tourists must be aware of the timings of the operation of the national parks before they plan their visits. Otherwise, their visit may go in vain. For example, *the best time to visit the Ranthambore National Park in Sawai Madhopur, Rajasthan, is from October to March.* One may see the migratory birds at this time. However, for wildlife enthusiasts and photographers who wish to spot the tigers and other rare fauna, April to June, that is, the summer season is the ideal time as animals move out in search of food and water owing to high temperatures. The park is closed for visitors during monsoons, that is, from July to September.

Likewise, the state rooms of the famous *Buckingham Palace* are open for tourists only from August to September and during some specific days in winters and springs.

Even, the *Keukenhof Tulip Garden in the Netherlands*, being the world-famous garden in Europe for its blooming bulbs and the most beautiful spring flowers which include more than seven million tulips, hyacinths and daffodils, is open only for two months in spring from March end to May end. Therefore, tourists may plan their visits accordingly. Hence, knowledge of the best time to visit an attraction is very important.

Total Time Duration

It is important for a tourist to be aware of the total time required to be spent at an attraction before planning his/her visit. Especially, if he/she is travelling to multiple attractions, he/she must know the ideal time that he/she may spend at one attraction so that he/she may plan his/her itinerary accordingly. The total time spent by the tourists generally depends upon the interest of the tourist. An art lover would spend more time at an art gallery, whereas a historian or a student of archaeology may like to spend more time at historical sites. For example, *an artist who has a keen interest in paintings may spend days and months at the 'Louvre Museum', the world's largest art museum, appreciating the paintings of the museum.* As this museum is home to the most valuable masterpiece of art, that is, the Mona Lisa portrait by Leonardo da Vinci, it is the most visited museum in the world. Thus, this museum is an ultimate destination in itself for those tourists who are art lovers.

However, the total time to be spent at an attraction would depend upon the number of days one has in hand at a destination and the number of attractions that the tourist is planning to cover during his/her visit to the destination.

Entry Ticket

Many attractions may charge an entry ticket for getting an access inside them, though in many attractions, there is free entry. Generally, most of the attractions such as historical sites, artificial structures, forts, national parks, botanical gardens, museums, galleries and theme parks have an entry ticket to be paid by the tourists. The idea of charging entry fees is to allow limited authorized access to the attraction and to use the money in the maintenance of an attraction.

A tourist while visiting an attraction must be aware of the amount of entry ticket that is chargeable. *It may be noteworthy to mention here that the charges of entry tickets for domestic tourists may be different from that of foreign tourists.* Many tourists may also buy entry tickets in advance online so as not to waste their precious holiday time standing in long queues to buy the ticket.

Making Reservations in Advance

Many popular attractions may be crowded during the peak seasons when there are hordes of tourists visiting an attraction at the same time. Thus, the best way to see an attraction is to plan one's visit in advance. Thus, it is always advisable to make advanced reservations by the tourists to avoid any delays in their scheduled itinerary and not to waste their precious time standing in queues to get the tickets. For example, *while visiting France, during peak season, it is advisable for a tourist to buy the entry tickets in advance, especially for visiting the top storey of the Eiffel Tower to avoid being stranded for long hours at the attraction due to the heavy rush of tourists.*

Also, generally, when the tourists travel to watch the famous shows in an attraction, for example, the *Lido Show in Paris* or *Light and Sound Show in Andaman and Nicobar Islands in Cellular Jail,* they may make reservations in advance rather than getting no reservation on non-availability of seats due to heavy rush during the peak season.

Arranging Travel Documentation

Some attractions require travel documentation and permits for visiting them. It is important for the tourists to be aware of such requirements, if any, for visiting such attractions. It is also advisable to preferably arrange for the necessary documentation before the arrival at the attraction so that the visitors may not have to waste their time in queues waiting for the permits. For example, to visit the *Nicobar Islands in India,* not only foreigners, but even the domestic tourists are required to show permits at check posts before travelling there. Likewise, for visiting *Nathula Pass, in Sikkim, India*, domestic tourists are also required to take special permits for visiting there that may be arranged in advance, if possible.

Photography and Videography Policy

In many attractions, taking photographs and doing videography are not permissible due to security reasons and religious beliefs. At some attractions, it is allowed but with some charges. At some attractions, it may be allowed without paying any extra charge. Therefore, tourists must be aware of the policy of attraction regarding photography and videography.

Gathering Knowledge about the Points of Interest at the Attraction

Every attraction has some points of interest that are a 'must-see' for tourists. It is essential for a tourist to have prior knowledge of such stoppage points before he/she starts the tour of an attraction. A tourist must gather information about the history and significance of these points of interest before he/she visits these attractions. This helps the tourist to relate and appreciate the attraction more when he/she actually visits the attraction. For example, while visiting the *Grand Canyon in Arizona, USA*, that is famous for its deep gorges, rock formations and ridges, a tourist might visit or engage in the following activities:

- Take a helicopter ride
- Visit to the Grand Canyon Village
- Walk to the Bright Angel Trail and Rim Trail
- Raft at Colorado River

Likewise, while visiting the *Madame Tussauds Museum in London*, a tourist must take the exciting 'Spirit of London Taxi Ride' besides appreciating the wax statues of famous celebrities.

Popular Activities at an Attraction

At many attractions, activities are organized for the tourists within an attraction to make their visit more interesting and unique. It is important for the tourists to be aware of such activities taking place and know the timings of the activities at which they are performed along with their duration.

For example, at many forts in India, shows are organized for the tourists that highlight the legacy of these forts. *The Light and Sound Show at Red Fort, New Delhi*, is one such example.

Likewise, the *Laser show and 7D show at Guru Gobindgarh Fort, Amritsar*, and various activities such as horse rides, camel rides, traditional Punjabi dance performances and local street food of Punjab are showcased for the tourists to keep them engaged at the fort. Such activities that showcase the rich culture of Punjab make the visit of guests at the fort more exciting, meaningful and engaging.

Likewise, tourists are taken for elephant rides at *Amber Fort, Jaipur*, followed by a visit to Hathigaon (elephants' village) where the guests can ride, paint, feed and bathe the elephants which are an exciting activity for the guests.

Things to Carry

There may be restrictions on carrying of specific items at an attraction that may vary from one attraction to another. Thus, it is important for tourists to know about the list of things that they may take or may not take at an attraction. In general, the tourists may carry the following items at an attraction:

- Umbrella
- Water bottle
- Sunglasses
- Hats or caps
- Sunscreen lotion

Knowledge of Dos and Don'ts at an Attraction

Every attraction has its own set of rules and regulations that a tourist must abide by. It is expected of a tourist to have a thorough knowledge of these norms of the attraction so that they may not be unnecessarily stopped from entering these attractions or unnecessarily harassed due to ignorance of the rules they might violate unintentionally. Also, having knowledge of the rules gives them enough time to make preparations for themselves for visiting those attractions. For example, in the case of mountain excursions/beaches/holy shrines, tourists are expected to follow a specific protocol before visiting them. Some prior preparations may be required on the part of the tourists.

In case of a group of tourists going for a mountain excursion, they may ensure the following:

- Eat light before travelling
- Wear warm clothes
- Wear comfortable sports shoes that are not slippery
- Take camphor and keep smelling it as it might help in dealing with less oxygen in the air
- Carry medicines
- Keep hydrated at all times

Also, while visiting the holy shrines, a tourist must observe specific rules and regulations practised in these sacred places. For example, while visiting St. Peter's Basilica in the Vatican, the tourists are advised to cover their arms and knees before entering the Church. Therefore, the tourist must not wear sleeveless dress or shorts while visiting the Church.

Likewise, while attending a gurudwara, the place of worship for the Sikh community, visitors must keep their head covered to give respect to their religious beliefs.

Likewise, while visiting amusement parks, the tourists must take care of their safety by wearing safety belts during rides and they may not take selfie sticks inside the theme park if is not permissible.

Even, at many places, the tourists may have to walk a lot or climb many stairs like while visiting *Batu Caves in Malaysia*. Thus, the tourists must wear sports shoes and not heels which might hurt their feet eventually.

Therefore, before visiting any attraction, a tourist must be aware of the uneven terrains, distances and so on so as to prepare accordingly.

MANAGEMENT OF ATTRACTIONS

Generally, attractions are managed by attraction authorities. These attraction authorities may sometimes be independent bodies like non-profitable organizations or government bodies. Some of these may be private bodies, for example, the *City Palace at Jaipur*, famous for the two largest silver vessels in the world, is a privately managed body that comes under the aegis of royal family HH Maharaja Padmanabh Singh. Likewise, *the Buckingham Palace, London*, and *Glamis Castle, Scotland*, are all managed by private bodies.

However, the management of attractions is not only the job of the tourism authorities but also the tourists. Maintaining the hygiene of the attractions is equally the responsibility of tourists. Therefore, the tourists must behave responsibly while visiting the attractions.

Some of the ways in which the tourists can contribute towards the management of attractions are as follows.

Cooperating for Security Check

Before visiting an attraction inside, the tourists must cooperate for the necessary security checks at the entry points of an attraction. It may be the individual screening, that is, passing through the metal detector gates or getting their hand baggage screened through X-ray machines. Cooperation with the security staff at an attraction helps in the proper management of an attraction.

Maintaining Discipline

During peak seasons, most attractions are flooded with hordes of tourists. While visiting these attractions, the tourists must stand in proper queues before entering the gates of the attraction and at various points of interest at the attraction. Even for taking a picture at a particular point of interest, the tourists must follow the proper queues. Even while speaking to others, the tourists must keep a check on their volume of speaking. Maintaining discipline is very important for tourists.

Being Mindful of Others

The tourists must maintain the overall discipline at an attraction. Generally, at most of the attraction points, one would see a number of other tourists also who may be coming on their own or in a group. Therefore, it is important for the tourists to be mindful of other tourists and not to misbehave at the attraction or argue unnecessarily and spoil the fun of other tourists while visiting the attraction. The guests must behave and maintain the dignity of the place being visited.

Maintaining Hygiene

The tourists must help in keeping the attraction clean by throwing the garbage in the dustbins only. They should not litter around.

Observing the Dos and Don'ts

Every attraction may have certain rules and regulations to be followed. The tourists must ensure to abide by the rules and observe the local sensitivities of the attraction like not clicking pictures where photography is prohibited.

SUMMARY

Attractions form the fulcrum of the tourism industry. They may be of different types. There may be different ways of exploring an attraction. Tourist attractions must be tourist-friendly so as to keep the visit of the tourists comfortable and relaxing. They must offer an array of facilities to the tourists. To make the best out of the visiting attractions, tourists must have prior knowledge of many things about an attraction before they actually visit it. Since the whole tourism activity revolves around attractions, it is important to manage the attractions effectively and efficiently. However, management of attractions is not only the job of the attraction authorities but also the tourists. Tourists must respect the norms and regulations laid out by the attraction authorities and use the facilities in a proper way so as to keep the attraction in a good and sustainable condition not only for the present but also for the future generations. An attraction must create a strong recall value in the mind of the tourists by giving him/her a memorable experience and reasons to visit the destination again.

ACTIVITIES

Activity 1

List out the five major attractions of the following destinations:

- Dubai
- Singapore
- New York
- Amsterdam
- Melbourne
- London

Activity 2

Visit an attraction around your city and carefully observe it.
Present a write-up of the visited attraction that may include the following:

- Location of the attraction
- Its history and importance
- Best time to visit the attraction
- Amenities at the attraction
- Rules and regulations to be followed at the attraction

Activity 3

Identify the cities/countries of the following attractions:

- The Colosseum
- The Keukenhof Garden
- Times Square
- Statue of Unity
- The Glass Bridge
- SoHo, Little Italy and Chinatown
- Piccadilly Square

Accessibility: Part I

LEARNING OBJECTIVES

The given chapter shall clarify the following:

- What is the role of the transportation sector in the tourism industry?
- What are the various modes of transportation in the tourism sector?

BOEING 777: A GAME CHANGER FOR EMIRATES!

- Emirates (international airlines of Dubai) has recently unveiled the world's largest fleet of New Boeing 777 aircraft that flies to nearly 100 cities on 6 continents, carrying millions of passengers across the globe each year.
- Also known as the seventh wonder of Boeing, Boeing 777 is the world's largest twin-engine aircraft with six luxurious suites and has three million parts provided by more than 900 suppliers. Truly it is a 'game changer' for Emirates.
- The suite's design is inspired by Mercedes Benz, giving utmost elegant and unforgettable experience to the passengers of Boeing 777.
- The six exclusive private suites are fully updated with features such as temperature and lighting controller, mini bar, closet, entertainment gadgets and recliner chairs with zero gravity setting.
- People who have paid for first class and business class can enjoy the private chauffer service in luxury transfers by cars arranged by Emirates.
- Want to see the Boeing 777 without moving? Check out the Emirates website to enjoy a 3D virtual tour of the luxurious plane.

INTRODUCTION

For tourism to flourish in any destination, an important factor is the accessibility of a destination. Whenever any visitor plans to travel to a destination for his/her holiday vacation, he/she thinks of travelling only to those destinations that are easily reachable or approachable through different modes of transportation. In other words, destinations that are better connected by different modes of transportation are the first choice of a traveller as compared to those destinations that are difficult to reach. The tourist footfall in a destination increases as its connectivity with other destinations increases. Thus, transportation forms an integral part of the tourism sector. In other words, we may say that transportation is the lifeline of the tourism industry.

As accessibility of destinations evolves and develops, the tourist arrival increases. In other words, we may say that accessibility is an indicator for increased tourism receipts to a country. Thus, we may say that transportation and tourism have a cause and effect relationship.

Transportation systems refer to the modes or means by which passengers are transferred from one point to another. In the tourism sector, the tourist leaves his/her home for another destination to experience tourism or perform tourism activity. Here, his/her home is the point of departure and another destination is the point of arrival. Thus, the tourist uses a means of transportation from his/her point of departure to reach the point of arrival and back. He/she also uses the means of transportation to discover the different attractions within a destination.

As the tourism sector has dynamically evolved becoming one of the important sectors of the economy, the means of transportation are also evolving. In fact, new modes of transportation have evolved to become a revolutionary way to travel to a destination. New safety features and technological advancements are being radically incorporated in the transportation systems to make them safer and user-friendly for the travellers.

It is important for a destination to have airports, runways, well-connected roads and highways, rail links, railway stations, bus stands, bus stations and the other required infrastructure for transportation. It is imperative for the transportation authority to not only construct a new infrastructure of transportation but also maintain the existing transportation systems.

TRANSPORTATION AS A TOURISM PRODUCT

Today, with the rapid development in the transportation sector, many means of transportation have become stand-alone attractions in themselves. Tourists look forward to using these unique transportation systems to enhance their travel experience and contribute to the local economy. In fact, many transportation systems of the world showcase and market themselves as an experiential tourism product.

Rickshaw rides, trams, animal safaris and cable car rides are some attractive modes of transportation that tourists want to experience when they visit a destination. Few transportation systems of the world are the preserved heritage of the countries. Trains such as *Palace on Wheels in India, Maharajas' Express, Kalka–Shimla toy train* and *Darjeeling Himalayan Train of India* and *Puffing Billy*

Heritage train of Australia are few examples of preserved heritage of the countries. Likewise, Singapore Airlines and Emirates and many other similar airlines market themselves as unique experiential products. Similarly, when tourists visit Chandni Chowk, they are excited to experience the cycle rickshaw ride.

FACTORS AFFECTING THE CHOICE OF TRANSPORTATION

While choosing to travel by a means of transportation, the following factors may be considered by a traveller.

Safety

Safety is the top priority for a traveller. Many travellers who are extra cautious may choose the safest mode of transportation while planning to travel to a destination. Generally speaking, air travel is the safest mode of transportation as the number of accidents that occur on flights are the least. Similarly, many travellers may not be comfortable travelling by road due to the fear of accidents. Therefore, they may choose travelling by train which they may consider to be a safer option. However, this would always depend upon an individual's perception of safety. A traveller may use a mode of transportation according to his/her own perception of safety. For many travellers, travelling by ships or yachts may not be a very safe option to try. They may, therefore, refrain themselves from using this mode of transportation.

However, few safety measures also need to be exercised by a traveller while using the modes of transportation. Wearing seat belts, life jackets while taking water rides, not walking inside the moving vehicle such as cable car, boats and coaches, driving slow and using helmets while biking and learning about the emergency procedures that may be needed in case of emergency landings are some of the ways that travellers can ensure their safety while using the various modes of transportation.

Comfort

An important criterion when a traveller thinks of using a means of transportation is the comfort that a traveller feels while using a mode of transportation. Comfort may be defined by the least time to reach a destination with least botheration. The comforting factors within a mode of transportation may include the comfort of chairs, sleeping facility, facilities for food and beverages, ease of navigation and so on. For long distances, few people may prefer travelling by air as it may mean taking less time to reach a destination that reduces the discomfort of travelling by train or by sea that may take hours or sometimes even days together to reach the same destination. Likewise, for covering a shorter distance, many travellers may feel more comfortable travelling by train, while some may be more comfortable travelling by a private taxi. Thus, based on their perception, comfort may mean different to different travellers.

Comfort may also refer to the ease of using a mode of transportation with minimum effort. While using the public modes of transportation in foreign countries, travellers must learn the ways of using buses, trams, trains and so on. As in most of the transportation systems, the ticket system has been replaced by smart cards, travellers must know how to use the smart cards, how to top up the cards, recharge them and so on. They may buy smart cards online or from designated places/stations and recharge them online. While using a mode of transportation, the travellers must know where to touch the card in the bus or the train station. It is important to familiarize oneself with the usage of modes of transportation before using them.

Time

A traveller may choose a kind of transportation depending upon the time he/she may have in his/her hand to travel to a destination. If he/she wants to reach a destination far from his/her point of origin that may be accessible by air at the earliest, he/she may prefer to travel by a flight rather than by a train. However, while travelling by air, the traveller must keep in mind the reporting time to reach, that is, 2–3 hours prior depending upon whether one has a domestic or an international flight and the time required to reach the airport. However, if a place is in close proximity from one's point of origin, the traveller may plan his/her travel by a taxi or his/her own car that may take less time to reach a place.

Distance

Distance is another major factor to be considered while choosing a mode of transportation. For places that are quite at a distance, for example, travelling between continents, travelling by air is the only fastest option unlike sea travel that may be very time-consuming. Sometimes, travelling by air is the only option available. Travelling by train is also an ideal option for travellers to cover reasonable far-off distances. However, some travellers may also prefer to travel by road for longer distances, especially those who have a passion for self-driving. Although it is a much convenient option for those who want to take stopovers at different points of interests, it can also be a little taxing for the travellers. This may again depend upon one's personal preference and ease of one's comfort.

Budget

Many travellers who are price conscious always compare the prices of travelling by different means of transportation. Generally, such travellers will choose the cheapest mode of transportation to reach their point of arrival. For travellers who have flexible travel plans, they may plan their travel according to the dates when the fares of flights are the cheapest.

However, for many travellers, budget is not a constraint. For them, the comfort and experience of travelling are more important than the price of travelling. For example, travelling by luxury train, Maharajas' Express, is an experience of its own kind. Likewise, travelling by cruises like Royal Caribbean Cruises is another unmatchable experience that a traveller may not like to trade off with any budget constraints.

Days and Timing of Operation

It is very important for the traveller to check the timing of operation of the mode of transportation. The vehicle should be operating on the day of departure and arrival as per the travel plans of the traveller. Moreover, its timing should match with the timings that the traveller is planning to leave his/her destination. Travellers who have flexible timings may travel by air or train, otherwise they may hire a car or drive down to reach their destination if they want to leave for a destination at a scheduled time that suits them. However, this is only valid for the shorter distances where the traveller can travel by road.

Number of Passengers Travelling

While choosing a mode of transportation, a traveller may also check the total number of travellers who are travelling and the viable option that may work for him/her depending upon the best deal that he/she may get on the mode of transportation. For example, for a family of five members while travelling on a domestic sector from Delhi to Dehradun, the travellers may compare the price of travelling by air vis-à-vis travelling by a taxi. The cheaper option may be the first choice for such travellers. This will also depend upon the capacity of the vehicle to accommodate the maximum number of passengers without compromising on the safety of passengers.

Health Issues

Many travellers have health issues associated with different modes of transportation. Some travellers who have air sickness do not prefer to travel by air. If a place is accessible through a rail network or road, he/she may opt for that option. Likewise, many travellers may have motion sickness while travelling by road. Such travellers may not prefer travelling by cars or taxis.

THINGS TO KNOW BEFORE CHOOSING ANY MODE OF TRANSPORTATION

Before choosing ay mode of transportation, the traveller must know about the following:

- Different classes of travel in the mode of transportation, if any.

- Facilities in the mode of transportation such as Wi-Fi and mobile charging points.
- Operational timing of the mode of transportation.
- Days of operation of the mode of transportation.
- Routes on which it operates.
- Kind of clothing suitable for the mode of transportation, for example, in biking tours, tight clothes should be avoided. Likewise, for horseback tours, the travellers should wear hard hats.

KINDS OF TRANSPORTATION

There are different kinds of transportation systems of the world. Every mode of transportation has its own advantages and disadvantages. This may also depend upon the perception of travellers.

Now, let us have a discussion on each of the transportation systems of the world popularly used by the travellers while visiting destinations.

Air Transportation

International air transportation and international tourism share a powerful synergy. Even the remote destinations that have developed an efficient network of air transportation have enabled themselves to be considered as tourist destinations. Even until today, most destinations of the world are almost completely dependent on air transportation for inflow of tourists within the country.

Air transportation is the fastest means to cover longer distances where even the distance between the continents can be covered within hours. Travelling by air is an experience one of a kind. The feeling of being in the clouds can give an adrenaline rush to a traveller. Following are the modes of air transportation.

Travelling by Airlines

Airlines are one of the most preferred modes of transportation by travellers who want to experience convenience and save upon time to cover the long distances in the shortest period of time. Especially while travelling through continents and countries, sometimes travelling by air is the only option. Even if the countries are accessible through the other modes of transportation, they may be very time-consuming and may not suit the traveller as today he/she is more time-starved than ever before. In fact, airlines are considered as the main mode for international tourism.

Airlines now have become an experiential tourism product where tourists travel to experience the hospitality, luxury, comfort and pleasant in-flight services. Tourists prefer to fly with those airlines that offer excellent customer service. The airlines business is continuously becoming competitive with deregulation paving the way for the new competition. Different airlines are positioning and differentiating themselves in unique ways with their USPs to yield the best returns. People may choose to travel with FSCs or low-cost carriers LCCs depending upon their budgets and the distance between the destinations. The visitor traffic has phenomenally increased in the last decade in most of the travel destinations due to the emergence of LCCs. Catering to different markets of consumers, these LCCs primarily target fare-conscious leisure and business travellers and cater to those small airports neglected by big competitors. LCCs also offer flights at high frequency that supports increased tourist traffic at a destination.

Scheduled airline carriers refer to those flights that operate according to a published timetable with regular or frequent flights on fixed routes and are open to direct booking by the public. Non-scheduled flights, also referred to as charter flights, are generally reserved by tour companies and offered to the passengers as a part of the package. They may also be chartered/rented by anyone who can pay for the entire aircraft along with the crew. These may be called private charters which do not have a regular airline routing. Privacy, luxury, flexibility in choosing the timing and destination of flying according to their need, convenience and comfort are the main reasons for hiring of charter planes by travellers. The only deterring factor for travellers in hiring the charter flights is the huge cost involved that is charged generally per hour along with fuel surcharges and other fees.

Most of the world airlines or total air tourist traffic, that accounts for approximately 290 passenger and cargo airlines, is represented by the trade association that formulates civil aviation policies, resolves issues, and ensures a safe, secure and sustainable air transportation industry. The association that registers both scheduled and non-scheduled air services is IATA.

Travellers may book their flight tickets through travel agents or may book on their own through metasearch engines such as *Skyscanner, Kayak* and *Google Flights* or various OTAs such as *Travelocity, Expedia, Priceline* and *Agoda. Recently, Amazon in India has also launched the domestic flight bookings in collaboration with Cleartrip.*

Travelling by Helicopter

For many tourists travelling by helicopter is an attraction. Many destinations of India such as *Kerala, Andhra Pradesh, Maharashtra* and *Tamil Nadu* are promoting heli-tourism that encourages tourists to travel to the destination by a helicopter. Hilly areas such as *Northeast India* and the *Himalayas* that are not easily accessible are increasingly being promoted as heli-tourism destinations. Also, for travellers for whom mobility may be an issue, travelling by helicopter is an ideal choice to reach places at high altitudes. *Vaishno Devi Shrine in J&K* and *Hemkund Sahib in Uttarakhand* are few examples where pilgrims have the option of travelling through helicopters due to their difficult terrains. *Pawan Hans* is the national helicopter carrier in India. With the fleet of more than 50 helicopters, the helicopter service provider of the Government of India is primarily responsible for all helicopter operations within India.

Many destinations promote a *helicopter joyride* that gives an opportunity to the traveller to enjoy the aerial bird's-eye view of the destination and, thus, helps in increasing the tourist footfall. It doubles the joy of the traveller to enjoy the thrill of flying and exploring a city through helicopter rides. *A few examples of city helicopter rides are the Delhi helicopter ride, Mumbai helicopter ride famous for the most amazing skyline view, Joy Ride Gangtok Aerial View, Sydney city helicopter ride and Dubai helicopter tour.* Some of the other famous rides worth taking on a helicopter are as follows:

- The Grand Canyon helicopter ride
- The Great Barrier Reef, Australia
- Niagara Falls, New York, USA
- Fox Glacier, New Zealand
- Victoria Falls, Africa

Cable Car Rides

Another epic piece of engineering that is a great way to soar in the high skies and discover the iconic city settings is the cable car ride also called the gondola ride at many places. In cable cars, one can get to see an unbeatable aerial view of the places around. One can watch breathtaking views, gushing waterfalls, snow-clad mountains, 360-degree panoramic views and most beautiful sceneries with the see-through glass surrounding the cable car. Travelling on a cable car being suspended at a very high altitude above the sea level may give a scary feeling to the tourists, but at the same time, is very thrilling. Some of the famous world cable car rides are as follows:

- Cable car ride in Mt Titlis, Engelberg (world's first revolving cable car called Rotair)
- Table Mountain Aerial Cableway, South Africa
- Genting Skyway, Malaysia
- Cable cars in San Francisco, USA
- Cable car ride in Sentosa Island, Singapore
- Gondola Ride in Gulmarg and Patnitop, J&K, India

Water Transportation

One of the oldest modes of transportation is water transportation. The sea and rivers have always attracted the attention of travellers. The first intercontinental travel during older times was only possible through sea travel. Navigating through the waters can be a unique experience for a traveller. Many destinations of the world are promoting nautical tourism that is being increasingly seen as an important segment of the tourism trade. *As nautical tourism is a big business, it focuses on promoting water travel with water activities, especially during summers.* For many tourists who love spending vacations in the waters, sailing is an ideal choice.

Now let us discuss the different kinds of water transportation used by a tourist.

Ocean Cruises

One of the most 'extraordinary' and a 'stand-alone experience' that makes travellers sense awe and leaves them spellbound is spending their vacation travelling in a cruise. Today, cruising is a key thrust area and it is increasingly being marketed as an 'experiential travel tourism product'. *World's finest luxury can be experienced in cruises.* Cruises are large vessels that transport passengers from one point to another. A traveller thinking of spending an extravagant vacation would think of spending a vacation at cruises. Guests get spoilt for choices onboard. All kinds of facilities that a traveller can think of on a holiday, for example, swimming pools, multi-cuisine restaurants, spas, ice rinks, gyms, golf course, badminton court and so on can be found at cruises. The best part about cruising is that every morning travellers wake up to the new location, which is an experience of its own kind. The travellers may join the ship at the port and then go for *shore excursions* during the day led by knowledgeable guides. The reservations for shore excursions may be made in advance.

Many cruise companies market themselves for different segments of cruises. Many honeymoon couples and families spend their vacation in cruises enjoying the scenic views of the seas. In fact, cruises are the new venue for extravagant family celebrations such as weddings and anniversaries. They are also one of the most sought choices for corporate incentive travel. Many travellers may also opt for the *fly-cruise holiday* that includes flying to the country from where the cruise departs. This option gives the travellers an opportunity and flexibility to explore another destination at their own pace as they may customize their holiday and choose to arrive at the location a week or two before the cruise departure date or either extend their stay on land after the completion of the cruise trip. In both the arrangements, they have enough time to explore the destination to its fullest.

Most of the world's popular cruises are from North America.

The leading destinations for cruises are as follows:

- The Caribbean
- The Mediterranean
- Northern Europe
- Australia/New Zealand
- Alaska
- Asia
- Greenland
- Galapágos Island
- Antarctica

Some of the leading cruise companies of the world are as follows:

- Royal Caribbean International
- Norwegian Cruise Line
- Disney Cruise Line
- Princess Cruises

- Cunard
- Viking Ocean Cruises
- Star Cruises
- MSC Cruises
- Dream Cruises

India has also recently joined the bandwagon of cruise liners by launching its first premium cruise liner 'Karnika' from Mumbai.

River Cruises

These are other popular modes of water transportation. River ships are comparatively smaller in size as compared to ocean cruises and therefore can carry fewer passengers. They may have basic facilities as compared to a large cruise ship. For example, *while cruising through the river in Singapore, pre-recorded commentary runs onboard that unfolds the different facets of Singapore along with the interesting facts on scenic points that the travellers may be passing by.*

Some of the other famous river cruises that can be experienced in different rivers of the world are as follows:

- Thames River, London
- Yangtze River Cruise, China
- Seine River, Paris
- Brahmaputra River, Assam
- Amsterdam cruise
- Chicago River, Chicago

Ferries

Ferry on River Thames, London

Travellers also prefer to travel on ferries that are vessels to carry passengers and cargo in the small water bodies like river waters. Ferries are popular among tourists for day excursions. For example, *while visiting Goa, many travellers take ferry rides to Mandovi river.* They  enjoy gala dinner, DJ night, Goan cuisine and local drinks on ferries. Some other famous day tours on ferries are:

- The Staten Island Ferry in the USA between Manhattan and Staten Island in New York passing through the Statue of Liberty

- Ferry on Australia Sydney Harbour
- Day boat glass ferries at Alaska
- Ferry ride from Port Blair to Havelock Islands, Andaman and Nicobar Islands

Hovercraft

A hovercraft is a boat which operates on water. It may travel on land, ice, mud and other surfaces. It is also called the air-cushion vehicle. It is considered as a safer option than boats. To increase the length of stay at a destination, it a much-needed tourism injection introduced by many destinations. It is manned by a pilot. Some of the famous hovercraft rides can be experienced in the following waterbodies:

- Puri Beach, Puri, Odisha, India
- RK Beach, Visakhapatnam, India
- Lake Pukaki, New Zealand

Boats

Tourists also use boats to move from one point to another. Many interesting activities take place on boat tours that are world-famous. For example, *the snake boat race of Kerala is quite popular among tourists, where race competitions are organized among travellers and locals in snake boats.*

Some of the famous boat tours in the world are as follows:

- Maid of the Mist, Niagara Falls, USA
- Rhine Falls, Switzerland
- Boat ride at Ganga Ghats, Varanasi, India
- Boat ride at Kumarakom Backwaters, India (wooden boats in Kerala are called *kettuvalom*)
- Boat ride at Dal Lake, Srinagar, J&K, India (wooden decorated boats are called *shikara*)
- Boat ride at Nakki Lake, Mount Abu, India
- Boat ride at Naini Lake, Nainital, India

Boat Tour at a Lake in Boston, USA

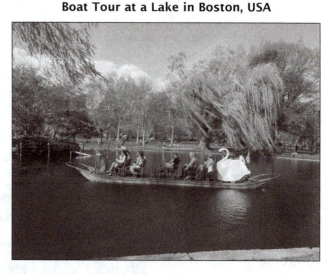

Yachts

Chartering yachts for a holiday is a luxurious and unforgettable getaway for many tourists. One may explore the exotic coastlines and cruise through the crystal-clear waters in the beaches of the world, pass through the fishing villages, enjoy the breathtaking sceneries, dock in any port and then explore the cities surrounded by seas. One can also enjoy the exciting onshore activities, water activities and explore the bays. One can also anchor yachts near one of the islets and enjoy in seas.

A yacht is a watercraft used for pleasure or sports. For yacht to operate, destinations must be sailor friendly. Many travellers book private yacht charters to sail in the seas. Safety in such cases is top priority for the tourists. Weather conditions, sailing conditions and required infrastructures are some of the important factors while considering sailing in the yachts.

Sailing on yachts may appear to be very comfortable for the sailing tourists, which gives them independence and ensures the tourists' privacy unlike in cruises where they have to share the spaces with other tourists.

Perfect destinations for yacht charter holiday are as follows:

- Monaco
- Croatia
- Sicily
- Thailand
- French Riveria
- Fiji
- British Virgin Islands
- The Bahamas

Water Taxi

It is also called a water bus that transports passengers from one point to another. It is a watercraft that may be used for both private and public transportation. The water taxis have a fixed schedule and fixed stops like a taxi. Some of the famous water taxi tours in the world may be experienced in the following places:

- Water taxi in Venice
- Water taxi in Dubai
- Water taxi to Fort Lauderdale in Florida

Gondola Ride

Many destinations of the world are famous for narrow canals where travelling is possible only through boats called 'gondolas'. *Gondolas are flat-bottomed rowboats that are quite popular in Venice.*

These gondolas carry a fixed number of tourists for a fixed time at a fixed price. Taking a gondola ride at Venice can be an experience of a lifetime for a traveller. There are *oarsmen also called gondoliers* who oar the gondola and sail it through the canals. One may book a gondola ride online or near the gondola ride where there is an office that books and makes reservations for the tourists who are interested in taking the ride.

SUMMARY

Transportation is an important component of the tourism industry. A traveller has a myriad of choices to choose from the modes of transportation while planning his/her holiday. Transportation is not only a medium for getting transported from one point to another, but it is also an experience in itself that is an important part of a traveller's overall experience. The journey is as important as the destination. The traveller may consider a number of factors while choosing transportation. A traveller may choose to travel by air, water, road or rail transportation. Whatever mode of transportation he/she may choose for his/her journey, he/she must be provided with comfort and ease of travelling. It defines his/her overall impression of a holiday.

ACTIVITIES

Activity 1

Identify the countries to which the following airlines belong to:

- KLM
- Emirates
- Qantas
- AirAsia
- Cathay Pacific
- British Airways
- United Airlines

Activity 2

Think of starting your own transport company. Which business of transportation would you propose? Justify your answer with valid reasons. Also, work out in detail the technical modalities involved in setting up a transport business.

Accessibility: Part II

LEARNING OBJECTIVES

The given chapter shall clarify the following:

- What are the modes of road transportation?
- What are the other kinds of land transportation?
- What is rail transportation?

LONDON TUBE: FIRST-EVER UNDERGROUND METRO!

- World's first underground metro, London Tube or London Underground is a public rapid-transit system, serving the London region and some parts of the UK.
- Opened in 1863, London Tube has carried about 117.39 million passengers in 2019–2020.
- Now, the transit has air-conditioned carriages, intermittent Wi-Fi signal and convenient connectivity, which makes the overall journey of passengers very comfortable.
- This transit system has about 270 stations and 250 miles (400 km) of rail track.
- Oyster cards are used by metro users in London who prefer using contactless payment method.
- If you are planning to visit London to do some sightseeing and visit some of the London's best attractions, use a London Pass.

INTRODUCTION

Road transportation is one of the very important means of transportation for the travellers. Many travellers prefer to travel to destinations by road with good connectivity. The following modes of road transportation may be used by the travellers.

Own Car

Many travellers are comfortable driving fairly long distances that are well connected by roads. Thus, they may visit a destination using their own private vehicles. Construction of highways and drive-through restaurants and wayside amenities like public conveniences have made travelling very comfortable for the travellers choosing to travel by road. However, this option is generally exercised by those travellers who have a passion for driving and do not suffer from any motion sickness while travelling by car. They may feel more independent and comfortable in an unknown destination with their own private car that may be available round the clock at their discretion during their holiday.

Taxis

Many travellers who are not comfortable driving on their own or are not aware of the routes may contact the local transporters to give them a chauffeur with a car. Chauffeur-driven cars may be from compact cars to SUVs or luxury cars. Many tourists may also book a package through a travel company that also arranges chauffeur-driven cars for the clients for the entire holiday duration along with other travel arrangements. Many travel companies also give an option to the tourists to book taxis online through their website or through their app like *MakeMyTrip*.

Also, with the advent of new mobile taxi apps, many travellers book their ride on taxis through the apps on their smartphones. Taxi apps such as *Uber, Ola, Savaari* and *Meru* are widely used by travellers, especially within the cities and sometimes for travelling between the destinations that are easily accessible. The travellers are charged according to the distance or the number of kilometres covered.

Car Rentals

Drive tourism is trending among travellers. Many travellers prefer to explore destinations on their own by renting an automobile and driving it to visit the interiors of a destination. With the advent of technology and the ease of using the global positioning system (GPS) for navigating the destinations, travellers are increasingly hiring cars when they reach a destination. One can either book online the kind of car one wants through a car rental company or either book the car on reaching the country. Many car rental companies have counters of their own at the airports. The traveller can look for the best deals on the type of car available along with fuel charges and the car insurance, which the traveller can compare with other car rental companies and finally book through the car rental company where he/she finds the deal most suitable according to his/her decided budget.

Using the car rental for exploring the destinations gives the traveller freedom to travel as and when he/she wants. He/she can be on an auto mode without any timebound pressure hanging on him/her. The traveller has the flexibility of altering his/her plans according to his/her choice. For example, if a traveller is feeling unwell and he/she wants to take a day's break, he/she may decide to stay back as he/she does not have a prior booking of any mode of transportation.

Also, it allows the traveller an opportunity to visit the interiors of a city as he/she has the car at his/her own discretion and at his/her own pace. He/she can enjoy the countryside views that may come in his/her way. Countries such as *Scotland*, *Spain* and *New Zealand* can be best experienced through driving down the most breathtaking views of the nature that one crosses by passing through the interiors of the destinations.

Another advantage of travelling by car is that the traveller has no problem of the luggage. The luggage can be transferred from one point to another without any issue of weight.

Some of the examples of car rentals companies of the world include *Enterprise, Avis, Hertz, Budget, National, Alamo, Dollar, Fox, Europcar* and so on. Some of the popular car rental services popping up in India are *Zoomcar, SelfDrive, Justride, Carzonrent, Bookmycab, Savaari* and so on.

Coach

Coaches are very comfortable for long distances when people are travelling together in groups for sightseeing tours. Travellers can travel within the city, between states, regions and countries by a coach. Travelling together in groups on the coaches can be more fun and frolic.

Coaches are basically operated by either coach operators or travel agent/tour operator who operates package tours or local tours. Multiple attractions are covered in a day. Some tours may be panoramic where the driver does not stop at an attraction but just passes by important points of interest giving passing commentary on attractions. However, sometimes coaches may stop for a few minutes for a *photo stopover*. However, in regular sightseeing tours, coaches may stop at designated parking spaces of the attractions being visited.

Coaches come in different sizes according to the number of passengers they can accommodate and in different makes. Many famous coach companies such as *Mercedes Benz* and *Volvo* offer coaches which are very safe, luxurious and comfortable to travel in. Many coach operators such as *Cosmos* and *Globus* offer escorted package tours in Europe, America and some other parts of the world. Within Europe as countries are in close proximity, tourists may travel by coach from one country to another. They may pass through the cross-border controls of the country and get their passports stamped during entry and exit points. Likewise, travellers may travel from *Singapore to Malaysia* by coach. Similarly, a tourist may travel from *Belfast in Northern Ireland to reach Dublin in the Republic of Ireland* by a coach within two hours operated by a private transporter.

Motor coach operators like Globus may provide the following features:

- Reclining seats with headrests, individual air-conditioning vents and extra legroom
- Sound system

- Daily seat rotation
- Free Wi-Fi
- Video monitors
- Emergency restrooms
- Experienced and professional drivers
- Sustainable travel
- Smoke-free coaches

Hop-on Hop-off Buses

HOHO buses are one of the most popular means of exploring a destination. They are one of the most convenient and economical ways of sightseeing at a destination. Generally, these are open-top double-decker buses that cover all important attractions of a city in one go and run audio recorded commentary for the tourists in different languages. Some buses may have guides while others may have driver-cum-guides giving live commentary to the visitors while passing by the attractions. The open views through the buses while sitting at the double-decker rooftop is a treat to the eyes and a great way to see the bustling city life for the tourists. These buses have a very high frequency of turning up for tourists. Many onboard facilities such as *Wi-Fi, multilingual audio-guided devices, maps* and *guidebooks* may be provided for the tourists.

HOHO buses operate on fixed routes where the bus stops at fixed attractions for a fixed time. While travelling by HOHO buses, the traveller has the flexibility of travelling to as many attractions as possible. A traveller can hop off one bus to see an attraction of his/her choice and then hop on another bus to get to the next attraction with the same ticket or the pass. These buses generally operate throughout the day.

The HOHO buses are generally operated by the government authorities. The travellers can avail discounts and passes depending upon the number of days that a traveller has for sight-seeing and the number of passengers travelling together in a group. The tourists may choose a pass ranging from one to three days and enjoy the unlimited hop-on and hop-off.

Some of the popular HOHO buses are as follows:

- HOHO buses in Delhi, India
- HOHO buses in London
- HOHO buses in Singapore
- HOHO buses in Boston
- HOHO buses in Barcelona

Buses

Using public buses is the best way to explore a city. Many countries of the world have excellent transportation system where the travellers buy tickets or visitor passes to explore the city by bus. Visitor passes always have special deals for the tourists who are there for a few days at the destination to explore it. Buses allow the travellers to have a panoramic view of the destination. The tourists may visit different attractions on a bus. However, the traveller must know the timings of operation of buses and the bus numbers that may be in the timetables published by the bus authorities, which may take the tourists to the nearest point of an attraction. Moreover, travelling through buses is generally an economical option for travellers as compared to other modes of transportation.

The online bus ticket reservations have been revolutionized by redBus, the largest online community of bus travellers in the world connecting over 2,300 bus operators. A traveller may make his/her bookings through redBus mobile app or through the website. redBus is now owned by the *Ibibo travel group.*

Trams

Another interesting way to explore the cities is taking the trams and visiting the cities. Trams operate on their laid tracks using electric power. Many countries of the world operate trams that are very interesting rides. Some of the famous tram systems of the world are in *Kolkata, India; Melbourne, Australia;* and *San Francisco, USA.* Many countries also have free tram zones where there is no ticket for using the trams. For example, *in Melbourne, Australia, few areas have been designated as free-tram zones where the travellers are not required to buy the tickets.*

Using these public transportation systems, a tourist gets the feel of living like a local of the destination. He/she also gets an opportunity to peep into the local life of the commuting passengers watching those striking conversations, observing their office timings and so on. Being on these transportation systems gives an opportunity to the traveller to get an insider's perspective.

One of the must-try trams is in Melbourne, Australia, which has a restaurant inside it, the Colonial Tramcar Restaurant. The traveller can have a delightful luxurious dining experience relishing the sumptuous local Australian delicacies on a moving restaurant tram that has a vintage decor.

OTHER MODES OF LAND TRANSPORTATION

Some other modes of land transportation used by tourists are as follows.

Animal Safaris

Taking a ride on animals is a very interesting activity. In earlier times, animals were used to transport passengers and goods from one point to another. Some of the famous animal rides are as follows:

- Tonga rides in Agra, India
- Camel rides in Dubai, the UAE
- Elephant ride in Kerala, India
- Yak safari in Ladakh, India
- Dog-sledding in Alaska, USA, and Tromsø, Norway

- Horse carriage rides—the Royal Carriage Tour, Victoria, Australia; Central Park Carriage Rides, New York, USA; Horse carriage ride near Gateway of India, Mumbai

Jeep Safaris

The Jeep safaris are also very popular among the tourists who want to explore the hidden treasures of nature. For adventure enthusiasts who may be planning to explore the rugged terrains or beautiful countryside, driving on their own can be a very thrilling and challenging experience on Jeeps. In Jeep safaris, the travellers have the flexibility of taking stopovers wherever they want. Jeep safaris are also common for exploring wildlife in national parks and wildlife sanctuaries where the tourists are escorted in Jeeps by a tour guide and the drivers who are experts in driving in jungles. Some of the famous Jeep safari worth taking are as follows:

- Desert safari, Dubai, the UAE
- Jim Corbett National Park, India
- Jeep safaris in Tanzania
- Jeep safari in Amber Fort, Rajasthan, India
- Jungle safari in Ranthambore, Rajasthan, India
- Jeep safari in Ladakh, India
- Jeep safari in Lahaul and Spiti, Himachal Pradesh, India

Palanquins

Palanquins are generally used for senior citizens and people with special abilities for whom mobility is an issue. Palanquins are a very common mode of transportation especially at pilgrimage places in India where the older people are made to sit inside a palanquin and then they are carried from one point to another by two people who carry the burden of the passenger sitting in the palanquin on their shoulders. Some of the places where palanquins are still used are as follows:

- Amarnath Yatra, Pahalgam, J&K, India
- Vaishno Devi, J&K, India
- Kedarnath, Uttarakhand, India

Biking and Motor Biking

Biking is another mode of transportation popular among travellers to explore the interiors of a city. There are designated biking stands, especially near public transportation systems, public spaces or attractions from where the travellers can hire bikes per hour on payment basis. Biking allows the travellers to get an insider's view of a city. Besides helping the tourists to stay fit during their vacation, it allows them to explore the interiors of a destination thoroughly and also discover the countryside views. For cycling buffs, the bumpy rides across the rugged terrains are experiences and adventure that such travellers are looking for.

Some of the famous biking destinations are as follows:

- Amsterdam, the Netherlands (cycling capital of the world)
- Christ Church, New Zealand
- Pyrenees cycle tours, France
- Girona and Costa Brava cycle tours
- Mountain biking tours in Sikkim and Garhwal, India

Many travellers also go for mountain biking expeditions in India to paddle across the rugged terrains. Motorbiking is also opted by many tourists, especially to explore mountains. *Ladakh and Himachal Pradesh in India are famous destinations among foreigners and domestic tourists for motor biking.*

Many travel companies offer travel packages to destinations that may be explored through bikes or motorbikes, especially for travellers seeking adventure and offbeat experiences.

Rickshaw Rides

These are tourist attractions in themselves. Travellers, especially from other countries, enjoy these rides that are quite popular in India. These rickshaws are modified versions of bicycles with a cabin at the back for two people to be seated and a driver riding on it. Sometimes they may be decorated to look aesthetically more beautiful so as to attract the tourists. Seeing the city life sitting on a rickshaw or tuk tuk and passing by the narrow roads can be a unique experience for the tourists. For example, *Chandni Chowk in India* is very popular for its rickshaw rides, especially among the foreign tourist. Likewise, *trishaw in Melaka* decorated with flashing lights, bright flowers, souvenirs and flags is an attraction in itself for the tourists to experience.

RAIL TRANSPORTATION

The mode of railways has created massive strides in the tourism industry. Lakhs of travellers prefer to travel by railways. Convenience, safety, affordability and the opportunity to witness the breathtaking scenic views of the countryside are the reasons for travellers preferring to travel by this mode of transportation. In India, this is the most popular mode of transportation for travelling across the length and breadth of the country with more than 13 million passengers travelling daily through railways. *The formation of IRCTC by the Indian Railways has been instrumental in spurring the 'rail tourism' in the country along with the entire catering of railways.* Working in collaboration under the aegis of the PPP model, the organization aims at working in association with state tourism departments, tour operators, transporters, hoteliers and so on to promote rail tourism in the country. *IRCTC is the tourism arm of the Indian Railways.* It is a public sector enterprise under the Ministry of Railways that provides a complete range of travel and tourism services along with the hospitality to rail passengers. It is responsible for feeding millions of travellers pursuing their journey by the Indian Railways. *It is also considered as one of the world's largest e-commerce portals with a number of rail tourism products and a catering service also. It runs many special trains such as Maharajas' Express and the Buddhist train Mahaparinirvan Express.*

To promote tourism through trains, various packages for domestic destinations are offered for leisure destinations and pilgrimage destinations including those of *Bharat Darshan* packages that cover pan-India tours. Recently, packages are also being marketed by IRCTC for visiting international destinations.

Many special trains have been launched for promoting rail tourism. Some of these include the following.

Tourist Trains

- Statue of Unity train (originates from Pune)
- Vande Bharat Express (India's first semi-high-speed train that runs between Delhi and Varanasi)

Luxury Heritage Trains

- Maharajas' Express (awarded 'world's leading luxury train' from 2012–2018)
- Fairy Queen Express (oldest rolling locomotive of the world that started in 1855)
- Royal Rajasthan on Wheels
- Palace on Wheels
- Royal Orient Train
- The Deccan Odyssey
- Golden Chariot

Pilgrimage Trains

- Shri Ramayana Express (covering the holy destinations associated with the life of Lord Rama)
- Buddha Express Special Tourist Train
- Mahaparinirvan Express (covers the Buddhist circuit)

Hill Trains

- The Joyride for Darjeeling Himalayan Train, Darjeeling, India
- Kalka–Shimla Railway (conferred world heritage status by UNESCO in 2008 and recorded as the greatest narrow-gauge engineering in India)

- Kangara Valley Railway
- Matheran Hill Railway

Some of the worth-taking train rides in the world are as follows:

- Scenic Railway, the Blue Mountains, Sydney, Australia (world's steepest passenger railway at 52-degree inclination)
- The Toy train in Vaduz, Liechtenstein, Europe
- The Puffing Billy train

The Puffing Billy Train, Melbourne

in Victoria, Australia (In this train, the station master gives a running commentary on the importance and uniqueness of this train as it is Australia's premium steam railway that has been given an old fashion look that adds to the thrill of the guests. While passing through the scenic landscapes, the station master fabricates a story and fills it with humour and narrates it to the travellers that leaves the travellers spellbound)

Some of the best high-speed trains and rail networks of the world are as follows:

- Bullet train, Japan
- Maglev, China
- Eurail, Europe
- BritRail, Britain
- TGV, France
- Amtrak, USA

SUMMARY

Many travellers may opt for road transportation for visiting destinations. Different modes of road transportation include travelling by own cars, taxis, car rentals, coaches, buses, trams and HOHO buses. Some travellers may travel by other modes of land transportation through animal safaris, Jeep safaris, palanquins, rickshaw rides, biking and motorbiking and so on. Rail transportation is one of the most preferred modes of transportation by many travellers. In India, IRCTC promotes rail tourism by running many special trains. Heritage trains and toy trains are promoted as tourism products by railway authorities in India.

ACTIVITIES

Activity 1

Identify any five major heritage trains of your country and discuss the destinations they travel to.

Activity 2

Identify the transportation systems that you would use while travelling within the following destinations as a first-time traveller. Give reasons as to why you would choose that means of transportation.

- Venice
- Scotland
- Melbourne
- Singapore
- New York
- Shanghai

Activity 3

Identify the airports and major air carriers that fly to the following countries/cities:

- Singapore
- London
- Paris
- The Netherlands
- Thailand
- New York
- Chicago
- Mumbai

Accommodation 14

LEARNING OBJECTIVES

The given chapter shall clarify the following:

- What are the factors that affect a traveller's choice while choosing a kind of accommodation?
- What is a hotel, and what are the various types of hotels?
- What are the various types of rooms in a hotel?

LANGAR: WORLD'S LARGEST COMMUNITY KITCHEN!

- Also called community kitchen in English, langar is a kitchen in gurudwaras (a holy place of worship for Sikhs) offering free vegetarian meals to everyone irrespective of their religion, caste, ethnicity and so on.
- World's largest community kitchen is Guru Ka Langar in Golden Temple, Amritsar, that serves 100,000 people in a day and on an average more than 100 quintal wheat flour, 25 quintal cereals, 10 quintal rice, 5,000 litre milk, 10 quintal sugar and 5 quintal pure ghee are used a day. Isn't that amazing?
- The langar concept was introduced by the founder of Sikhism, Guru Nanak, around 1500 AD, who believed in equality and humanity. The purpose of langar is to spread the virtue of sitting in a community and eating together as it teaches that all humans are equal.
- Langars are also organized by the Sikh community during the time of crises such as floods and earthquakes. The people voluntarily help everyone in need by offering food, shelter and safety to the victims of distress.

- The volunteers who serve in the langars are called *sewadars*. Anybody can volunteer at these langars and help in the day-to-day chores.
- Many city tours in Delhi and Amritsar offer tourists an unforgettable experience where foreigners are taken to gurudwaras to witness the langar and volunteer in the services there. They also get to enjoy the holy *prasad* (a devotional offering made to God) besides learning about the local community.
- Langars are truly an example of excellent hospitality of India!

INTRODUCTION

Stay is an important part of the tourism activity. According to the definition of tourism, a traveller is qualified to be a tourist only if he/she travels for more than 24 hours out of his/her domicile. Therefore, while travelling to a destination, stay is an important component of the tourism phenomenon. The basic need of a traveller while travelling is the need for a shelter in an unknown land. He/she wants a place where he/she can get a bed to sleep and meals to eat. For him/her, finding a shelter to spend a night is the first priority while visiting a destination.

The accommodation industry has evolved over the decades. From hotels to guest houses, tented accommodations to recreational vehicles, the accommodation industry has undergone a dramatic transformation. *Accommodation basically refers to a provision for staying at a place. It may or may not include meals.*

The hospitality and tourism industry go hand in hand. While the tourism practitioners consider the hospitality industry as a part of the tourism industry, the hospitality industry experts consider tourism as a part of the hospitality industry. However, in common parlance, we may consider both the sectors as synonymous sectors that are complimentary and supplementary to each other. Both domains may be considered as each other's backbone that depend on each other for their sustenance.

The hospitality industry is a multi-billion-dollar industry today, which primarily focuses on customer service, comfort, exclusivity and offering world-class amenities. The industry sustains itself on the disposable incomes and leisure time of the guests.

Broadly speaking, the hospitality industry is a service industry that is necessarily experiential-based. Basically, the various businesses and services involved in the provision of accommodation and F&B services to both the tourists (leisure and business tourists) and the locals of a destination who want to enjoy and experience luxury during their leisure time come within the ambit of the hospitality industry. In simple words, it is combination of lodging/accommodation, and F&B services.

Travellers require not only a place to stay, but they also need food and beverages to sustain themselves when they travel to another destination. This places the F&B industry in a strategic position to cater to the taste palettes of different international travellers visiting the country. In fact, there is a whole gamut of gourmet travellers primarily visiting destinations for different culinary experiences. This may be referred to as food tourism, gastronomical tourism or culinary tourism. Thus, the various establishments primarily engaged in making food, snacks and beverages for consumption of tourists and locals of a destination may be considered as a part of the F&B industry. The F&B industry ranges from a quick-service restaurant, a full-service restaurant, a bistro, a takeaway, tea and coffee shops, cafes to all kinds of catering establishments that may be outdoor catering or industrial catering. It basically involves restaurant management, food management, food presentation and beverages.

Some also consider the entertainment industry as a part of the hospitality industry that comprises the sports and gaming sector, movie or theatres, events, theme parks, cruises, nightclubs, casinos, bars, marinas and so on.

However, in the given chapter, we shall confine our discussions to the first aspect of hospitality industry, that is, the accommodation industry.

When tourists visit a destination, they expect warm hospitality from the service providers and the local community of a destination. Especially, for a country like India, where the ethos of *Atithi Devo Bhava* runs in the Indian traditions and value system, which connotes that the 'the Guest is God', the guests need to be treated most respectfully and with utmost courtesy during their visit to the country. Thus, hospitality industry involves a warm reception of guests by offering them unparallel services more than they expect. It involves a step beyond customer satisfaction, that is, 'customer delight'. It would not be wrong to say that *Indian hospitality is all about pampering and spoiling the choices of the tourists visiting the country.*

Even across the world, hospitality has been redefined from time to time by various international hotel chains such as *Marriott International, Four Seasons Hotels and Resorts, Hyatt Hotels, Hilton Worldwide, Wyndham Worldwide, InterContinental Hotels Group, Choice Hotels, Jin Jiang International, Accor, Best Western* and *Rosewood Hotels and Resorts*, which are known for their exemplary service. The new hotel brands also that have forayed the hospitality industry are millenial-friendly, family-oriented, design-driven and customer-loyal. Luxury resonates with today's travellers when they think of best world hotel chains. Talking in the context of India, some of the famous hotel chains in *India are Oberoi Hotels and Resorts, Taj Hotels, Palaces, Resorts and Safaris; the Leela Palaces, Hotels and Resorts and so on.* though in the past few years India has seen a massive proliferation of international multinational hotel chains entering the hospitality industry.

ACCOMMODATION AS A TOURISM PRODUCT

Accommodation is absolutely one of the most important parts of the hospitality industry that offers a place to stay on a temporary basis for travellers visiting a destination for any reason.

People travelling around the world are ready to spend thousands of dollars per night just to buy a comfortable space to sleep. From inns to hotels and from self-catering apartments to B&B, the today's traveller has a myriad of choices to choose from.

As the new-age traveller has become necessarily experiential in nature, for him/her staying in a different form of accommodation such as underwater hotel, tree-house hotel and ice hotel is an experience in itself to be cherished for a lifetime. Many travellers look for out-of-the-box experiences for staying in a destination. For them, accommodation is an important tourism product in itself. It is an experiential product that the tourists want to have the feel of while away from home. As the traveller stays in an accommodation for a substantial time of his/her total travel, the kind of stay matters to him/her. Many travellers are quality conscious. They want luxurious and exotic stays where they can have a larger-than-life celebration such as a stay in *Burj Al Arab, Dubai* and *Umaid Bhawan, Jodhpur*. However, for some backpackers, basic and modest accommodation is good enough.

FACTORS FOR CHOOSING AN ACCOMMODATION

The factors that a traveller may consider while choosing any kind of accommodation are as follows.

Budget

One of the major factors while choosing an accommodation would be the budget that the traveller is willing to spend on his/her stay during his/her vacation. Depending upon the limit of budget, the traveller may choose an accommodation from a luxurious hotel, a cruise, a castle to a budgeted accommodation like a youth hostel or a B&B inn.

Safety and Security

One of the most important needs of a traveller is to feel safe and secure at the type of accommodation he/she is choosing to stay in, so it should be free from any fear of crime or theft. For travellers who play safe may not like to stay in tented accommodations outdoor or in caravans or self-catering apartments. For them, staying in a hotel may be a safer choice to exercise while choosing an accommodation. However, this perception may vary from person to person.

Comfort

The most important need of a tourist is to feel comfortable at the accommodation. Comfort may mean different to different people. Some may want a cosy stay that may mean a small but a hygienic space with basic amenities, while for some comfort may mean luxurious stay with comfortable beddings, good furniture and soothing decor with facilities such as private swimming pool, spa facility, outdoor facilities and huge spaces within the accommodation.

Level of Social Interaction Required

Many travellers choose accommodation according to their interest for socializing. For tourists who want to interact with people from different cultures, staying in youth hostels may be an ideal option. While some may stay in homestays or B&B inns with the host community to understand their cultures, those looking for privacy may prefer to stay in hotels or self-catering apartments. This depends upon one's requirement for personal space.

Need for Self-esteem

For many travellers staying at a good accommodation is a symbol of status. They want to brag about their experiences to their friends and relatives. For them, staying in a lavish or a decent accommodation may be a kind of their regular lifestyle that they even want to maintain when they go to another destination.

Amenities

Tourists may choose an accommodation depending upon their need for amenities. Facilities may vary from one accommodation to another. For tourists who are backpackers and need the modest amenities may stay in youth hostels, tents, B&B inns and so on. However, travellers looking for a complete range of amenities may prefer to stay in hotels, cruises and so on.

Types of Traveller

The choice of accommodation may vary depending upon the kind of traveller. Business travellers may have their own criteria for choosing an accommodation. For them, an ideal choice may be hotel or apartment hotels. Likewise, for women solo travellers, safety may be a top priority while choosing an accommodation. They may, thus, prefer to stay in hotels where hotels have designated floors only for women travellers with female housekeeping and room service staff to give them a protected environment in a hotel. Tourists with special abilities and senior citizens may also prefer to stay in those accommodation properties that have accessible toilets, ramps and so on to cater to their special needs. Yet youngsters may prefer to stay in a hostel, while a family on a vacation may prefer to stay in a resort.

Need for Novel Experiences

For tourists looking for novel and offbeat experiences, staying in a forest lodge or a caravan may be the first choice, whereas travellers looking for regular experiences and not wanting to try anything new would prefer to stay in a hotel or a guest house.

Level of Self-service

Many travellers do not want to do the household chores such as making food and doing laundry on their own during their vacation. Such travellers may not prefer staying in self-catering apartments, tents and so on. Instead, they may prefer staying in hotels, lodges, guest houses and so on. However, tourists who prefer to work on their own may prefer staying in self-catering apartments, caravans and so on.

A DISCUSSION ON HOTELS AND THEIR TYPES

The most popular and one of the most used kind of accommodations for a traveller is a hotel. Hotels basically cater to both business and leisure travellers who are looking for an overnight stay or long-term stays along with provision of meals. They provide both lodging and boarding for the tourists on a temporary basis. They provide a place for resting, relaxing, having fun and getting pampered while on a vacation.

Hotels may be located in city centres, airports, suburbs, railway stations and so on. Most of the clientele of hotels are business travellers who generally stay for a night. Hotels may offer an array of facilities for travellers based on their star ratings that may range from 1 to 5 star ratings. It has a common reception area, multi-cuisine restaurants, room service, swimming pools, spa facilities, housekeeping services and so on depending upon the category of hotel that one may be staying in.

There are different choices of hotels available for the tourists to choose from. Some of these are as follows.

On the Basis of Location

Hotels may be classified on the basis of locations that are as follows.

Airport Hotels

Hotels located near the airport of a destination generally providing hotel shuttle services are called airport hotels.

Downtown Hotels or Commercial Hotels

Hotels located in the city centre or the heart of a destination preferred by business travellers like *New York Marriott Downtown Hotel in Manhattan* are called downtown hotels.

Suburban Hotels

These are the hotels located in suburbs of a city away from the hustle and bustle of the city. These hotels are generally preferred by travellers looking for tranquillity.

Motels

These are also called motorist hotels which became popular in the USA when travellers initiated self-drive concept by their own cars or rented cars. These hotels are *generally on highways* that provide a resting space for the enervated tourists where they can take an overnight stay to recharge their batteries for continuing their road travel next day. These are generally modest kind of accommodation generally on roadside offering basic amenities such as a parking space, gas and fuel stations and garage.

Resort

Resorts are scattered units of accommodation that are in natural areas/areas of scenic beauty such as beaches, mountains and ski areas that are generally spread over a larger area. They may be single-storey or double-storey buildings. Resorts may have independent cottages that are stand-alone units within the vicinity of nature. These resorts generally cater to the holidaymakers who are looking for rest and relaxation. Resorts offer an array of recreational facilities such as spas, gyms, swimming pools and activities for the relaxation of travellers besides the regular accommodation and meals. Resorts are generally meant for families who are looking for a getaway and planning to stay for a longer duration as compared to hotels where the stay of travellers is generally overnight. Therefore, they are more family-oriented and generally the duration of stay here is more as compared to hotels. However, resorts may also be booked by corporates for business travellers for organizing business meetings, conferences and so on. Many resorts also offer free services such as complimentary water activities and complimentary airport transfers depending upon the kind of package that one may have booked. In short, resorts are destinations within themselves.

Resorts may be classified into the following:

- Seaside resorts
- Ski resorts
- Hill resorts
- Destination resorts
- Spa resorts
- Theme-based resorts
- Health resorts
- Wildlife resorts

Some famous resorts in India are as follows:

- Kumarakom Lake Resort, Kerala
- Banasura Hill Resort, Kerala
- Ananda Spa Resort, Rishikesh
- Shaam-e-Sarhad Village Resort, Kutch, Gujarat
- The Oberoi Vanyavilas, Ranthambore

Floatel

These are luxurious floating hotels that sail in the waters, especially in the high seas. These may be considered as cruises/ocean liners that offer facilities of a 4–5–star category hotel depending upon the budget that one is ready to spend for his/her vacation. Cruises are both a means of transportation and a source of accommodation. Cruises are large ships where passengers have the provision of staying in the sailing cruise itself. The cruise travel is jam-packed with scintillating activities, exquisite cuisines and an opportunity to explore new lands every day. During the daytime, the tourists may visit the 'shore excursions' and during the night they sail in the cruise. A luxury cruise has full facilities for travellers on board, which may include multi-cuisine restaurants, cafes, shopping arenas, ice-skating rinks, golf course, gyms, swimming areas, pool facilities, ball rooms, discotheques, bars and pubs and so on. A tourist can have some incredible moments of his/her life staying at the cruises.

Boatel

These may be referred to hotels on the boat. Here, the traveller can have a unique experience of moving in a water body that may be a lake or a river. Staying in a boatel is a treat for nature buffs. Some of the examples of boatels in India are of the intrinsically carved walnut-wooden house-boats in *Srinagar, Kashmir,* on the Dal Lake, where the tourists can enjoy the impeccable Kashmiri hospitality, Kashmiri cuisine, that is, Wazwan food and witness the passing by *shikara*s (small boats) selling lotus stems while relaxing in the houseboat amidst breath-taking views of the Himalayas. Another example may be of *kettuvallam* in Allepey, Kerala, where the tourists can enjoy navigating through the lush backwaters and lagoons seeing the remote and tranquil locations.

Roatel

These may be referred to as *hotels on wheels* or *rotating hotels*. These may be heritage trains that offer facilities of a 5-star category hotel such as *Maharajas' Express* and *Royal Rajasthan on Wheels*.

On the Basis of Clientele

On the basis of clients staying in the hotel, hotels may be classified as follows.

Business Hotels

Business hotels cater to the corporate clientele who may be CEOs, MDs, directors, middle management, dealers, buyers and businessmen who have come to network, do business or attend a meeting, conference or an exhibition or are on an incentive trip at a destination. Such travellers prefer staying in business hotels that are in proximity to the airport, railway stations or either in the central markets where the connectivity of transportation is good.

Business travellers may require services such as Wi-Fi, table desk, conference rooms, convention centres, LED projectors and interactive digital boards within the hotel depending upon their purpose of business visit. The idea is to facilitate every business traveller to do his/her business comfortably at the hotel. Such travellers are a more constant source of income for the hotels as they give the business throughout the year as compared to the leisure travellers who are generally seasonal travellers. Also, the business travellers may have a larger movement of people in one go that means a big business opportunity for a hotel. The entitlements of business travellers are also quite high that makes them spend more as their trips are sponsored by the companies as compared to leisure travellers.

Luxury Hotels

These hotels are preferred by upper-class travellers who look for lavish facilities and maximum comfort. Such travellers do not mind paying enough provided they are offered with the best quality of services. These hotels may further be categorized into super deluxe/deluxe categories depending upon the services they provide.

Budget Hotels

These hotels generally offer minimal amenities and thus charge a nominal tariff from the tourists. These hotels are ideally more suitable for those tourists who are mainly backpackers having a low budget like *Ginger Hotel in New Delhi established by Roots Corporation of India.*

On the Basis of Theme

Hotels may be theme-based. A discussion on each of these is as follows.

Heritage Hotels

These are the former old palaces, castles and residences of royal kings that have been converted into heritage properties for the tourists. Tourists who wish to get a royal treatment and enjoy the old charm with present-day amenities prefer staying in these heritage properties. Many of these that are popular in India are in Rajasthan. These may include the *Umaid Bhawan Palace, Jodhpur* (one of the best hotels in the world); *Taj Rambagh Palace, Jaipur;* the *Oberoi Rajvilas, Jaipur;* the *Oberoi Udaivilas, Udaipur;* the *Leela Palace Hotel, Udaipur* and many more.

Ecotels

Ecotels may be referred to as eco-friendly hotels that aim at inspiring the tourists to act as responsible tourists by taking care of the environment. Such hotels use eco-friendly products, recycle things and work towards environment sustainability. To become eco-certified hotels, they must abide by the standards set out to become an ecotel by the concerned government authorities in a country. For example, *Orchid, a 5-star ecotel based in Mumbai and Pune, India, is Asia's first certified ecotel.* It is committed to being eco-friendly by being sensitive towards energy efficiency, water conservation, environment protection and community involvement.

Boutique Hotels

Boutique hotels cater to the affluent class of society. Guests who are looking for an exclusive style and a theme with top-class services may stay in these establishments. These hotels may generally be theme-based hotels. They are much smaller in size and maintain a unique kind of decor.

Spa Hotels

Spa hotels are popular among tourists who want to relax, rejuvenate and seek wellness treatments like taking a spa with a focus on their health. Thus, spa hotels provide specialized amenities and services such as steam, sauna, physical fitness activities, wellness education, massages and healthy cuisine. An excellent example of a spa hotel in India may be of Ananda Spa which is considered a luxury destination spa in the Himalayan foothills that focuses on holistic living, healthy organic diet, fitness, Ayurveda, Yoga and vedanta along with various international wellness experiences to maintain one's physical as well as mental health. The tourists may go for various treatments here such as detox, stress management, weight management, meditation and Yoga.

Capsule Hotels

This concept that initially emerged from Japan is steadily becoming a global trend. It is an affordable, hygienic and safe accommodation for travellers. Capsule hotels are also called *pod hotels* where the rooms are in the shape of a capsule. These hotels are ideal for travellers who are generally looking for an overnight accommodation. These hotels are more popular among solo travellers, travellers who are low on budget, business travellers who have very short stays in a city and travellers looking for an offbeat experience during their holiday. Such hotels may have a very small space for a bed for tourists with charging points and a television inside the room. The rooms are very compact and good enough for those people who can accommodate themselves in less space. There may be common space for almirahs or lockers to secure their personal belongings and common toilets to be shared by the people staying in the hotel. *There is very less human intervention as everything is technologically driven.* Everything has to be punched by the traveller to have access to anything in such hotels. An example of a *first Pod hotel in India is UrbanPod that has recently opened in Mumbai,* which is an experience in itself for the travellers.

Furthermore, the classification of hotels may be according to the following criteria.

On the Basis of Meal Plans

Breakfast Being Served in a B&B

- European plan (it includes room tariff without any meals)
- Continental plan (it includes room tariff with continental breakfast)
- American plan (it includes room tariff along with all meals that include breakfast, lunch and dinner)
- Modified American plan (it includes room tariff along with breakfast and one major meal that may be a lunch or a dinner)

On the Basis of Size

- Small hotels
- Medium hotels
- Large hotels
- Mega hotels

On the Basis of Amenities and Services

- 5-star hotels
- 4-star hotels
- 3-star hotels
- 2-star hotels
- 1-star hotels

On the Basis of Ownership

- Independent hotels
- Chain hotels

TYPES OF ROOMS

Hotels may have different types of rooms depending upon their category. Let us have a discussion on the kinds of rooms that a hotel may have based on their occupancy type.

Single Room

A room with a single-bed facility is called a single room. It is generally preferred by those guests who are looking for single occupancy.

Twin Room

A room with occupancy for two independent people with two single separate beds separated by a bedside table is referred to as a twin room.

Double Room

A room which has a double bed facility for two people who share a common bed (generally preferred by couples) is referred to as a double room. The double beds may come in two sizes—king-size double bed and queen-size double bed. The king-size double bed is bigger in size as compared to a queen-size double bed.

Double–Double (Twin Double) Room

A room for a family with two double beds with separate headboards is referred to as double–double room.

Triple Room

A room meant for three people which may have more than two beds is referred to as triple room.

Standard Room

A standard room is a basic room in a hotel which has minimalistic facilities for the guests. These rooms are generally small in size and do not offer views such as pool view, ocean view and garden view.

Superior Room

This kind of room is better than the standard room in terms of amenities available and its size. It is much bigger than the standard room and may offer a better view to tourists from the room.

Deluxe Room

The rooms which are well furnished and have amenities within the room such as a TV, fridge, kettle for making tea, writing table, a dressing table and an attached bathroom with toiletries are referred to as deluxe rooms. These may be a single deluxe room or a double deluxe room. These are the better-quality rooms than standard or superior rooms.

Duplex Room

Two rooms on two different floors connected with each other by a staircase are referred to as a duplex room.

Lanai

A room facing a scenic area that may be a garden, a waterfall or any other landscape may be referred to as a lanai.

Penthouse

A luxurious room at the top with access to the terrace that gives a bird's-eye view of the city is called a penthouse.

Suite

A room (or sometimes more than one room) with a living room is called a suite. These may be preferred by guests who want luxury, comfort and more space. Business travellers also may prefer such suites and thus, these may also be referred to as executive suites or business suites.

Presidential Suite

Suites that redefine opulence with a grandeur bedroom (attached with a lavish bathroom with shower cubicles/bathtub, luxury amenities such as silk bathrobes and top-notch toiletries), a living room, dining space, a powder room, a private bar, a pantry with personalized butler services, a private swimming pool and a Jacuzzi are referred to as presidential suites. One may expect unparallel care with best of amenities such as a pillow menu, complimentary champagne and chocolates while staying in a presidential suite.

Studio

A room with a single bed and a couch that can be transformed into a bed is called a studio room.

Sico/Murphy Room

A murphy bed is a bed that is attached to a wall or a closet and folds out whenever required. Thus, rooms that have a murphy bed or a sofa bed which allows the room to be converted into a living room or a meeting room during the daytime and a bedroom during night-time are called sico or murphy rooms.

Cabana

A room that may offer a view of a swimming pool with the swimming pool adjoining to it or may have a private swimming pool within the room may be referred to as a cabana.

Connecting Rooms

Rooms that are connected by virtue of a door inside that allows them access to the rooms without going out in the lobby area but have separate entrance doors from outside are called connecting rooms.

Adjacent Rooms

Rooms that are nearby or close to each other across an area are called adjacent rooms.

Adjoining Rooms

Rooms that share a common wall with each other without any connecting door in between are referred to as adjoining rooms.

Accessible Rooms

These are also referred to as disabled rooms which meet the requirements of people with special abilities. These rooms are generally placed on the ground floors to provide easy access to disabled guests with entrance ramps and disability lifts for access to ballrooms and so on. Generally, the F&B services are also located on the ground floors.

These rooms may be specially designed with wide automatic doors, disabled toilets with low-level washbasins and bathtubs, emergency pull cords, grab rails and so on. As per the government laws, hotels must maintain a limited number of accessible rooms for such guests.

Besides the above, the hotels may have the following types of rooms or floors for the guests:

- **Smoking/non-smoking room:** Some hotels may provide a small percentage of rooms as smoking rooms which are preferred by smokers as the flamy consumption of tobacco is allowed inside the rooms. Such rooms have an extended facility of ashtray and matchsticks whereas in a non-smoking room, smoking is prohibited for the guests.
- **Executive floor:** A dedicated floor in a hotel for executives is called as an executive room.
- **Female executive floor:** Rooms specially assigned to female guests for their safety and security on a particular floor are called female executive floors.

SUMMARY

The term hospitality has been redefined from time to time and is undergoing a radical change. When a traveller visits a destination, he/she expects a safe and hygienic place to stay. Accommodation is an experiential tourism product for the traveller that adds value to his/her total travel experience. The tourism sector offers multiple opportunities for the hospitality sector businesses. Not only this sector generates income for a country, but it also provides employment to people in large numbers. Unlimited employment opportunities are created in a country through this sector. It also helps in sustaining the local community of a destination by providing them with a stable source of earning their bread and butter. This sector equally contributes to the infrastructural development of a destination by building quality hotels and other supplementary accommodation and F&B outlets, which eventually improves the quality of life of the local residents of a destination. As this industry flourishes at an exceptional pace, it is an exciting and innovative career option for professionals planning to serve the guests.

While choosing a type of accommodation, there are many factors that affect a traveller's choice of accommodation such as safety, budget, kind of services offered, comfort, level of social interaction required, self-esteem, type of travellers and many more. Hotels are one of the most preferred and oldest forms of accommodation opted by many travellers. They may be classified on the basis of location, clientele, theme, size, ownership and so on. Hotels may also have different types of rooms based on their occupancy. These may be single room, double room, triple room, twin room, suite, cabana, duplex room and so on. The traveller must choose the room according to his/her requirement.

ACTIVITIES

Activity 1

Visit any three hotels in your destination, preferably of different categories. Observe and seek information in each hotel regarding the following:

- Category of hotel
- Existing departments in the hotel
- Its USP
- Amenities available for the guests
- Different types of rooms
- Any other special amenities

After having visited the hotels and having gathered the information, make a comparative analysis of the hotels and make a detailed presentation of the same and present it in front of the class. Share, discuss and then debate.

Activity 2

Seek the interview of the hotel staff of three different hotels. Ask them to narrate incidents or difficult situations that they may have encountered while dealing with difficult guests.

Ask them the situation first and then the solution of how they handled the situation.

Come back to the class and discuss your experiences with the other classmates. To make it more interesting, share the incident first without giving the solution. Seek solution from your classmates first and then share the solution that the hotel came up with.

Alternative Forms of Accommodation

LEARNING OBJECTIVES

The given chapter shall clarify the following:

- What are the types of accommodation available for a tourist?
- What are the challenges posed to the hospitality industry?
- What are the emerging trends in the hospitality sector?

A GRACIOUS HOSPITALITY ALONG THE WORLD'S MOST LUXURIOUS ROYAL RIDE AT MAHARAJAS' EXPRESS!

- Want to experience a royal ride in the most luxurious train? Maharajas' Express is at your service!
- Maharajas' Express is a luxury tourist train owned and run by IRCTC, covering more than 12 destinations across India.
- Those who want luxurious Indian holidays and want to indulge in the cultural richness and history of India, booking a royal vacation with the Maharajas' Express and making the memorable expedition is a right trade-off.
- The train offers different itineraries covering different destinations that the tourists are free to choose according to their preferences. While passing by the different locations, tourists can catch a glimpse of cultural lifestyle, atmosphere, traditions and festivals.
- The train is equipped with luxurious suites, restaurants, bars, lounge, massage centre, gym, conference room, Wi-Fi facility and so on.

INTRODUCTION

Hotels are one of the oldest and most usable forms of accommodation by maximum travellers. However, to accommodate the tourist traffic, especially during the peak tourist seasons or during the events, the number of hotels at a destination may not be enough. Thus, it is important for destinations to create and develop alternative forms of accommodation that may be preferred by the other set of travellers.

A detailed discussion on each of the alternative forms of accommodation used by tourists is as follows.

YOUTH HOSTELS

The youth hostels are an exciting accommodation choice for young travellers who prefer to interact with the fellow youth, thereby facilitating cultural exchange between each other. Youth hostels are also an ideal option for budget travellers/backpackers who are looking for a very economical option to stay.

Youth hostels generally create a social ecosystem connecting travellers of different background with each other. Such tourists avail membership for staying in youth hostels by paying a certain membership fee that gives them the access to stay in any youth hostel of the world.

The rooms are generally in dormitory style where travellers have to share the room with other travellers from different parts of the world unless one specifically requests for a single room that may also be subject to availability. Sometimes rooms may have to be shared with roommates of different genders unless a special request is placed to share the room with a person of the same gender only.

The youth hostels have a shared kitchen, common dining area, library facility and toilet facilities for the travellers staying there.

Two very popular hostel chain brands popular in India among backpackers or low-budget travellers are 'Zostel' and 'Moustache'.

B&B INNS

These inns provide a basic stay to the traveller with the provision of a private room with a bed and a breakfast meal. These inns may not have lavish facilities for the travellers. However, for many budgeted travellers staying in B&B inns is the first choice, as they may be of the opinion that the whole day is generally spent in sightseeing and exploring the city that they barely get time to spend at the accommodation. Thus, they may be able to manage with a modest accommodation.

In some B&B inns, the host generally stays with the guests, though in a separate space. In such cases, the travellers may like to interact with the host who may provide them with the breakfast. *For the tourists, getting an opportunity to interact with the host is a highlight of their holiday.*

SELF-CATERING APARTMENTS

Self-catering apartments are the self-contained units or apartments where the traveller has to cater to his/her own needs during his/her stay. Such apartments cater to those travellers who want more space/are travelling for a long duration on a holiday/are travelling with kids or either joint families who prefer to stay together. These apartments are well furnished and equipped with cooking utensils, cutlery, crockery, cleaning equipment, refrigerator, microwave oven, washing machine and the other required basic facilities such as proper bedding, dining table and furniture, which make the stay of tourists very convenient. The advantages of staying in a self-catering apartment are as follows:

- These are one of the most spacious accommodations with all the necessary facilities that give the feel of a home away from home to the traveller. The children also feel more comfortable due to the spacious area of the apartments. In a single room in a hotel, the guests or the children may feel claustrophobic.
- For many tourists, food is a major issue in another destination. The tourists may be allergic to certain foods or may have certain health issues due to which they may not be comfortable trying the local food of a place. Still, for many, the local food may not suit their taste palettes. For such tourists, self-catering apartments are a convenient choice that allows them to make their own food in the kitchen/pantry of an apartment according to their own taste.
- Self-catering apartments are a good choice for those travellers who prefer independence and flexibility. The tourists comparatively feel free to be on their own terms and conditions unlike in a hotel room where one is bound by rules.
- The tourists can also do their own laundry while on a holiday (especially a holiday which is of a longer duration), which is a great respite for them.
- The tourists have more privacy as compared to staying in a hotel.

These apartments may generally be privately owned or sometimes operated by hotel chains. In the privately owned apartment, the owner may be staying at a different location and may have let out the whole apartment for the tourists. These days many privately owned apartments are registered with AirBnB.

Sometimes, hotels like *Hyatt* may own independent fully furnished apartments that have rooms, living room, dining area, washrooms, kitchen and so on. The travellers can comfortably stay in the *hotel-owned apartments, also referred to as aparthotel,* with no interference of the hotel staff unless and until it is really required. However, these aparthotels offer all the services by the hotel such as housekeeping, meals, laundry, room service, concierge and so on.

The guest may be free to use the common facilities offered by the hotel such as conference rooms, spa facilities and swimming pools.

CAMPING

Camping is also an outdoor adventure activity for many travellers. It is an offbeat experience where travellers stay outdoors for at least a night away from home. The camping sites are also called *open-air hostels or tourist camps*. Many adventure tourists going for hiking while visiting adventure destinations may pitch in their tents within the vicinity of nature. *Tourists may also do camping in deserts, open areas and areas hosting the festivals besides the mountainous regions.* Tents may vary in their quality and amenities provided. However, tents must be strong enough to have the tenacity to stand by the extreme weather conditions.

Living within the limited means in a designated space of a tent is an experience that teaches the lessons of life to a traveller. Pitching the tent together can be a good team-building exercise besides being a recreational activity. Some of the interesting camping sites are as follows:

- Camping in Rishikesh for white water rafting, India
- Camping during Rann of Kutch festival, Gujarat, India
- Camping during a full-moon night in Jaisalmer, Rajasthan, India
- Night camping with campfire in Wayanad, Tamil Nadu
- Camping at Yosemite National Park, California
- Camping at Sahara Desert, Morocco
- Camping at Lake District National Park, England
- Camping at Ladakh, India

GUEST HOUSES

Guest houses are generally private homes that have been converted and furnished to cater to the needs of the guests with independent rooms for different guests. Tourists staying in guest houses may expect modest facilities. There may be a caretaker to take care of the guests and prepare meals for them. The public areas may be for the common usage of the guests staying in the guest house. Guest houses may be company-owned or privately owned.

LODGES

Staying in a lodge is an unforgettable experience of its kind. Many travellers prefer to stay in the vicinity of natural settings. They like staying in those independent units that may be made of natural materials such as wood, thatch and stone. Lodges may vary depending upon their location or facilities. Some of these are as follows:

Eco-lodges These lodges are constructed in eco settings which are made of natural products. These may offer recycling services, eco-friendly toiletries, energy-efficient lighting, locally sourced food, organic linens and towels, water conservation methods and various sustainability-focused initiatives.

Forest Lodges Anyone who is interested to stay in the wilderness and enjoy the adventures should stay in forest lodges that are generally around national parks, wildlife sanctuaries, forests and so on.

Luxury Lodges Luxury in these lodges can be defined by facilities that are offered such as private golf, helicopter flights, spa facilities, personal swimming pools and Jacuzzis that one may ever imagine of a perfect holiday.

CARAVANS

Caravans are a popular choice among holidaymakers. *Caravans may also be called recreational vehicles or RVs.* These are mobile accommodations where travellers may drive around the city in the caravan, explore the city during the daytime and park the vehicle in their parking lots wherever required to take rest in the night. The trailers that are loaded with home facilities are generally towed behind a vehicle. Caravans have comfortable bedding facility, en-suite toilets, a small kitchenette or a pantry, air conditioners, television, Wi-Fi facility, microwave oven, refrigerator, washing machine, in-built GPS system and so on to facilitate the tourists to have a comfortable stay in these moving vehicles. However, manoeuvring the caravans may not be an easy task for the rooky drivers, especially in foreign countries as trailers are hard to move.

These are very popular modes of accommodation in the UK, Australia, Europe and North America. In India, the state of Madhya Pradesh has initiated the concept of caravans.

Caravans may be static and may be stationed on caravan parks. *Caravan parks are the open spaces designated for parking the caravans.* In other words, they are permanently placed on site. They may have on-site facilities such as swimming pools, showers, cafes, playgrounds, electricity and water supply and waste disposal. For travellers who do not prefer staying in caravan parks that may affect their privacy, finding a single caravan site like a farmer's field is the viable option. These are generally self-catering accommodations where the traveller has to do things on his/her own. These provide great flexibility and freedom to the travellers. These are generally oriented towards families seeking a holiday.

However, *Campervans* are more convenient and popular among the holidaymakers. These are equipped vans with all the facilities of a home to make the stay of travellers convenient. Due to their small size, unlike motor homes that are large vehicles and the large caravans, these are compact and thus, comfortable to drive. However, due to the limited space in these as compared to caravans and motor homes, less number of people can be housed in campervans.

HOLIDAY PARKS

It is an important category of accommodation that is highly popular in Europe and the USA. These are the dedicated open spaces or grounds for camping sites, parking caravans and campervans.

HOMESTAYS

Homestay at Glasgow, Scotland

Staying with the locals of a destination in their homes and their residential areas is an attraction in itself for many tourists. The idea of getting an opportunity to interact with the local community and seeing the local culture closely while getting all their individual attention is the motivating force that pushes the traveller to use this kind of accommodation. Besides, the travellers may feel safer and secure in a protected environment of a local family who can guard them against any tourist traps that they may fall into.

In homestays, the tourist stays with a family in their home like a family member and may use complete facilities of the hosts such as their kitchens and bathing spaces by paying for their stay to the family. Sometimes, the tourists may gain invaluable suggestions and guidance from the local hosts about the local sights to be visited, local foods to be tried, local festivals or events to attend and local activities to be tried, which actually make the holiday experience of a traveller more worthy and meaningful. Certain local experiences that may not be even mentioned in the guidebooks are treasure secrets only hidden within the locals. Sometimes, the hosts may also take their guests for enjoying local activities such as making them cook the local cuisine, food tasting of the authentic local home-cooked food, visiting farms, taking a tour of coffee plantations and going for orchard picking. Homestays can be a pleasant experience only when the host is hospitable and concerned about the traveller who is visiting him/her. However, travellers who prefer privacy, staying in homestays may not be a very good idea.

In India, many states such as *Himachal Pradesh, Uttarakhand, Sikkim* and *Ladakh* are actively promoting homestays to boost the local economy and showcase the local culture to the tourists while also focusing on sustainability and eco-friendly practices.

FARM STAYS

For those wanting to experience the rural and rustic life and fresh and clean air, farm stays are ideal, especially for weekend getaways. As agritourism has picked up in many parts of the world, more and more tourists have started preferring to stay in farmhouses with the idea of staying close to nature. These are the perfect choice for those tourists who are looking for a simplistic way of living away from the hustle and bustle of metro life. One can find a natural environment here and peace of mind for a healthy living.

The travellers may experience authentic rural life experiences in the farm stays. Some of the activities that travellers may indulge in while staying in the farmhouses are orchard picking, plucking fruits and vegetables, cow milking, taking spice tours, going for village walks, tasting farm fresh ingredients, cattle feeding, horse riding, taking cooking lessons, doing plantation, birding, practising Yoga and meditation, taking mud baths and so on.

GLASS HOUSES AND GLASS IGLOOS

Staying in glass houses is a great getaway for many travellers. Such travellers may enjoy spectacular views of nature through the glasses surrounding the house that adds to its beauty. In the night, the tourists may draw curtains/blinds to maintain privacy. Although igloos are generally made up of snow, glass igloos are another version of igloos. *Glass igloos are very popular in Finland where tourists visit to see the famous Northern Lights* that are an unparallel experience of its own kind for a traveller. Staying around ice all around in glass igloos can be an incredible experience for a traveller. Thermally insulated walls keep the igloos warm for the tourists. The igloo is ideal for two travellers who can be easily accommodated. *Husky safaris, ice fishing, cross-country skiing, snowmobile safaris* and so on are some of the popular activities that travellers can experiment staying at the glass igloos. One of the most famous glass igloos is the *Kakslauttanen Arctic Resort in Finnish Lapland* famous for viewing the Northern Lights.

TIME SHARE

This is also a trending concept of accommodation industry that involves vacation ownership of a place. Under this kind of arrangement, multiple tourists buy a particular time slot or a specific time period during a year for a property to share and use that property. People buy membership plans for a lifetime according to their budgets and book their holidays either in hotels, resorts, condos, houses or villas. For example, companies such as *Hilton Grand Vacations Club, Disney Vacation Club, Marriot Vacation Club, Club Mahindra, Sterling Resort, Toshali Resort* and *Country Vacations* promote this concept of time share resorts.

COTTAGES

Cottages generally refer to compact homes in the countryside. These may be used as weekend getaways or summer retreats. These are private homes that are given on rent to tourists for private stays. These may be generally around natural settings such as lakes, mountains, countryside, vineyards and the sea.

VILLAS

A stand-alone house generally in resort hotels that provides bedrooms with living rooms, a private swimming pool, Jacuzzi, balcony and so on to the guests who are looking for more luxury, space and extra privacy is referred to as a villa. Villas are bigger in size as compared to cottages where two or more families can stay together on a holiday.

CHALETS

These are houses that are made of wood with gently sloping roofs. These are more popular in Europe, especially in European Alps. *These are also called Swiss Chalets as these were traditionally found in Switzerland.* Many tourists prefer staying in these cosy wooden houses.

CASTLES

Castles are the private fortified residences of nobles or lords where they used to live once. Castles are generally located near the countryside away from the hustle and bustle of the city and, thus, a perfect retreat for young couples. If a traveller wants to take a regal vibe from the awe-inspiring antique-filled interiors of a building, then he/she must stay in a castle. Castles may have rooms or suites with medieval decor made of stonework or wooden beams. Castles are a popular accommodation choice for holidaymakers, especially visiting the UK and Europe.

LIGHTHOUSES

For those planning to take a coastal break and enjoying the pristine views of nature with sea stretching out all over and fresh air to breathe in, staying in a lighthouse is the right choice. *Many travellers celebrate their vacations in a lighthouse, especially on special occasions of life like anniversary, birthdays or proposing someone for marriage.* However, one should be ready to climb the steps to reach the rooms. Generally, the stay at lighthouses may not be of more than overnight duration unless one books a package for two or three nights. *Stay in lighthouses is quite popular in the UK, especially in Ireland and Scotland.*

HOLIDAY HOMES

From cottages to a complete independent bungalow to a duplex, the feeling of staying in a big house is a dream come true for many travellers. Holiday homes may be an ideal choice for travellers who prefer luxury and comfort. These are generally privately owned additional properties by an owner in some other location from his/her regular residence where he/she may stay occasionally during his/her vacation. Sometimes, these may be rented by an owner to holiday vacationers for a few days to stay in the holiday home and avail all the utilities on payment basis.

CHALLENGES OF THE HOSPITALITY INDUSTRY

A few challenges for this industry are as follows:

- Maintaining consistent quality
- Maintaining customer loyalty
- Integrating technology in the industry
- Increasing globalization and competition
- Revenue management
- Packaging of hospitality services as a single value proposition by not only providing hotel reservations but also offering packages by including airport transfers, sightseeing tours, freebies and so on
- Dealing with the attrition rate in the hospitality sector
- Talent management

NEW TRENDS IN HOSPITALITY

Following are the emerging trends in the hospitality sector.

Sustainability

Increasingly, the hotels are taking the subject of sustainability quite seriously. From incorporating greener practices to eco-friendliness, the hospitality businesses are actively engaged in promoting the concept of sustainability not only to their similar businesses but also to the tourists staying in the hotels. Using various sustainable and energy-saving materials, nature-based products for construction, using smart technology, creating policies for water conservation like requesting the guests not to get their linen and towel changed every day, promoting vegetarian and vegan options and so on are some of the ways in which the hotels are practising sustainability in their business models. Some hotels have stopped using plastic straws in their mission to save the environment. *Using energy- and cost-saving Internet of Things (IOT) technology to control and adjust the heating in rooms is the new step towards creating sustainable rooms.*

Personalization

Today's guest needs personal attention and personalized services by the hotels. Thus, hotels have developed mechanisms to provide a personalized touch to their services. For example, hotels may delight their repeated guests by greeting them by their first names by using the booking data that may contain their preferences and dislikes that they may have shared with the hotel staff or the hotel staff may have observed.

Branding

Branding is a visible important trend seen in the hospitality sector where every hotel is promoting itself under a particular sub-brand catering to a particular segment of the market. The market segments can identify the sub-brand and choose the hotel according to their budget and its location.

Smart Hotels

Hotels are increasingly turning to smart hotels by making use of IOT. They are using IOT to enable devices to make use of Internet connectivity that can send and receive digital information. Smart devices are associated with smart room technology in hotels that enables smart room controls, voice-controlled entertainment, faster guest services, automation and improved responsiveness. Even the smartphones of the guests can interact with the in-room technology like they can control the room's temperature. Also, the smart speakers or smart hub like Alexa by Amazon that allows hotels to implement smart voice control can aid in controlling room lights, drawing of curtains, turning the television on or off, playing music and so on at the command of the guest using voice recognition through the IOT technology.

Through the use of smart technology like a smart hub, the guests can have a faster access to services by clicking on a screen, sending voice messages to take the room service and so on.

Use of Robotics

Another trending aspect of the hospitality industry is the use of robotics and artificial intelligence (AI) as butlers, receptionists, bellhops and so on. The hospitality industry is being redefined by the emergence of robots equipped with AI who respond to human speech and reply to queries. For example, in Japan, the *Hotel Henn na* opened in the year 2015 in Nagasaki introduced robotic staff for check-in and check-out of guests to increase the efficiency of hotel operations. Although in 2019, they had to reduce the robotic staff by more than 50 per cent as a lot of time and money went in repairing the robots. Many guests also complained that the robot could not answer basic queries raised by them. A similar example is of *China's Smart LYZ Hotel in Chengdu*, which is almost entirely automated.

Use of Virtual Reality and Augmented Reality

Hotels are also incorporating the concept of virtual reality through giving a virtual tour of their hotel rooms to the guests before their booking of hotel room that gives them a fair and a realistic picture of how their room would look like when they actually visit the hotel. Using graphics and information overlays to enhance the real-world environment, augmented reality assists the guests by providing interactive tourist information maps in the hotels, creating entertainment opportunities and so on.

Health-conscious Customer

As the new consumer turns more health-conscious and aware of what he/she is putting into his/her body, he/she is opting for healthier food options. Thus, to keep pace with the changing preferences of the consumers, the hotels have to change their menu options with more low fat, grilled, vegetarian, organic, gluten-free and vegan options. Likewise, the drinks offered also have to be healthy and organic to cater to the growing health-conscious market.

A further detailed discussion on the emerging trends of hospitality which are relevant to the tourism phenomenon also has been discussed separately in Chapter 31, 'Emerging Trends in Tourism'. The trends are as follows:

- Couch surfing
- Work away
- House sitting
- Staycation
- Types of travellers

SUMMARY

Today's traveller has an array of accommodation choices to choose from. He/she may stay in a youth hostel, B&B inn, self-catering apartment, castle, time share resort, glass house or glass igloo, cottage, chalet, villa, lighthouse, farm stay, lodge, homestay and so on. The hospitality industry is facing a number of challenges that it needs to cope with. Many new trends are emerging in the hospitality sector such as sustainability, personalization, smart hotels, use of technology such as virtual and augmented reality and robotics, and evolution of new health-conscious consumers.

ACTIVITIES

Activity 1

A group of friends wants to visit Goa for four nights/five days. Which kind of accommodation arrangement would you suggest them if you were their tour operator? Also justify why would you suggest that accommodation over others?

Activity 2

Divide the class into different groups depending upon the strength of the class. Ask each group to make a presentation of a unique accommodation idea that they may like to sell. Every group must make an appropriate sales pitch, convincing the other group members to stay in that kind of accommodation. The students must give a detailed proposal of the unique accommodation idea, discussing in detail the highlighting features of the accommodation, its location, the proposed budget of the accommodation per night and the merits of staying in that accommodation. After the presentation gets over, the house may be open for a discussion where the other students may pose questions related to the presentation from the group presenting the idea. The teacher may then evaluate each group and declare the one that has the best unique idea and the presentation.

16

Amenities

LEARNING OBJECTIVES

The given chapter shall clarify the following:

- Why are amenities significant for tourists?
- What are the amenities that must be present in a destination to ensure the comfort of tourists?

MASS TRANSIT RAILWAY: THE EASY WAY TO TRAVEL IN HONG KONG!

- Travelling and exploring Hong Kong's world-class attraction is made easy with quick and efficient mass transit railway (MTR) system. It is one of the world's best public transportation system.
- MTR covers all major districts in the territory which also includes stops at the boundary with Mainland China (Lo Wu Station and Lok Ma Chau Station).
- These trains are known for being immaculately clean, well signposted, cheap, regular and super convenient.
- MTR system has introduced amenities such as free Wi-Fi at every station in Hong Kong. It also has facilities such as tactile flooring and Braille plates for passengers with disabilities, public washrooms, shops, banks and takeaway food outlets.
- Purchasing tickets for the visitors has been made easy with automated machines conveniently placed at every station.

- The passengers make payment through contactless payment card called Octopus card, which can also be used to pay for rides on MTR, buses, minibuses, ferries, trams and taxis with Octopus readers.

INTRODUCTION

With tourism becoming an important contributor to the global economy, tourists are travelling for different reasons to different destinations. Thus, destinations may try to market themselves internationally in different ways to woo tourists. However, in spite of the vigorous efforts of destinations to market themselves, many destinations may still not be the top priority for a traveller. One of the reasons as to why travellers may not wish to visit a destination may be lack of amenities there.

Some travellers may term a destination as more 'tourist-friendly' as compared to others. There may be many factors that qualify a destination to be tourist-friendly. Besides the receptive attitude of the host towards the guest, the other factor that makes a destination 'tourist-friendly' is the presence of amenities at a destination required from a tourist perspective. Hence, the presence of amenities at a destination has become an important competitive factor today for a destination to qualify as a 'tourist-friendly' destination.

A destination can offer a high-quality and consistent experience to the tourists only if it has basic and advanced amenities to facilitate the holiday of tourists at a destination. Attractions may bring a tourist to a destination, but it is the presence of reasonable amenities that sustains the tourists at a destination and makes their stay comfortable and enjoyable. Lack of amenities at a destination may become a deterring factor for the tourists to visit a destination in the future.

Thus, destinations of the world must focus on offering world-class facilities to the guests so as to make the guest feel at home and to ensure that the comfort of the guest is given utmost importance.

From the tourist's perspective, there may be many amenities. Now let us try to understand each of these in detail.

PUBLIC TRANSPORTATION SYSTEMS

Accessibility within a destination is an important parameter for a traveller visiting that destination. Getting around the city can be a task for a new visitor. For many budgeted travellers, public transportation is the first choice to explore a city. Travelling on public transportation systems can be an experience in itself if the public transportation system is strongly connected and easy to understand. Travelling through local public transportation with locals enriches the experience of a traveller as he/she gets an idea how the locals live and lead their common daily lives travelling from one point to another.

The presence of reliable and affordable bus networks, trams, train networks, local trains, airlines, car rental facilities, motorbikes, bicycles, ferries, local taxis, auto-rickshaws, cycle rickshaws and tuk tuk makes the travel of the tourists more comfortable and convenient at a destination. Along with the good network, a strong infrastructure of train stations, subways, tram stations, bus stands, bus shelters, airport terminals, car rental designated parking and bicycle stands is a must to facilitate the travel of tourists at a destination. Thus, the presence of a good public transportation system at a destination that connects the whole city is an important amenity for the travellers.

PUBLIC TRANSPORTATION SMARTCARDS

Most of the public transportation systems of the world offer smart cards technology. The idea of using the smart cards ticketing systems for visitors is to make their travel easier, quicker and more affordable. These smart cards are value for money while travelling from one point to another. On buying these rechargeable cards, one may top up the cards based on one's frequency of travel.

The smart card ticketing system for using public transportation may not be bought on buses or trams. One has to buy them in advance. Generally, these cards are available through card vending machines at bus stands/train stations/tram stations besides being available at customer care. Sometimes, they may be purchased/recharged from local supermarkets/local shops also. Alternatively, one may also download the relevant travel apps for the cards and get them recharged online. At some destinations, these cards may also be accessible for tourists at major tourist points such as airports, railway stations, visitor centres/tourist information centres, hotel concierge desks and backpacker hostels besides the above-mentioned places.

Destinations may offer special visitor smart cards catering to the needs of the tourists that may be valid for a few days depending upon the stay of the tourists at a destination. For example, *the 'Myki Visitor Pack' for tourists visiting Melbourne, Australia,* is generally used by overseas visitors where there are deals and discounts for visiting major tourist attractions in Melbourne, while in *Sydney, the Opal card* is generally used. Likewise, tourists in *London use Oyster cards.*

It is important to mention here that some cards can be used for multiple modes of transportation at a destination. For example, in Melbourne, tourist can use the same myki card for boarding buses, trains and trams except in the 'free tram zones' in Melbourne. A visitor Oyster card gives access to journeys on trams, tubes, buses, River Bus, London Underground, most national services in London and so on.

TOURIST SIGNAGE

Map of Luss Village, Scotland

In recent years, the concept of drive tourism has been trending. Many tourists choose to travel to destinations by road on their own. While visiting a destination for the first time, the tourists may not be very familiar with the routes of a destination. Also, while driving to countryside areas or natural trails, the Internet connectivity may not be strong enough due to which GPS may also stop functioning. Losing track of the route can be a frightening experience for the tourists. Thus, in such situations, the presence of proper signage with the names of destinations and their proximity mentioned in miles/km can be a great sigh of relief for the tourists. *Basically, the signages are universally recognizable pictograms recognized by tourists.*

Although signage at a destination may appear to be a basic facility, however, many destinations underestimate the importance of signage at important points. *Signages are like lamp posts that direct the tourists to unknown routes.* With the help of signage, tourists can self-drive/self-ride to different tourist destinations more easily and comfortably. In other words, the tourists can be on their auto mode. Signages assist the travellers to reconfirm their routings with GPS. Lack of signage at destinations can leave the traveller baffled.

Some of the important functions of signages are as follows:

- They aid the motorist in safe and easy navigation by guiding him/her in finding appropriate routes.
- They also assist the tourists in exploring a range of services and attractions available nearby.
- Besides guiding the tourists, the signage also play a functional role in promoting a destination and making it more appealing with the use of visuals.
- Presence of signage gives people a sense of place and increases their awareness of the nearby points of interest.
- Signages make the travel of tourists more comfortable and smoother.
- It is more likely that the tourists will return to the same destination or recommend their friends and relatives if they find it easy to move around.

Generally speaking, the signage for tourists are in the local language of the destination being visited. However, many destinations may also have signage in the language of tourists who visit that destination in maximum numbers there. *For example, in the USA, besides English language, signages are also displayed in Chinese/Mandarin language as for the USA, Chinese travellers are one of the largest inbound markets who have a language barrier of understanding English.*

Signage may be of different types.

Gateway Signage

The gateway signage are at the approaching/exit points of a destination/state/territory borders generally put up by the government authorities. These generally indicate 'welcome' to the guests on entering a destination and saying 'thank you' at the exit points for paying a visit to a destination.

Digital Signage

Some destinations may also have digital signages that help tourists to explore destinations with interactive information.

Photography Signage

Many destinations have photography signage on roads that suggest the motorists of a photography point approaching that may be a few yards away. These indications assist the motorist in keeping his/her vehicle slow if he/she decides to take a stopover for clicking the photographs at the scenic point. For example, *while travelling by car from Edinburgh to Isle of Skye in Scotland, one may come across some spectacular locations for clicking pictures.* At every worthy picturesque point approaching, there are proper photography signages at yards or a mile away on the road to suggest photography opportunity for the tourists.

Signage for Wayside Amenities

Many tourists who prefer to travel by road expect basic amenities on a road to have a safe and convenient travel. Thus, tourism authorities to promote drive tourism and highway tourism ensure to maintain certain wayside amenities for the weary travellers so that they may take frequent stopovers whenever required. Therefore, signage for the following amenities may be put up at the highways:

- Restrooms
- Drinking water facility
- Motels and dormitories for short stays
- Food courts, kiosks and drive-through restaurants
- Parking space
- Repair shops
- Local shops

- Filling stations
- ATMs

INTERNATIONAL SIM CARD

While travelling overseas, an important challenge for a traveller is to buy an international SIM card. Generally, international SIM cards are country-specific. Tourists use the international SIM card of a country as their calling rates are quite cheap as compared to one's own country home-mobile provider.

However, the data plans and calling plans may vary from company to company offering the SIM card. One may choose the package and plan depending upon one's length of stay in a country, one's local usage of the Internet, the need of staying connected with family and friends and also upon one's budget that one is ready to spend. The traveller also has the option of buying the international SIM card/global cards from his/her own country before he/she departs for another country.

For planning to visit one single country, an international SIM card is the given option. However, *for globetrotters travelling to more than one country, global cards such as Uniconnect, Matrix Cellular and Roam1 are an ideal option.* Otherwise, the traveller may end up wasting his/her precious time in looking for local SIM card for every country and then keep changing the SIM card on his/her mobile every time he/she arrives at another country making the whole process more complicated for him/her.

Wi-Fi Facility at Humayun's Tomb, New Delhi

FREE WI-FI HOTSPOTS

Today's traveller has become heavily dependent on the Internet for planning his/her travel. For him/her, the Internet is a magic wand that will resolve his/her every travel query.

As most travellers these days travel on their own, they rely on the Internet for accessing travel apps, using GPS for travelling from one point to another, finding nearby attractions, exploring local markets and the best restaurants of the city to eat at. Besides these obvious reasons, the most important reason for today's travellers is to stay updated on social media for posting their pictures on social networking sites like Facebook, hash-tagging the posts on Instagram and sharing their live status and stories of their unique travel experiences such as

attending a festival/concert, trying one's favourite local food at a destination with others and many more such similar travel experiences.

When the tourists travel to a destination, they may use the Internet data plan on their smartphone to stay connected with their family and friends. However, when a tourist is planning an overseas travel, the international SIM card with the Internet usage plans that a traveller may buy for his/her smartphone comes out to be generally very expensive. Accessing the Internet in another country can turn out to be an expensive affair as one's usage of the Internet would be heavy. Therefore, many countries offer free Wi-Fi zones in their cities to facilitate the usage of the Internet for the travellers. One may have access to the free Internet at airports, hotels, restaurants, cafes, pubs and bars, public spaces, shopping malls and at important tourist attractions.

Offering free Wi-Fi services helps the traveller explore the destination free of charges. It means that the moment a traveller reaches a destination, he/she is provided with the free Internet connection on his/her smartphone on entering the authorized Wi-Fi password code. He/she may have to register his/her mobile phone and sign in to his/her email id or alternatively install an app (e.g., Wiman app in Hungary) to use the public Internet connection. However, the surfing speed (in mbps) may vary from country to country. One may also note that the surfing speed in few countries is restricted on the basis of usage duration.

Some of the countries in the world that have free Wi-Fi services at most of the locations are Ireland, Portugal, Denmark, Canada, the USA, Romania, the UK, Germany, Switzerland, Latvia, Finland, Singapore, Slovenia and so on.

VISITOR INFORMATION CENTRE

Another very important amenity from a traveller's perspective is the presence of a Visitor Information Centre at a destination operated by the government authorities. Many destinations are not able to effectively realize the importance of giving information to the guests in the right way at the right time and at the right place as they are not able to manage their Visitor Information Centres well. This may not be able to leave a favourable impression in the minds of the visitors.

The Visitor Information Centres are generally located at main accessible tourist points, that is, at airports, bus stands, train stations, around major tourist attraction areas, in the city centre or in the local shopping market areas and so on.

The advantage of seeking consultation at the Visitor Information Centre is that being government-owned bodies, the information given here is more genuine and reliable as compared to limited information from other sources. One may also get more choices and avail better deals and discounts on conducted tours operated by Visitor Information Centres.

Some of the basic functions of the Visitor Information Centres are as follows:

- The basic objective of the Visitor Information Centre is to give the detailed and authentic information of a destination to the tourist. The Visitor Information Centre may be manned by tourism professionals who have an expertise in suggesting to the visitors about the major attractions to see, good places to stay in, famous restaurants, cafes and pubs to visit and the kind of activities to indulge in during their visit to the destination.

- They may also suggest the possible public transportation systems available at and between destinations. For example, if a traveller wants to travel between Northern Ireland and Republic of Ireland by bus, the Visitor Information Centre may suggest the operating bus links, bus numbers, the ticket prices and the frequency and timings of bus services from Belfast to Dublin.
- Generally, they may also give the information related to HOHO buses available for the city sightseeing for the tourists such as their timings of operation, frequency of boarding and the kind of deals on taking the HOHO bus services.
- The Visitor Information Centre may also suggest itineraries according to the interest of the travellers. For example, for people who are looking for some element of surprise and fun, the Visitor Information Centre at Belfast, Northern Ireland, recommends a 'steam and jazz tour' in Belfast which consists of a ride on the 1960s-restored train hauled by a vintage steam locomotive that takes the passengers to a mystery destination along with a jazz band that plays the local music. The train may halt at any station in the Northern Ireland Railway Network. The tour generally operates 5–6 times a year for locals as well as the tourists where they are taken at an unknown destination that is a surprise for them.
- The Visitor Information Centres also provide important maps, brochures and pamphlets suggesting important itineraries to be covered by a tourist on his/her visit to the destination or a country.
- The staff at the visitor centre also assists the tourists with the bookings and reservations for the tours/itineraries/important shows/attractions and so on. For example, while in Belfast, North Ireland, the staff at the Visitor Information Centre may suggest and book a tour for the tourists to 'the Titanic Museum' and 'the Giant's Causeway tour'.
- The staff at Visitor Information Centre also assists the tourist by comparing the prices and services of package tours offered by different travel companies/tour operators with comparisons on charts and deals that may be best suited for them.

DIGITAL INFORMATION KIOSKS

Many destinations have digital information kiosks at major tourist attraction points or local tourist markets. The tourist can just trace their locations around these digital kiosks and find out all the important information about the place they are planning to visit.

CHARGING POINTS KIOSKS

Many destinations in order to facilitate the tourists and the local hosts have charging points for their smartphones at important locations so that the guests may charge their mobile batteries in case they have exhausted. This is a great respite for tourists as most of the tourists nowadays use smartphones for accessing the Internet so as to easily navigate around the city, which depletes their batteries very fast.

Also, as many destinations of the world have introduced *hybrid cars* that the tourist may hire to practise sustainability, charging points may also be introduced at different points in a destination that may help in charging a car, if required during travel.

CAFES AND RESTAURANTS

The presence of good cafeterias, restaurants, pubs and bars makes a destination livelier for the guests as many travellers during their travel spend a reasonable time at these points. For some travellers, the local food to be tried at specific local locations may be the most important attraction to be covered in their itineraries.

LAUNDRY SERVICES

Personal hygiene during a holiday is of prime concern for a tourist. For travellers who stay in hotels or self-catering apartments, washing facility may not be a problem. While the tourists staying in hotels can give their dirty clothes for washing in a laundry, the tourists staying in apartments equipped with washing machines may wash the clothes on their own. However, many budget travellers, especially backpackers who generally travel on longer vacations and stay in budgeted accommodations such as hostels and B&B inns, find it a challenge from where to get their clothes washed as they may be travelling light with very few clothing options. Also, such travellers have a restriction of budget. For such travellers, destinations must offer laundry services to its tourists.

Providing laundry services to the guests as an extended facility makes the stay of guests at destinations more convenient and comfortable. Destinations may offer a *launderette facility* to their tourists where they arrange coin-operated washers and dryers where the guests can wash their dirty clothes. Many launderettes may be completely automated, whereas in some launderettes, there may be helpful attendants who may assist a tourist with the functioning of washing machines.

Although the primary clientele of launderettes may be the foreign tourists, however, the local community may also avail the services within their residential areas.

SUPERMARKETS

Supermarkets are a storehouse of basic food amenities and toiletries. Supermarket stores generally serve the local community. However, many tourists who travel for a longer duration to a destination, and especially those who stay in self-catering apartments, find them very useful. While staying for longer durations, eating out every day can be an expensive affair that every traveller might not be able to afford. Besides affordability, the tourists may get tired with eating out every day and in some circumstances, the local food might not even suit them. In another limiting case when couples travel with young kids on long vacations, giving kids hotel food all the time may not be a healthy option for them. In all such cases, preparing food for oneself seems to be a viable option. To make food, the tourists have to buy all the daily grocery requirements such as milk, bread, eggs, yoghourt, cereals, fresh vegetables, fruits and sometimes ready-to-eat foods that can be catered to by the supermarkets.

Also, many times while packing his/her stuff for travelling, the tourist may have missed out to carry a few items. In such a case, he/she may buy his/her personal necessities from the local supermarket. Yet for many tourists, supermarkets are an attraction that they visit to spend their spare time, see what the locals buy and sometimes even buy the famous local stuff during the destination for their own consumption. Thus, supermarkets offering quality products are an important amenity for the tourists where they can shop according to their needs and find food or other stuff of international standards.

PHARMACY SHOPS/HOSPITALS

While travelling to a destination, due to weather change, a tourist may fall ill or he/she may report headache, nausea, cough, cold and body aches due to long travelling hours. Some even may report motion sickness due to a long road journey, while some may report lack of sleep or body aches due to jet lag while travelling overseas. In all such cases, the traveller would require a medicine to cure his/her health so that he/she may be able to enjoy the rest of his/her holiday time happily. Every traveller may not carry a pack of medicines with him/her while travelling. Even if some tourists have already packed their medicines, they may have missed out on a few. Therefore, a destination must have enough pharmacy shops at airports, major tourist areas and local markets where generic medicines are available for the tourists. Likewise, there must be enough good hospitals at a destination.

TOURIST POLICE STATIONS

The safety and security of the tourist should be of prime concern for the government at a destination. Tourists are the most susceptible to frauds by the locals as they are unaware of the laws and the functioning of the society of the foreign country that they are visiting. The common problems faced by them may be theft, sexual harassment, overcharging by local shopkeepers and local transporters and cheating by unauthorized guides at tourist attractions due to which they are bound to feel insecure. The presence of tourist police at airports, railway stations and at major tourist areas assures them of their safety and keeps the crime under a check, making the visit of tourists more comfortable and secure at a destination.

For a destination to become more tourist-friendly, it should have dedicated tourist police stations that specifically cater to the challenges and issues faced by the tourists at a destination. The tourist police posted at these police stations must be well trained and have an expertise in dealing with the grievances faced by the tourists (both domestic and international) at a destination.

PUBLIC PARKS

Public parks are an important attraction for the tourist, especially the well-maintained parks with amenities for the tourists. However, public parks may also be classified as an important amenity for a destination as tourists may not always wish to spend time at tourist attractions, local markets or cafes of a destination. On the other hand, the tourist may be looking for an open space where he/she may spend good quality time with himself/herself and with others while experiencing local life. Public parks are a good place for picnicking activity where one can bask under the sun and enjoy the bounties of nature. Public parks must have reasonable amenities for the tourists to spend quality time. For example, *in Hyde Park, one of the eight royal parks located in Central London,* some of the facilities that the visitors may avail are as follows:

- Deck chairs (on paid basis)
- Public conveniences
- An open gym
- Accessible toilets
- Waterside cafe
- Wi-Fi facility
- Disabled parking

Likewise, the facilities available for tourists in Central Park, located at the centre of Manhattan, New York, are as follows:

- Visitor centres giving information on the kind of attractions and the guided tours that one may take inside the park
- Audio-guided devices
- Virtual tours
- Restrooms
- Benches
- Picnic tables

- Trash cans
- Wi-Fi facilities
- Refreshments
- Maps of central park
- Signage for alerts and closures

Thus, to attract tourists, public parks must have reasonable amenities.

AUTHORIZED FOREIGN EXCHANGE COUNTERS/DEALERS

Many tourists while travelling overseas may plan to exchange their currency and buy the local foreign currency on reaching the destination itself. Therefore, this facility must be available for the travellers. Thus, destinations must have authorized foreign exchange agents either at airports/local markets or at major tourist areas where the tourist can have easy access to them to get their currency exchanged.

FREE CASH WITHDRAWALS

Many destinations offer a free cash withdrawal facility for the tourists where there are no charges levied on using the ATM card or debit card for withdrawing the money. However, many international destinations have a basic surcharge on the amount of money being withdrawn by a tourist at a foreign destination.

Washroom Facility for Tourists

PUBLIC CONVENIENCES

Every destination must have the basic public conveniences for the tourists. During long journeys, guests may wish to use the public toilets. Not only toilets should be clean and hygienic, but they should also have the necessary toiletries such as hand wash, hand dryer, tissue rolls, sanitary pad dispensers, dustbins and clean washbasins to facilitate the tourists. Many of the toilets may be paid ones for the tourists' use. Therefore, the tourists may carry loose coins so as to be able to have access to the locked toilets.

PUBLIC SPACE UTILITIES

While a tourist travels to a destination, he/she may be expecting basic amenities that may be available at public areas like in local markets. Therefore, the government must create basic facilities not only for the usage of the local community but also for the tourists. These may include the following:

- Restrooms
- Drinking water facilities
- Garbage cans and waste management
- Public benches for people to relax
- Street lights/lamps preferably using green energy
- Uninterrupted flow of electricity and water supply
- Telephone booths
- Rain shelters
- Waiting rooms
- Parking lots
- Pots and planters for aesthetic appeal of attractions
- Souvenir shops
- Accessible roads, wheelchairs and accessible toilets for people with special abilities
- Pedestrian walkways
- ATM machines
- Green landscaping
- First-aid centres
- Installation of CCTV cameras

SUMMARY

The above discussion has been indicative of the fact that amenities at a destination are a pull factor for the tourists for bringing them to a destination. The absence of the basic amenities at a destination will definitely dissatisfy the guests. Today's traveller wants a comfortable stay at a destination. He/she wants his/her travel to a destination to be hassle-free and eased out. The presence of maximum amenities at a destination creates a favourable impression of a destination in the mind of the tourists. Tourists may wish to come back and spread a positive word of mouth among others if they find world-class facilities at a destination. This may in turn increase the tourist footfall at a destination.

ACTIVITIES

Activity 1

Based on the amenities given in the chapter, carefully examine your city that is your home town. Now prepare a list of amenities that exist in your city and also enlist the amenities that do not exist in your city. Now based on the prepared list, discuss whether your city qualifies as a tourist-friendly destination or not. Share your thoughts with the class. The same list may be prepared in the chart form and presented in the classroom with a discussion on each of the amenities. In case, there are students representing the same city, the same activity may be conducted in groups.

Activity 2

Based on the discussion above on amenities, take a chart and divide it into two parts. Now, list out the 'must-have' amenities and 'could-have' amenities that a destination should have. Give reasons for having chosen and considered the 'must-have amenity' over the 'could have amenity' in a destination.

Based on the strength of the class, the same activity may be carried out either individually or in groups.

Activities at a Destination

LEARNING OBJECTIVES

The given chapter shall clarify the following:

- What are the factors that a tourist might consider while choosing an activity at a destination?
- What are the activities that the travellers indulge in while travelling to a destination?

AURORA SPOTTING IN MAGICAL LAPLAND!

- Want to see Santa Claus's official hometown? Visit Lapland, the largest and northern-most region of Finland, famous for the Northern Lights.
- People from all over the world visit *Rovaniemi*, the capital of Lapland, as it is known to be the *home of Santa Claus*.
- In the summer, the sun sometimes never sets. For 73 days each year, the sun is visible 24/7. June is the perfect time to visit Lapland when you can expect 21–24 hours of light a day.
- The Northern Lights are visible every other night in Lapland, if the skies are clear. The other activities to go along with Aurora spotting are snowshoeing, cross-country skiing, snowmobile safaris, ice karting, husky-dog-sledding and reindeer safaris.
- Tourists can book a 'snow igloo' on AirBnB. The igloos are built by the hosts each winter where they are provided with beds/sleeping bag and lights. Tourists can also enjoy sleeping under the Northern Lights if they are lucky to witness one.
- The Snow Castle of Kemi in Lapland is the biggest snow fort in the world. It has a chapel, a restaurant and a hotel for those who want a chilly experience.

INTRODUCTION

Entertainment is a very important element of tourism. When tourists visit a destination, they wish to be thoroughly entertained there. Thus, many tourist destinations offer world-class entertainment opportunities to the tourists to lure them. Therefore, many cultural and entertainment organizations including other service providers of the tourism industry engage in providing an array of activities for the action-seeking tourists. In other words, we may say that activities are an important source of entertainment for the tourists at a destination. As today's traveller has evolved preferences, he/she is looking for action-packed holidays with new experiences. Thus, travelling is all about activity-based holidays now.

Activities are an important motivating factor for travellers while choosing a destination for their vacation. Travellers visit destinations to get an unforgettable experience of their lifetime. Their visit might include travel to diverse destinations to see the vibrant and diverse cultures, experience the breathtaking beauty of places or try new activities to get an overall feel of a destination. Many destinations internationally package and market themselves for particular activities that go synonymous with the name of that destination. For example, *when travellers think about Rishikesh in India, the 'white water rafting' activity resonates in our mind.* We may divide the tourism markets on the basis of activities that the tourists may be seeking at a destination, which include clubbers, music lovers, foodies, party lovers, nature lovers, socialisers, action seekers, culture seekers, explorers, shopaholics and so on.

CONSIDERATIONS WHILE CHOOSING ACTIVITIES AT A DESTINATION

Travellers may like to pursue an activity on a holiday. However, there are many factors that may or may not lead travellers to choose an activity at a destination. Some of the factors are as follows.

Interest

An important factor is the interest of a traveller. A traveller will only plan doing an activity during his/her holiday time if he/she has an interest or a passion for it. Otherwise, he/she may avoid doing it. Many tourists have a love for waters. They may, thus, opt for water activities while planning their vacation. *In India, they may plan to either visit Goa or Andaman and Nicobar Island to indulge in water sports and adventure that may include surfing, snorkelling, scuba diving, parasailing and so on.*

Age

One of the prime concerns for choosing an activity may be determined by the criteria of one's age. A tourist may be interested to do an activity, but he/she may not be able to pursue it due to the age factor. For example, certain rides at amusement parks have the restriction of age and height. Thus, even if a child wants to do that activity, he/she may be constrained by his/her age factor. Likewise, many teenagers are not allowed to visit night clubs, casinos, taste wine in wineries and so on that they may like to do at a destination.

Budget

Money may be a deterring factor for a traveller while wanting to do an activity. Many travellers may not do an activity due to their budget constraints. For example, *helicopter rides, skydiving and so on are expensive activities* that a tourist might not be able to afford.

Time at Hand

A traveller may be interested in pursuing an activity at a destination. However, he/she may not have enough time to do the activities. This may happen due to his/her hectic itinerary that may be already packed with other attractions to be visited, which may leave him/her with no or hardly any time to pursue all activities of his/her choice at a destination.

Also, at times, certain activities are carried out in the peripheries of a destination that are far off from the main city. This means that the tourist needs to spare the whole day for doing the activity as well as to travel to the excursion point. Thus, if the duration of stay at that destination is short, the tourist may not like to limit himself/herself to one activity only. He/she may rather prioritize other activities over that activity that may consume his/her entire day.

For example, *many water activities such as scuba diving and underwater walk in Andaman and Nicobar Islands, India, are organized in Havelock Island, Neil Island and North Point, and Cinque Island,* and it takes almost an entire day to reach there and do the activity. If the tourist has a short stay in that destination, he/she may not be able to spare enough time to pursue that activity.

Timing of the Activity

Many activities are carried out on particular days and at specific timings at a destination. This may sometimes not match with the itinerary of the tourist. Thus, he/she may not be able to do that activity as he/she may have alternative things prioritized at a destination or he/she may just want to relax at a destination. For example, certain shows and plays at various attractions may take place at particular timings only such as *the Parade at Disneyworld happens in the evening and fireworks happen in the night*. Thus, a tourist must have the whole day with him/her to see those spectacular shows. Likewise, *the Sound and Light Show of Gardens by the bay at Singapore* happens in the late evening in the dim light. A tourist has to plan his/her visit in such a way that can match with the timing of the show.

Physical Stamina

Many activities may not be tried by travellers due to their physical health conditions or strength that may not allow them to do the activity. For example, for pursuing adventure activities, a traveller must be in good health condition.

Ease of Comfort

Many travellers may not be comfortable doing certain activities. They may fear doing certain activities. For example, a traveller may not be comfortable playing polo on the elephant or a camel. A kid may fear taking rides in an amusement park. In such cases, he/she should not be forced to do an activity that he/she may not be comfortable doing.

Sometimes the ease of comfort may also be defined by one's past experiences. If the traveller's past experience while doing an activity may not be very pleasant or he/she may have heard of a mishappening with someone while doing that activity, he/she may not opt for the activity out of the fear associated with it. For example, if while going on a boat tour in the past, the traveller's boat got upside down, the traveller may fear from taking a boat ride in the future. In fact, he/she may totally avoid it.

TYPES OF ACTIVITIES

There are a number of activities that a traveller may choose to do while visiting a destination. A list of activities that the travellers may pursue while travelling to a destination is as follows.

Sightseeing

This is the most popular tourist activity that includes a visit to a destination to see the various points of interest/attractions. Travellers may have top attractions in their bucket list that they might want to cover while visiting a destination. They may like to visit castles, museums, art galleries, amusement parks, historic sites, important landmark buildings, countryside, towns, villages, gardens, religious buildings, zoos, aquariums and so on according to their personal interests and passion. Regardless of age and health factor, this is an activity that travellers prefer doing with least resistance.

To visit these attractions, the tourists may take a package tour that includes either a full-day or a half-day sightseeing tour. These sightseeing tours may be operated by tour operators on *SIC basis* (i.e., seat-in-coach basis) where the travellers get the panoramic tours on a coach with other members of the group travelling together through the same tour operator. Alternatively, they may take a HOHO bus service to visit the city attractions on their own. Otherwise, the travellers may walk down, use public transportation or hire private taxis to explore the city attractions.

For example, while visiting Singapore, the sightseeing tour would generally include a visit to the *Merlion Statue, Marina Bay Sands, the Esplanade, Singapore Flyer, the modern skyscrapers of the Central Business District (CBD), Orchard Road, Chinatown, traditional shophouses of Clarke Quay and Boat Quay* and so on.

Bird Watching/Watching Wildlife/Marine Life

Many bird enthusiasts and wildlife enthusiasts visit destinations for watching birds and fauna in their natural settings. They may visit national parks, natural reserves, wildlife sanctuaries, wetlands, aquariums, tiger reserves, forests and zoos that are a wealth of tropical birds, different species of animals and rich biodiversity. Such travellers may go to watch the fauna in Jeep safaris, do photography and capture the wildlife in their lens or feed the animals, wherever allowed. Some of the famous wildlife attractions are as follows:

Sea World, Indonesia

- Bharatpur Bird Sanctuary, Rajasthan, India
- Dubai Dolphinarium, Dubai
- Feeding kangaroos in Phillip Island, Australia
- Jurong Bird Park, Singapore
- Jungle Safari in Tanzania

Travel Photography

Many travellers visit destinations for just clicking pictures of a destination. For some, it may be a passion, whereas for some it may be a business opportunity. They may visit the iconic attractions, capture them in their camera lens and then post the pictures and images clicked either in their travel blogs or on social networking sites. They may even sell the photographs to the travel magazines or other tourism industry service providers. *For example, a photographer may visit Norway just to capture the Northern Lights in his camera lens.* Likewise, many travellers who are professional photographers may visit India 'the land of festivals' to click colourful images of the people and the festivals like the *Lathmaar Holi of Barsana in Mathura, Uttar Pradesh, India.*

Shopping

The top to-do activity for shopaholic travellers is shopping at the destination being visited. Especially, this is a popular activity among women travellers. Many destinations of the world position themselves as shopper's paradise such as *India, Dubai* and *Singapore*. Shopping is considered as an important activity for a destination as it gives impetus to the local economy.

Thus, travellers are generally encouraged to purchase the local stuff of a destination so as to encourage the local artisans and craftsmen to preserve their craftsmanship and help them in sustaining their livelihoods.

Travellers may visit the famous local streets, local markets, haats, exhibitions, shopping emporiums and shopping malls of a destination. Travellers may also specially plan their travel to a destination during the shopping festivals so as to get the best deals at the place. For example, one of the largest shopping festivals in the Middle East is organized by Dubai, 'the Dubai Shopping Festival', annually to increase the tourist footfall by offering deals and discounts on products in every mall, global village, flea markets and local hideouts.

Some of the famous shopping areas of the world are as follows:

- Nanjing Road, Shanghai, China
- The Grand Bazaar, Istanbul, Turkey
- Deira Gold Souk (world's renowned largest gold bazaar in the world), Dubai, UAE
- Deira Spice Souk, Dubai, UAE
- Chandni Chowk, Old Delhi, India
- Khari Baoli for spices, Chandni Chowk, Delhi, India
- Flea market at Anjuna Beach on Wednesdays in Goa, India
- Queen Victoria market and Dandenong market, Melbourne, Australia
- Ibn Battuta Mall, Mall of Emirates and Dubai Mall at Dubai, UAE
- The Harrods shopping Mall, London, UK
- Orchard Road, Singapore (Asia's famous shopping street)

Cuckoo Clocks, Blackforest, Germany

Travellers may also shop for local specialties of the destination either for themselves or for their family and friends. These souvenirs are lifetime memories. Tourists may buy the following souvenirs while visiting a destination:

- Cuckoo clocks from Black Forest, Germany
- The Taj Mahal miniature from India
- The cashmere scarf and the Scottish Whiskey from Scotland
- Windmills, cheese and wooden shoes (Klompen) from the Netherlands
- Swiss watches, knives and Swiss chocolates from Switzerland
- Godiva chocolates from Belgium
- The Statue of Liberty miniature, New York, USA
- Cosmetics from South Korea
- Spices from India

Amusement Parks, Rides and Shows

Amusement parks and theme parks are an important activity centre as well as an attraction for tourists where the tourists can spend days or at least a whole day engaging in various different activities. They may engage the tourists in various activities like taking rides, watching shows such as magic show, puppet shows, parades and fireworks. Some of the famous amusement and theme parks are listed as follows:

Amusement Ride at Disneyland, Los Angeles, USA

- Disneyworld, Florida, USA
- Disney's Hollywood Studios, Orlando, Florida, USA
- Universal Studios, Singapore
- Wild Wadi Water Park, Dubai, UAE (outdoor water park)
- Ski Dubai, UAE (first indoor ski resort in the Middle East)
- Ferrari World, Abu Dhabi, UAE (the largest amusement park of the world)
- EsselWorld, Mumbai, India
- Chokhi Dhani, Jaipur, Rajasthan, India

Adventure Activities

Many travellers now visit destinations with the specific purpose of pursuing adventure activities. Travellers may indulge in *soft or hard adventure activities* depending upon their level of comfort. Soft adventure activities are less risky and can be done with ease and, therefore, appeal to more tourist segments as they require less physical effort such as biking, hiking, walking and camping.

On the other hand, hard adventure activities require one to move out of the comfort zone as they involve an element of risk such as trekking, mountain climbing and rock climbing.

Another classification for adventure activities may be as follows.

Land-based Adventure Sports

These activities are performed on the land. Some of these are as follows:

- Trekking
- Mountain biking

- Sand dune bashing
- Sand boarding
- Skiing

Water-based Adventure Sports

These activities are performed in the water. Travellers who are water lovers may love to do such activities. Some of these are as follows:

- Surfing
- Parasailing
- Snorkelling
- Scuba diving
- Underwater walks
- Canoeing
- Kayaking
- White water rafting
- Windsurfing
- Sailing
- Flyboarding
- Wakeboarding

Aerial-based Adventure Sports

These activities are performed in the air and involve a lot of risk.
Some of these are as follows:

- Sky diving
- Bungee jumping
- Cliff diving
- Paragliding
- Para motoring
- Hang gliding
- Hot air ballooning

Travellers may choose to do any kind of these adventure sports depending upon their interests and their level of comfort with the activity along with their physical fitness. For example, many international travellers who are passionate about *scuba diving visit Havelock Islands in the Andaman and Nicobar Islands, India,* to learn and take training lessons on scuba diving, staying for days and months on the island. Likewise, adventure tourists interested in *skydiving* would travel to destinations such as *Australia, the USA* and *Dubai* to pursue it. Destinations such as *South Africa* and *New Zealand* are the leading players in adventure tourism.

Watching Shows

Many destinations of the world are known for their spectacular shows. When travellers visit such destinations, the shows are the top priority for visitors to see. For example, *Las Vegas is famous for shows which are organized by many hotels there.*

Some of the famous shows of the world at different destinations are as follows:

- Songs of the Sea Show, Sentosa Island, Singapore
- The Lido Show, Paris
- The Acrobatic Show, Shanghai, China
- The Garden Rhapsody Light and Sound Show at Gardens by the Bay, Singapore
- The Light and Sound Show, Red Fort, New Delhi
- The Dubai Fountain Show
- The Tiger Show at Dreamworld, Gold Coast, Australia
- The Tiger Show, Pattaya, Thailand
- The Shamu Show at SeaWorld, San Diego
- The Sea Lion Show at SeaWorld, Indonesia
- The Dolphin Show at SeaWorld, San Diego
- Walk with the Lion Show, Mauritius
- The KÀ Show at Las Vegas, USA
- Fountains of Bellagio at Bellagio Hotel, Las Vegas
- Zangoora Show, Kingdom of Dreams, Gurugram, India

Joy Rides

Another must-to-do activity for travellers at a destination is to take joy rides at the famous transportation attractions. Some of the worth-taking joy rides are as follows:

Shamu Show, SeaWorld, San Diego

Dolphin Show, SeaWorld, San Diego

Puffing Billy Train, Melbourne, Australia

- The helicopter ride at Grand Canyon
- Las Vegas Strip helicopter tour at night
- Niagara Falls helicopter tour
- The helicopter ride at Melbourne, Australia
- Seaplane flight in Dubai
- Singapore cable car ride at Sentosa Island
- Cable car ride on Rotair, Mt Titlis, Switzerland (world's first revolving cable car revolving at 360 degrees)
- San Francisco cable car ride
- Toy train ride at Kalka–Shimla Railway, India
- The Scenic Railway Ride, Blue Mountains, Sydney (steepest passenger railway in the world)
- Puffing Billy Railway ride at Melbourne, Australia
- The Darjeeling Himalayan Train ride

Safaris

Going for camel safaris/elephant safaris/jeep safaris is one of the highlights for many travellers while visiting many holiday destinations. These are not-to-be-missed activities. Some of the must-to-do safaris for the travellers are as follows:

- Desert Safari, Dubai
- Yak Safari, Ladakh, India
- Camel Safari, Jaisalmer, India
- Double-humped Camel Safari at Nubra Valley, Ladakh, India
- Elephant Safari, Kerala, India
- Jeep Safari, Ranthambhore, India
- Night Safari, Singapore

Taking Local Tours

Many travellers prefer taking local walking tours/Segway/bike tours/motorbike tours and so on to understand and explore a destination better and to gain its local insights. Taking food walks, heritage walks, nature walks and so on are one of the best activities to indulge in for travellers while visiting a destination. For example, many travellers may take a local tour of how to make copper bells, pottery making, handloom weaving and so on to learn about the tradition of Bhuj, a small town in Gujarat. Some of the other examples of famous walking tours are as follows:

- A heritage walk at Ahmedabad, India (a world heritage city declared by UNESCO)
- A walking tour in Melaka, Malaysia (a world heritage city declared by UNESCO)

- Food walk at Chandni Chowk, Old Delhi, India
- Textile tour at Bhuj, Gujarat, India
- Walking tour at Florence, Italy
- Segway tour, Rajpath, New Delhi, India
- Cultural tour to the Thar Desert, Rajasthan

Yoga and Meditation Retreats

Many travellers may visit destinations for learning and practising Yoga or attending meditation sessions. Yoga and meditation are important activities that keep the mind calm and help in the overall well-being of a person. Due to the origin of Yoga in India, it is an important destination for travellers who want to learn the art of Yoga while visiting India. People visit Rishikesh, Haridwar, Goa, Dharamshala, Varanasi, Auroville in Puducherry, Kerala and so on to understand and assimilate the art of Yoga by attending various retreats and courses.

Attending Ceremonies

For many travellers, attending ceremonies at destinations is an activity that may be very exciting for them. Some of the famous ceremonies worth attending for travellers are:

- The Ganga aarti at Varanasi, India
- The Beating Retreat Ceremony at Wagah Border, Amritsar, India
- The Changing of the Guard Ceremony at the Buckingham Palace, London, UK
- The Disney Parade at Disneyworld, USA
- The Palki Ceremony at Golden Temple, Amritsar, India
- The fireworks at Disneyland, Hong Kong

Playing Sports

Sports are a passion of many travellers. Travellers may visit destinations to participate, to learn or to watch sports. Some of the popular sports activities are as follows:

- Playing polo on camels/horses
- Playing golf
- Go karting
- Horseback riding
- Playing martial arts
- Playing Jiu-Jitsu
- Ice skiing
- Ice skating

Fishing

Fishing is another interesting and exciting activity for many travellers. Such travellers enjoy it as a popular pastime to spend their vacations. Sea fishing enthusiasts and mariners may be fond of deep-sea fishing.

Attending Events

Events are another important activity that travellers may wish to indulge in. In fact, many travellers plan their visit to a destination during the time of an event. Some of the special events that may attract a tourist are as follows:

- Weddings (e.g., attending a grandeur Indian wedding of a friend or a relative)
- Attending musical concerts like Sunburn Festival, India
- Special personal events such as anniversary and birthday celebrations
- Sporting events (e.g., rugby match, Formula 1 Australian Grand Prix 2019, Melbourne)
- Cultural festivals (such as Lohri of Punjab, India and La Tomatina festival of Spain)
- Business events (such as International Trade Fair and International Book Fair, New Delhi, India)

Participating in Product Demonstrations

Participating in product demonstrations is an important activity for travellers that they may enjoy doing while visiting a destination. Some of the popular factory visits and demonstrations attended by travellers are as follows:

- Attending a class on bread making in Paris on a French Bakery tour
- Visiting the Chocolate Factory, Philip Island, Australia
- Visiting the Cheese and Shoes Factory, the Netherlands
- Visiting the Murano Glass Factory, Venice, Italy
- Visiting the tea factory, Assam, India
- Visiting the coffee plantations in Chikmagalur, Karnataka, India
- Visiting the wineries, vineyards and distilleries, Scotland
- Visiting the Black Forest in Germany for cuckoo-clock demonstrations

Attending Theatre/Opera/Ballet/Music

Another pastime activity for travellers is to watch theatrical performances, operas, ballets and other dance performances at a destination. Some worth attending performances are as follows:

- Watching opera at Sydney Opera House
- Watching plays at National School of Drama, New Delhi or at Prithvi Theatre, Mumbai
- Enjoying the Irish music at Irish pubs
- Watching theatrical performances at Piccadilly Circus, London

Manly Beach, Sydney, Australia

Exploring the Coast

Visiting seaside resorts and destinations by the coast may be a top choice activity for beach bums. Travellers may spend a quality time of their holiday on the sea beach just basking in the sun, tanning their bodies or enjoying the wafers with a dip while chit-chatting with the family/friends. Some may relax in the beach shacks, whereas some may participate in the water sports being offered on the beach.

Nature Park, Phillip Island, Australia

Volunteering Activities

Many travellers spend their vacations in a fruitful way by engaging in social service activities. They may visit a destination with the objective of volunteering to associate themselves with a cause. They may engage in the following volunteering activities at a destination:

- Teaching the poor kids
- Working in an old-age home
- Aiding the farmers in organic farming
- Spreading awareness of hygiene and sanitation
- Creating an awareness about the environment among the host community

Dining

For many travellers, eating and drinking at local cafes, eateries, restaurants, fine dining restaurants, pubs and bars is a popular pastime that they look forward to. Trying the local cuisine on the local streets of a destination is also on the itineraries of many travellers. Every country of the world may have its own rich food that may be again a combination of regional cuisines that are representative of the culture of the country. For example, for many travellers, *India is a land of 'curries and spices'.* Some of the best foods that people may try while visiting destinations in the world are:

- Desert safari with barbeque dinner in Dubai
- Visiting Paranthe Wali Gali in Chandni Chowk, Old Delhi
- Taking a dumpling tour at Nanjing in China
- Trying the Punjabi Thali of Punjab, India, with Lassi

Indulging in Spa

Certain destinations of the world specialize in offering spa facilities as they may have natural thermal springs which are a rich source of minerals that can heal anyone of their skin diseases besides relaxing and rejuvenating them. Many travellers may pamper themselves by indulging in relaxing therapies and treatments during their vacations. Some of the famous destinations of the world that offer spa facilities are:

- Tuscany, Italy
- Ananda Spa in Rishikesh, India
- Kerala, India
- Turkey for *hammam* (Turkish bath)
- Budapest (spa capital of the world being a home to large number of hot springs)
- Bali in Indonesia

Cruising/Boating

Spending an evening on the cruises by the river and witnessing some of the panoramic spectacular views of a city is a favourite pastime for many travellers. Some destinations may also offer gondola rides and boat tours to woo the tourists.

Some of the famous cruises/boat tours in the world are:

- Gondola ride in Venice, Italy
- Maid of the Mist, Niagara Falls, USA
- Sunrise boat tour of Varanasi at river Ganges, India
- Boating at Purana Qila, New Delhi, India
- Chicago river cruise (it is generally a 60–90 minute tour to view the world-famous architectural marvels of more than 40 skyline buildings of Chicago cruising through the Chicago river with an ongoing commentary of a knowledgeable on-board tour guide)
- Singapore river cruise
- Huangpu River Cruise, Shanghai, China
- Dhow Dinner Cruise, Dubai

- Mandovi River Cruise Goa, India
- Cruise at Seine River, Paris

Enjoying the Nightlife

Many travellers just visit a destination to enjoy the vibrant and electrifying nightlife there, to party and just to hang out with friends. For such travellers enjoying the nightlife, having beach parties, partying at discotheques, pubs, jazz clubs, bars are an idea of spending an ideal vacation. Few cities of the world that become alive in the night offering non-stop after-hours entertainment to the tourists are as follows:

- Las Vegas
- Tel Aviv
- Goa
- Mumbai
- Amsterdam
- Paris
- London
- Bangkok
- New York
- Miami

Gambling

Another popular way of spending one's holiday is gambling in casinos, an activity famous among the casino players. Many destinations are known for casinos in the world. Some of these where travellers visit in numbers to play in casinos are as follows:

- Las Vegas, Nevada
- Macau, China
- Atlantic city, New Jersey
- Monte Carlo, Monaco
- London, UK
- San Juan, Puerto Rico
- Aruba, the Caribbean
- Genting Highlands, Malaysia

Spelunking/Caving

For many cavers, caving is an important adventure activity at a destination that interests them. Cavers may move in groups to explore caves and to know and understand the world inside the caves. Travellers may visit those destinations that are famous for caving. Some of the destinations of the world famous for caving are as follows:

- The USA
- France
- Italy
- Australia
- New Zealand
- Slovenia
- India

Research Expeditions

Visiting destinations for doing research is an important activity for researchers. Researchers may be doing research pertaining to the climate, flora and fauna, culture, archaeology and so on of a destination. For example, botanists may be visiting various botanical gardens and parks to study the flora of a destination. Thus, primarily travelling for research-related to a particular field may be an activity for such travellers.

SUMMARY

Travellers choose and visit those destinations that are famous for a particular activity. The choice of any activity may be affected by various factors such as the time in hand or timing of an activity, one's budget, personal interest, one's health condition, age and ease of comfort. There are myriad activities to choose from that a destination may have to offer. Some of the activities that tourists can enjoy at a destination are sightseeing, shopping, doing adventure activities, taking rides, bird watching, safaris, visiting amusement parks, doing travel photography, attending local events, taking local tours, dining, volunteering, watching shows, attending ceremonies and product demonstrations, going for river cruises, exploring the coast, fishing, playing sports, enjoying the nightlife, indulging in spas, going for Yoga and meditation retreats, exploring the coast, playing in casinos, caving, doing research and so on.

Thus, it is important for the destinations and tourism industry to understand that activities play a significant role for travellers in choosing their destinations. Therefore, the destinations must realize that if they are offering an activity as a tourism product, they must package and market it well so that travellers are clear about the value proposition being offered by the destination. This may lead to an increase in the tourist footfall to a destination.

ACTIVITIES

Activity 1

Imagine you have the choice of going on a vacation for a week. Now which destination would you choose, and which activities would you opt for? Deliberate and share your views with the other classmates.

Activity 2

Create a festival of your own that you would like to promote in your area. Discuss the reasons for promoting the festival along with the detailed plan to organize the festival. Have an interesting tagline along with a logo to attract the tourists. Specify the tourism markets, the travel arrangements that you would do for the guests and the list of activities that shall be included in the festival along with a desirable all-inclusive travel package for the tourists.

Activity 3

Identify the souvenirs you may purchase from the following cities/countries:

- Switzerland
- India
- Istanbul
- New York
- Black Forest
- Sydney
- Brussels
- Paris
- Singapore
- Kashmir

Case Studies

B.1. AN ACTION-PACKED HOLIDAY

Introduction

A couple living in Delhi decided to travel to a new place. They had visited many destinations before, but this time they wanted something different. After a tonne of discussions, disagreements and research, they stumbled on a marketing campaign called 'There is nothing like Australia', which caught their attention. After reading about Australia on its official website and listening to their friends talk good things about Australia who had recently been there, the couple finally chose their next destination. Australia offered a variety of fabulous activities and new experiences which were exactly what they wanted on their trip.

After finalizing their destination, they started to make a list of the things that they wanted to experience in a month's vacation.

Australia's Marketing Campaign

- With the objective to re-establish its credibility and reinstate the flow of tourist traffic within the country amidst the outbreak of Bushfires that had either led to cancellation or postponement of traveller's plans, the Australian Tourism Board unveiled in March 2020 its existing marketing campaign to a modified version that says **There Is Still Nothing Like Australia**.
- Tourism Australia advertised its another campaign 'Come Live Our Philausophy' in 2019 to elevate Australia's character and its people. This global campaign was worth 38 million dollars.

They found a number of fun activities to do in Australia and set their itineraries as follows.

Melbourne

They booked their tickets through Qantas airways and then they flew to Melbourne, which is the capital city of Victoria and also famously known as the 'coffee capital of the world'. After reaching Melbourne, which was their first stop and recovering from the jet lag, the couple started with the first thing in their itinerary.

Local Sightseeing

The couple took a HOHO bus and went for a city tour.

They first visited Melbourne's CBD where they visited the Federation Square, art-filled laneways, art galleries and so much more. They also had a shopping spree in Queen Victoria Market. Then, they saw the giant Melbourne Cricket Ground, which is considered as Australia's favourite stadium. Just 4 km away from the centre of Melbourne, the duo also met beautiful animals in the Melbourne Zoo.

To give a perfect end to their city tour, the couple had one of the best dining experiences in the Colonial Tramcar Restaurant. The award-winning restaurant is a converted fleet of three vintage tramcars where the duo tasted amazing local cuisine of Australia.

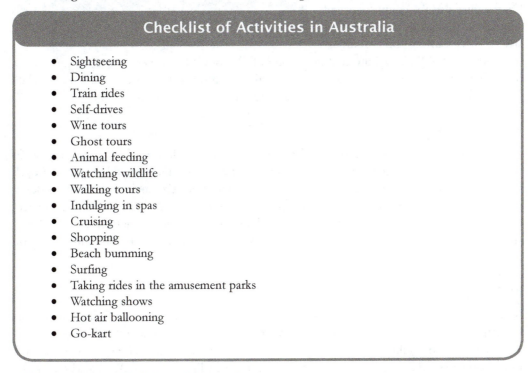

Checklist of Activities in Australia

- Sightseeing
- Dining
- Train rides
- Self-drives
- Wine tours
- Ghost tours
- Animal feeding
- Watching wildlife
- Walking tours
- Indulging in spas
- Cruising
- Shopping
- Beach bumming
- Surfing
- Taking rides in the amusement parks
- Watching shows
- Hot air ballooning
- Go-kart

Williamstown Walking Ghost Tour

The couple had a spooky and fun experience in a two-hour guided walking ghost tour through King William's town. They visit scary hidden alleyways, morgues and the opium den used in *Miss Fisher's Murder Mysteries*.

The Great Ocean Road Tour

After a lovely city tour, the couple planned an excursion for the next day and enjoyed one of the world's most scenic coastal drive on the Great Ocean Road. The 400-kilometre-stretch has amazing beaches, clifftops and gor-geous nature. The couple decided to hire a car on rent and self-drive on the Great Ocean Road to enjoy the real scenic views. Enjoying the breath-taking limestone pillars known as the Twelve Apostles was truly fantastic. Spending an entire day at one of the most important landmarks of Australia was worth every second.

Twelve Apostles, Victoria, Australia

Puffing Billy Railway Ride

On the third day, the couple boarded Australia's most favourite heritage steam train Puffing Billy Railway. Opened in 1900, Puffing Billy Railway is one of the finest preserved steam railways in the world. They both enjoyed a relaxing journey in the beautiful steam train ride as they travelled through the dense rainforests of the Dandenong Ranges in Melbourne.

Yarra Valley

From Melbourne, the couple drove about an hour to reach the oldest wine region in Australia—the Yarra Valley. They tasted special sparkling wine and enjoyed exquisite French cuisine in various wineries and bistros. Their day would not be complete without a ride on hot air balloon at the 'Global Ballooning Australia'. From high above, they could see a spectacular view of vineyards, scenic landscapes and mountains. Exactly what the Yarra Valley is all about. A tour of De Bortoli's vineyards and winery sealed their day with bliss and amazement.

Philip Island

Next day, the couple set their course for some adventure, so they went to Phillip Island, just 90 minutes away from Melbourne. Hand feeding kangaroos and watching the Penguin's parade in the natural and wildlife parks were the best experiences for the duo. Hungry for some thrill, those two had a great time go-karting at go-kart tracks in Philip Island. After a whole day of fun, a trip to the chocolate factory was a must!

Hidden Laneway

A friend of theirs told them not to miss the tour of Melbourne's laneways. In a 2.5-hour tour, also known as walking tour, they visited quirky cafes and drank amazing coffee. Art displays in the beautiful galleries brightened their whole day. In the end, they bought souvenirs at funky shops and decided to visit a beach.

St Kilda Beach

Just 6 km from the Melbourne city centre, the couple spent a nice evening strolling St Kilda beach. This 700-metre-long beach is located in St Kilda, Victoria, offering a beautiful atmosphere to relax.

Royal Botanic Garden

Another day, another exploration. The Royal Botanic Garden surprised the couple with forest therapy, harp meditations, a solar tour in Melbourne observatory and not to forget the whole baggage of tranquillity and relaxation at the peaceful lakes. They did not forget to buy some souvenirs from gift shops present inside the gardens.

Peninsula Hot Springs

After a long week of exploration and adventure, it was time to relax at the most amazing natural hot springs and day spa in the Mornington Peninsula, an excursion from Melbourne. The couple visited Peninsula Hot Springs to soak in the natural thermal hot springs. They also enjoyed a nice Turkish steam bath (*hammam*) and the most relaxing wellness treatments.

Go-karting, Phillip Island, Australia

Sydney

After a lovely 10 days in Melbourne, the couple travelled to the harbour city—Sydney—which is the oldest and most urbane city in Australia. Both of them were excited to experience a different kind of activities in Sydney.

Sydney Opera House

Their first stop was one of the world's most artistic and most bustling performing arts centres. They spent their time enjoying opera performances in the Opera House and loved every second of it.

Opera House, Sydney, Australia

Sydney Harbour Bridge

Next, they visited the famous Sydney Harbour Bridge (also known as 'Coat Hanger'). Being amongst a few climbable bridges, they met lovely climbers and enjoyed the spectacular view during their climb. The best way to enjoy this venue is on foot and the experience was truly iconic.

The Blue Mountains Scenic Train Ride: World's Steepest Train

The best way to combine adventure and scenery was riding on the steepest passenger train in the Blue Mountains. The Scenic Railway, known as the world's steepest train, gave them a thrill-filled tour of the Three Sisters, Katoomba Falls and Jamison Valley. Just 100 km west of Sydney, they had great fun riding cable cars, skywalks and nice little cafes at the top of the hills.

The Blue Mountain Scenic Train, Sydney, Australia

Nepean Belle River

The couple had fun riding on the paddle wheeler cruises and enjoyed the serenity of the Nepean Belle River. The gorges are truly hidden gems of Sydney.

Bondi Beach

After an amazing adventure, the duo decided to have some beach fun. Time spent at one of the most iconic white sand beaches was indescribable. They had an amazing time surfing and water sporting the whole time. The relaxation and adventure were worth spending an entire day at Bondi Beach.

The Grounds Market Tour

Last, they went to the local Sydney market in Alexandria, where they saw amazing performances, bought great local products and soaked in the lively atmosphere of the grounds market.

Gold Coast

As beautiful as Sydney is, there is no way the couple were going to miss enjoying fun activities in Gold Coast. Just one and half hour's journey via flight from Sydney, Gold Coast is very popular for its theme parks, beaches and ancient rainforests.

Surfers Paradise Beach

One of the most famous beaches of Australia, particularly Gold Coast, is the Surfers Paradise Beach. Both of them spent a nice day surfing, swimming and relaxing a quiet time on the golden sands.

A Visit to the Amusement Parks

The adventure lovers visited the Dreamworld which is Australia's biggest theme park. They had a lot of fun in this park as it had over 40 rides and attractions including the Tower of Terror II, one of the tallest and fastest thrill rides in the world. They were also astounded to watch the tiger show.

The next day, they went to meet their favourite movie characters in Warner Bros. Movie World. They screamed their gut out on many adventure rides including the DC Rivals HyperCoaster and also enjoyed amazing performances.

Surfers Paradise, Gold Coast, Australia

Dreamworld, Gold Coast, Australia

They also visited Australia's number one Marine Park, the Sea World, where they met various marine animals, had fun on the water rides and learned about animal rescue and conservation projects.

Gold Coast Hinterland

In their last day of the Australian tour, the couple chose lush greenery over warm and golden sand. The untouched, unspoiled rainforests and scenic mountain views gave a perfect end to an amazing, adventurous and spectacular tour.

Conclusion

This case study is focused on the activities a tourist can indulge in when they travel to a new destination. The couple wanted an action-packed holiday and visiting Australia was a dream come true. Their expectations were fulfilled by indulging in the activities such as kangaroo feeding, amazing train rides, wine tasting, surfing, thrill-filled theme parks and so much more. The couple went home happy and satisfied after their adventurous holiday in Australia.

Learning Outcomes

- There is a particular segment of tourists who wants something different than mere sightseeing. They want to indulge in various activities and experience new things to do.
- It is the responsibility of destination authorities and private players to develop various activities which can attract the tourist to a destination. Not only they should create opportunities for various activities at a destination, but they should also position and market a destination in the right way in order to increase tourist traffic to a destination.
- The travellers seeking activities during their holiday must research well on the activities that a destination provides before they decide to choose a destination to avoid any cognitive dissonance in the future.

Points for Discussion

- How is travelling with the travel agency different from travelling on your own? Discuss the pros and cons.
- Australia is a big destination with diverse communities and individuals. What are the problems a tourist may face after travelling to such places?

B.2. RYANAIR

Introduction

So let us paint a picture together. You work hard for days and months to go on a vacation that you have been dreaming about for some time now. You gather all your money, make a budget, make an itinerary and daydream about all the things you are going to do when you reach your destination. You expect everything to go as smoothly as butter, just like you planned. Yet life somehow finds a way to give you a little detour. And that is exactly what happened with Amiksha and Anand. While travelling to London from Dublin, by Ryanair, they faced an unfortunate situation. Prior to two hours before their check-in time, the couple reached the airport on time excited to leave for their next destination, London, as they were travelling to many destinations in the UK. Now, one would think that while travelling by an airline, you do not require a lot of information. You pay for your ticket, pack your luggage, check in at your required time and climb aboard to fly in the skies. Alas, things were not that simple and the couple learned that the hard way, especially with Ryanair. After reaching the airport, the couple went to the check-in counter of Ryanair to complete their check-in process. When they met the staff and showed their passport ID proofs, they were asked to pay €110 to which the couple shouted as to why they had to pay this hefty amount when they had already paid a heavy amount of €197 for the ticket. They were told by the lady sitting on the check-in counter that since they had not done their check-in online, they had to pay this amount as a penalty. Now, the couple was in a deep state of shock. They did not know that Ryanair has a requirement to check in online before 48 hours to 2 hours from your scheduled flight. And the passengers who are not able to do so? Well, they pay a fee of €55 (£48). Our unlucky couple was one of those people. They either had to pay that enormous fee of €110 or not board the plane at all. And no amount of explanations or resistance could get them out of this tragic state of affair, and they had to do what they were asked to. The whole trip cost them €307. The airlines argued that they were informed through an email and that it is the responsibility of the passengers travelling to be aware of the rules of the airlines that they are travelling with.

Conclusion

This case is about a couple who faces an issue with the airline due to their ignorance on the check-in policy of the airline. The happy trip of the couple turns out to be a nightmare for them when they get to know that they have to pay a heavy penalty for not having checked in online with the airline.

Learning Outcomes

- The rules and regulations with respect to check-in, baggage allowance and so on vary from airline to airline.
- It is always advisable for the traveller to check with the respective airlines their check-in policy, especially those travellers who are travelling on their own to avoid any surprises later.

Points for Discussion

1. Is the airline at fault or is it the couple's fault? What is your take on the same?
2. What would you do in such a situation?

B.3. HOTEL HELL

Introduction

Three workaholic women, working in different and hectic fields, needed to blow off some steam and wanted to spend some relaxing time with each other. Being best friends, they rarely had any time for themselves, let alone for each other. One day, one of those three decided to make a plan for the weekend as a small get together was overdue. Working life in Mumbai can be very stressful, so they chose to go on a road trip to the outskirts of Pune which is famous for its greenery, hills and quiet atmosphere. They got together one evening and started a search for some place to stay. Their requirements for the accommodation were very simple—clean, safe, easily accessible and good vicinity.

In this digital era, booking accommodations is very easy and instant. Online apps such as Trivago, Booking.com, Oyo, Goibibo and AirBnB provide accommodation services to the users without much hassle. Knowing this, three of them picked the most recognized app and looked for a hotel which matched their needs. The choice of their destination was outside the city because they wanted a calm environment. This meant a reduced number of choices for accommodation.

After a lot of scanning, they found a hotel which promised everything they required. A peaceful area, safe and most importantly, photos displayed on the app were of squeaky-clean rooms, the area around the hotel was just as they wanted, and the building looked very assuring. They analysed every detail advertised on the page thoroughly. Most of the reviews given on the app were positive, which was enough assurance for them.

After a long and fun ride to Pune, they reached their destination. The area looked pretty decent, and the hotel building seemed reasonably decent. They parked their car and went inside. As they entered, to their horror, the reception area smelled of alcohol and the atmosphere was very unsettling. Because they had already paid for the rooms through the app, there was not much they could do. They desperately needed some time to relax so they hoped for the best and completed the check-in process. After they entered their room, everything fell apart. It seemed like the room was not cleaned after being used by the last guest who must have stayed there. They could see the spider webs in most of the corners in their room, and the bed had a few bugs on it. The wall paint was chipped almost everywhere, and the window could barely shut. It was the saddest, underwhelming and unclean room they have ever seen. 'How could the photos be this misleading?' they said. Not only that, the condition of the bathroom was horrible, the TV was not working, every corner smelled very odd and the neighbouring rooms were packed with idiotic men who were roaming around in the lobby area and kept staring at the girls which made them feel very uncomfortable. It was the most horrifying moment for them. Still making the best out of the situation, they tried to enjoy each other's company as they were too tired to find another place to stay.

After a disappointing night, they decided that it was enough and registered a complaint to the app authorities. After a long and painful conversation, the only thing hotel staff could do was clean the rooms a bit. Sadly, it did nothing. After a while of discussion, those three decided to leave the place and find another one in the city. It was not what they had planned, nor they felt any relaxed.

Soon the weekend was over and their wish for a relaxing outing was filled with disappointments.

Conclusion

When a traveller decides to visit a destination, he/she ensures a few things in advance. Like transportation, itinerary, shopping for the needful things and most importantly accommodation. This study is based on an incident faced by three working women who wanted to have a peaceful weekend with each other, but instead, they faced a big issue with the accommodation. They expected the best and got something worst instead. Not only they had a horrible experience at the hotel, but also their agenda of having a relaxing outing failed. Because of the misleading photographs and false hotel information on the app they used, their whole perspective and trust in the online accommodation process became non-existent.

Learning Outcomes

- Accommodation is an important component of tourism, just as important as transportation. Nowadays, many online apps and websites for booking accommodations are uploading misleading photos of the hotel properties, which creates a negative impression on the mind of tourists.
- False or half information about the accommodation is bad for the reputation of a hotel, the app as well as the destination. Thus, it is the responsibility of the service providers to ensure that the information given about a property is honest and factual on the app.
- Tourists should always call the property and reassure about their requirements. Paying on arrival is the best option if tourist and travellers are unsure about the properties.
- Women's safety is more important nowadays. If the situation is not comfortable, then they must opt for another plan rather than compromising for the sake of a few reasons such as budget, tiredness or limited time for a vacation.
- Nowadays, women are increasingly travelling. Thus, hotels should give special attention to the needs of female travellers and must have an independent floor dedicated to women only. They should have dedicated women-only housekeeping staff and

rooms with decor suiting to the taste of women in general. All these few steps by a hotel ensure the safety for women travellers and also show their sensitivity towards this sect of emerging travellers.

Points for Discussion

- The case mentions that three girls chose to stay for a night in the hotel despite the condition of the hotel rooms. Did they make the right decision? If not, discuss the possible alternatives by keeping their agenda in mind.
- Many travellers nowadays are facing issues with online accommodation apps. Discuss a few accommodation issues and give suggestions on how to solve such problems.
- Did you have any similar experience? Share it with the class.

B.4. THE WI-FI FAILURE

Introduction

A famous novelist from the USA, George Perry, had come to India to work on his upcoming publication. The novel he was working on involved the adventures of a young girl in the Indian subcontinent who consequently gets lost within the jungles of the Himalayas. That is why the writer wanted to draw direct inspiration from the actual land where the story was supposed to take place to give an authentic feel to his writing. George had heard about India that it is a preferred destination among the writer community because of its world-famous hospitality and also because India proved to be a rather pocket-friendly destination. Therefore, he booked a hotel in a remote village called Ramgarh in Uttarakhand, to stay away from the hubbub of the marketplace and get on with his work peacefully. He specifically selected the hotel after checking that it provides 24-hour free Wi-Fi connection as it was very important to him to keep doing his research for the novel alongside and also for keeping in touch with his publisher. Checking for availability of Wi-Fi was very important for him as he was aware that the mobile network is weak in that remote area.

His first two days were very pleasant as his work went on smoothly without any disturbance as the amenities provided in the hotel were top notch. But on the third day, the weather condition in the village started getting bad due to which the electricity connection was lost, and as a result, the Wi-Fi stopped working. Also, the hotel did not have the backup facility with which the Internet could still work. The absence of power backup in the hotel further infuriated George. Thus, it became difficult for George to email the preview of the first chapter to his publisher that night as the Wi-Fi had stopped working. Not doing so would have put the contract in jeopardy. Thinking about the repercussions of his contract,

George got into a scuffle with the management as they had assured him that he would not have any problem with the Wi-Fi connectivity during his two-months stay. However, the hotel management responded by saying that it was very seldom that they lost electricity connection in that area, and they had not anticipated that the weather conditions would deteriorate to this level.

George was taken aback by the lack of basic amenities in the hotel. He was so frustrated that he did not want to spend a single minute in the hotel now. He felt cheated and despondent. Finally, George packed his bags and left the hotel immediately. Dissatisfied with the service of the hotel, he wrote a blog on the Internet about his awful experience and discouraged other writers from coming to India for their travel inspiration.

Conclusion

Stay is a very important part of travel. Thus, when a tourist makes his/her booking with the hotel, he/she expects all the amenities to be in order as promised by the hotel. However, when his/her expectations are not met, he/she feels disappointed and deceived. The same happened with George Perry when the 24/7 Wi-Fi that was initially promised to him, remained a distant dream. As a result, his work was affected and his whole idea of coming to India was dashed to the ground. His bad experience not only affected the future business of the hotel as he posted his negative feedback about the hotel but also it shattered the image of the country in his eyes.

Learning Outcomes

- Every destination is different from another destination in terms of the amenities available there. Thus, when a tourist visits a remote destination, he/she must moderate his/her expectations accordingly.
- The communication regarding the amenities between the hotel staff and the tourist must be very clear from the outset.
- Hotels must post correct information about their amenities on the websites.
- Before making any reservation with the hotel, the tourist must also educate himself/herself about the hotel through the reviews posted by the guests who have stayed in that hotel.
- The service providers of the tourism industry must not only promise impeccable services that the tourist would be provided with when they visit their destination but should also ensure to deliver their promise of giving those quality services.
- A bad word of mouth about the services of the tourism service provider by the tourists can badly affect the reputation as well as the business of the service providers.

- The image of a destination also gets affected when the tourists go unhappy from a place.

Points for Discussion

1. Was the hotel at fault in the above case, and if so, what was the fault?
2. According to you, being a hotelier, what will be your plan of action if such a situation arises?
3. In the above case, what are the things that the hotel should have considered while making the reservation of the tourist?

SECTION

C

THE TRENDING HOLIDAYING

The given section has been introduced with the objective of orienting the budding tourism aspirants to the pragmatic aspects of the tourism industry. This section is more of application based. It discusses the grassroots-level issues that travellers face once they decide to visit a destination. It is very important for the readers to understand the mindset of tourists that how they actually conceive the idea of travelling to a destination. The given section shall delve deep into the behavioural patterns of tourists while planning their holiday to finally understanding the technicalities involved in executing the plan of a holiday.

It starts with a discussion on how travellers plan their vacation with a focus on the factors that the travellers consider while choosing a destination for a holiday. It then elaborates on the various stages that a traveller goes through. From dreaming about a destination to its conceptualization, booking and finally visiting the destination, the traveller evolves at every stage of travel. If a traveller decides to visit a destination internationally, he/she may have to complete a number of travel formalities. Chapter 20 on travel formalities would elaborate on the various formalities and documentation procedures required for travelling abroad. This chapter is very important for the budding tourism professionals to be aware of and have knowledge of the various processes required for travelling abroad such as having a passport and visa, knowledge of foreign exchange regulations, airlines regulations and airport information required. Travel may induce stress for many. Thus, a chapter (Chapter 21) has been dedicated to travel stress that shall discuss the various sources of travel that causes stress for the traveller. It shall be followed by a discussion on the pre-departure checklist that acts as a ready reference for the tourist when he/she visits a destination.

At the end of each chapter, there are activities related to each chapter, which students may practise in their classrooms. Also, every chapter has interesting information for students to know, organized in the boxes that the students are advised to read to increase their knowledge of tourism. After the completion of chapters in the section, there are certain case studies related to the section for the students to read, comprehend and analyse, followed by questions to be answered.

Thus, after going through the section, the learners would know the following:

- What are the processes involved in planning a vacation?
- What are the various stages of travel?
- What are travel formalities?
- How is travel a source of stress?
- What are the things in a pre-departure checklist?

So let us continue our journey of learning and try to understand the intricacies of the travel trade.

Till then, happy learning, dear readers!

18

Planning a Vacation

The given chapter shall clarify the following:

- What are the various decisions that a traveller may have to take before arriving at a final decision of choosing a holiday destination?
- What factors affect the choice of a traveller while choosing his/her final destination for travel?

GOD'S OWN COUNTRY: KERALA!

- Kerala, a state in India, is a dreamland for tourists. For people who want to indulge in the wild vibes and serenity of nature, Kerala is the place to go!
- Tourism has developed brilliantly over the past few years by including amazing tourism products for tourists such as learning folk art of Kerala, trekking expeditions on popular spots such as Chimmony and Thusharagiri, village life experiences, boating in Kavvayi islands and so much more!
- People travel from far away to taste *sadya*—a traditional three-course feast which is served on a plantain leaf and eaten with hands. *Sadya* includes an amazing variety of around 40 vegetarian dishes.
- You can energize your cells and rejuvenate your body, soul and mind through Ayurvedic and Panchakarma treatments, as Kerala is the 'land of Ayurveda' in India.
- Kerala is also known for its vibrant and energetic festivities and celebrations. Art, culture and tradition come together in beautiful performances which win the tourists' hearts.

- To reach the core of Kerala's life, tourism offers many close-to-soil activities such as bathing the elephants, walking through the woods and camping experiences, traditional fishing and so much more to see like the famous Chinese fishing nets in Kochi!

INTRODUCTION

Holidays have become the latest fad for spending one's discretionary income. Although the reasons for holidaying may be different, one thing that brings travellers together is a novel experience that everyone is looking for. When a traveller conceives an idea of a vacation, he/she has a number of concerns to be addressed to.

Planning for a vacation is the foundation of a good holiday. Whether the duration of a holiday is less or long, it is important to plan one's holiday. Paying attention to the minutest details can help a traveller have a hassle-free trip. Also, through planning one can get sufficient time in hand to streamline one's travel arrangements in advance and plan accordingly if things do not work out. Moreover, the better and earlier one has planned for a holiday, the greater would be the chances of getting better deals on flights, hotels and packages. Thus, planning one's holiday intelligently in advance is very important.

In an extremely competitive environment where every destination is competing at its best for its lion share to attract more tourists, the traveller finds himself/herself in a *Catch-22 situation* to choose an ideal destination for his/her holiday from a myriad of choices that he/she has at his/her discretion like never before. A traveller has to take a number of decisions before he/she leaves for his/her final holiday destination.

Now, let us have a detailed discussion on the various decisions that a traveller may have to take while planning his/her holiday.

WHY TRAVEL?

The starting point for a traveller may be the need for a change from his/her status quo. Any traveller before planning his/her vacation must be clear about his/her idea of vacation. The clarity of one's purpose may help him/her to plan his/her vacation and more specifically his/her destination accordingly. Some travellers just travel to a destination for a getaway or to take a break from the mundane routine. Therefore, they do not believe in keeping their itineraries hectic as their sole purpose is to relax and chill as much as possible with enough rest breaks. Accordingly, some may particularly opt for a beach destination just to relax around the beach, while some plan to relax by visiting a luxury and a wellness spa destination. For example, many tourists visit *Ananda Spa in the Himalayas, Uttarakhand, India,* to relax through a spa treatment. While for some, just staying in a hotel for a change of environment from home and relaxing in the hotel may be enough to recharge their batteries.

However, some travellers may visit a destination with the sole objective of exploring it as much as possible. They may wish to pack their day with all-day sightseeing points leaving no room for rest.

Many other travellers especially travel for a particular purpose. These purposes may vary such as exploring the mountains, experiencing the wilderness, attending a festival, experiencing the culture of a destination, taking a medical treatment, attending a destination wedding, indulging in adventure, satisfying one's taste palette, watching sports and many more.

On the basis of clarity of purpose of travel, the tourist may choose the kind of destination and the kind of itinerary that may compliment with his/her purpose of travel. For example, a couple going on a honeymoon will have a different set of consideration of destinations where they can find enough solace and privacy. They may choose to travel to a beach destination, visit mountains or visit any other dream destination of their choice. Some of the overseas destination for honeymooners may be Switzerland, Mauritius, Maldives, Fiji Islands, the Bahamas and so on. Alternatively, for honeymooners planning to visit India, the destinations may be Himachal Pradesh, Goa, Sikkim, Kerala and so on.

WHERE TO TRAVEL?

Once the purpose of travelling to a destination is clear within the mind of a traveller, the most important question that he/she struggles with is the place where to travel. Many similar destinations may be catering to his/her purpose of travel. Especially, in today's scenario where every destination is marketing itself in enticing ways by giving every reason to the traveller to travel, the traveller may get confused with the myriad of choices. Few filters that may further bring clarity of thought for the traveller may be as follows.

Choosing a Domestic or an International Destination

The first filter for choosing a destination may begin from whether the traveller wants to visit within his/her own country or visit outside his/her country. For choosing to travel outside one's own country, the time and budget may be the biggest constraints besides the ease in getting visas and some other factors that may deter a traveller from visiting internationally.

Choosing from Number of Destinations to Travel

It is also important for a traveller to be clear prior his travel that whether a traveller wants to travel to a single destination or multiple destinations. In case of multiple destinations, the traveller must be clear about the number of days he/she wants to spend at each destination and the destination which he/she wants to travel first. He/she must basically decide on the number of stopovers he/she may wish to take, that is the number of cities/countries he/she wishes to visit at one time. While travelling to multiple destinations, time management is very important. To make most of one's time, one must start his/her travel early to a destination or either travel at night wherever possible so that he/she has enough time during the day to explore the city/destination.

Many tourists also have a tendency of clubbing the transit destinations as a stopover destination to explore it. For example, *many tourists while flying to London on Etihad Airways may wish to spend two or three days at Abu Dhabi, the transit point of Etihad Airways.*

FACTORS FOR CHOOSING A DESTINATION

There may be many factors for consideration while choosing one's final destination of travel. Some of these factors are as follows.

Number of Accompanying Travellers

A lot depends upon the number of travellers travelling together. When a large number of travellers are travelling together, everyone's choice needs to be considered for choosing a destination. There are more chances of conflict of interests as everyone may have a different destination for a holiday in their mind. Some may just be looking for an activity-based holiday, while some may be just planning to relax. A common liking of a destination where everybody mutually agrees for should be the destination chosen for travel.

Also, in some limiting cases, for a traveller, the increase in the number of travellers may lead to an increase in the overall travel expenditure that may affect the traveller's decision for choosing a holiday destination. For example, for a couple planning to travel to a foreign country, Australia may be an ideal choice. However, if the same couple has to travel with two kids, the budget may then become an important consideration. The family may then change their choice of the destination to a more pocket-friendly destination such as Thailand, Indonesia, Singapore, Malaysia and Dubai. However, this may not hold true when two nuclear families may be consciously choosing to travel together by contributing equally to the travel budget.

Accompanying Travellers

A lot depends upon who is travelling with you. To a large extent, the accompanying traveller may affect your holiday destination choice. Travelling with parents/spouse/kids/friends/relatives would connote different images of different destinations in the mind of the same traveller.

In case of solo travel, the traveller's choices of a destination may be different. However, if the same solo traveller is travelling with his/her spouse, his/her choice of a destination would change. Likewise, for an Indian family travelling with young kids, the consideration set of destinations may be different. They may prefer to visit 'kids-friendly' destinations where the kids may have a variety of attractions according to their likings such as amusement parks, theme parks and entertainment centres. Thus, while travelling overseas with kids, the family may consider either of the following destinations offering kids-friendly products such as *Disneyland in Hong Kong, Disney World in the USA, the Universal Studios and Sentosa Islands in Singapore, Ferari World in Abu Dhabi, and Desert Safari and Dhow River Cruise in Dubai* and so on. Likewise, Indian families with young kids may take their kids in India to *Darjeeling for Toy train, Jim Corbett in Uttarakhand for seeing the wild-life, Jaisalmer for camel rides or Delhi to show heritage sites* depending upon the interest of kids. Therefore, while travelling to destinations with kids, kids become an important decision-making authority for the parents whose choices determine the decision of the holiday destination.

River Cruise

Sometimes it may so happen that in a family, there may be a senior citizen who is physically challenged. Therefore, in such a case, the family would only opt for those destinations within India that are accessible and cater to the special needs of such handicapped travellers.

In yet another case, a group of three girlfriends planning to go on a bachelorette's vacation before getting married would plan to go on a destination that offers fun, nightlife, beaches, shopping, interesting adventure activities along with a safe environment. Therefore, they may choose to travel together to *Las Vegas, Florida, Thailand, Bali* and so on so as to create lifetime memories together. Similarly, a group of college boys going together would prefer to go to adventure-based destinations like mountain treks or beach-based destinations.

State of Health

While choosing a destination, one's state of health is very important. Many travellers base their decision of destination on their state of health. *Some travellers may have health issues that emanate due to travel such as motion sickness, seasickness and air sickness.* Otherwise also, a person may not be medically well due to a health issue like a backache, high blood pressure or any other related medical issue. Thus, such travellers may not prefer visiting those destinations that affect their health or further deteriorates it. Those destinations may simply be chucked out by them while planning their vacation. For example, *an asthmatic patient may avoid travelling to Ladakh*, India, due to lack of oxygen in the high altitudes of the region. Similarly, a traveller having backache or motion sickness may not travel to those hilly areas where road travel is quite curvy and bumpy as the traveller may feel nauseated and uneasy. Thus, one's state of health may restrict his/her choice of a destination.

Proximity

Another deterring factor to travel is a destination's proximity to one's residence. Many travellers prefer to visit only nearby destinations due to the paucity of time in hand. They may be constrained to choose a destination due to its long distance. Even while travelling to multiple destinations, distance may be a deterring factor. Many tourists who avoid long air travel may avoid visiting long-haul destinations.

Budget

Budget may be one of the most important considerations for a traveller. The choice of a destination to a larger extent is determined by one's readiness to spend a sufficient amount for one's holiday. For example, few destinations of the world are quite pocket friendly when compared with other destinations of the world. These may be some countries such as *India, Nepal, Sri Lanka, Bhutan, Vietnam, Cambodia, Laos, Philippines, Indonesia* and *Thailand* that are comparatively cheaper as compared to some countries such as the *UK, Europe, the USA, Japan, Canada* and *Australia,* which are more expensive holiday destinations. However, this may vary with respect to the traveller's country of origin, his/her proximity with the other country and his/her value of currency versus the country that he/she is visiting. Accordingly, the traveller may look for choices based on his/her budget requirements.

Some travellers may be low-budget travellers who just want to visit and explore destinations with the idea of spending a minimum on their travel and stay. Such travellers may be categorized as backpackers who are just looking for very basic facilities during their travel. They are rough and tough travellers ready to face any hardships. They may stay in hostels or other budgeted accommodation. Many of them may opt for couch surfing (staying free of cost at others' accommodation) to keep their stay economical. Such travellers may rather spend more on sightseeing and other tourist activities. They may not be very keen to spend on their stays. However, for some travellers, budget may not be a constraint. They may want comfortable travel and stay during their travel. This is again subject to one's personal choice and perception.

Another aspect would be of budget spent on preparations for travelling and holidaying. This may include buying travel essentials and clothing according to the place to be visited. Many travellers staying in tropical region temperatures while visiting destinations with cooler environment have to purchase enough winter clothing for the travel that may increase their overall budget. For example, a tourist travelling within India from Mumbai to see snow at Himachal Pradesh will have to purchase enough winter clothing for himself/herself that may increase his/her budget.

Effective Holiday Time

Quality time that one can spend at a destination is a major determinant for a traveller while choosing a destination. To travel, one must have enough time in hand. While planning a vacation, a traveller must be calculative of his/her effective holiday time at a destination. *Effective holiday time refers to total vacation time minus travel time. In other words, it may refer to the time left out or available at a destination after deducting the to-and-fro travel time for reaching the destination.* In case of international travel, one also has to take into account the jet lag time on reaching the holiday destination that further reduces the effective holiday time. The idea is that one must have enough time at the destination to explore it and make sense of it. Lack of effective time or quality time that a traveller may get to spend at a destination may affect his/her choice of the holiday destination. For example, due to the paucity of time, many working professionals prefer short weekend getaways nearby where they can get to spend maximum time at the destination and minimum time on travelling.

Gender

Another important factor that may influence the choice of a destination for the travellers may be their gender. Women travellers are more conscious about their choices of travel. For them, safety at the destination is of paramount concern. They may choose only those destinations where they feel free to explore without any fear of being harassed or troubled by anyone in the destination. In fact, service providers in the tourism industry are also quite gender-sensitive. Various travel agents offer special packages for women travellers keeping in mind their specific requirements. *Even the hospitality industry is conscious about the specific needs of women travellers as hotels have dedicated rooms and sometimes separate floors for the women travellers.* In fact, many destinations of the world are positioning and marketing themselves as destinations safe for women travellers to lure this emerging segment of the market.

Age

Earlier, age was a prime factor in deciding one's travel. However, with the changing times this factor is becoming less determining. Nowadays, irrespective of any age barrier, people travel to destinations. As they say, 'age is just a number'. However, having said that, the fact is that the mobility of senior citizens may accordingly reduce as compared to youngsters. They cannot afford to have hectic itineraries. Also, sometimes, the purpose of travel may change according to the age differences.

In the context of India, many senior citizens prefer to visit pilgrimage places in order to attain salvation before death. For example, *Hindus in India wish to visit Chardham for salvation while Muslims visit Haj in their lifetime for salvation.* However, this may not always hold true. Many old-age foreigners, on the contrary, travel to explore destinations and relax their minds. They may also travel to beach destinations or other places just to chill and enjoy the slow pace of life. Likewise, youngsters may travel to destinations that offer excitement and adventure. Their idea of holiday may be of visiting mountains, beach destinations, indulging in adventure activities and so on. Thus, the choice of destination may be influenced by one's age at times.

Food

Food may be another major constraint for choosing one's destination of travel. Many travellers do not choose certain destinations to travel due to the lack of food options available for them in that destination. For example, mostly visitors who follow Islam religion only prefer Halal meat. Therefore, few destinations such as *Malaysia* and *Turkey* are offering Halal as a tourism product (Halal Tourism) in which one of the main aspects is the Halal-certified restaurants that only serve Halal meat that is in consonance with the Islamic religious values. Hence, for the Muslim travellers, these countries are definitely the preferred choice.

Likewise, certain countries of the world such as *South Korea* and *Denmark* offer very limited options for the vegetarians, Jains (who neither eat onion nor garlic), vegans and people allergic to seafood. Thus, automatically, these countries would not be the first choice for such travellers.

Extent of Travel Documentation

It is very important to understand that the travel documentation will vary from country to country. However, tourists prefer visiting those destinations that have less documentation barriers. With elaborate documentation required such as permits and the long time for visa processing, many destinations may simply be out of the consideration set for many visitors, especially if the traveller has less time for his/her holiday. On the contrary, destinations that have simple visa procedures or VOA become a pull factor that attracts the tourist to these destinations. Thus, for destinations to be tourist-friendly, they must have VOA facility and easy documentation procedures.

Awareness about Tourism Destinations

Awareness precedes the choice. A person will only choose that destination to travel if he/she is aware of it. If a destination has not marketed itself well, the traveller may not think of visiting there. However, if a destination has been well marketed, the chances of being considered as a vacation destination are more, if it matches the traveller's purpose and meets his/her other requirements.

Language Spoken at the Destination

Further, the language spoken at the destination to be visited may affect the choice of a traveller while choosing it. If a traveller is not aware of the local language of a destination and English is not the general mode of conversation in that destination, then the traveller may be forced to choose another destination where people speak English. In this case, the language limits the choice of a destination.

Image of a Destination

Image affects a traveller's choice of a destination. Many destinations evoke strong images in the mind of a traveller. With more clarity of image of a destination, the traveller can match his/her purpose of travel with the kind of product offered by the destination. Hence, the image of a destination that a traveller carries in his/her mind affects his/her choice of destination.

For example, many Indian travellers particularly interested to go for scuba diving in India may plan their vacation to Havelock Islands in the Andaman and Nicobar Islands. While planning to visit a beach destination, the traveller may think of travelling to *Mauritius* famous for its white sands and water adventure activities. Alternatively, he/she may plan to travel to *Gold Coast, Australia,* famous for its beaches and being a 'Surfer's Paradise'. For a traveller interested in visiting distilleries, he/she may plan to visit *Scotland.* For tourists from India, destinations such as *Thailand, Cambodia, Vietnam* and *Indonesia* evoke images of a 'pocket-friendly' destination. Thus, the image of a destination in the mind of the traveller strongly affects his/her choice of a destination.

WHEN TO PLAN A HOLIDAY?

The most important question that a traveller juggles with is when to travel. For many families, taking an annual holiday is a ritual. This is again subject to the following factors.

Holiday Entitlement

Many families may plan their travel either during summer vacations or winter vacations when their children have vacations. This is also subject to both parents being working parents who may get paid holiday approved at the same time. Mostly, working professionals in foreign countries, especially the USA, Europe and Australia get holidays during the time of Christmas and New Year's Eve. Therefore, they plan their travel around Christmas time. Thus, holiday entitlement and vacations would be the first pushing factor for the families to plan their vacation.

Personal Circumstances

Choosing the time to travel for one's holiday may vary from one traveller to another depending upon his/her convenience and circumstances. This may vary from case to case. In case of business-class families, they may not have enough time to spare for a holiday as leaving one's business on others can be a risky proposition. Therefore, they may only plan to take a holiday when it may be lean season for their business. Also, one's urge for a change from one's routine and availability of time would be the determining factors while wanting a vacation.

Best Time to Visit

Another important factor that travellers consider while planning a holiday is the best season time/best time for the destination to be visited. Although some travellers may visit a destination during any season due to certain compelling factors such as low prices, holiday entitlements and so on, however, many travellers prefer to travel to a destination only during its season time. Every season may not be the best time to visit a destination due to scorching heat, chilling winters or monsoons. For example, for a tourist to visit Northern Europe during winters, it may not be the appropriate time as it shall be too cold for the tourists along with the shortened days to explore the place fully. Besides, many things may be closed. Therefore, ideally, travellers visit North Europe during summers from April onwards until July which is the best season to visit North Europe and also other parts of Europe.

Likewise, many foreigners and Indians may plan to visit *Ladakh, India*, during summers. It is important for them to be aware that being the coldest season from mid-November to March when the temperatures dip to sub-zero with frequent snowfalls, the region of Ladakh gets completely cut-off from rest of India by road, with only very few roads open. Most of the lakes also get completely frozen as there are frequent snowfalls. However, there are only a few adventure tourists who can dare to survive and acclimatize themselves in the extreme temperatures arrive between mid-January and mid-March to do the famous 'Chadar Trek' that involves walking on the frozen *Zanskar River* in the Ladakh region.

However, travelling during the season time may not be a choice for many travellers. One reason may be the prices of flights, hotels and all local package tours may be escalated by local service providers due to the tourist visiting a destination in numbers. For example, all the hotels, flights and other local arrangements have skyrocketed prices in Goa every year in December due to the heavy rush during the Christmas and New Year's Eve celebrations. Another reason may be the quality of services that drop at the destination due to the over usage of tourism resources. Also, many tourists may not be comfortable travelling in the presence of hordes of tourists. Instead, they may prefer deserted destinations, with less people around. This may depend upon an individual's liking. Some may like seclusion, while some may be looking for crowded areas to spend their vacation time.

Special Events

Another time of choosing an ideal time of spending one's vacation at a destination may be a special festival or an event taking place at a destination. For example, *many Indians travel to Goa for special celebrations during Christmas and New Year's Eve.* Likewise, many foreigners visit *Rajasthan, India, during the world's largest cattle fair, the Pushkar Fair, that takes place generally in the month of November* that is the best time to see and soak oneself in the colours of festivities, traditions and cultures.

Special Personal Celebrations

Yet another best time to plan one's vacation is around one's special day celebrations. For example, many travellers may plan to travel to destinations around their special lifetime occasions such as *anniversary celebrations, birthday celebrations, pre-wedding celebrations, wedding celebrations, honeymoon time and babymoon time.* These special occasions are a time to unwind, rejoice and celebrate these events with one's own family and friends away from routine life.

HOW TO TRAVEL?

There are many decisions that require the attention of a traveller. A traveller needs to be clear in his/her mind as to how he/she should plan his/her holiday. Few aspects that a traveller may decide on before he/she departs for the tour are as follows.

Booking Behaviour

On finalizing the destination by the traveller, he/she must decide as to how he/she wishes to book his/her holiday. The booking behaviour of a tourist may vary from person to person. Some travellers may prefer to *book on their own via online bookings, while some may prefer to make their booking through a conventional travel agent.* Generally, the booking behaviour of the traveller will depend on his/her ease with technology and whether he/she is a frequent traveller or a first-timer. Generally, first-time travellers visiting out of country may prefer to make their bookings through a travel agent, whereas frequent travellers may prefer to visit on their own by making their own online bookings. Also, in some limiting cases, the travellers may use a combination of both online booking on their own and leaving few bookings for the travel agent. Every traveller may follow any of the above-mentioned arrangements.

However, if the traveller has chosen to make his/her travel arrangements through a travel agent/tour operator, then the next decision that is critical to his/her travel is to decide which travel agent/tour operator he/she would like to book his/her holiday with. This may in turn depend upon the credibility of the travel agent, recommendations by friends and relatives, the kind of package and itinerary being offered, the services offered, the price and discounts, if any, offered and so on by the travel agent/tour operator.

FIT/GIT

Another important question for a traveller while planning to go on a vacation, if travelling through a travel company, is to decide whether he/she wants to travel alone (FIT) or whether he/she wishes to travel in a group (GIT). Both ways of travel have their own advantages and disadvantages. Many first-time travellers, especially while visiting foreign destinations, prefer to travel in groups due to the fear of unknown in a new place. They may feel unsafe travelling on their own. Such travellers may feel safer in the presence of others and hence, prefer to travel in a group. Still, some others also travel in a group to foster friendships and develop camaraderie. For them, 'the more, the merrier' may hold true. However, certain travellers prefer to be on their own and explore newer unknown places for themselves. For them, the factor of 'unknown' is excitement in itself. Thus, while planning the vacation, a tourist must decide prior if he/she wants to travel alone or in a group.

MAKING OTHER TRAVEL ARRANGEMENT DECISIONS

It is not that easy to travel to a destination, especially when one is travelling with one's family. A little planning before travelling is very important for safe and a comfortable travel. Thus, timely planning of travel arrangements is a wise decision. *Choosing on how to travel, that is, the mode of transportation by surface/rail/sea/air is an important decision that a traveller must take while deciding to travel.* Likewise, an appropriate way to travel internally within the cities is an important decision that a traveller must take while planning his/her vacation.

Another important decision that a traveller must decide on is the *type of accommodation* where he/she wants to stay. The choice of accommodation for the tourist may range from a hotel, a guest house, an apartment, a resort or any other similar kind of supplementary accommodation. Also, choosing the location of stay whether a downtown area, a suburb area, an airport vicinity and so on is one of the important decisions that a traveller must take while planning to stay in an accommodation.

Similarly, while making arrangements through a travel agent, many variant packages may be offered by the travel agent of the same destination that may vary in terms of services and prices offered. This may also baffle a traveller. He/she must, therefore, match the inclusions, exclusions and extras with the budget that he/she can afford and then choose a final package. Also, while making the final booking of a package, the traveller must properly revisit similar itineraries of different travel agents to be able to compare more effectively the various travel packages and opt for the best package that may be in the best interest of his/her holiday. If the traveller is travelling internationally and making his/her booking on his/her own, then he/she may decide from which company he/she should book his/her travel insurance with, which operator he/she should buy his/her SIM card from, which authorized agent should he/she buy his/her foreign exchange from and so on. Finally, he/she must also decide on the mode of payment (debit card/credit card, cash/demand draft and so on) by which he/she wants to book his/her holiday. This may in turn depend upon the policy of the travel company through which he/she is booking his/her travel arrangements.

SUMMARY

As discussed, there are a myriad of decisions to be made by the traveller while planning his/her vacation. As 'a stitch in time saves nine', it is always better to take time to plan one's vacation and take informed travel decisions. A good holiday requires meticulous planning with an eye for detail. It requires a traveller to take the decisions pertaining to the following:

1. *Why should he/she travel to a destination?* Indicates his/her need and purpose of travel.
2. *Where does he/she want to travel?* The choice may be a domestic or international destination/one or multiple destinations to be visited that may again be influenced by various factors such as one's budget, time in hand, proximity to one's residence, one's health, number of travellers, age, gender, accompanying travellers, language and food criteria at the destination being visited, ease of documentation, the image of destination and marketing awareness created by the destination authorities/travel companies.
3. *When does he/she want to travel?* This in turn depends on various factors such as one's holiday entitlement, the best time to visit the destination, any event taking place at the destination and any personal event celebration at a destination.
4. *How does he/she want to travel?* This involves taking decisions regarding his/her booking behaviour—if he/she wants to book on his/her own or through a travel agent, FIT or GIT—whether he/she wants to travel individually or in a group, other travel-related arrangements and so on.

Therefore, a traveller must spare enough time to work out the details of his/her holiday so that he/she can have a hassle-free and comfortable travel later.

ACTIVITIES

Activity 1

Plan a trip for visiting the East Coast of the USA with your family. Discuss in detail your itinerary covering the destinations that you wish to visit in the East Coast. Also, elaborate in detail the various travel arrangements that you would make on your own.

Activity 2

Prepare a detailed adventure trip itinerary for a group of friends for 10 days. Elaborate it in detail with the destination of your choice.

Activity 3

A couple wants to visit Eastern Europe for their vacation. They have 12 days in hand for their vacation. Suggest an appropriate itinerary.

Travel Stages

LEARNING OBJECTIVES

The given chapter shall clarify the following:

- What are the various stages that a traveller goes through when he/she plans his/her holiday?
- What are the major characteristics of each stage of travel?
- What strategies should tourism marketers adopt to woo the travellers at each stage of their travel?

DUBLIN: THE FRIENDLIEST CITY!

- Have you ever been to a place where people welcome you with open arms and make you feel at home? Welcome to Dublin!
- Being a city of rich culture, lively atmosphere, friendly neighbourhood and music, Dublin is also the largest and the capital city of Ireland.
- The famous *Black Taxi Tour* in Belfast provides a wide range of tours including political mural tours, ultimate *Game of Thrones* tours covering film locations like Dark Hedges, open art galleries, peace walls and a trip down history-lane.
- *The popular Giant's Causeway is listed by UNESCO as a world heritage site.* You can take a bus tour from Belfast to explore Bushmills, Carrick-a-Rede and Giant's Causeway in one day.
- The Library of Trinity College is the largest research library in Ireland. The Library contains about five million books including the *Book of Kells*, also known as *Book of Columba*, which is considered as Ireland's finest national treasure.

- The most iconic shopping area in Dublin is *Grafton Street* which has buskers and 'living statues', adding life to the ambience.
- *Dublin Literary Pub Crawl* is a tour which provides the audience with first-hand experience of charming streets, pubs with literary significance, listening to anecdotes and stories about famous authors, watching performances where actors bring literary work to life and so much more!
- People can enjoy seven floors of fun by visiting the famous *Guinness Storehouse* brewery where they can taste the most iconic beers on rooftops and listen to iconic beer tales of Ireland.
- Want a spectacular day trip? Take a ride on the *DART Train*, which offers a scenic route around the coast of Dublin Bay.
- *Temple Bar* is a cool and quirky pub, popular among artists and poets. Traditional live music sessions are a daily occurrence, and it is a must-visit place to fully experience the best of Irish culture.

INTRODUCTION

Every traveller goes through various stages of travel when he/she plans his/her holiday. *Travel stages may be referred to as the various steps that a traveller is involved in from the moment he/she thinks of going on a holiday to eventually taking the trip and then coming back home with a bundle of experiences and memories of the vacation.* However, it is important to mention here that, every traveller may not go through every stage. Some spontaneous travellers may make instant travel plans in the wink of an eye without any planning. Thus, the travel stages experienced may vary from one traveller to another.

Travel stages are important for the tourism and hospitality service providers as they may devise different marketing strategies for the traveller at different stages of planning his/her vacation.

Travelling can be a very exciting activity. Every person is a tourist at one point of his/her life, though his/her reasons for travel may be different. Some may travel to a destination for beach bumming, while some may travel for spelunking. Still, many may travel for rejuvenation and relaxation by taking a wellness treatment at a destination. Whatever may be the reasons for travel, travelling involves a number of stages. A detailed discussion on each of these is as follows.

DREAMING STAGE

Travelling predominantly begins in the mind of a traveller. This stage is the beginning of the need of a traveller to visit a place. However, this need may vary from person to person. A traveller may feel the need to escape from his/her routine seeking a change in his/her regular life, whereas another traveller may wish to see an attraction at a destination or simply visit his/her friends and relatives. Thus, every traveller may have a different idea of a holiday.

The traveller at this stage may find himself/herself baffled. However, this may not always hold true. While some travellers may have a clear destination in their bucket list where they wish to travel to, others may not be very clear as to where they exactly want to visit, though the thought of travelling somewhere may be very clear to them in their minds.

At this stage, the travellers may be influenced by various factors. Sometimes, a thought may be spurred to travel by reading an article about a destination in a travel magazine or watching a travel show where the traveller is fascinated to travel to that destination. Sometimes, social media may also evoke the interest of a traveller to visit a destination when he/she sees the exciting travel posts and pictures of his/her near and dear ones. To put it simply, this marks the beginning of dreaming about a destination by a traveller.

Hence, the action plan for travel actually initiates when the traveller takes a conscious decision of taking a break and going for a holiday.

The following strategies may be adopted by tourism service providers at this stage:

- The tourism marketers must aggressively create awareness among the tourists about a destination with a clear positioning strategy as to what exactly is the tourism product that they are offering, to whom they want to offer the tourism product and how their destination has a competitive advantage over other destinations offering similar tourism products, if any. For example, *New Zealand is clear about its positioning strategy as it promotes itself as an adventure destination to the adventure enthusiasts.*

- The tourism destination marketers may aggressively promote their tourism products through organizing various marketing campaigns tailor-made to a specific target market by advertising in electronic, print and social media so as to evoke strong images of the destination in the mind of a traveller. For example, *the Israel Ministry of Tourism these days is aggressively promoting Israel as a tourism destination, especially the cities of Tel Aviv, Jerusalem, Eilat, Nazareth (the cradle of Christianity) with the tagline 'the land of creation'.* They have also launched the *interactive trip planner* that helps the travellers to plan their holiday. They are promoting various tourism products such as *wellness tourism in the Dead Sea, culinary tourism, bike tours, Segway tours* and *pilgrimage tourism in Nazareth.*

- The ultimate objective is to evoke an interest in the mind of the traveller by bringing a destination into the consideration set of a traveller and eventually creating a strong liking and a desire in the mind of the traveller so that he/she starts seriously considering the destination for his/her vacation.

CONCEPTUALIZATION STAGE

Once the day-dreaming is over and the traveller is really keen and sure to go on a vacation, this stage begins. Planning is an inevitable part of travel and is very crucial for a hassle-free experience later. *This is the preliminary stage of travel that involves a lot of research and preparation on the part of the traveller. It is the most time-consuming stage.* It involves an active participation of a traveller. A good homework done at this stage lays the foundation of a good holiday.

The decisions/typical characteristics pertaining to this stage are as follows.

Choice of a Destination

The most mind-boggling decision for a tourist would be to travel to which destination. Should he/she visit within his/her own country or travel abroad? What is his/her real purpose of travel? The traveller must be very sorted in his/her thoughts right from the beginning. Clarity of purpose to travel plays an important role in deciding a destination. Some other factors that may affect his/her choice of a destination may be an image of a destination, the best time to visit the destination, the climate at the destination, one's level of awareness about the destination, one's personal interest and liking for the destination, one's budget, time at hand and the ease of documentation required in case choosing of travelling abroad.

The interest of travelling to a destination may also depend upon a traveller's active search on review websites like *Tripadvisor* that may give him/her effective comparisons on the pros and cons of visiting a destination.

Sometimes, a word of mouth spread by friends and family may also influence the choice of a traveller while choosing his/her destination. In fact, social media plays a significant role in shaping the choice of today's traveller. Pictures and stories posted by friends and family on social networking sites such as *Facebook, Instagram* and *Snapchat* or videos posted on YouTube may infuse an idea of travelling to the same destination by a traveller who may yearn to get a similar experience as shared by his/her close friends or family. One may also be inspired by reading the travelled passengers travel blogs and their stories and any interesting anecdotes shared by them that may further be a push factor to travel. Many mobile applications like *Pinterest* may have tools for planning one's trip that may also push the traveller to plan a holiday. Even, many destinations have *interactive trip planners* that may help them plan their trip more effectively.

Also, exciting deals given by airlines, hotels, travel apps, packages offered by tour operators and marketing activities carried out by the destination management organizations may induce the traveller to visit a destination.

How to Travel?

The most important decision when a traveller decides to travel and has decided upon his/her destination of travel is whether he/she should make his/her travel arrangements on his/her own or travel through a tour operator/travel agent.

If the traveller is making travel arrangements on his/her own, then he/she may start searching for individual websites that may be giving him/her best deals on buying individual tourism products that again requires a lot of research and effort on the part of the traveller. In case, he/she does not wish to make bookings on his/her own, he/she has an option of booking his/her holiday through a travel agent/tour operator. Again, when he/she decides to travel through a travel company, he/she may decide whether he/she wishes to travel individually or in a group. This may depend upon the choice of the traveller. Some travellers who prefer privacy would prefer to travel alone while some traveller who believe in socializing with others and feel that being with more people addresses their security concerns may prefer to travel in groups.

He/she may take a customized package tailor-made to his/her requirements from the travel agent/tour operator. Alternatively, if a traveller prefers to travel in a group for various reasons, then he/she may opt for a ready-made package tour that the travel company may be offering. In both cases, travelling through a travel agent/tour operator is more convenient and hassle-free for a traveller where the planning and execution of the tour is the job of the travel company. While taking a fixed package tour, the traveller may also decide upon the kind of package he/she may wish to book, in case there are variants of packages being offered for the same destination.

While choosing to make travel arrangements through a travel company, a traveller may get baffled by the number of competing choices of tour operators who may be offering similar exciting packages and discounts on the destinations that the traveller may be interested in. In such cases, a traveller should rely upon the credibility of the brand, the kind of services offered by the travel company and his/her past travel experience with the company, if any. He/she may also review the websites to read the feedback of the travelled passengers or take the referrals from his/her friends, if they may have travelled with the same company in the past. This may aid him/her in making an informed decision.

Learning about the Destination

Once the destination has been finalized by the traveller based on his/her filters discussed above, and if he/she has decided that he/she wants to travel on his/her own, the next thing expected of him/her is to do good and sound homework regarding the chosen destination.

A traveller must start spending a lot of time gathering and seeking maximum information and knowledge about a destination. A traveller must be well-read before he/she travels to a destination, even if he/she is making arrangements through a travel company. This enhances his/her overall experience of travel as he/she can connect more to a destination when he/she actually visits it. Also, he/she can be on auto mode, reducing his/her dependence on others, if he/she has insights on a destination.

It is important for a traveller to gain a thorough understanding of the various facets of a destination during this stage on how to reach the destination, how to travel within the destination, which mode of transportation to use, which places to shop at, which eateries and restaurants to visit, which attractions to visit and so on, especially if he/she is planning to travel on his/her own without taking a package tour from a travel company. A traveller must also learn about the local sensitivities of a destination before he/she plans to travel there so that he/she does not hurt the locals' sentiments. His/her timely research can help him/her save a lot of money as well as precious time.

Planning an Itinerary

A traveller must plan his/her travel intelligently. However, in case a traveller opts for a fixed departure/customized tour through a travel company, where the complete itinerary has been customized by the travel company, then he/she may sit back and relax.

However, while travelling on own, the traveller may consider the following two points:

- Itinerary must be planned in a proper way so that time is not wasted in backtracking.
- Itineraries should not be too active as in action-packed that puts a traveller to a difficult regime. The idea is to take a holiday and not punish oneself just ticking one's checklist with ultimately no time for relaxation.

The attractions and destinations to be packaged in an itinerary would depend upon the number of days that a traveller has in his/her hand and his/her areas of interest. A traveller must filter the attractions that he/she wishes to see at the destination depending upon his/her personal interest. He/she must decide on the kind of accommodation he/she wishes to stay at, the kinds of cafeterias and restaurants he/she wants to visit, the kind of activities he/she wishes to indulge in at the destination and so on. A prior planned itinerary can always save his/her time and at the same time his/her holiday would be more organized.

Deciding upon the Expenditure

Every traveller may have a set budget which he/she may think of spending on his/her vacation. A traveller, thus, must decide the amount of money within which he/she may plan his/her travel, stay, sightseeing, shopping and so on. He/she must also set aside the money that he/she is likely to spend on eating his/her everyday meals, the entry fees of the monuments and so on. However, it must be borne in mind that the traveller may also keep aside extra money for meeting contingencies, if any, that may happen during the tour. However, especially while travelling overseas, one must be wary about the permissible limit of currency allowed by a country. A traveller should not be ignorant of the *Basic Travel Quota (BTQ)* rules.

Planning the Documentation

If any documentation is required to be done to enter a destination (if he/she is travelling internationally) or an attraction (certain attractions require permits even for domestic tourists) at a destination, a traveller must have a prior knowledge of it. A traveller must find out the appropriate documentation such as *visa requirements, health certificates* and *special permits*, if any, required and, therefore, must complete all the formalities before travelling to a destination while travelling abroad.

The following considerations may be kept in mind by the tourism service providers at this stage of travel to woo the traveller to his/her destination:

- At this stage, the tourism marketers must offer variants of packages catering to the different requirements of travellers from premium to budget travellers.
- They must focus on building their strong brand image and brand recall.
- They must understand the psyche of the traveller and how he/she behaves while making a purchase. In other words, they must do research on tourist's consumer behaviour, tourist profiles and so on who are visiting the destination that may be used for launching new tourism products or altering the existing tourism products, if required.
- Travel companies and tourism authorities promoting destinations must have relevant self-explanatory websites that can be used by travellers to refer to for searching authentic and complete information about a destination. The websites must be a one-stop shop within themselves providing comprehensive information about a destination from the tourist perspective that he/she may be looking for.

BOOKING STAGE

Booking one's holiday is now a step forward towards the realization of one's dream of a vacation. After the research is thoroughly completed and the traveller is completely sure of his/her travel arrangements where to book from, he/she may start with his/her initial bookings.

When booking on own and not through any tour company, it is advisable to do the direct bookings in advance with the various service providers/travel portals separately so as to not to face any non-availability of flights and accommodation during one's travel that may upset a traveller later. This may happen especially during the peak season at a destination where even the prices are escalated for making any travel booking. Thus, blocking the tickets or making reservations in advance saves the money of the tourists. Besides, booking in advance can give early bird deals to travellers that may save their money.

Generally, the traveller has to pay the complete amount of money before departing for the final tour. However, sometimes he/she may give an initial booking amount as a token for finalizing his/her trip with a particular service provider and then keep paying partial payments before his/her final departure or either pay in one go depending upon the policy of the service provider and his/her personal paying capacity. One may make the payments by debit cards/credit cards/cash/cheque/DD that may be the policy of the service provider. While booking one's tour, a traveller must carefully read all the terms and conditions of the service provider, the refund and cancellation policy of the service provider and the inclusions and exclusions given in the deal.

The same procedure may be followed while making arrangements through a travel company.

The following considerations may be ensured by tourism marketers and service providers to attract the tourists at this stage of their travel:

- Provide easy and friendly interfaces on the websites for travellers so as to enable them to make their booking on their own without any hassles.

- The booking procedure must be easy and understandable stating clearly the terms and conditions of the booking along with the cancellation policy.
- There should be no hidden costs or clauses while booking that may upset the travellers later.
- The mode of payment must be easily understandable for the tourists and there must be multiple modes of facilitating payments.

PRE-DEPARTURE STAGE

This is again both an exciting and a strenuous stage for the traveller. It is exciting because while packing one's bag, a traveller starts getting the actual feel of going on a holiday. The feel-good factor of travelling can be very thrilling for him/her. However, it may be strenuous because of packing involved at this stage.

Some of the typical preparations at this stage of travel are as follows.

Referring to Pre-departure Checklist

Before packing, a traveller must prepare a checklist of things that he/she must carry with him/her before travelling. It is advisable for him/her to carry the items according to the place being visited.

During his/her final packing, he/she must tally his/her items packed with this checklist. This may help him/her not to miss on any item when he/she travels. The general items that one may carry on a tour are as follows:

- Clothes according to the place being visited
- Personal toiletries
- Generic medicines
- Electronic accessories including chargers, power banks and universal adapters (in case of travelling abroad)
- Things to eat
- Rain gear
- Sunglasses

This is just the basic list of travel essentials. A detailed discussion on this has been given in a separate chapter, 'Pre-departure Checklist for Travellers'.

Packing

Packing intelligently with all the things needed to carry for the travel is important. Otherwise, the tourists may have to unnecessarily spend money in another destination purchasing things of daily usage. Tourists must ensure that they pack their stuff and personal belongings within the permissible limits in case they are travelling by air. The weight of the check-in and cabin baggage must be in conformity with the norms of the airlines. Otherwise, a traveller may end up paying a good amount for excess baggage. He/she must also be aware of the items that may or may not be carried in cabin baggage.

However, the rule of the packing is that one must travel light, especially in foreign countries such as Europe, the USA and Australia where one has to carry their own luggage in a hotel.

Other Formalities

Before travelling, a traveller may have to do the following formalities in case of his/her international travel:

- Documentation for visa processing
- Travel insurance (to safeguard oneself against the unforeseen situations)
- Arrangement of an international SIM card
- Conversion of currency according to the county being visited

The following strategies may be adopted by the tourism service providers at this stage:

- The travel companies must facilitate the travellers who have booked a tour through them with a pre-departure checklist so that the travellers may refer to the checklist for their packing.
- Travel companies may also facilitate other travel arrangements for travellers by providing them with travel insurance, SIM cards and foreign exchange conversion in case of travelling abroad. This facilitation by the tour operator where the tour operator acts as a one-stop shop for all the travel solutions can make the travel more convenient and comfortable for the traveller.
- They may also provide extra goodies to the travellers such as travel bags, passport and ticket jackets that may delight the travellers besides aiding the travel companies in marketing themselves.

DEPARTURE STAGE

This is the most awaited and the most exciting stage for a traveller as this is the time, when the traveller is ready to leave his/her home towards his/her realization of dreams.

It involves the travelling part of the journey. For many travellers, journey is more important than the destination. It may be seen as an opportunity for social cohesion with others. Yet for others it might be about enjoying the views of nature en route the journey.

The traveller may travel by different modes of transportation depending upon the distance, accessibility and time that he/she may have in his/her hand. Sometimes, the mode of transportation may be an experience in itself for the tourists. With the tourism industry becoming necessarily experiential, many transportation systems are being packaged as attractive tourism products in themselves that promise a thrilling travel experience to the traveller. For example, travelling by luxurious and heritage trains such as *Palace on Wheels, India; Darjeeling Toy Train, India* and the *Puffing Billy Railway in Melbourne, Australia;* and the cruises and luxurious yachts are all memorable journey experiences for a traveller.

Outside View from Puffing Billy Train, Melbourne, Australia

Travelling can be an experience of a lifetime, provided the experience is pleasant. However, many exogenous factors may spoil the fun of a traveller. For example, a delay in flight due to a bad weather condition or a technical glitch, breakdown of a coach, a strike at a destination, a natural calamity at a destination, an outbreak of an epidemic, bad medical condition of the traveller himself/herself and so on may affect the travel plans of a traveller.

However, hectic travelling journeys for long hours may have negative repercussions for the travellers. It may disturb their sleeping patterns during the long journeys on flights and trains that may affect their health eventually.

At this travel stage, the tourism service providers may adopt the following strategies towards the travellers:

- Make the journey of travellers as comfortable as possible by providing a quality mode of transportation, a good network of roads and highways, world-class infrastructures such as runways, airports and railway stations and so on.
- Making navigation of travellers easy in case they want to travel on their own by providing free Internet connectivity and signages so that they can use GPS technology.
- Enable their promises on providing an impeccable experience and warm hospitality services to a traveller en route journey.
- Provide an experiential travel to the travellers. Many international airlines such as *Emirates* and *Singapore International Airlines* provide world-class air travel experiences to their guests.
- The transportation companies must aggressively try to sell themselves here by competing on different competitive propositions. For example, *Volvo buses position themselves on the attribute of the safety of travellers*.
- The airports and railway stations of a destination must also facilitate the tourists by providing all kinds of amenities for the guests such as a help desk, Wi-Fi services, cafeterias and shopping arcades.
- If the traveller is travelling through a travel company, it must send the tour leaders to accompany the guests during departures so that the tourists may not face any problem during the departure of the tour.

ARRIVAL STAGE

This is the beginning of the realization of one's dream at a destination. Until now, the traveller was only imagining the destination, but this is the moment when his/her dreams shape into a reality. The tourists may feel the 'wow factor' of being at the destination or being at the place that he/she always dreamt and longed for. For many tourists, it is a soul-quenching experience of being at their dream destination. However, a traveller must be guided by the rule of 'expect the unexpected' at this stage of travel as his/her experience at a destination may be full of pleasant or unpleasant surprises.

This is the stage where the real execution of the tour begins with one's initial set travel plan. This is the time when reality hits the expectations of the tourist. Few characteristics of this travel stage area as follows.

Services by Service Providers

This is the stage for a destination to sell itself at its best. On arriving at the destination, a traveller may come across various service providers with whom he/she may interact for the first time. These are the 'moments of truth' for a traveller. On the basis of his/her interactions and the quality of services provided by the service providers of the tourism and hospitality industry such as immigration officers, airport representatives, cab drivers, hoteliers, restaurateurs, local transporters, tour guides and tour leaders at the destination, a traveller may form a positive or a negative impression about the destination in general.

Bunch of Experiences

This stage is all about experiences and experiments. The experience of staying in different kinds of accommodations, travelling in different modes of transportation, pursuing different tourism activities, visiting different tourist trails and eating out at different places can just leave a traveller bizarre and in a super-excited stage. The feel of experiencing different cultures at a different place can be food for soul for the traveller. Also, on visiting the attractions that once a traveller imagined of, the traveller may be in a state of complete ecstasy. Based on the opportunities of spending one's leisure time, activities for entertainment and places to hang-out, a traveller may make judgements about a destination. The more immersive experiences a destination has to offer, the more are the chances of a traveller feeling joyful at a destination.

Attitude of Host Community

The behaviour of the host community also plays a significant role in attracting the tourists to a destination. If the hosts are receptive and welcoming, they create a 'feel-good factor' for the tourists. Friendly hosts create a favourable impression in the mind of the traveller. *Many of the friendliest cities in the world such as Cork, Galway and Dublin are based in Ireland.*

Tourist-friendly Destination

A destination must be tourist-friendly to invite the tourists to the destination. To keep the trip of the tourists enjoyable and memorable, the destination must have amenities that can facilitate their stay there.

Use of Technology

Today's traveller may heavily rely on technology on arrival at the destination. He/she may use the Internet for accessing websites, travel apps, use google maps to search and explore the places around and to stay connected with his family and friends. Therefore, now destinations must be smart cities easing the use of technology for the travellers that may create favourable impressions of the destination in the minds of the travellers. *Dubai and Barcelona are examples of the smart cities that have opted the smart technology.*

Jet Lag

While travelling overseas, due to travelling in different time zones, tourists may feel the jet lag. It may take time for the traveller to cope with the jet lag, which is generally three–five days depending on traveller to traveller and the difference in the time zones.

Cultural Shock

Many tourists may also face cultural shock on arriving at a destination. When tourists travel to different destinations, they may observe the different cultures of different destinations that may be different from their own culture. Sometimes it may be pleasant, while sometimes it may be a cultural shock for them. However, it is important not to disrespect the natives' culture and show tolerance for their culture.

Contingency Planning

At this stage, the tourists must also be well prepared to face any deviations from his/her planned trip. A traveller must understand that everything may not always happen as planned by him/her. Many a time, various unplanned unwelcoming situations may hit the traveller that he/she may be unprepared for. For this, the traveller must have a contingency planning if things do not work out according to his/her pre-decided plan.

For example, if a couple is travelling with a kid and the kid is suffering from high fever, then the couple may have to drop their plan of continuing their trip and immediately attend to the child and retire back home. Some other unforeseen situations that may happen with a traveller during the trip are loss of his/her passport, loss of his/her luggage, pickpocketing, meeting an accident, being hospitalized or any other situation that may totally spoil the tour of a traveller. Thus, a traveller must always be flexible enough to change his/her plans as and when the situation arises.

Monitoring the Tour

The tourists must also monitor if their plan is in accordance with their laid-out travel plan. Sometimes, a traveller may have decided to hire the services of a particular car rental company to travel around the country. However, on arriving at the country, he/she may not be able to book that car rental service due to the non-availability of cars of that particular brand. In such a case, a traveller may not be left with any other option but to book the car of another brand at a much higher price if he/she does not want to spoil the fun of his/her vacation. Therefore, for a traveller it is important to monitor his/her extra expenditures from the pre-decided budget that he/she may have set earlier. It is also important for tourists to keep monitoring their other expenditures on the trip. Many travellers make proper excel sheets to monitor their overall expenditures. On daily basis, they keep noting down the expenditures they are incurring for making their travel arrangements.

As far as the travel companies are concerned, the tour leaders on the tour, leading the travellers, must ensure that they follow the itinerary as promised to the travellers. The tour leaders on package tours are responsible for monitoring the overall tour, whereas in case a traveller is travelling on his/her own, he/she must monitor his/her tour on his/her own.

Behaving as Responsible Tourists

The onus of a pleasant experience at a destination not only lies with the host community but also with the tourists who are visiting that destination. It is important for the tourists to act locally according to the destination being visited and respect its local culture. The tourists can act as responsible tourists by keeping the destination clean by not littering around, by following the rules set by the attraction authorities while visiting the attractions, by purchasing the local stuff to boost the local economy of a destination, by not engaging in any kind of unlawful activity at the destination like shoplifting and so on.

At this stage, the tourism marketers and service providers must focus on the following:

- Facilitate the tourists in every possible way by providing amenities and services to make the destination tourist-friendly
- Educating the host community to treat the tourists with respect
- Educating the tourists to behave as responsible tourists while visiting the destination
- Delivering the services as initially promised

- Focusing on delighting the tourist and not just satisfying him/her
- By welcoming the guests warmly and creating pleasant 'moments of truth' for them

RETURNING STAGE

This may be the hardest stage for a traveller to end his/her vacation time at a destination as bidding farewell to the place may not always be pleasant. Eventually, every holiday comes to an end and the traveller must ultimately come back to his/her home. Many people fear and get anxious with the very thought of going back home and getting back to work and facing the same reality and following the same routine once again. Although if the duration of travel is too long, tourists may also be looking forward to coming back home.

However, a traveller may be feeling more energetic and emotionally charged after spending a good holiday vacation. If the destination could not match to his/her level of expectations, then he may not wish to come back again. If the traveller is satisfied with his/her travel experience at the destination, then he/she may like to repeat the destination and spread a positive word of mouth among others.

Some of the typical preparations at this stage of travel are as follows.

Carry All Your Personal Belongings

Once again in preparation for arrival to one's own place of residence, it is time to pack again. Before returning home, tourists must not forget to bring back their personal belongings from the destination. They must ensure that they bring back everything that they had packed.

Tax Refunds

Shopping is one of the main activities of a tourist. Many travellers may buy souvenirs from the place as a token of remembrance from the destination for their own self or their friends and relatives. In many countries like the Philippines, buying *Pasalubong* (homecoming gift) is a tradition for home-coming. It is mandatory for the tourists to buy souvenirs for their family and friends when they return home after a holiday.

However, while doing shopping of valuable items, especially while in another country, the tourists must be aware of his/her own country's custom duty rules. Sometimes, he/she may have to pay heavy duties, especially on expensive electronic items purchased, when he/she returns to his/her home country.

While shopping in a foreign country, before returning home, the tourists must also ensure that they take their tax refunds at the airports/other designated places like malls (like in Singapore) on showing their shopping bills to the concerned authorities at the foreign holiday destination. Since the tourists are not the residents of a country, they are not supposed to pay taxes on the goods purchased. However, the taxes paid on shopping can only be refunded by a traveller, if he/she claims for them at the airport of the departing country along with the proof of purchase. However, the conditions for claiming tax refund may vary from country to country. For example, in Singapore, the tourists can only claim tax refund if they have spent more than $100 (including GST) on shopping. Moreover, the tourists may claim refund on 7 per cent goods and services tax (GST) paid on their purchases.

Thus, a traveller must have knowledge of tax refunds as well as the rules of refund prior to his/her travel so that he/she may be able to save a fortune while returning. If travelling through a travel company, it is the job of a tour leader to remind his/her guests about the tax refunds.

Currency Conversion

While returning from overseas, a traveller may choose to return the foreign currency at the airport or in the local markets of a country, if he/she does not want to carry the foreign currency back. He/she may get it converted into his/her own currency.

The following strategies may be adopted by tourism marketers at this stage:

- The tourism service providers must take the valuable feedback of the tourists. They must attentively go through their challenges that the tourist faced at the destination and work on the suggestions given by the tourists.
- The tour operators must appreciate the feedback given by the tourists and take it as a gift that may help them to improve their services.
- They must maintain a liaison and networking with the travelled passengers for maintaining their future business.
- They must follow up their feedback, comments and compliments.
- They must ask the travellers to post their testimonials on social networking web pages of the tour companies. This builds up the credibility of the tour company as well as the destination and, thus, increases the confidence of other prospective travellers to travel to a destination with the tour company.

HANGOVER STAGE

The hangover for many tourists may stay for a longer time. They may keep going through the pictures of their trip captured as memories in their camera. They may post their vacation pictures on social networking sites like Instagram using hashtags such as *#throwback* and *#major missing* reflecting that they are still not able to accept that the holiday time is over. Many tourists share stories of their travel with friends and relatives. *While some may take on the Internet and write their own travel blogs, others may create their own travelogue, post vlogs and so on to share their experiences with the world.*

Many travellers may already start imagining about their next dream destination in their bucket list and holding on to their old memories until they make the new ones.

The various marketing strategies adopted by tourism service providers may be as follows:

- To keep the memories of travel fresh in the minds of travellers, tourism marketers must organize informal get-togethers with the ex-paxs (travelled passengers).
- Various travel websites may encourage travellers to post their pictures by organizing photography competitions on social media or asking them to share their interesting stories on their websites which may keep the travellers engaged to their memories of a traveller and spread a positive word of mouth among the prospective travellers.
- Tourism marketers must start sending 'Teasers' of the new destinations for the next holiday of the traveller.

SUMMARY

From dreaming to actually travelling to a destination, every traveller steps forward towards his/her realization of travel dreams with each passing travel stage. A traveller generally undergoes eight different stages of travel which have typical characteristics that define them. The eight stages of travel are as follows:

- Dreaming
- Conceptualizing
- Booking
- Pre-departure
- Departure
- Arrival
- Returning home
- Hangover stage

At every stage, the traveller behaves differently and so does the role of tourism and hospitality marketers changes and evolves with every passing stage of travel. However, these stages are just indicative of a typical traveller. These may vary from traveller to traveller.

ACTIVITIES

Activity 1

Identify any five major websites/travel portals/apps commonly used for booking an international airline by the travellers.

Activity 2

Identify any five major websites/travel portals/apps used by international travellers to book their accommodation.

Travel Formalities

UNITED NATIONS WORLD TOURISM ORGANIZATION (UNWTO)

- A United Nations (UN) agency, UNWTO, is a leading tourism organization in the world that focuses on promoting sustainable, responsible, accessible and universally acceptable tourism.
- It offers leadership support to 159 countries along with 6 associate members and 500 affiliate members that include organizations such as private sector, tourism associations, educational institutes and local tourism authorities involved in tourism.
- It aims at creating travel synergies and improving tourism competitiveness by engaging in global tourism agendas such as economic growth, environmental sustainability, international policies on tourism and development.
- It is also responsible for implementing the Global Code of Ethics for Tourism besides encouraging tourism as a tool for achieving SDGs.
- Its headquarters is based in Madrid, Spain.

INTRODUCTION

Travelling within one's own country is much easier than travelling abroad. This may be due to the elaborate set of travel formalities required to be completed by a traveller before departing for an international destination as compared to negligible or very fewer travel formalities while travelling within one's own country. Thus, we may say that travelling abroad is not a cakewalk. Sometimes, travelling can be a daunting experience as it requires a lot of preparations. Many formalities are required to be carried out before one's actual travel. Any laxity shown in not complying with any travel formality may lead to cancellation of travel plans that can be very emotionally disappointing for a tourist.

Although, generally, the travel formalities for visiting most of the countries remain the same, there may be slight variations concerning some of the countries being visited. Sometimes, this may also depend upon one's purpose of travel. Complete awareness of travel formalities for visiting a country is always in the interest of a traveller for a smooth and hassle-free travel experience later.

Travel formalities may refer to the requisites required to be fulfilled by travellers for visiting a country. All the necessary documents and endorsements are a part of it. This is the first checkpoint for a traveller when he/she decides to travel abroad.

Now, let us have a detailed discussion on each of the formalities required to be fulfilled by a tourist before his/her actual travel abroad.

PASSPORT

A passport is a legal document that proves that you are the bona fide citizen of a country. It is an important proof of one's identity. It is the most reliable piece of identification that is universally acceptable.

Most of the countries in the world require a passport to enter them. It enables travellers to travel internationally. *As a thumb rule, a passport must be valid for six months from the date of travel.* In other words, it means that the validity of a passport should not expire when the tourist is overseas. However, in certain countries such as Canada, it is required for the travellers to have their passport valid up to six months from their return date. Thus, it is pivotal for travellers to thoroughly check the passport rules before travelling internationally.

In India, the passports may be issued by Regional Passport Offices (RPOs) that comes under Consular Passport and Visa (CPV) Division of Ministry of the External Affairs (MEA).

Passports issued in India may be of the following types.

Ordinary Passport

This kind of passport is issued to the ordinary/regular citizens of India for tourism, study or business purpose. It is generally *navy blue* in colour. Generally, a passport is issued with 10 years validity and has 36 pages. However, for seasoned travellers such as business travellers or leisure travellers who travel frequently, a Jumbo passport is a better option as it has 60 pages that reduces the hassle of a traveller getting it reissued frequently.

Official Passport

This passport is issued to the officials who are representing the country on government duty. It is generally valid for five years or even less depending upon the nature of assignment of the government official and his/her position. It is *white* in colour.

Diplomatic Passport

This passport is issued to the Indian diplomats/delegates or top-ranking government officials representing the country for a duration of five or less years depending upon the nature of the assignments and their position. It is *maroon* in colour.

Biometric Passport

This passport is also known as an *e-passport or digital passport*. This passport was first issued to the then President of India, Pratibha Patil in the year 2008. Such passports are traditional passports that have an embedded electronic chip that stores all the data of the traveller that may be used to authenticate the identity of the passport bearer. The advantage of an e-passport is that it allows quick and easy access through the security gates of an airport. In India, it is being issued to the diplomats and officials in the first phase and shall be rolled out to the general public in a later stage. The chip has a storage capacity of 64 kb in memory that can store the photograph, fingerprint and other biometrics, and it can record up to 30 visits of the passport holder. However, biometric passports may be of different configurations issued by different countries of the world.

CONTINUOUS DISCHARGE CERTIFICATE (CDC)

Continuous Discharge Certificate is a document issued by the Government of India only to the *seamen* of the country. It is the seafarer's identity that is mandatory for them to carry while onboard. This document is also official evidence of a seamen's travel time. Each time a seaman signs off from the vessel, the master of the ship signs the CDC certifying his/her experience on board. The document is generally valid for 10 years and needs to be renewed within six months prior to the date of expiry.

LAISSEZ-PASSER

It is a travel document that is issued by the UN to officials of the UN, International Labour Organization (ILO) as well as to employees of other organizations such as World Health Organization (WHO), World Trade Organization (WTO), UNWTO, World Bank, International Monetary Fund (IMF) and a few more international organizations. It may be issued by the office of UN in New York and Geneva as well as by ILO.

VISA

Visa is a licence to travel internationally. *It refers to the Visitor's Intended Stay Abroad.* Most of the countries in the world require a visa to enter. This is the legal permission granted by a country that authorizes a traveller to enter its border. The grant of visa is at the discretion of the authority that may be an *embassy, a consulate or high commission.* However, *Visa Facilitation Services (VFS)* may act as a facilitating agency for the collection of documents for the travelling passengers by acting as an interface between the embassy and visiting traveller.

There are different types of visas depending upon one's purpose of travel. These may be tourist visa, business visa, student visa, transit visa, working visa and many more. Tourists travel to destinations generally on tourist/visitor visa or business visa (if the tourist is travelling for business or visiting a destination to attend an exhibition/conference) and so on. However, tourists travelling for medical reasons may visit India on a medical visa.

Generally, *visas have a limited validity* within which the traveller must return from another country to his/her home country.

Obtaining visas can be a cumbersome and tedious task. It requires a lot of documentation that may vary from country to country. Generally, for grant of visa, one must submit one's original passport valid for six months from the date of travel, passport size photographs as per the embassy specifications, visa form duly signed by the traveller, bank statements generally of last six months before the date of applying for the visa and return tickets. In many countries, for grant of visa, proofs of traveller's stay such as his/her address of hotel accommodation, complete itinerary, travel insurance and all other financial documents are necessary besides the above-mentioned documents. For grant of Schengen visa and many other visas, like the UK visa, all these documents besides many other documents are necessary. However, visa documentation also depends upon the type of visa the traveller may be applying for. For many countries such as Sri Lanka, Mauritius, Singapore and many more countries such elaborate documentation may not be required. Thus, visa regulations may vary from country to country. The processing time of visas also varies from country to country.

The grant of visa may depend upon the traveller's personal credentials, financial credibility, background check, the purpose of travel and the relation of his/her country with another country where he/she wants to go. If one is transiting through a country and wants to visit that destination, one must not forget to take a transit visa. The traveller must check the rules of transit visa valid for the country through which he/she is transiting.

Generally, *visas may be stamped, or a visa sticker may be pasted on a passport. However, sometimes, it can be a separate document also, like it is for the UAE.* On grant of visa, travellers must check the validity of the visa, length of stay on it, its type granted, passport number and correct name of the passport bearer if that has been spelt properly or not on the visa. These things must be thoroughly checked to ensure one's seamless travel.

Many countries, in order to increase the influx of tourists in a country, grant VOA. It also eases one's trouble of arranging all the documentation, standing in long queues for submitting the documents, facing the interviews and then waiting for weeks together for grant of visa. It means that when a traveller reaches a country, he/she will be granted the visa by the immigration authorities. However, this is always at the discretion of immigration officers who after intriguing the traveller and going through his/her passport details grant the VOA when they are satisfied with his/her background check. *Countries that grant VOA to Indian tourists are Thailand, Cambodia, Indonesia, Fiji, Mauritius, Sri Lanka, Vietnam and so on.* However, many countries may not even require tourists to get a VOA. The tourist may enter the country without a visa. This again depends upon a country's political equation with another country. Countries such as *Seychelles* have introduced this concept to increase the inflow of tourists in the country. Many nationals including Indians may travel to Seychelles without taking a visa. The tourists may be issued a permit by the immigration authorities on reaching there that makes the international travel very smooth and hassle free from the them.

In order to increase the inflow of tourists, India has also started VOA for citizens of many countries. E-visas (electronic visas) have also been initiated by India to fasten the procedure of getting visas. The citizens of 169 countries at present who are eligible for e-visa do not need to visit the Indian consulates abroad. They can apply for the e-tourist visa from their homes. However, there are certain restrictions attached to this kind of visa. *ETA is an electronic travel authorization through which a traveller can apply online. It is also called e-visa or tourist VOA (TVOA).* The ETA must be taken in advance of the traveller's departure from the country that he/she is coming from. Once the application has been approved, the traveller receives intimation via email of the e-tourist visa (eTV) to visit India. When the traveller reaches the country, he/she may take the printout of the eTV to show to the immigration authorities in India and provide his/her biometric information at the airport, and then visa will be stamped in the passport upon arrival in India. However, this is subject to many terms and conditions. *The e-visa is presently given under four categories that include eTV, e-business visa, e-medical visa and e-medical attendant visa.* Others have to follow the regular procedure of taking a visa.

In the case of Indian government officials travelling on an official assignment abroad, *visa notes are issued to them by the CPV Division.* Here, for the passport holders holding official or diplomatic passports, the visa processing time taken is less as compared to the procedure for availing visas on regular passports.

However, it is important to mention here that the visa requirements keep changing from time to time for different countries of the world.

FOREIGN EXCHANGE

While travelling abroad, it is important for tourists to carry enough finances that can cover their planned travel. Tourists must carry the local currency of a country to meet their daily expenditures.

It is important to mention here that tourists cannot take an unlimited amount of currency during their travel. The *Foreign Exchange Regulation Act (FERA)* regulates the amount of currency that a tourist can carry for his/her expenditure during his/her travel abroad. This may be referred to as BTQ. According to Reserve Bank of India (RBI) regulations, Indian travellers on private visits abroad cannot carry more than $10,000 in one calendar year for tourism purposes out of which only $3,000 may be carried in the form of cash. The rest of the amount may be carried in the form of travellers' cheque/banker's draft, credit cards and so on. The same must be purchased from authorized dealers (banks) on a self-declaration basis. However, there are exceptions to this rule while travelling to a few countries.

Business travellers are allowed to carry the limit of $25,000 per trip. Any amount being taken above this must be declared to customs before a traveller leaves his/her country. Otherwise, the traveller may be detained by the customs. However, the BTQ may vary depending upon one's purpose of travel like medical treatment.

CASHLESS CARDS

While travelling internationally, travellers may carry debit cards and credit cards that are generally acceptable with a few exceptions besides the cash. However, it is important to note that banks which issue debit/credit card generally charge fees for international transactions. A traveller must check with his/her bank for these details before he/she travels abroad. It is also suggested that the travellers must carry transaction receipts with him/her back home so that he/she may verify the transactions against his/her bank and credit card statements when he/she reaches his/her country.

TRAVEL INSURANCE

Anything unforeseen can happen with a traveller during his/her travel. Thus, a traveller must be prepared for meeting any contingency. Getting travel insurance done before one's travel is always in the interest of a traveller. *Travel insurance is a safety valve that gives coverage and protection to the tourist against any theft, loss of passport, damaged luggage, lost or stolen luggage, any accident and so on that might happen during one's travel.* Also, in case, a tourist falls ill during his/her travel especially in countries such as the UK and the USA where the treatment can cost a fortune of money, it can become very difficult for the traveller. *The Overseas Mediclaim Policy which is a part* of *travel insurance is a prudent choice by travellers* today to safeguard themselves against any uncertain situation that they might counter and the heavy medical expenses that they might have to incur. For travelling to certain countries, getting travel insurance is mandatory to apply for the visa.

Adequate coverage of insurance is a must. Thus, a traveller must buy a comprehensive travel insurance policy that covers him/her against any unexpected cost from any insurance company and he/she must keep a copy of the same along with its manual, in case, he/she needs to get travel insurance done. Many travellers may opt for *Cancel for Any Reason (CFAR)* travel insurance policy that helps in recovering the 50–75 per cent of the trips' prepaid cancellation costs, in case he/she cancels his/her trip due to any reason.

HEALTH REGULATIONS

As per the WHO, certain vaccinations before travel are imperative in the interest of global public health. Many countries of the world are still affected by diseases that are vaccine-preventable. Without taking vaccines, travelling to these affected countries can lead to increased illness and deaths. Thus, before travelling to a country, a tourist must check if he/she is required to take any vaccinations as per the requirements of the law.

While travelling to certain countries affected with yellow fever, such as African and South America countries, yellow fever vaccinations are necessary. *As per the International Health Regulations, yellow fever immunization is required for entering these countries. A yellow card is proof against one's vaccination for yellow fever that travellers represent at an international entry point generally.* Only registered Yellow Fever Vaccination Centres can provide this kind

Yello Fever Vaccine Card

Yellow Fever Vaccine Card Information Inside

of vaccine and a certificate for the same. It is advisable for the travellers to take the vaccination 10 days prior to being in that endemic area. *Yellow fever vaccination is lifelong.*

Likewise, vaccinations are required for *meningococcal disease and polio for pilgrims visiting Saudi Arabia.*

In fact, most of these countries only grant a visa to the tourists on submission of their yellow card or any other vaccination certificate that is mandatory.

CUSTOMS REGULATIONS

Every time, the traveller leaves his/her country or arrives at another country, he/she is required to pass through the customs authorities posted at the airport. The customs officials are responsible for seizing any merchandise that may pose to be a threat to the health and environment of the country. *They levy a customs duty on import or export of goods and ensure that no commercial goods in large quantities are being sent or purchased without paying their customs duty.*

Thus, it is very important for a traveller to check the regulations of customs before he/she travels to a country.

It is obligatory for a traveller to declare the things that he/she carries from his/her own country or purchases at another country with complete honesty. If the traveller is carrying foreign exchange above the permissible limit, he/she must declare it fully.

There are two channels at the airport that the traveller may pass through. If the traveller is carrying any dutiable items that are above the permitted customs limits or carrying any prohibited item, he/she must pass through the **Red Channel** otherwise he/she may pass through the **Green Channel** if he/she is carrying goods within the permissible limits.

TRAVEL ADVISORIES

It is advisable for the travellers, before they plan their travel, to check the travel advisories issued by the governments of countries that are issued in the public interest of their citizens.

Travel advisories suggest their citizen travellers the countries that are safe to travel and the precautions that must be observed by them while visiting different countries. Besides giving information about the security conditions in a country, travel advisories suggest the local laws and rules of a country, the entry and exit requirements, any possible health hazards or health restrictions in the country, where to find help when travelling in that country and so on.

This important piece of advice helps the travellers make informed decisions and to travel safely when they are in another country. It is generally advisable for the travellers to check the travel advisories twice. First, they should check it before they book their holiday for the country and second, they should check it when they are about to depart their country as security conditions may change during this period. In the case of India, the travel advisory is issued by MEA.

REGISTRATION

Registration is also an important formality required to be adhered to by the foreigners in India. When a foreigner is granted a visa for more than six months for visiting India (it may be a student, research, employment, missionary visa, etc.), he/she is required to register himself/herself with the nearest *Foreigner's Registration Office (FRO)/Foreigners Regional Registration Office (FRRO) within 14 days of his/her first arrival as per the regulations of the country*. The FRROs are based in New Delhi, Mumbai, Kolkata, Amritsar and Chief Immigration Office in Mumbai. In the rest of the country, the *superintendents of police (SP)* of districts act as registration officers for foreigners. In case, any foreign tourist wants to extend his/her stay or get his/her visa converted or wants to change his/her address or get exit permits, he/she is required to visit the FRO for the same. However, with the launch of *e-FRRO (Electronic Foreigners Regional Registration Office)* scheme recently launched by the Government of India, visiting FRROs/FROs would not be required, but only in exceptional cases. The registration can be done online, as well.

FOREIGN COUNTRY LAWS

Every country has a social structure. When tourists travel to the other country, it is important for them to be aware of their culture, religious practices, lifestyles and so on. It is important for the travellers to check the local laws and rules of a country before they travel. Obeying the laws of the country being visited is the moral as well as the legal responsibility of a traveller. Local sensitivities must be adhered to. For example, while visiting the places of worship such as churches, temples, mosques and synagogues, a tourist must be mindful and watchful of his/her behaviour and clothing that does not disrespect the sanctity of these religious places. Likewise, in certain countries of the world such as India, *drinking and smoking publicly are prohibited. Likewise, in Singapore, eating chewing gum is banned.* Thus, before travelling to a destination, a traveller must be aware of these local laws in order to avoid paying any penalties or facing any punishments in a foreign country.

AIRLINES REGULATIONS

It is equally important for a traveller to check the regulations of airlines on which he/she is flying. Travellers must check with the airlines *the checked baggage allowance, the carry-on baggage allowance and the restricted items before flying* with the respective airline. This allowance may vary from airline to airline. It may also depend upon one's class of travel, that is, economy, business or first class. *Generally, according to the weight system of international airlines, the baggage allowance for checked baggage is 20 kg for economy class, 30 kg for business class and 40 kg for first class.* However, it further depends on one's purpose for travel. For example, if seamen are travelling abroad for months, on showing the seamen's ticket, they may be allowed up to 40 kg even in economy class. The same may hold true for students travelling abroad on a student visa.

The same allowance restriction may hold true for carry-on or cabin baggage where the rules may vary from airline to airline depending upon the class of travel, the routes on which the airlines fly, the size of the aircraft and the frequent flyer status of the traveller. Generally, as a thumb rule as defined by IATA the cabin baggage may have a maximum length of 22 inch (56 cm), width of 18 inch (45 cm) and depth of 10 inch (25 cm).

Likewise, a traveller must be very thorough with the items that are permissible to be carried in the aircraft. *Many items such as liquids and sharp items like knives are prohibited in carry-on luggage.* Thus, before travelling abroad, he/she must be fully aware of the airline regulations so as to avoid any penalties or delays while travelling.

SUMMARY

Although completing the travel formalities seems a tedious task, doing things at the right time can save time and money of a traveller. A traveller must get familiar with the rules and regulations of a country that he/she is visiting. He/she must fulfil all the basic requirements for travelling abroad. Knowledge of passport and visa requirements, local rules, visa rules, foreign exchange rules, use of bank cards, airlines regulations, health regulations, travel insurance and so on can smoothen travel and make it hassle free for a traveller.

ACTIVITIES

Activity 1

Think of any five famous countries that are promoting tourism on a large scale. Identify their tourism authority along with their tagline for promoting tourism in the country. Also discuss their visa rules and documentation procedures.

Activity 2

Which are the top five sources of tourism markets in the world? Discuss their reasons for being at the top five positions besides discussing their positioning strategy towards the tourism markets. Also discuss their local laws to be followed by the tourists.

21

Travel Stress

LEARNING OBJECTIVES

The given chapter shall clarify the following:

- Is travelling a source of stress?
- What are the reasons that lead to stress before the actual travel, during travel and post travel?
- What are the other factors that lead to travel stress?
- What are the different ways in which a traveller can combat stress?

YOGA AT INTERNATIONAL YOGA FESTIVAL

- India, being the birthplace of Yoga, is a spiritual retreat for many tourists. The Incredible!ndia campaign by MOT, Government of India, aims at promoting Yoga as a wellness tourism product to the world.
- Various Yoga retreats and festivals are organized in India along with the International Yoga Day (21 June) to attract various tourists in the country.
- Every year, to attract tourists in the country, the *World's International Capital of Yoga*—Rishikesh in India—hosts the famous International Yoga Festival.
- To encourage a healthy lifestyle through Yoga, Uttarakhand Tourism Development Board and Parmarth Niketan (an ashram in Rishikesh) in association with MOT, Government of India, have been organizing International Yoga Festival since 1999.
- The week-long annual Yoga festival aims at detoxification and purification of the body, mind and soul.

- Some of the ancient techniques and asanas of Yoga such as *Pranayama, Hatha Yoga, Yog Nidra, Reiki* and various meditation sessions are organized to ensure overall well-being and emotional stability of a person.
- A lot of veteran gurus and Yoga practitioners conduct Yoga sessions during the festival to teach the spiritual benefits of Yoga to the tourists.
- The 2020 International Yoga Festival was successful in attracting people from over 76 countries throughout the world.

INTRODUCTION

There is a myth that comes with travel that travelling is always a pleasant experience for travellers given the fact that many have become vagabonds. There is a lot of focus on the advantages and benefits of travelling. Many opine that that one of the major benefits of travelling is that it reduces stress. In fact, travelling is seen as an antidote to stress and anxiety caused by one's mundane routine.

However, there is no discussion on the kind of stress generated due to travelling. Travelling may not always be a pleasant activity. Sometimes, it may in itself become a source of stress. It can be a stressful experience too. As also suggested by Crotts and Zehrer, travelling is a stressful activity.[1]

Travelling has become a way of life for many. It is an exciting activity that involves seeing places around the world. It is also an opportunity to learn and gel with people from different cultures of the world. However, some people may long to travel, while for some, travelling may not be the first choice. Many people may feel uneasy while moving out of their comfort zone and being in an unknown space.

Travelling may not be everyone's cup of tea. It may be a source of stress for many. Some people prefer being at home without a change in their status quo. For such people, travelling may be a disruptive activity, affecting their comfortable lifestyles. For such people, if they have to travel, then travelling becomes a source of stress rather than a source of joy.

For many travellers, stress may be induced due to the fear of travelling or other related factors. No matter how well a person may have travelled, he/she would always undergo some kind of stress before or during the travel. Even if the traveller is repeating his/her destination of travel, he/she may feel a few jitters every time he/she travels.

FACTORS RESPONSIBLE FOR TRAVEL JITTERS

There are many factors that contribute to the jitters of a traveller. Some of these are discussed below. For the sake of the understanding, the sources of stress due to travel have been divided into three categories:

[1] Crotts and Zehrer, Vacation Stress: The Development of a Vacation Stress Model among US Vacation Travellers.

- Pre-travel stress
- On-tour stress
- Post-tour stress

Pre-travel Stress

Now, let us have a detailed discussion on the sources of anxieties and fears that may induce stress for a traveller before his/her actual travel begins.

Travel Companion Matters

Not everybody can be a pleasant company to travel with. Every traveller may not be lucky enough to choose his/her travel companion. Sometimes, a traveller may be bound to travel with other family members, relatives or friends with whom he/she may not be comfortable with. For example, youngsters may not be comfortable travelling with their parents or grand-parents. They may prefer travelling with their friends of the same age. Also, while travelling with relatives for a destination wedding, a traveller may not be very comfortable with the relatives that may create stress for him/her.

Likewise, if a daughter is taking her old-aged parents on a pilgrimage journey, she may be so worried all the time about their health and safety during the trip that the whole vacation may become strenuous for her. Similarly, during business travel, one may have the obligation of travelling with one's colleagues or boss. In both cases, the traveller may not be very comfortable to travel with them. The journey may become stressful for the traveller.

Travelling with kids can also be very strenuous. Taking care of young toddlers, especially during long journeys, can get very difficult. Kids may feel very restless and throw tantrums during journeys. They may also get very cranky due to change of places. Packing for the kids can be another big task in itself for the parents. Kids may also suffer from high fever, lose appetite during travel and get uncomfortable while travelling. They may easily get tired while visiting places and may sometimes demand to go back home. Also, while travelling with kids, security is a major concern for the parents. All this leads to stress for a parent travelling with his/her kids.

Travelling with expecting mothers, people with special abilities, senior citizens, people with a medical history or people who are very selective about eating, for example, *vegetarians, vegans, Jains (who neither eat onion nor garlic)* may be a source of stress for a traveller.

All such travellers, as mentioned above, demand special attention and care from the accompanying traveller that may eventually spoil his/her fun and also create stress for him/her.

Pre-tour Planning

Planning before travelling can be a big source of stress for the traveller. Travelling is not as difficult as planning because *it is a very time-consuming activity*. Any pitfall or callous approach, shown at this stage of planning, can totally mar the experience of a traveller's vacation. This stage requires a lot of patience on the part of the traveller as he/she has to do a lot of research and homework before finalizing his/her travel arrangements and making his/her travel itinerary.

A traveller may have to *visit various websites, do online research, visit travel blogs, compare travel websites, take the packages from travel agents/tour operators or consult travel magazines/travel guidebooks* to make his/her travel arrangements. *It can be very baffling and a risky exercise for the traveller.* It may be baffling because a traveller has a number of choices to choose from. As a traveller may plan and book his/her arrangements to the best of his/her knowledge, there is a risk if things may not turn out as he/she expected. He/she may make travelling mistakes while planning his/her tour.

Sometimes, the following questions may bother a traveller:

- Which destination should I travel to?
- If travelling to multiple destinations, which destination should I first travel to?
- Should I book travel arrangements on my own or do the bookings through a travel agent?
- Which travel agent should I make my bookings with if booking through a travel agent?
- Which websites or apps should I make my bookings from that are more credible if I am travelling on my own?
- Which attractions should I visit in a city?
- Should I rent a car or use public transportation to explore the city?
- Should I take surface transportation for inter-city travel or take internal flights?
- Should I stay in a hotel or an apartment?
- Which is a better option for me—to buy local currency and local SIM card at the destination when I reach there or should I buy prior from my own country?
- Which SIM card should I use that gives me the best deal?
- Do I need a visa to travel to the country?
- Do I need an international driving licence to drive in the country?
- Should I take travel insurance? If yes, to what extent should I take my coverage for the travel insurance?
- How much money should I carry with me on the trip?
- Are credit cards accepted in the other country?

The above-mentioned questions create confusion in the mind of traveller that he/she must sort out before travelling to a destination. One has to be decisive on many aspects of travel that may be a source of stress for the traveller.

Even veteran travellers find their confidence shaking at this stage as they can never be 100 per cent sure of the quality of travel arrangements that they are making.

Financial Stress

Travelling is a big expense. People spend a fortune of money to make their dreams of spending vacations come true. A traveller may have been saving an extra penny for years to have a good holiday in his/her lifetime.

Travelling involves extra spending from one's routine. One must have enough discretionary income to travel to another destination. However, the budget may vary from traveller to traveller.

Nowadays, travelling has become a symbol of status more due to the social media effect. Many people travel to destinations with the sole idea that their friends, neighbours or relatives are also travelling. *This is called as the exhibition effect where one travels to show off to others rather driven by the fact that he/she loves travelling.* This may put the traveller in a certain kind of stress, especially financial stress, because everyone may not be able to afford an overseas holiday. Everyone cannot afford a luxurious annual holiday. However, the social pressure may be so immense that it may force a traveller to imitate others and push himself/herself beyond his/her financial limits. The expenditure spent on the whole travel can be very taxing for the traveller. He/she may have to take loans to travel, lend money from his/her friends/family or the bank that may ultimately land him/her to financial debts.

Thus, a traveller must set a realistic budget for travel based on his/her income and savings, as the saying goes that 'one must cut his/her coat according to his/her cloth'. Therefore, a traveller must set his/her own financial limits within which he/she must spend during his/her vacation.

To keep the travel budget low, a traveller must make his/her bookings in advance before his/her vacation begins, as the traveller can get better deals and discounts on bookings earlier. Last moment bookings are generally more expensive.

Travelling in Odd Hours Causes Pre-trip Anxiety

For travelling to destinations, a traveller needs to move out of his/her comfort zone. The very thought of travelling in odd hours might discomfort him/her as it may disrupt his/her sleeping patterns and overall health. Many travellers complaint that their eating pattern is also disturbed while travelling. They are not able to eat on time due to odd hours of travelling. For example, most of the international flights generally fly late in the night or in the early morning, so if a traveller has to catch a flight for early morning, he/she may not have a sound sleep due to the fear of waking up early in the morning, and he/she keeps on ensuring that the alarm clock rings in the morning on time so that he/she does not miss on his/her flight. As a result, the traveller may have pre-trip anxiety that may lead to a sleepless night for him/her. *Many travellers may report jet lag due to flying in different time zones that disturb their body clocks.*

Fear of Unknown Causes Stress

Although for many travellers, unfamiliarity at a destination is a charm in itself, for many travellers, the fear of unknown makes them feel uncomfortable and insecure. The fear of being in an unknown territory sometimes can be a nerve-wracking experience for the traveller. Visiting a destination for the first time and not being aware of the usage of local transportation systems, the local sensitivities of the place, the kind of food one will get at the destination and so on may create fear in the mind of the traveller. Fear may also arise out of the language barriers that may make the communication with the host community difficult for the traveller, thereby making his/her stay at the destination more difficult.

For some travellers, visiting another destination which has a totally different culture from their own culture may lead to a cultural shock that they may not be very comfortable with. For example, *a traveller from Saudi Arabia may find the culture of American people very liberal. Likewise, American tourists travelling to Saud Arabia may find their culture very conservative and hence may find it difficult to adapt with*. This may, however, vary depending upon the perception of a traveller.

The following questions may further bother a traveller:

- Would the accommodation I am going to stay in be safe for me and my family?
- Is the destination safe to visit?
- Would I get the food according to my preference?
- Would I get medical aid easily, in case I get unwell?
- Would my credit card work in another country?

Packing May Be Stressful

Packing can be equally a stressful activity, especially if one is planning a long holiday. One must not forget the long list of things that one must carry, especially when travelling overseas. For example, for old-aged travellers or travellers with a medical history, packing of medicines is very important. Likewise, while travelling with infants and toddlers, packing can be very taxing. Children have their own set of requirements.

While travelling overseas, one must pack things keeping in mind the international regulations of a country. Also, if travelling by airlines, one must check the check-in and cabin baggage regulations that may vary from airlines to airlines and from country to country. Certain items are prohibited to be carried in cabin baggage. The traveller must be aware of all these details. Sometimes, it becomes very strenuous for the travellers to adjust their luggage so that it is not overweight.

For travelling on a longer duration, one must start the packing early as one may get hanky-panky if there is a pile of stuff for the last moment still waiting to be packed.

However, no matter the packing may be completed, the traveller may keep fearing always that he/she may have missed on something while packing and this stress lingers on till he/she finally leaves his/her home.

Leaving One's Home for Travel May Be Strenuous

Staying disconnected with the home can get quite difficult for a traveller. Especially, in the case of nuclear families, when they travel for longer durations, travelling may be strenuous as leaving home unattended for days can be intimidating due to safety and security concerns.

It is, thus, advisable for a traveller to prepare a checklist of things to do before leaving his/her home. This helps him/her to cross-check and be assured that everything has been checked and looked into before he/she leaves his/her home for the vacation that may keep him/her relieved off stress during vacation. For example, before leaving, one has to ensure that all electrical appliances are unplugged so as to avoid any mishaps. One must also ensure that all the doors and windows are locked besides checking of the closure of gas connections and so on.

Besides the above-mentioned reason, leaving the loved ones behind if they are not travelling with you can also be a source of stress for the traveller.

Pre-trip Excitement May Cause Stress

Many travellers are so excited to travel that it becomes a source of stress for them. They may not able to sleep properly because of the adrenaline rush of travelling to their dream destination. The very thought of travelling in the next morning may lead to butterflies in their stomach that may not allow them to sleep causing stress.

On-tour Stress

Things may not always work out according to the traveller on the tour. This may create stress for the traveller. A detailed discussion on each of these is as follows.

Travelling May Lead to Health Stress

Travel may not suit everyone. Many travellers have health concerns while travelling. Their health suffers and may deteriorate during travel. *The odd timings of travel, the disruptive patterns of eating, facing extreme temperatures at a destination and so on may lead to serious health issues for a traveller.* Many people suffer from 'Turista' which is a gastrointestinal illness caused by long odd hours of travelling.

It may so happen that on arriving at a destination, the traveller may not be able to adapt to the local food of the place. It may not suit him/her and thus it may deteriorate his/her health condition. Sometimes, the water also may not suit him/her. Thus, many tourists report insomnia, ill health, indigestion, acidity, constipation and so on during travel.

Some travellers may suffer from air, motion, sea, altitude sickness and so on due to which they may fear travelling.

For taking care of their health on the tour, travellers may observe the following:

- It is advisable for tourists to eat light and take medicines during long travel.
- Get the travel insurance done to safeguard themselves against any unseen health incident.

- Travellers must also get proper health vaccinations done while travelling to countries in Africa and South America where health vaccinations are mandatory.
- Travellers who are taking controlled medicines as suggested by the doctors must carry the prescriptions of the doctor as documentary evidence with themselves.
- Tourists must also be aware of the nearby doctors and hospitals to reduce their travel stress, if the need arises, as they may feel that they are in control of the situation.
- They should also choose travelling to those destinations that suit their health. For example, if a traveller knows he/she has altitude sickness, he/she may avoid going to destinations like Ladakh in J&K, India, where there is a lack of oxygen in the air.

Fear of Flying/Air Travel

Many travellers may have the phobia of travelling by air. For many travellers, travelling by air is not less than a nightmare. Such travellers may get very uncomfortable and anxious with the very thought of being in the air without anything beyond their control. The feeling of being in the air may be further aggravated by the turbulence in the flight that may become another major reason for being frightful in the air.

Besides, being a fearful experience, it might seem to be a very tedious process to travel by air for a traveller due to the long procedures and the situations associated with travelling by air. The following may be the sources of stress related to air travel:

- Reaching the airport one and a half hour before for the domestic flight and three hours for the international flight on time
- Long and complex airport handling procedures
- Cooperating with airport security
- Waiting in long queues at the check-in counter
- Paying for 'extra' baggage in case it is found in excess
- Paying for not doing the online check-in with some airlines (where it is mandatory such as Ryanair)
- Waiting for a long time at the airport to board the flight when the boarding starts
- Dealing with flight cancellations, flight delays or overbooking
- Fear of missing on the next connecting flight due to delay in the flight
- Stress due to less transit time in case of connecting flights
- Long duration of flights especially long-haul flights
- Fear of feeling claustrophobic in the flight
- Loss of luggage or damaged luggage at the arriving destination
- Buying of foreign exchange or SIM cards at the airports
- Reclaiming of tax refunds at the destination visited before departing for home country

Long Journeys Can Be Daunting

Long journeys can be daunting for a few travellers, especially for those with multiple health issues. Also, for senior citizens, expecting mothers, mothers travelling with infants, people with special abilities and so on, long journeys can be quite strenuous. In long journeys, either in trains/flights/buses, the travellers may not be able to sleep or eat properly. They may face issues such as indigestion, acidity, constipation and high fever due to long journeys and disrupted routine patterns.

Meeting the Expectations of Travel Companion

Travelling alone and with others are two different scenarios. Travelling with others who have different expectations from the trip may get difficult to manage. For example, for three friends, who are travelling together, they may vary in their expectations. For one traveller, holiday may mean relaxing in the hotel and waking up late whereas for the other friend, it may mean, waking up early and exploring the destination to its maximum whereas still for the third friend, shopping may be a priority.

Therefore, while travelling with multiple travel companions, it is always good to discuss each other's expectations from the holiday before its start and accordingly plan the holiday itinerary in such a way that everyone's expectations are met. This can help to avoid stress.

Expectations from a Tour

Many travellers keep very high expectations from their tour. They assume that their trip will meet all their expectations. They believe that whatever quality of services they are expecting at the destination, the same will be delivered at the destination. However, this may not always hold true. Sometimes, there may be a big gap between what the traveller expects and what he/she gets. There may be a difference in what is being viewed on the Internet versus what is the reality when one actually visits and consumes the tourism product. Thus, if the product does not match with the expectations of a traveller, it may eventually become a source of stress for him/her during the trip.

As a thumb rule, it is always advisable for a traveller to be mentally geared up for any kind of experience on the tour. He/she must understand that things may not always work according to his/her whims and fancies, no matter how well he/she may have planned his/her trip. The services provided by the service providers at the destination he/she is visiting are beyond his/her control. The only way to keep himself/herself calm is to moderate his/her expectations before the start of the tour and take things as they come to him/her. A traveller may be guided by the mantra of 'expecting the unexpected' when on a tour so as to make the most out of it.

Unexpected Situations during Travel Cause Stress

Anything may happen to a traveller during the tour. Certain things may happen at the destination due to exogenous factors that may be unpredictable and beyond anyone's control. Certain situations may arise out on the part of service providers while many situations may be created due to the negligence of the traveller himself/herself. Whatever may be the circumstances, such unforeseen situations may absolutely spoil the fun of the traveller's holiday.

Some situations that may happen with a traveller that he/she may be unprepared for are as follows:

- Natural calamities at the destination, for example, floods, earthquakes and so on during one's travel
- Outbreak of an epidemic
- Meeting a road accident
- Traffic jams
- Coping with extreme weather conditions
- Flight cancellations or flight delays
- Closure of attractions due to a sudden strike
- Cancellation of hotel bookings
- Issues with the tour operator
- Loss of one's luggage
- Loss of any travel document such as the passport
- Getting cheated during shopping or when being guided
- Wrongly made reservations

Such unforeseen circumstances are beyond the traveller's control that may happen to him/her during the tour. Thus, they may become a source of stress for the traveller.

Missing Home Leads to Stress

Some travellers keep getting nostalgic about their home and keep missing it even while on a holiday. For them, 'east or west, home is the best' works. For such travellers, being away from home creates stress. They may keep missing their family members, their own space and bed or their home-cooked food. The only panacea for such travellers is to get back home as soon as possible and reunite back with the family members and friends and come back to the same routine as early as possible.

Post-travel Worries during Travel Causes Stress

Many travellers face post-trip blues during their tour only. They may be sooner eloped by depression and anxiety where they may forget to enjoy their present vacation in anticipation of the future. The fear of holiday getting over may strain them. The following thoughts may bother them:

- Will I reach back home safe and secure?
- Would everything be okay back home when I reach home?
- How much work will be piled up for me when I join back the office?
- How much homework will be piled up for my children?
- How will I do the unpacking?
- How will I deal with the finances for the coming month?

Such travellers are busy spending time worrying all the time about the future that leads to stress for them during the tour. They forget that they must enjoy their holiday now, which they may have earned with difficulty and may have been dreaming about and planning for months. Future may be taken care of later.

Post-tour Stress

This refers to the stage where travellers start worrying once they have completed their vacation and are back home. Some travellers keep thinking rather overthinking about their holiday and the time gone by. Some post-tour worries may be as follows:

Unpacking Is Stressful

Coming back and unpacking can again be a stressful task. Putting dirty clothes for washing, keeping the things in place and looking after the whole house that has been unattended for days can take a long time for the traveller to get back to his/her routine. This may be very discomforting for the traveller.

Worrying about the Good Times Gone by Causes Stress

A traveller may keep worrying about having the time of his/her vacation over. He/she may not be able to come at terms with his/her daily routine and life. He/she may still be thinking about the time spent and not able to accept the fact that his/her holiday is over as good times do come to an end.

For such kind of travellers, it is advisable to get back with their routines at the earliest and also to start planning their next vacations so that they do not feel depressed and upset with the thought of holiday that is over for them.

Overthinking

Many people are trapped in their process of overthinking. Sometimes, the traveller may think about the choices that he/she has left for booking a particular tour or hotel. He/she may keep thinking about the opportunity lost in not being able to book that option. He/she may undergo the cognitive dissonance of not booking his/her particular travel arrangement that may become an unnecessary source of stress for him/her. He/she may keep thinking about what better he/she could have done to make his/her holiday much better. He/she may keep finding his/her travel mistakes and keep criticizing himself/herself for the things that did not work out according to his/her plan.

It is advisable for a traveller in such cases not to brood over his/her past holiday experience. *He/she must treat bygones as bygones.* Instead, he/she must learn from his/her travelling mistakes that may help him/her to plan his/her future holiday better.

Other Factors

Till now, we have discussed the pre-tour, on-tour and post-tour travel worries. Now, let us discuss some other factors that may also lead to travel stress for a traveller.

Travelling Overseas Can Be Strenuous

Travelling to a new country can be strenuous, especially for first-time travellers. While travelling abroad, there are a lot of fears and anxieties that arise out of the different travel requirements that one has to meet and the fear of being in someone else's country. The travellers may feel less safe in a new country as he/she may not know anyone there. The fear may also arise out of the ignorance of laws and the systems of another country that one needs to follow while visiting there.

Especially for first-time travellers, the fear of unknown may be a source of stress for them. *They may be ignorant about the airport handling procedures, immigration procedures, visa formalities, currency regulations and conversions, baggage regulations and any other related documentation like travel insurance, health certificates, special permits etc.* The list of formalities for travelling abroad is endless that may create stress for such travellers.

Frequent Travelling Can Be Stressful

For people who travel occasionally, travelling may be an activity that they may look forward to. However, for people for whom travelling is not a choice, but a compulsion, travelling may become a stressful activity. For many working professionals, such as people working in a corporate setup, people working in navy and tourism industry, travelling is a part of their job. Such people may not always enjoy travelling as it may disrupt their daily living such as exercising routine, food habits, sleeping patterns and family life that may become a source of stress.

Travelling to Unsafe Destinations Creates Stress

Many travellers may not prefer to travel to those places that carry reminiscence of unpleasant experiences for them. For example, if a traveller visited a destination once and suddenly there was an outbreak of a flash flood, and he/she was narrowly rescued, he/she may not like to visit the same destination again due to his/her bad experience at the destination earlier. Likewise, if some friend was robbed or pickpocketed at a destination, and he/she shared that incident with the traveller, the traveller may not choose to travel to that destination.

Also, many destinations across the world are not very safe to travel to. Many travel advisories are also issued by the government organizations that suggest their citizens avoid travelling to those countries. *The reason may be an outbreak of a civil war in that country, a political crisis, communal riots, terrorist attacks, crime and theft, natural disasters, an outbreak of a disease and so on.* If one has to travel to that destination due to the nature of his/her job or if he/she has already made his/her holiday booking for which the cancellation charges may not be refunded, he/she may hesitate to travel and get nervous with the thought of travelling to that destination.

Solo Travelling

For many travellers, travelling solo can be a nightmare initially. Although travelling solo may have been chosen purposely by the traveller, the initial anxiety and fear of travelling alone can be quite scary for the traveller. The traveller may feel insecure at the destination and feel uncomfortable for not having anyone to share his/her anxieties with.

TIPS FOR TRAVELLERS

The following may be practised by a traveller to reduce anxiety before, during and after the travel:

- Practise deep breathing
- Practise meditation
- Continue with the exercise routine even when on a holiday
- Have a pre-departure checklist for packing always
- Keeping things in perspective is important for travellers
- Try to be in the moment and enjoy being at a place

SUMMARY

Travelling can be a source of stress too. Anything before, during and after travel can make a traveller uneasy. Not only people who do not like travelling but also people who have health issues due to travelling or for whom travelling is mandatory and part of their jobs may not like to travel, and thus, it may be a source of stress for them. However, travel stress may vary from person to person. Some people may not take any stress at all, while some may take it moderately. Some may take it and never admit. However, some worrying people by virtue of their worrying nature may keep taking stress from the planning of taking a holiday until the time they return. In all cases, stress due to travel is inevitable.

ACTIVITIES

Activity 1

Do you take stress during travel? If yes, what are the sources of your stress?

Activity 2

You may have gone on a vacation with your family or friends. Revisit any of your personal travel experiences and cite any incident or any situation that might have caused stress to you during your travel. Elaborate and share with the class your source of stress and any corrective measure if you took to combat that stress.

BIBLIOGRAPHY

Crotts, J. C., and Zehrer, A. 'The 7 Stages of Business Travel Stress.' *Harvard Business Review*. 2012.
———. 'Vacation Stress: The Development of a Vacation Stress Model among US Vacation Travellers.' *Tourism Review* 67, no.3 (2012): 41–55.

22

Pre-departure Checklist for Travellers

LEARNING OBJECTIVES

The given chapter shall clarify the following:

- What are the things that a traveller must carry with him/her on a tour?
- What can be the basis of classification for packing the travel essentials by the traveller?

SMART LUGGAGE FOR SMART TOURISTS!

- Travelling with the bag or a suitcase loaded with high-tech capabilities is the latest fad now.
- A futuristic approach and innovative technology have made the luggage fully advanced and smart.
- The high-tech features of smart luggage include device charging, remote controller operating system, Bluetooth-enabled locks, motion-sensing technologies, LED battery indicator, GPS tracker, electronic scales, solar charging capabilities, and so much more!
- However, smart bags with lithium-ion batteries, which may cause a fire hazard in the plane, have been stopped by the IATA and the International Civil Aviation Organization (ICAO). Instead, travellers may buy smart luggage with easily removable batteries that may be removed and kept in the cabin luggage.
- Smart luggage prevents identity theft, tracks your luggage and keeps your devices charged during long journeys besides adding more to the style.

INTRODUCTION

Packing is an inevitable part of travel. When a tourist visits a destination, he/she has the intention of staying there. Thus, he/she has to pack all his/her personal stuff so that he/she may not face any difficulty in the destination being visited. While visiting a destination, packing is an important aspect of pre-departure preparations, and packing is an art that comes with practice.

At times, travellers may travel for months to a destination that may be domestic or international. Be it travelling for few days or few months, packing can be strenuous. In all likelihood, while doing a number of preparations when planning to travel, a traveller may forget to pack certain important things due to the stress and pressure of packing, which he/she may regret later. For travelling happily, doing smart packing at the right time is very important. For smart travelling, a traveller may refer to a pre-departure checklist.

While packing, it is advisable for a traveller to carry certain essential items that he/she may require during his/her visit to a place. For not missing out on any essential item, he/she may refer to a list of travel essentials while doing his/her packing for a destination. *This list of essentials that a traveller may refer to for packing before his/her departure is called a pre-departure checklist. Thus, this list acts as a ready reckoner or a reference point for the traveller as he/she may do his/her packing according to the pre-departure list, thereby not missing out on any item to be carried.*

In the given chapter, we have discussed the list of essential items to be carried from an international traveller's point of view when he/she travels globally. However, by and large, the list may also remain the same for domestic travellers, only with a few exceptions. Now, let us have a detailed discussion on the pre-departure checklist that a traveller may refer to while doing his/her packing.

IMPORTANT DOCUMENTATION

Carrying the right documentation during travel is very important for a traveller. Missing out on any kind of documentation may upset the traveller later and cause unnecessary stress for him/her. The following documentation may be carried by the traveller on tour.

Travel Documents and Their Photocopies

The most important document for a traveller visiting overseas is a passport that should be valid for six months from the date of travel. *Along with the passport (always attach the old passport also, in case you have one), a traveller must have a valid visa to travel to a foreign country.* Generally, the visa is stamped on the passport. However, a few countries also give paper visa that the travellers must not forget to attach to their passports.

A traveller may also carry the printed copy of e-ticket though he/she may have the soft copy of the ticket on his/her mobile. He/she may also carry the printout of overseas travel insurance policy along with him/her in case of international travel. In case he/she wishes to drive internationally, he/she must not forget to pack his/her international driving licence along with other travel documents.

During outbound or domestic travel, showing photo ID by the travellers is mandatory at airports during check-in at the airlines counter and at hotels during check-in procedures that comply with the security norms. Therefore, it is important for a traveller to carry his/her original ID proof to be produced during the travel. In case of international travel, a passport is the most important ID proof for the airlines and the hotels. In case of domestic travel, pan card, driving licence, Aadhar card and so on are also acceptable within India. The domestic documents may vary from country to country. The airlines and hotels may take a photocopy of ID proof and give back the original ID proof to the client.

Along with all the original copies of travel documents, it is advisable for travellers to carry a set of photocopies of each travel document that may be required in case a traveller loses his/her originals. Also, before leaving his/her home, he/she may scan all the documents and keep a soft copy of all the travel documents in his/her email ID.

In case of group travel, when travellers are visiting an international destination on a tour package through a travel company that has made all the travel arrangements for them, a tour leader carries the necessary photocopies of the documentation of guests. Still, it is advisable for the guests to carry one set of photocopies of all travel-related documents just to be on the safer side.

Detailed Itinerary

It is advisable for the tourist to carry a detailed itinerary of his/her tour that may contain the details of the day-to-day tour programme. Especially if the duration of the trip is long and the traveller is covering multiple destinations, a detailed itinerary becomes very handy. A detailed itinerary may contain information about the sightseeing attractions to be covered each day and the address of accommodations to stay in, besides the proposed activities to be done by the traveller at the destinations.

Passport Size Photographs

Travellers must also carry their own passport size photographs that may be required in case he/she loses his/her passport in another country.

Transportation Tickets

Besides the flight tickets, a traveller may carry printed copies of booked travel tickets on buses, trains or any other reservations made for special rides at the destination. For example, *a traveller may have booked an online gondola ride at Venice in advance or a train ride from London to Paris on Eurostar.* He/she may carry a printed copy of the same with him/her though these days mostly electronic tickets are acceptable on smartphones that are received via email from the local transporters.

Hotel Voucher

It is a written confirmation of services promised by the hotel to the client/tour operator/travel agent. It contains the confirmed occupancy details of the stay of clients along with their check-in and check-out details and any services to be availed by them at the hotel. A traveller must carry the same document with him/her while on a tour. In the case of group travel arranged through a travel company, the tour leader carries the copy of hotel voucher for his/her guests.

Reservation Confirmations

If a traveller has made any bookings for special activities at a destination in advance, such as a *Desert Safari along with dinner at Dubai* or *hot-air ballooning at Jaisalmer in India*, he/she must carry the printed copy of such advanced reservations with him/her.

Maps

It is advisable for a traveller to have all the necessary maps of a destination with him/her before he/she travels to that place. This helps him/her to figure out places with much accuracy, and he/she can make more sense of the destination being visited. Generally, if a traveller has booked through a travel company, the itinerary file may contain printed maps of different destinations being covered during the tour. However, if a traveller has made his/her own travel arrangements, he/she may himself/herself print the required hard copies of the maps of the destinations and attractions being covered before the start of the tour. Alternatively, at the destination, he/she may also seek the help of Google maps, whenever required. However, that is always subject to the connectivity of the Internet with the smartphone. Otherwise, the traveller may also collect various maps on reaching a country's airport or visitor's information centre.

Travel-related Books

Besides the maps, a traveller may carry additional city guidebooks, language guides and phrase books to learn more about a destination during the journey. He/she may learn local jargons and phrases from the language book to interact with the locals at a destination.

In-house Contact Sheet

If a traveller, has made his/her bookings through a tour operator then he/she must have the contact list of an in-house staff of the company in case he/she has to speak to them in times of emergency.

List of Important Emergency Numbers

A traveller must keep a list of all the important telephone numbers, that he/she may require in case of an emergency at a destination. Alternatively, he/she may save the same in his/her cell phone directory. The important contact numbers may include the local numbers of his/her country's embassy in another country, the contact details of the hotel he/she is likely to stay in, the local police station/hospitals/ambulance number contact numbers and so on.

Business Card, if Required

Travellers may also carry their personal business card on a tour. This card may be used for fostering new friendships and expanding their social network with other travellers whom they may meet during the trip.

PERSONAL TRAVEL ESSENTIALS

A traveller may carry the following personal items while on a tour.

Backpack

A traveller must always take a smart backpack with him/her during the trip besides a proper suitcase. He/she may keep his/her own essential stuff in his/her backpack that he/she may require every day. It may include a power bank, charger, water bottle, any important travel document, notebook and a pen, items of personal hygiene, deodorant, hand sanitizer, any food items and so on. This may give him/her hands-free mobility and real comfort. Alternatively, he/she may carry a duffel bag according to his/her own convenience.

Travel Lock

Although it sounds frivolous, it is very important for a traveller to carry a travel lock. A traveller must keep his/her luggage properly locked at all times to prevent any theft and keep it secure. First, while travelling by airlines, he/she must lock his/her baggage to avoid any pilferage. Even when he/she is travelling out for local sight-seeing of the destination, he/she must keep his/her bags locked in the hotel room.

Travel Document Holder

While travelling abroad, a traveller may secure all his/her travel documents such as passport, ticket, boarding pass, foreign currency, debit cards, credit cards and travel insurance in a travel document holder. Besides being a more secure place, it also gives a smarter and an overall professional appearance to a traveller that adds on to his/her confidence.

Cash

A traveller must carry enough money with him/her while on a tour that may be required at every step for making local travel arrangements, eating food, trying different activities, doing shopping, giving tips and porterage charges at hotels, making a payment towards entry fees for visiting an attraction (wherever required) and so on as debit cards or credit cards are still not accepted everywhere. Besides spending cash on the regular transactions during travel, a traveller may also require cash for incurring any incidental expenditure in case of an emergent situation arising during the tour.

However, a traveller must ensure that in the case of international travel, he/she must carry the cash in the form of the local currency of the country being visited. However, the cash must be within the prescribed limits as per the BTQ rules. Above the permitted cash limit, he/she may carry the money in the form of travellers' cheques. He/she may also carry few dollars with him/her (that may be converted into the local currency of a country later) besides the local currency of a country that is generally universally acceptable.

Plastic Money

A traveller may choose to travel cashless while carrying plastic payment cards without any tension of losing any money. *He/she may carry plastic money in the form of traveller's cheques and international credit/debit cards to make cashless transactions.* However, a traveller before travelling must check prior at the destination with the authorities if doing cashless transactions is easily permissible within a country or not. However, as a safeguard, a traveller must carry some cash also with him/her to avoid facing any trouble later during his/her travel. *At many places, loose coins of small denominations are required; for example, while having access to chargeable public toilets, the traveller has to insert loose coins.* Even at many local markets, especially while doing street shopping when buying local stuff, many shops only accept cash. Thus, carrying some cash is always in the interest of the traveller.

Diary

Many travellers have the habit of writing journals while travelling. They continuously pen down their own travel experiences and also list out the names of attractions that they visit for their own future memories. Thus, to make notes of important things, such travellers must carry their own diary on the tour. Diary may also be used for noting down everyday expenditures being incurred by the traveller during the tour. Alternatively, the travellers may use their smartphone or a tablet for making their notes or noting their expenditures.

Pen

A traveller may need a pen for making his/her necessary notes of his/her expenditures or penning down his/her thoughts and experiences on the tour. He/she may also need the pen to fill the forms at the airport/flight while disembarking wherever required. Therefore, he/she must carry a pen with him/her on the tour.

Envelope

A traveller generally wants to keep a check on the expenditures he/she is making on the tour. On returning, he/she may like to tally the amount spent with the bills that he/she may have collected during the tour. Keeping bills in one envelope makes things more organized and streamlined for the traveller later. Therefore, he/she may not miss on any receipts that may help him/her in tracking his/her expenditures accurately. Also, the same envelope may be referred to by the traveller for submitting his/her bills of shopping at the airport while collecting his/her tax refund for the shopping done during his/her international travel.

Alternatively, the envelope may also be used by the travellers for keeping the cash.

Toilet Kit

A traveller must carry his/her personal items that may include a shaving kit, extra razors, shampoo bottle or shampoo sachets, travel soaps, pouch detergents, shower gel, hair gel (in case he/she uses one), comb, toothbrush, toothpaste, mouthwash, floss, sunscreen lotion, moisturiser, night cream, hair oil, lip balm, nail cutter, small mirror, earbuds and so on in a toilet kit. To minimize the space occupied by toiletries, such as shampoos, shower gels and moisturizers, a traveller may pack the same in small quantities in small travel bottles in separate toiletries bag or plastic disposable bags where there are fewer chances of leakage of these liquid items. Notably, during long-haul or transit flights, a traveller may carry this little travel kit with him/her to freshen up. He/she may also use this kit every day during the tour as many hotels do not provide toiletries.

Female Items

Besides the toilet kit, a lady traveller may also pack feminine hygiene products such as sanitary napkins, toilet spray, tampons and so on and all her makeup stuff, artificial jewellery, accessories, scarves, clothes, slippers, sports shoes, formal shoes to attend any special evenings or any other thing required for travelling to a destination. Along with all the above-mentioned items, women travellers may also carry *pepper spray* in their bags, especially in case they are travelling solo. The pepper spray acts as a safety guard for the women that may be used in case of any mishappening with her.

Sewing Kit

A traveller may need a sewing kit anytime. Any cloth may get torn that may be required to be stitched. Notably, in foreign countries, this can become a task for the traveller to buy a sewing kit due to the difficulty in locating the shop where it may be found and the expense to be incurred for buying it. It is, therefore, advisable for a traveller to carry with him/her a small sewing kit from his/her place of departure that may include colourful threads besides needle, scissors, buttons and safety pins and so on.

Wet Tissues/Face Wipes

A traveller may get weary during the long journeys on the tour. Hectic day's itinerary may make him/her feel very tiresome and may make him/her sweat if the weather is hot and humid. The same may be reflected in his/her face.

Therefore, to look fresh and feel fresh, a traveller may use wet tissues/face wipes, and thus, he/she must carry the same with him/her on a tour.

Deodorant/Perfume

A traveller must smell good. In hot weather, while going from one place to another, he/she may sweat, and therefore, his/her body odour may smell foul. He/she may himself/herself feel uncomfortable along with other tourists who may come in contact with him/her.

It is, therefore, advisable for a traveller to carry a small bottle of perfume/deodorant/cologne with him/her on tour to maintain a good body odour at all times.

Hand Sanitizer

Personal hygiene is very important for a traveller. While using local modes of transportation, the hands of a traveller may get dirty. Also, at many places, he/she may not get water to wash his/her hands. He/she may like to eat something, but his/her hands may be dirty. Therefore, for his/her personal hygiene, a traveller must carry a sanitizer with him/her at all times on a tour.

Mouth Freshener

A traveller must have a pleasant breath. When he/she speaks, he/she should not smell bad. Thus, he/she may carry a mouth freshener with him/her. If possible, he/she may also rinse his/her mouth with mouthwash, especially after the meals.

Caps/Hats

Travellers may also carry caps/hats that act as a shield in hot weather besides providing a sporty look to the traveller.

Sunglasses and Eyeglasses/Contact Lenses

Travellers may carry sunglasses with them to a destination to protect their eyes against the heat. Besides sunglasses, travellers who use eyeglasses may carry an extra pair of glasses with them on the tour along with the glass case. The reason is that if the spectacles break, a traveller may be under duress. His/her valuable time might go wasted in locating an optician. This may cost him/her significant time and money. Likewise, travellers who wear contact lenses may carry extra lenses, solution for cleaning the lenses and the contact case. It is also advisable for travellers to carry the prescription of the optician with the vision number in case the travellers loses/damages his/her eyeglasses at the destination being visited.

Food Items

A traveller may have a hectic itinerary during the tour. He/she may get hunger pangs in between. Moreover, he/she may not like the local food of the place. Even if he/she likes the local food, he/she may not have enough time to hunt for local restaurants and eat food that may delay his/her scheduled tour programme for the day. Therefore, it is always advisable for a traveller to carry doses of small energy packets with him/her. He/she may carry small portions of snacks with him/her that may include dry fruits or energy bar, wafers, cookies and so on that may give him/her instant energy besides satisfying his/her hunger pangs so that he/she enjoys an uninterrupted sightseeing at the destination.

He/she may also carry zip locks with him/her to keep any foodstuff fresh which he/she may be carrying for his/her own consumption.

He/she may also take *ready-to-eat food* from his/her destination or buy one at the destination if he/she wants to eat the native food of his/her place or try the food of other places.

Water Bottle

As tourists remain on their toes due to their hectic itineraries while visiting attractions, they may get tired, dry up and dehydrate, especially during the hot weathers. *Therefore, it is always advisable for travellers to carry their own collapsible refillable water bottles which occupy less space and are easy to carry.* The traveller may keep drinking sips of water to keep himself/herself hydrated at all times. Alternatively, he/she may have to buy mineral water bottle every few hours that may cost him/her money and time in locating the nearest shop from where he/she can buy the water from.

TRAVEL COMFORTERS/FACILITATORS

These things are not essential to carry. But if a traveller carries these items, his/her trip becomes more comfortable.

Neck Travel Pillow

To make his/her travel comfortable during long flights, a traveller may carry a neck travel pillow with him/her. Although most of the international airlines also give neck travel pillows to their passengers, he/she may even then take his/her own neck travel pillow that he/she may be more comfortable with. He/she may use the same in coaches too during the long journeys to take small naps and relax during the journey.

Eye Blinders/Sleep Masks

During transit flights, when there are long halts at airports, the eye blinder is a useful item for taking a nap at the airport. Although airlines also generally provide the eye blinders during long journeys, it is advisable for a traveller to carry his/her own eye blinder.

Mesh or a Collapsible Laundry Bag

Many travellers go on tours for a long duration that may cover multiple destinations. A traveller may have dirty clothes that he/she may not be able to wash on the tour at the hotels due to the scarcity of time. Therefore, he/she may carry a separate collapsible laundry bag or a mesh that may be placed in his/her suitcase as it occupies less space besides keeping the clean clothes separated from the dirty clothes. He/she may keep this mesh in the hotel room to put his/her dirty clothes in it. On checking out of the hotel, he/she may pack this mesh back in his/her suitcase that keeps the used clothes separated from unused ones.

Travel Blanket

A traveller may carry a travel blanket to keep himself/herself comfortable and warm during the journeys. Although in long international flights, travellers get a travel blanket, the same may not be the case while travelling by trains or buses. Thus, it is advisable to carry one's own cosy light travel blankets that occupy less space and are convenient to carry besides being more hygienic.

Packet Organizers

For a better and a convenient packing in the primary check-in baggage (a large suitcase), a traveller may make use of packet organizers that help in keeping the stuff stacked in organizers. Making use of *compression sacs, packing cubes, pouches* and *folders* make the packing a lot more organized by packing the things in fewer spaces with minor wrinkles on clothing. This helps a traveller in locating his/her material more easily and also keeping the things back in place quickly besides keeping the stuff clean.

Rain Poncho

Weather is beyond anyone's control. A traveller may have a plan to explore the city, and it may seem to be a rainy day. Therefore, a traveller, instead of postponing his/her travel plan, may venture out in the rain for his/her scheduled sightseeing wearing a raincoat or poncho. This may keep him/her as well as his/her backpack dry, in case he/she is carrying the same.

It is better to carry a rain poncho instead of an umbrella as it occupies less space in packing. The hands of a traveller also remain free, and he/she thus feels more comfortable.

Local SIM Card

While travelling abroad, a traveller must carry a local SIM card of the country he/she is visiting if he/she has not activated his/her international roaming. He/she must also ensure that he/she has a net pack for better connection and easy access on a tour as he/she may find the free Wi-Fi only in the hotel or at the airport.

Money Belt

As a traveller may be carrying quite some cash, he/she may for security reasons carry a money belt/neck wallet or an extra hidden pocket that may help him/her to keep his/her cash safe from the pick-pocketers. These gears help a traveller to place the money close to him/her.

Sling Bags

A traveller may carry a sling bag to keep cash or any other important item while travelling. Besides, storage, it gives a smart look to the traveller.

Beach Bag

While travelling on beach vacations, a traveller may also carry a foldable beach bag that may contain a *beach towel, beach hat, water-resistant phone pouch, sunscreen, sunglasses, reading material* and so on.

ELECTRONICS

It is an era of technology. Today's traveller has a high dependence on the electronic items. Following is the list of electronic gadgets that he/she may carry with him/her on a tour.

Smartphone

A smartphone is not less than oxygen for a traveller. A traveller may have to make important emergency calls or stay connected with his/her family while on the tour. Also, he/she may have to make use of the Internet for seeking any necessary information such as finding a good local restaurant and attractions to visit. For travelling to different places, he/she may even have to keep track of the routes by using Google navigation maps. Therefore, a smartphone is a must for a traveller. It is the best companion of a traveller today.

Electronic Accessories

A traveller must carry the charger of his/her smartphone with him/her. As the battery of the smartphone may be fast consumed due to usage of the Internet by the traveller, he/she may charge his/her phone from time to time with a charger before the battery of mobile goes dead.

He/she must also carry a *memory card* for data storage as he/she may take lots of pictures during the tour through his/her phone. Alternatively, he/she may carry a camera of his/her choice for capturing his/her travel memories. *Professional photographers or travellers who like doing photography may carry digital single-lens reflex (DSLR) with them on the tour.* They may also carry an extra lens if required for the DSLR.

Music lovers may like to listen to music on their mobile phone or watch a movie during a flight/train/bus. For the same, the traveller may carry his/her earphones so that other co-travellers may not get disturbed due to loud voices. Alternatively, he/she may also carry head-phones to listen to music to save the battery of his/her phone.

Besides, the above, a traveller must not forget to *pack the data cable and chargers of his/her laptop, iPad, Bluetooth headset, music speakers, iPod* and so on while going on the tour depending upon the things that he/she wants to carry.

Power Bank

A smartphone as compared to other phones consumes more battery. Therefore, besides carrying a charger, a traveller must have a battery backup for his/her mobile. He/she may take a charged power bank for charging his/her mobile on the tour.

Universal Plug Adapter

When a traveller is travelling to a foreign country, he/she may carry a universal plug adapter with him/her so that he/she may not find any difficulty in charging his/her mobile or any electronic equipment such as laptop, video camera and tablet that he/she may require during the trip.

Flashlight

These days mostly all mobiles have an inbuilt torch. However, in case the battery of the mobile phone is discharged, a torch may be required. Travellers, especially going on treks and passing through dark patches in the night or otherwise exploring the city in the night where there are no floodlights, may require to use a torch. Therefore, he/she may pack a flashlight in his/her suitcase as he/she may need it anytime during his/her travel.

OTHER TRAVEL ESSENTIALS

First-aid Kit

Contingency planning is an essential part of the trip. A traveller must plan things in advance to meet any unforeseen circumstances on the tour. He/she may fall sick on the tour or may injure himself/herself. Carrying the first-aid kit helps in dealing with such situations. The first-aid kit generally includes first-aid manual, bandages, adhesive tapes, scissors, cotton, antiseptic solution, antiseptic wipes, antibacterial ointment, thermometer and instant cold packs. It also includes some essential medicines that are painkillers such as Paracetamol, Disprin, Ibuprofen, antacids, motion sickness pills, altitude sickness pills, allergy medicines, Vicks, Strepsils, sun-burn relief, multivitamins and insect reliever medicine.

In case, a traveller is taking any regular medication, he/she must take his/her doctor's prescription while on a tour.

Insect Repellents

To avoid insect bites by mosquitoes and so on at a destination, a traveller must pack an insect repellent or a bug spray in his/her luggage. Many dreaded diseases like dengue fever can be avoided by the travellers using these insect repellents.

Disposable Plastic Bags and Sickness Bags

A traveller may also carry disposable plastic bags with him/her on a tour. He/she may bring them to pack any damp item such as his/her towel or any other personal stuff. He/she may also need it to put any kind of trash while eating inside the car or coaches, or sometimes, if he/she wants to vomit on the coach due to motion sickness issue, he/she may use the sickness bags.

TIPS FOR PACKING

The following tips may be considered by a traveller while packing his/her stuff:

- A traveller should always be guided by the rule of travelling light.
- It is always advisable for a traveller to carry one suitcase with a trolley that makes it convenient for him/her to carry.
- At the same time, he/she may also pack carry-on baggage with him/her in which he/she keeps his/her all necessary items required during travel. A carry-on bag can be a backpack or a small bag with a trolley.
- It is also very important to save space while packing. It is advisable to pack the heavy stuff at the bottom in the suitcase, and any stuff that will be required on reaching the destination and any items like toiletries that are likely to leak to be kept at the top of the suitcase in separate plastic bags.

SUMMARY

The above list of things that a traveller may carry is comprehensive. This pre-departure check-list is handy for a traveller while packing for his/her holiday to a new destination. It aids him/her in not missing out on any essential item that may disappoint him/her later searching for it. However, a traveller must always be guided by the rule of the thumb to travel light. A traveller must carry the necessary travel documentation, personal items, travel facilitators and electronic items with him/her while going on a tour. Taking the right stuff with him/her at the right time helps him/her to stay comfortable and hassle-free on the tour.

ACTIVITIES

Activity 1: Paint a Picture

Distribute pieces of chits to students in the class. Ask them to draw two items each on the same chit that they must carry while travelling. Give them 10 minutes to draw. Now collect all the chits and distribute the chits at random to different students. As a result, every student shall get a different item with him/her that has been drawn by another classmate. Now conduct an extempore in the class. Ask each student individually to speak for a minute on the picture that he/she has on the chit he/she has received. This is a very exciting activity, and this will help the students to be more creative and also create a more intellectually stimulating environment.

Activity 2: Listing

Take a chart. Now use props on the chart to make funny representations of the items that a traveller may carry with him/her while visiting a destination.

Case Studies

C.1. NIGHTMARE BY A LEADING AIRLINES

Introduction

Michael is a travel blogger who gets invited to media press conferences and FAM trips all over the globe. He was living in Miami for a brief period in 2017 when he decided to choose travelling as his first preference. Being a traveller, he came across many airlines and received a number of experiences, good and bad, in his journey. In 2017, Michael was invited for a media travel conference in Newark, New Jersey, where he was going to meet high authorities and business tycoons in the media industry. Without wasting any time, he booked a flight to Newark from Miami. He packed his bags and set his course towards the airport. After going through the lengthy airport process, he finally boarded his flight in one of the most reputed airlines of the USA which was supposed to take off at 8 PM.

One hour later, the plane was standing still at one spot, and all the passengers were getting impatient. Little did they know that it was just the start of their nightmare. As an hour passed, the pilot made an announcement saying that they apologize for the inconvenience, and they request all the passengers to gather their belongings and proceed to deplane the aircraft. Michael looked around and saw irritated faces of his fellow passengers. He was slightly worried as the start of his journey became troublesome, and he wanted nothing to jeopardize his conference in Newark. Given no choice, he gathered his belongings and got down from the plane to proceed towards the common area where everyone from his plane was standing for further information. The airline crew apologized again for the trouble and announced that due to fault in the pilot's chair, they are waiting for a new aircraft and a new aeroplane crew. Michael did not understand that if there is a fault in the aircraft, why an entire crew replacement is needed. He thought that it must be the protocol, so he sat tight. After half an hour, the crew announced that the new aircraft has left from the hanger and will reach the gate by 10 PM. Listening to this, Michael relaxed a bit. Every passenger was already on the edge but there was nothing they could have done so they waited some more. Realizing the restlessness of all the passengers, the airport crew provided everyone with some snacks and water.

After a long wait, it was now 11 PM when another announcement was made that the plane has not arrived at the gate yet. They apologized again and said that they could not provide the passengers with a specific boarding time. By now, everyone was making rounds of the airport as they had no choice other than following instructions of the crew. Having enough from the airlines, one passenger requested for a recommendation for different airlines, and she got a response that she has to take it up to the service centre and talk to an agent. Michael was getting impatient now. He asked the crew whether the plane was going to arrive at 11:45 PM as it was shown on the screen, and the operator lady replied with a simple no. Another misleading information was given by the so-called one of the leading airlines of the country. This was the least that one could expect from such an airline. Judging the overall scenario, Michael knew that the flight was not going to leave till next day which made him wonder why they were not letting everyone go home or pay for their hotel and tell them the truth that flight was not going to leave till next day. It was the decent thing to do after making everyone wait for 4–5 hours and possibly more!

After a long wait and stressful atmosphere, the information screen now showed boarding time—6:00 AM. Everybody became irritated after they saw the screen. Then came the announcement saying that the flight is not cancelled, it is delayed till 6:00 AM. Therefore, everyone's luggage would stay with them, and passengers would be provided with vouchers for airport hotels. The airport vouchers offered a decent discount for the hotels, but the remaining amount was to be paid by the passenger. Every passenger was now furious and started yelling at the crew, demanding to cancel their tickets and refund the amount. The airlines strictly said that the current boarding passes will be used for 6:00 AM flight, and the flight is just delayed, not cancelled. By doing this, the airlines saved themselves from refunding the money of the passengers. They not only mislead their customers but also did not pay for the hotel tariff, did not provide proper food and also behaved very arrogantly with a few passengers. Michael talked to his fellow passengers and found out that this particular airline has a long and promising history of such mishaps and bad customer service. Michael had two choices in front of him. He could either wait at the airport till 6:00 AM with a few of the passengers, or he can spend a little more money and rest in a hotel room. He then chose to stay in a hotel room and relax until the boarding time. Next day, the flight was again delayed by 45 minutes but managed to arrive at last. Not happy with such kind of experience, Michael promised to never book future flights with this airline.

Conclusion

Being an avid traveller, Michael expected mishap from this airline as it has a record of bad services. Being the patient man among other fellow passengers, Michael kept his cool and waited without causing any fights, unlike some passengers. The airline was discreet with important information as it did not want to lose the money by refunding it to the passengers, which caused them to lose future customers. After causing so much inconvenience to the passengers, the airline should have taken better care in providing customer care services when they announced the 6:00 AM delay. They not only failed in that but also managed to lose a valuable customer who was going to a meeting with important people in the tourism industry where he must have shared his airport nightmare.

Learning Outcomes

- When a passenger pays a high amount for a flight, airlines must realize that the journey is also an important part for a customer. The airlines must stand by what they promise to the customer and must provide a decent service to them.
- Customer service must be a top-most priority for airlines. Airlines owe a responsibility towards travellers' safety, respecting their deadlines, on-time arrivals, providing correct information to travellers, providing hotels, food and so on during flight delays, behaving politely with the traveller and so on.
- Before choosing an airline, one must take appropriate time in reading travelled passenger reviews to avoid trouble.
- Stressful situations while travelling can cause negativity during the whole trip. One must remain calm and find appropriate solutions.
- It is easy to lose one customer but a challenge to gain one. One lost customer can spread criticism about their bad experience, which can cause the company to lose 100 more. Negative publicity in today's social media era can cause catastrophic outcome for airlines with bad customer services.

Points for Discussion

- If you were in Michael's situation, what would you do?
- After the airport scenario, Michael was going for a media conference where important people from the tourism industry were going to attend. Do you think it was bad timing for the airlines to give bad customer service? Why?
- Have you ever experienced an airport nightmare? Discuss.

C.2. NOT-SO-ORDINARY CHINESE TRAVELLERS

Introduction

In today's date, the Chinese outbound tourism market is growing at an impressive speed. Chinese tourists are among the largest outbound travellers in the world, as there were about 150 million foreign visits made by Chinese tourists in 2018. Data issued by the China Outbound Tourism Research Institute estimated that by the year 2025, the Chinese outbound tourism market would be worth $270 billion. The most visited outbound tourist places for Chinese travellers in 2018 were Thailand, Japan, Vietnam, Korea, the USA, Singapore, Malaysia, Cambodia, Russian Federation and Indonesia.

According to recent studies, it is believed that the Chinese people have a different system when it comes to travel planning and creating itineraries, which makes them different from the majority of international travellers. On average, Chinese tourists tend to spend a lot more when they visit foreign countries, more than they spend in their homelands. In 2018, they spent about $277 billion in foreign countries. In other words, they have a big hand in increasing other country's economy.

Many countries recognized their potential for travel and made creative marketing strategies to attract them. For example, the majority of restaurants represent Chinese food in their menu, many signages of many countries are in the Chinese language, many countries have opened tourism information centres in China and so much more!

Now, what makes Chinese travellers different from others?

Here are a few researched points to answer the above question.

They Travel in Groups

- It is known that average Chinese travellers prefer to travel in groups rather than solo travelling. The reason being that some of them might not speak or understand English very well so travelling in large groups and with travel agencies is a much safer option for them.
- They also prefer to make their travel arrangements through travel agencies to avoid the hassle of doing any research, creating the itinerary, visa processing, bookings and so on. They like having a relaxed holiday without any headache of taking care of travel plans.

They Use Social Media for Travel Planning

Majority of Chinese travellers plan their trips using social media platforms such as Weibo and Youku as their main channel. WeChat is the first application of preference for them.

Chinese Travellers

- Tourism-related forums dedicated to tourism such as Qyer, Tuniu or Baidu are highly appreciated by Chinese potential travellers.
- They use Baidu the almighty internet word of mouth (IWOM) and different video platforms to get a better idea of the destination.
- Tuniu is the most active social network specializing in mass-market online travel and positioning itself on leisure travel. It offers a wide range of advices as well as places for Chinese tourists about leisure travel to discuss their latest experience of the hottest places to go to.

Source: http://elib.bsu.by/bitstream/123456,789/166192/1/94-102.pdf (accessed on 5 August 2020).

They Make Short Travel Plans

Chinese travellers are believed to choose short travel packages. A study showed that Chinese travellers choose packages with short duration and maximum coverage, i.e., choosing a package with a trip to three countries in 10 days.

Chinese Traveller's Itinerary

- Generally, travellers from most of the countries select their itinerary which includes famous landmarks of a destination, unlike Chinese traveller who prefers visiting natural scenic attractions and theme parks.
- When it comes to shopping, the study shows that Chinese travellers spend 25 per cent on shopping while other travellers spend 15 per cent of their overall budget. Duty-free shops, boutiques and skincare shops are their favourites.

They Do Not Like Surprises

Chinese travellers tend to plan their entire trip 2–3 months before. They like to gain as much information possible about their trip beforehand and use websites available in their country for research purposes.

They Are Different from One Another in Terms of Requirement

- The majority of the total outbound Chinese tourists travel for business because of which they have specific needs. Business travellers from China require good speed internet service, 24 × 7 food delivery service, transportation service with good connectivity, ticket-booking services, three- to five-star hotel recommendations and good customer care services.
- Those who travel for leisure are more specific about tour packages. They want maximum entertainment, knowledgeable guides, recreational facilities such as spas, swimming pools, saunas, tennis courts, activity-oriented grounds and more!

They Are Specific with the Dates

Chinese people have a very specific timeline of holidays. They choose such a time for their travel trips when there is no peak season in destinations so that they can have an enjoyable and disturbance-free experience. For example, Chinese travellers spend the Lunar New Year Holiday week (late January–early February) abroad when there is more space on the ground and less foreign travellers.

Their Need to Make Mobile Payments

- Mobile payment is considered the first option amongst Chinese because it is easier and familiar, more secure, offers better deals and discounts and there is greater exchange rate transparency. The most popular online service used for payments by Chinese is Alipay and WeChat Pay.
- A recent survey states that more than 70 per cent of Chinese people use the mobile payment method in their day-to-day lives including travelling. The Chinese people are so used to removing mobiles from their pockets for making payments that they later realize that cash is required at some merchants.

They Have Specific Expectations

- When they travel to a destination and stay in a hotel, Chinese people expect a few basic amenities to be provided such as toiletries (toothbrush, toothpaste, shampoo, soap, handwash, etc.), home slippers, free Wi-Fi, kettle for making tea and all required necessities.
- Chinese travellers expect polite behaviour as they have a very low tolerance for rude behaviour. In the case of a complaint from Chinese tourists, the staff is advised to have an indirect, diplomatic and polite confrontation.
- When Chinese tourists give anyone their business card, it is advised to receive it with both hands. Respect and grace are considered very important among Chinese people.

They Are Difficult to Read

Chinese tourists are sometimes proven to be complicated travellers as it is slightly difficult to read them. It is very normal for the Chinese to hide their true emotions and speak diplomatically even when they have a big issue regarding their expectations from travel service providers.

Strong Chinese Beliefs

It is known that Chinese people avoid the number '4' as it is considered as devil's number. According to Chinese beliefs, the pronunciation of number four in the Chinese language resembles the word 'death'. This affects their choices such as buying more than or less than four things, not staying on the 4th floor when in a hotel and skipping the 4th floor when in an elevator.

Conclusion

This case is important to understand and appreciate the cross-cultural differences of different nationalities of tourists visiting a country. The case study shows that majority of Chinese travellers have a different set of choices and requirements. They put more thought into travelling than other international travellers. Countries and companies are tapping into their ideologies and making substantial changes to meet their expectations like the need for using mobile payments applications. Large tour groups are the safest option for them as Chinese travellers like to get the maximum outcome from little investment.

Learning Outcomes

- Every destination has its own cultural differences and patterns. It is important to understand cross-cultural differences and create mechanisms accordingly.
- There is a lot to learn from Chinese travellers. For example, digital payments can put stop to scammers and unreasonable expenses. To attract Chinese travellers, countries must have the option of cashless payments.

Points for Discussion

- Why do you think Chinese travellers are slightly different from other average travellers? Discuss.
- Digital payment methods can avoid tourists falling into scamming and overpricing traps. Discuss.
- Take an example of any other nationality and discuss their traits.

Bibliography

https://www.e-unwto.org/doi/pdf/10.18111/9789284421138 (accessed on 31 July 2020).

https://www.businesswire.com/news/home/20190204005351/en/2019-China-Outbound-Tourism-Market---Set (accessed on 31 July 2020).

https://www.pata.org/china-the-future-of-travel-demystifies-the-worlds-largest-outbound-tourism-market%EF%BB%BF/ (accessed on 31 July 2020).

https://www.marketwatch.com/press-release/china-outbound-tourism-market-size-is-expected-to-exhibit-usd-270-billion-by-2025-2019-07-31 (accessed on 31 July 2020).

C.3. THE GOAN CURRY

Introduction

Goa is a perfect blend of culture, warmth, lights, beautiful beaches and mouth-watering local cuisines. Because of its charm and what the city has to offer, every day, this destination is packed with tourists from all sides of the world. This is a huge boon for the tourism sector. As the tourism industry advanced, many MNCs, multi-cuisine restaurants, luxury hotels, night clubs, casinos and adventure clubs started their businesses in Goa. Along with the positives, this development has a negative impact on the local culture and regional flavours.

Many tourists like to choose staged experiences rather than finding ways to explore a destination's culture and regional background. This case study is focused on a tourist who had visited Goa 10 years back and fell in love with the local culture and regional cuisines. A few months ago, he decided to go on a vacation with his family to the same destination. He experienced that the originality of local culture and taste of regional cuisines are somewhere lost.

Background

The stereotype that Goa is not suitable for one to visit with their family is behind us, hopefully. A year ago, Gautami and her family went on a vacation in Goa. Her father, Mr Krishna, is a man with a premium taste. His demands were very specific and pre-planned—the best hotel with the most desirable room, great quality amenities and let us not talk about the demand for a room with a balcony and a seaside view. Travelling to Goa and not staying in a hotel room with the seaside view is an absolute no-no for Gautami's father. He also liked providing a great experience for his family. So naturally, the benefits were shared among all.

After checking into the hotel with a beautiful seaside view that cost around ₹5,000 per night, the food was almost just as pricey and did no justice to the name—authentic Goan curry. Every course that was selected by the family tasted premium, but the 'authentic' title was misleading. If you are travelling to Goa in search of local and authentic cuisine, then you expect something out of the usual and something you can only get by travelling to a certain region. It was very underwhelming considering that they paid a huge amount for one meal which said 'authentic Goan cuisine'. Truth to be told, the food was not something for which one had to travel to Goa. You can order a Goan curry in any restaurant near you, and it may taste the same. Everyone was very disappointed, especially Gautami's father.

Among the family of four, Gautami is the only one with a wandering soul. After lunch, she explored her neighbourhood and came across a mini restaurant. A small, poorly built outlet with a tiny welcome board designed like a fish placed on the top. A crowded space for customers to sit inside on very simple plastic chairs and four plastic tables. Very dull, badly structured, and frankly, the lack of customer is understandable, considering the first impression is not so great. But the aroma oozing out of that small place was filled with so much of flavour that you could tell even before eating that this place had made no compromise with their food.

There were no customers there, just the chef, one small boy, possibly a waiter and the owner of that place.

The kind smile of the owner was very welcoming to Gautami. Perhaps, he was more aware of Gautami's next step than she herself. She went inside the restaurant and asked, 'What smells so good?' The kind owner only questioned her back saying 'Would you like to try it?' There was no way she was going to deny that offer. After a good 6–7 minutes, the chef placed a steel plate full of different varieties of food in front of her. On one side, there was a huge dome of Goan parboiled rice (unpolished brown rice), a whole fish fry covered in their home-made spice rub, a bowl of fish curry made with coconut milk and a pink-coloured liquid known as Solkadhi (popular in Goa) which helps in digesting the food. The plate was spotless within a few minutes. The taste was so delicious that she urged her family to eat dinner at that small restaurant. Her father was very hesitant as it clashed with his ideology as a tourist that such places would be a complete waste of time and money. But by the end of that day, her entire family was just as amazed as the other customers in that restaurant. This experience proved that appearances are often deceptive. The expensive hotel where they were staying provided very basic tasting food at such a high price. You can probably get such food in any restaurants under the name 'Goan cuisine'. But that small restaurant gave them exactly what they were searching for—authentic regional cuisine.

Conclusion

Tourists who are in search of local and authentic food experience are often confused about where to start exploring. Their confusion gets no rest when a few of these big restaurants and high-end eateries present their food as 'authentic local cuisine'. Because of many reasons, small places that provide the real deal are ignored, and tourists are left unsatisfied. Not everyone is misguided but a majority of people are, especially those who love to relish the local flavours of a destination.

Learning Outcomes

- There are different segments of tourists who differ in terms of preferences, travel budget, interests and habits. It, thus, becomes imperative for the destination authorities to ensure that they are able to provide varied experiences and tourism products according to the requirements of different segments of the market.
- Every destination has a local culture. Local cuisine is one of the major subsets of a destination's culture.
- To understand the real culture of a destination and to taste the local flavours, tourists must come out of their comfort zone. Rather than going for staged experiences, they should seek the help of local people and tourist guides so that they can see the real insights of the local life of a place.

- It is always advisable for the tourists to visit local restaurants that help in elevating the local economy of a destination and bringing money to the local communities directly.

Points for Discussion

- From the above case scenario, what do you think would help such a tourist who wants the real Goan experience?
- The majority of tour guides see their benefit and take the tourists to the places where they are partnered with the hotels, restaurants and adventure spots. How does this affect the tourists?
- What measures should be taken to promote the small places which are authentic and genuinely work hard to provide a first-class experience for tourists?

SECTION

D

THE EXPERIENCE FACILITATORS

The given section is very important for the readers to understand and appreciate the role of various service providers involved in the delivery of tourism services for the tourists. It shall give a detailed account of how the various tourism professionals who are attached to tourists in different capacities are responsible for creating a memorable experience of a holiday for the tourists. The various service providers in tourism may be referred to as the touch points or experience facilitators of the tourism industry. This section initiates with an identification of the various types of touch points of the tourism industry, with a discussion on their brief roles and responsibilities and their contribution towards the tourism industry. It starts with the roles of travel intermediaries who may be travel agents/tour operators who are involved in making travel arrangements for the tourists due to their expertise in the travel trade. Then, this is followed by a detailed discussion on the job descriptions and job specifications of tour leaders, tour guides and cab drivers. Following this, there is an elaborate discussion on the role of government in promoting tourism.

At the end of each chapter, there are activities related to each chapter, which students may practise in their classrooms. Also, every chapter has interesting information for students to know, organized in the boxes that the students are advised to read to increase their knowledge of tourism. After the completion of chapters in the section, there are certain case studies related to the section for the students to read, comprehend and analyse, followed by questions to be answered. Thus, the given section shall help the learners to understand and appreciate the following:

- What are the various touch points of the tourism industry?
- Who are the travel intermediaries, and what are their roles?
- Who is a tour leader, and what is his role?
- What is the role of a tour guide?
- What is the role of a cab driver?
- What are the roles and responsibilities of the government in promoting tourism at a destination?

So are you all excited to learn more? Let us kick-start on our journey of learning new concepts of the experience facilitators.

Happy learning, dear learners!

23

The Touch Points of Tourism Industry

LEARNING OBJECTIVES

The given chapter shall clarify the following:

1. What are the various touch points of the tourism industry?
2. What are their roles in creating a pleasant experience for tourists at a destination?

VARANASI: THE SPIRITUAL AND SOULFUL CONNECTION

- Also referred to as *Banaras* or *Kashi* with ancient history dating back to as old as 11th-century BC, *Varanasi is one of the oldest, colourful and living cities in the world.*
- Known for its famous Ganga *aarti* at the ghats, an early sunrise boat tour on the River Ganges, millions of gods and goddesses, religious shrines, living traditions and customs and mouth-watering cuisines, Varanasi is truly the 'city of salvation' and the 'city of lights'.
- Although it is primarily a religious centre of Hindus, Jains and Buddhists, thousands of tourists, especially foreign tourists, visit this destination to witness the unique enthralling culture and legacy of this place.
- Since many Hindus come here to perform the last rites of their loved ones, many foreign tourists visit the ghats to witness the reality of life by seeing the rituals of death of Hindus.

- The various touch points of the tourism industry that include the tour guides, local travel agents, tour operators, local community and local merchandisers are happy and passionate to showcase their culture with utmost warmth and hospitability to the tourists.
- Varanasi is truly a feast to one's senses: *a city of sights, aromas and sounds!*

INTRODUCTION

The tourism industry is a *people-oriented industry*. It is by the people and for the people. Since this industry requires heavy involvement of human factor, the interactions between the tourism professionals/stakeholders and the tourists are very important. What a tourist expects at a destination and what he/she gets depends to a larger extent on the services provided by these service providers. Thus, we really need to understand and appreciate the role of each touch point in making the stay of tourists memorable at a destination.

Touch points refer to the various points of contact or interaction between the tourists and the businesses involved in the delivery of tourism services. In other words, it may refer to the various service providers or the stakeholders who collectively represent the tourism fraternity of a destination. Although the digital transformation may have phenomenally affected the tourism industry, the 'Moments of Truth' when the tourists meet the service providers at the destination are still a predominant aspect of this industry.

Every single touch point counts. It is imperative for all the touch points of the tourism industry to understand their roles and behave responsibly towards the creation of 'wow moments' for the tourists. A lacuna on the part of any touch point can leave the tourists despondent and unhappy if their expectations are not met by any of the service providers.

Now, let us have a detailed discussion on each of the touch points of the tourism industry who are engaged in the delivery of tourism services.

TRAVEL AGENTS/TOUR OPERATORS

One of the most important key people, with whom the tourists are in touch with the moment they decide to travel to a place, is the travel agents/tour operators. Not all travellers can make arrangements on their own. They may need the advice of an expert who can guide them well through the choices of holiday destinations that matches their interests. These travel consultants/holiday experts have tie-ups with various stakeholders of the tourism industry with whom they negotiate and put together their combined services as a tour package. Travel agents/tour operators have a great role in shaping the opinions and decisions of the travellers. Thus, they may also be called as *opinion leaders* who, to a large extent, influence the opinions of the tourists. Generally, the tourists approach them at the tourist-generating region where all the marketing activities of these tour operators/travel agents are aimed at. Thus, to maintain a positive impression on the tourists, the staff working for the tour operators/travel agents who are in touch with the traveller (generally the sales team, customer service team) must address their concerns courteously and politely, attend them patiently, answer their queries, guide them to the best of their knowledge and keep them regularly updated on every development of the travel arrangements. In short, they must happily be ready to serve the tourists in every way that they can.

AIRLINE STAFF

Most of the international travel takes place by air. Tourists fly for long hours before reaching their holiday destination. They are in touch with the airline staff who may be the ground-handling staff or the air hostess/flight steward in the flight. During this journey, the tourist must experience pleasant moments with the airline staff. Thus, the airline staff must behave professionally with the utmost care and hospitality with its passengers. *The spirit of service towards the guests should be at the heart of the airline staff.* Promptly resolving any issue of the passengers, serving them onboard meals, listening to the guests' requests, guiding them during their journey and so on are some of the ways in which the airline staff can politely deal with the passengers who are travelling with them.

Staff at Belgrave Station, Melbourne

RAILWAY AUTHORITY/STAFF

Many tourists may travel by many special trains such as heritage trains, tourists' trains and so on to explore the country-side of destinations besides enjoying the hospitality of the railway staff/authority. Thus, it is important for the staff/authority to be pleasant in their interactions with the tourists and make the journey of travellers as comfortable and memorable as possible.

IMMIGRATION OFFICER

These border controls ensure that only bona fide citizens of a country enter or leave the country. They ensure that the visitors meet the criteria for entering the country or exiting their own country. The immigration officers are responsible for checking passports and visas of the visitors and carrying out surveillance for stopping those passengers who fail to meet the criteria for entry/exit. They take the interview of the tourists (both inbound and outbound) and also take their biometrics in compliance with the rules set by the government authorities of a country. The immigration officers may be posted at airports/ports or other important border controls.

Although they interact with international visitors for a very short time, they carry lasting impressions on the tourists. Perhaps, they are the first point of contact for foreign tourists. A welcoming expression with a smile on their face instead of presenting a grim face can go a long way in comforting the tourists.

TRANSFER ASSISTANTS

Transfer assistants are one of the most important touch points of the tourism industry. The main job of the transfer assistants is to receive the guests on behalf of the tour operator with whom a tourist may have booked a tour package. Generally, the guests may be received at their first point of arrival at a destination that may be an airport/railway station/port and then transferred from the point of departure to the hotel. The transfer assistants who receive the guests at the airport may also be referred to as an airport representative (Airport Rep). In some limited cases, the person who receives the guests at the airport may also be the tour leader of a company.

The main job of the transfer assistant is to *meet and greet* the guests. The transfer assistants are a treat to the eyes of the tourists when they see a representative of the company as they are assured that they have someone on whom they can rely upon in an unknown destination. Generally, the transfer assistant carries a *placard* with him/her that he/she displays with the name of the guests written on it along with the name of the company on behalf of whom the guests have made their travel arrangements. This helps the guests to easily locate the transfer assistant. On meeting each other, they may be greeted by the transfer assistant who may then assist them with the luggage and escort them till the vehicle so that they may be dropped to the hotel.

On reaching the hotel, the transfer assistant facilitates his/her guests in their check in at the hotel. He/she may then share the day's itinerary with the guests depending upon their time of arrival at the destination. Likewise, the transfer assistants may also help in the checkout of the guests at the hotel during their departure time from the destination and then ultimately may assist the guests in the transfer from the hotel to their final point of departure along with their luggage. Since they are the initial point of interaction, their service-oriented attitude along with a pleasant smile can really make the first impressions of tourists very positive about the people of a destination.

TOUR LEADERS

An important key person and the face of the travel company who acts as a constant companion of tourists generally on group tours is the tour leader. He/she stays with his/her guests for the longest period on accompanied trips and takes care of them throughout the trip. A tour leader acts as the *spokesperson* of the destination as well as the company on behalf of whom he/she is representing.

Thus, it is very important for the tour leader to create a favourable image of the destination as well as the company that he/she is working for. His/she amicable nature and the way he/she takes care of the tourists can make or mar the overall experience of tourists about a destination. These tour leaders also have expertise in handling any kind of emergency that the tourists may encounter. Thus, tour leaders have a prime responsibility of creating happy and memorable moments for the tourists.

TOUR GUIDES

Tour guides are the 'experience enhancers' who add life to the places and the attractions. Being licenced by the government authorities, they provide access to important attractions, landmarks and other points of interest. They help the tourists in making sense of things and creating creative impressions about a place. Sometimes, these can be indelible impressions for a lifetime. It all depends on how the tour guide conducts himself/herself throughout the tour so that the tourists feel happy about a place. Thus, tour guides are an important touch point for the tourists at a destination.

Their expert insight, assistance and context make the visit of the tourist to a destination more meaningful and worthwhile.

HOTEL STAFF

The tourists spend a sufficient time of their holiday in the hotel. When they stay in the hotel, they interact with the hotel staff regularly. From checking in with the assistance of front office staff to seeking room service or talking to the housekeeping department, the tourists have several interactions with the hotel staff during their stay. Thus, the behaviour of hotel staff towards the guests makes a lot of difference to the guests. They need to be very hospitable and empathetic to the needs of the tourists.

RESTAURATEURS

Restaurateurs, whether they own a fine dining or local eating outlet, must be experienced enough in handling the tourist segments. Tourists may not be aware of the local food as to what to eat and whether it would be appropriate for their taste palette as it may be spicy or bland. The staff of the restaurant must assist the tourists in choosing the dishes patiently. If required, they must assist in explaining the local ingredients being used in the making of the food, ask their guests if they are allergic to any kind of specific foods, prepare the food keeping in mind the considerations of the guests and then serve the food with utmost hospitality and dignity to them.

TOURIST INFORMATION OFFICERS/SENIOR GOVERNMENT OFFICIALS

The government also plays a pivotal role in advising and framing the opinions of the tourists. Any information when it comes from the government side is considered to be more reliable and authentic. Tourists may consult the government websites of various tourism boards or may personally visit the tourism offices to gather information about the tourist attractions or any other important relevant information that they may require while visiting the destination. Tourists may seek information from the tourist information officers or the senior government officials posted either in the tourism boards or visitor facilitation centres. Thus, the government officials must have enough knowledge about the destination that may be a city, region, state or a country that they are selling, and they must be able to guide the tourists through the must-see destinations, itineraries to be covered, attractions to explore, tourism products to try, local eating outlets to visit, fairs and festivals to attend, activities to try and so on to make the most of their visit at the destination. Thus, to facilitate the tourists, they must be trained in soft skills so that they can politely resolve the queries raised by tourists so as to create a pleasant experience for the tourists. They must also have extensive knowledge of the destination that they are selling so that they can answer the doubts of the tourists and guide them to the best of their capacity. The right guidance can help the tourists to make the most of their limited time to be used in the most effective and useful way.

ATTRACTION AUTHORITIES

The various managers posted at the attractions are also an important point of contact for the tourists. Their behaviour with the tourists when the tourists enquire about any information pertaining to the attraction being visited by them or when they are buying the entry tickets from them makes a lot of difference. If they are happy to help and serve the tourists with a smile on their face and politeness in their voice, the tourists would feel good and at ease. Although the interaction time with the attraction authorities may be less, their demeanour can leave lasting impressions in the minds of the tourists.

HERITAGE INTERPRETERS

Tourism is all about showcasing and exploring the heritage of a destination. When tourists visit monuments and museums, they may hire the services of heritage interpreters. Heritage interpreters are the volunteers who have a keen interest in the heritage of a country. They are not tour guides. These heritage interpreters play an important role in interpreting the heritage of an attraction or a place and making sense of it for the tourists. Their presence at the monuments and other heritage sites brings life to the stoned buildings that have stood the testimony of time.

VOLUNTEERS

The role of volunteers in the tourism industry cannot be undermined. Volunteers may be generally youngsters who may want to be associated with tourism in some way. They may work on short-term tourism projects and tourism-related events to understand the function of the tourism industry. However, these youngsters aspiring to be tourism professionals have a lot of creative energy that may be tapped for the positive growth of this industry.

TOURIST POLICE

When tourists visit a destination, they may encounter any kind of unpleasant situations. It may be a theft, an eve-teasing incident, cheating by an unauthorized travel agent/tour guide/foreign exchange agent, overcharging by a merchandiser or a driver, loss of one's belonging like the passport due to one's negligence or any other incident that may require the intervention of local police. For the tourists, the local police are the custodian of the tourist at a destination. Thus, destinations must have dedicated tourist police specifically trained to handle the cases and situations faced by the tourists. In case of foreign tourists, procedures may be a little different. Thus, the tourist police must be adept in situation handling of foreign clientele and must be able to resolve any issue faced by them. Likewise, they must be able to intervene on any matter brought to them by the domestic tourist.

DRIVERS

The driver may be referred to as an experienced facilitator of the tourists. The drivers may be working for the tourist cabs, government taxis, tourist coaches, tourist buses, HOHO buses and so on that may operate on behalf of private owners, such as tour operators, transporters and car rental companies, or the government. A cab driver is overall responsible for the safety of his/her guests. His/her interaction with the guests generally is the maximum during the journey of travellers. In other words, he/she may be described as the companion of guests. A well-mannered, cultured and a professional driver can really make the journey of a traveller worth a while. He/she may be addressed to as pilot in some countries of the world.

PORTERS

Various porters at the railway stations and airports who are primarily responsible for carrying the luggage of the tourists interact with the tourists for a short time. Their service approach towards the guests, punctuality and professionalism play an important role in shaping the positive impressions of the tourists about the people of a destination.

HOST COMMUNITY

One of the most important touch points in facilitating the overall experience of tourists at a destination is the host community. The tourist-host interactions during their travel are pivotal in shaping the opinions of guests about a destination in general and whether they would want to return back to the same destination again or not. If the host community is receptive and friendly with the guests, they would feel comfortable at the destination and would spread a positive word of mouth about the destination. Thus, it is important to educate the host community about the positive economic and cultural benefits of tourists visiting a destination that prepares them mentally to receive tourists at a destination with a positive frame of mind. Likewise, the tourists also need to be educated to abide by the local culture of a destination when they are visiting a place. This helps in increasing the acceptability of host community towards the tourists.

MERCHANDISERS/SOUVENIR SELLERS

When tourists visit a destination, one of the popular activities that most of the tourists indulge in is shopping. They may like to buy local merchandise such as things of basic necessity or souvenir items that are local goods and specialities of a place. They may visit local markets, shopping malls, shopping emporiums and so on to enjoy shopping. Tourists, thus, get in touch with the merchandisers and souvenir sellers to buy souvenirs from a destination.

The integrity and honesty of shopkeepers in their dealings with the tourists and not cheating them by overcharging them go a long way in shaping the opinions of the tourists about the merchandisers. If tourists feel cheated by the shopkeepers, they may be disappointed and hence may frame negative impressions about a place and its people. Perhaps, they may not want to come back to the destination again and may also warn other tourists to be aware regarding the unethical practices followed by these shopkeepers that may eventually tarnish the image of the overall destination and its people.

Thus, the overall behaviour and attitude of merchandisers towards tourists affect them and play a pivotal role in shaping their impressions about the people of a destination.

SUMMARY

The tourism industry requires the collaboration and coordination of various touch points to create pleasant experiences for tourists. Touch points are the various stakeholders who maintain a close liaison with the tourists when they visit a destination. These may be the airline staff, immigration officers, transfer assistants, tour leaders, travel agents/tour operators, drivers, porters, hotel staff, restaurateurs, tourist information officers, attraction authorities, tour guides, heritage interpreters, volunteers, restaurateurs, local merchandisers, host community, tourist police and so on. To create a positive experience and to repeat the tourist to a destination, every touch point must incessantly work towards delivering impeccable services towards the tourists.

ACTIVITIES

Activity 1

Divide the class into groups and assign each group a service provider of the tourism industry. The number of service providers may be chosen at random and may depend upon the strength of the class. Now ask two groups at a time to debate as to why they consider their touch points contribution to tourism as more important over the other touch points assigned to the other group. Now decide the best group between the two. Likewise, keep rotating the groups and keep asking each group to take a stand for their touch points and support with appropriate logic and facts. Deliberate and debate! Finally decide the best group which has been able to defend itself with proper reasonings.

Activity 2

What are the various ways in which the host community can improve their relations with the tourists? Discuss.

Activity 3

Visit the local police station in your area and ask the police staff if they have received any complaint from a foreign tourist. If yes, ask them to share the nature of problems faced by the tourist and the corrective measures taken by the police to fix the issue. The same exercise may be repeated for domestic tourists.

24

Travel Intermediaries

LEARNING OBJECTIVES

The given chapter shall clarify the following:

- Who are the travel intermediaries in tourism business?
- What are their roles and functions?

FAITH

- FAITH is an apex body of the travel and tourism industry in India.
- It is an umbrella organization of 10 national tourism, travel and hospitality agencies of India which include ADTOI, ATOAI, Federation of Hotel & Restaurant Associations of India (FHRAI), HAI, IATO, ICPB, Indian Heritage Hotels Association (IHHA), Indian Tourist Transporters Association (ITTA), TAAI and TAFI.
- FAITH aims at strategizing and policymaking by associating with the central and state governments of India for creating growth opportunities and potential for the Indian tourism industry.
- By coordinating with fellow associations, FAITH also aims at creating better facilities for domestic and foreign tourists and creating a common ground for tourism industry where tourism-related issues and suggestions are addressed.
- In collaboration with MOT, Government of India, it also organizes the India Tourism Mart, which is a business-to-business (B2B) meet where foreign tour operators (FTOs) from all over the world participate.

As the tourism industry has leapt into the limelight, with travel becoming an important part of everyone's life, the need for tourism professionals who can manage the travel professionally has substantially increased. Travel agencies and tour operators play a pivotal role in the travel sector business. These travel intermediaries act as an important link pin between the tourists and the suppliers. Both are 'one-stop shop' for all the travel solutions for a traveller.

INTRODUCTION

When a traveller decides to travel, he/she may have two choices. He/she may book his/her travel arrangements either on his/her own or through a travel company. With the ease and approachability of various tourism service providers who are at one's fingertip due to the Internet technology, the traveller today can make his/her own ticket reservations, book his/her own hotel stays, take various coach or walking tours and make other various other arrangements while comparing various travel sites and going through the testimonials and reviews of other travelled passengers. However, while making bookings on his/her own, he/she is required to do extra homework and meticulously go through every detail before making any reservations. It involves prior planning backed up by excellent research and then some luck so that the traveller gets what he/she has expected during his/her holiday. In this kind of travel arrangement where the traveller makes the travel choices on his/her own, there is always an element of perceived risk because he/she is relying on his/her own research and instincts. It also involves a lot of hassle as the traveller has to do his/her homework properly right from the scratch looking deeply into the nitty-gritty of every travel arrangement that he/she is making.

Another popular option that has been conventionally followed by travellers has always been of relying on the services of travel intermediaries. It involves hiring the services of travel intermediaries to make their travel arrangements.

Here, travel intermediaries refer to the travel agents and tour operators who are involved in organizing, facilitating and delivering travel arrangements for the tourists. These travel intermediaries are entrusted with the complete responsibility of making all the travel arrangements for the tourists that may include making reservations on various modes of transportation, arranging visas, facilitating foreign exchange and travel insurance, creating itineraries with popular sightseeing places, making accommodation and meal arrangements, organizing activities on the tour and so on. In short, the complete headache of travel arrangements from their planning to execution is the job of these travel intermediaries. These travel intermediaries may also be referred to as travel consultants or travel experts who have expertise in the various tourism products.

ORIGIN

The first travel business was started by Thomas Cook, also known as the 'father of travel agency business', in 1845. He initiated the 'world's first travel agency' and started organizing excursions on railways and steamships through England, Scotland and Europe. Earlier, in 1841, he had organized a train trip of 22 miles for 570 members for the South Midland Temperance Association by buying bulk railway tickets and selling them to the members of the association that gave him an idea to start his own business. In 1855, he conducted the world's first international trip from England to Paris by offering a package tour to the travellers. This was the beginning of the business of travel agencies in the world.

OPERATING SYSTEM OF TRAVEL INTERMEDIARIES

The operation of the travel intermediaries may depend upon their size and scope of activities. These travel intermediaries may have *inbound, outbound* or *domestic operations* depending upon the segments that they decide to choose. Whereas some travel intermediaries may have all these departments (inbound, outbound and domestic) in place to diversify and grow in their businesses.

Generally, the travel intermediaries serve majorly two types of clientele, that is, the leisure and the business travellers. They may be leisure tour operators or MICE tour operators. However, some travel intermediaries may specialize and serve particular segments of markets and thus become specialized operators such as *wildlife, adventure, luxury, medical* and *niche tour operators* organizing special interest tours. Most of the revenues of most of the travel intermediaries are majorly driven by business travel though they may sell both leisure and business travel as business travel is a more perennial source of income as it takes place throughout the year.

Travellers may approach either travel agents or tour operators for making their travel arrangements. Although there might have been a difference between these two organizers, however, with the passage of time these lines are blurring as their functions and operations are almost the same. Now, let us have a detailed discussion on the slight variations of travel intermediaries for our understanding.

Principals

These may be called as *suppliers* in the tourism business. These may be airlines, hotels, railways, cruise liners, car rental companies, transport operators and so on, who hold an inventory of a particular tourism product. These suppliers may or may not sell directly to the public. On the contrary, they may sell their products through travel agents on commission basis or through tour operators on bulk purchase basis who may, in turn, either sell their products individually or combine them to make a tour package.

Travel Agents

The travel agent may also be called as a *retailer* in the tourism business. They may buy individual components of travel such as air tickets, rail tickets, car rentals, cruise tickets, bus tickets, sightseeing tours and hotel rooms from the principals and they sell these to the tourists without maintaining any inventory. *They may deal with one component of a tourism product, and thus, their size of doing business is small as compared to tour operators.* These agencies act as third parties that connect travellers with the suppliers and act as the agent for railways, airlines, cruise liners, car rentals and sometimes the tour operators. They may sometimes sell the product directly to the public or sometimes to the tour operators. These retailers operate on a commission basis on each transaction.

Tour Operators

Tour operators are also called as *wholesalers* who buy the travel inventory such as transportation tickets and hotel rooms in bulk and then may sell either directly to the tourists or through the travel agents. These tour operators buy individual components from various service providers called principals and then assemble them as a package. *These are sold as 'package tours' or 'inclusive tours' that are offered at an all-inclusive price.* These tour operators operate on a mark-up basis that refers to the difference between the retail price and wholesale cost. The size and scope of these businesses are larger as compared to travel agencies.

Sometimes, big tour operators such as Thomas Cook and Cox & Kings Ltd may also have their own tourism products such as hotels, coaches and airlines. Thus, they may be called as *manufacturers* of tourism products.

Ground Handling Agents (GHAs)

GHAs are responsible for making travel arrangements on behalf of the tour operator through whom the tourists may have booked their travel package. A tour operator may not have their own office at every place that may be a state or a country. Thus, for making all the travel arrangements of the tourists, the tour operator may liaison with the local operators at the tourist receiving destination who may be called as GHAs.

These GHAs (local agents) are responsible for organizing and coordinating all the *land arrangements* at a destination that may be within a country or overseas. This may include making return airport or railways station transfers, local transfers (travel by coach/taxi within the city), accommodation arrangements, food arrangements, sightseeing tickets, services of a tour guide, services of a tour leader or any other service required by a tourist at a destination. They ensure that the execution of the trip happens as initially planned by the tourists.

Travel Portals

These are online booking engine facilities that facilitate travellers to make all their travel arrangements on their own. *These are for both B2B and business-to-customer (B2C).* The travel portals have become an important source of making travel arrangements for travellers in today's time due to the advantages that they offer such as the convenience in making a booking at any time with value-added services. It makes the travel hassle-free and more economical for the traveller as he/she can make his/her booking at a much lower cost. One can also alter one's bookings depending upon one's change in the travel plan with perfect ease. These give discounted offers on travel, different options for booking instant accommodation bookings, car rentals, sightseeing tours and so on. *Some of the popular travel portals include Expedia, Travelocity, MakeMyTrip, EaseMyTrip, Cleartrip, Yatra and Goibibo.*

IMPORTANCE OF TRAVEL INTERMEDIARIES

There are various advantages of making travel arrangements through travel intermediaries. Some of these are as follows:

More Convenient

Vacation packages are the first choice for those travellers who do not want to bother themselves much. Here, everything has already been chosen for them that make it easier and more convenient for the tourists to plan a hassle-free trip.

More Secure

For travellers who are travelling for the first time especially overseas and are ignorant of the travel procedures, seeking the help of travel intermediaries is always a better choice for the travellers. They may feel more secure when they know there is someone on whom they can bank upon for making their travel arrangements.

Local Expertise

Travel intermediaries have deep insights into local places that they add to the itineraries of the tourists. They help the travellers see things that they might not otherwise have done on their own. They *filter the best options for the tourists* so that they can make the most of their time in a limited span.

Best Use of Time and Money

Travellers have limited time for their vacation. They may also have a limited budget which they may have planned to spend on their entire vacation. Given the limited time and financial resources, travellers through the sagacious and intelligent planning of travel intermediaries are able to optimize every minute of their holiday and every penny spent on realizing their dream vacation.

Psychological Relief

It is a big psychological relief for travellers that if anything goes wrong on the tour, they have someone to bank upon. In fact, they can seek the immediate assistance of the travel intermediaries when on a tour if they meet any unforeseen situation. They may lose a passport or may miss a cruise due to delay in a flight by the airlines. In such a case, the tourists may conveniently ask the travel intermediaries to make the desired changes in the itinerary if things do not work out as initially planned by them.

Human Contact

For many travellers, being able to contact a professional travel expert is a first choice instead of taking every single travel decision on their own. The traveller may have a feeling that there is the constant support of someone who guides him/her and advises him/her during his/her complete journey when he/she books his/her holiday to the time when he/her visits the destination. Talking to someone in person can be very gratifying for some travellers as compared to making decisions on own with the help of technology.

Group Travel

While a traveller chooses to travel in a group, it requires a lot of coordination with all the travellers who are travelling. Thus, in such cases that involve group bookings, making arrangements through travel intermediaries is always a viable option.

FUNCTIONS OF TRAVEL INTERMEDIARIES

The travel intermediaries perform the following functions:

Making Travel Arrangements

Travel intermediaries are responsible for making all the travel arrangements of the clients who make their bookings with them. This may include making all the advanced reservations on all modes of transportation that may include airlines, trains, coaches, any special rides such as cable cars and gondola rides, making reservations for rooms in accommodation as per the choice of the traveller, booking tickets for any shows or cultural performances and so on, buying entry tickets for sightseeing places and so on. Travel intermediaries ensure that the travellers have a seamless trip, and every minute of their trip is as enjoyable and organized as possible.

Making Travel Itinerary

A very important task for the travel intermediaries is to make a travel itinerary that is the most important part of a tour package. *A travel itinerary refers to a detailed daily tour programme that includes the starting point of origin, the various stopping points at the destination and the point of arrival.* Preparing itineraries is not an easy task. It must be backed up by vigorous research and personally visiting the destination before offering it for sale. Familiarizing oneself with the place is always important as one needs to be personally aware of the distances, timings or any challenges to be faced at the destination that the tour operator may consider while planning the itinerary of tourists.

Packaging and Costing

Travel intermediaries package the various individual components depending upon the needs and preferences of the traveller. On combining and integrating the various individual components, they do their costing that includes the actual cost being incurred in operating a tour and then add their mark up to be sold to the tourists.

Consultancy

Travel agents/tour operators clear the mist in the minds of a traveller. For example, a couple may want to travel on a honeymoon to a destination that they may not be clear about. Through posing questions such as the budget of the traveller, likes and dislikes and having knowledge of the climate and the best time to visit the destination, the travel agent/tour operator may provide either a domestic or an outbound honeymoon vacation option to the baffled travellers. Thus, due to their extensive knowledge about destinations, the travel agents/tour operators may provide consultancy to the travellers.

Providing Information

Providing updated information about a destination (including the domestic or an international destination) and any travel formalities required to visit a destination is the job of a travel intermediary. It may include the best time to travel in a destination, the climate at the destination, information about the country rules, the airlines regulations, the sightseeing places to be visited, the local festivals to be attended, the best restaurants to dine-in, the places to shop, information on visas, frontier formalities at the airport, health regulations, information about the transportation and accommodation to be used and so on.

Besides, the travel intermediaries may provide vital information to the tourists about the importance of getting travel insurance in the case of loss of luggage, theft, accident and so on during the travel that the travellers may not be aware of. Travel intermediaries must also inform *about the maximum foreign currency* that a traveller can carry with him/her while travelling overseas depending upon his/her purpose of travel. Providing such vital guidance can help travellers in making their travel more stress-free and relaxed.

Organizing Ancillary Services

Travel intermediaries may also facilitate the travellers with other travel documentation or arrangements necessary to travel abroad. The documentation may include assisting the client in taking visas, aiding in taking foreign exchange, helping with travel insurance, buying an international SIM card and so on.

Organizing Conferences/ Meetings/Incentive Trips/Industrial Visits

Many travel intermediaries who deal in corporate business tours (MICE tours) organize conferences and meetings for corporate clients. Right from choosing the venue for organizing the conference that may be a convention hall or a hotel to managing other logistics such as projectors, loudspeakers, podiums, mikes, registration counters, organizing airport pick-up transfers, hotel arrangements and fairground transfers, it is the complete responsibility of these travel intermediaries for making all the arrangements related to organizing a conference. These MICE operators may also organize *incentive trips and industrial visits* for the corporates.

Building Image

These travel intermediaries also act as 'image builders' of a destination as they help in promoting tourism in a country by promoting various destinations of a country. The destinations may be within or outside one's own country depending upon the operations of the travel company whether it is an inbound, domestic or an outbound tour operator. The travel intermediaries bring into limelight the various destinations by creating itineraries of destinations and offering them as packages, marketing them through various print, electronic and social media and also fighting the negative coverage of the place due to a crime or a terrorist attack that may have tarnished the image of a destination. They reassure the travellers to visit the destination again and thus help in rebuilding the image of a country.

LINKAGES WITH SUPPLIERS

The tourism industry does not exist in isolation. It works in tandem with various service providers who coordinate and synchronize their efforts to provide various tourism products as one package to the traveller. Smooth linkages in this industry form the edifice of a strong tourism business. Any lacuna on the part of any service providers may disrupt the overall tourism experience of tourists.

Travel intermediaries have the linkages with the following stakeholders of the tourism industry.

Airlines (Both Domestic and International)

To travel to destinations, travellers may opt to travel by air. Thus, many big travel companies that operate on a large scale have their own international and domestic ticketing departments, whereas small travel agencies that do not have their own ticketing departments may book the clients tickets through specialized ticketing agents that may be dealing in different airlines. Alternatively, some travel companies may have a direct liaison with the airlines' reservation offices through which they may book the tickets of their clients generally of those travelling in a group. They may block the airlines' inventory by sharing the group details with the airlines' office and later get the tickets issued near the dates of departure of the group.

Railways

Likewise, travel agencies must also maintain a close liaison with railways as they may be offering packages in which rail transportation is included.

Transport Companies

Many travel companies depend upon local transporters such as coach operators for internal transfers of its clientele who may be either travelling individually or in a group through the travel company. Internal transfers may include arrangements for transportation made by the transportation company for return airport transfers (airport-hotel-airport transfers), local sightseeing tours, fairground transfers (in case of business travel that may include travel from hotel to the fairground and then back to hotel) or any other transfers. Thus, it is important for the travel company to have a linkage with the transport company.

Cruise Companies

As cruising is one of the most trending holiday vacations opted by the new-age travellers, many travel agents have started dealing in marketing and selling cruise packages for various cruise liners of the world. Thus, they need to maintain a liaison with the cruise companies.

Car Rental Companies

As the interest of travellers has increased in self-drive holidays, they may ask the travel companies to provide them with cars on rents through which they can explore places. Thus, many travel companies who do not own their own cars have linkages with car rental companies such as *Avis and Hertz* that provide cars on rents. Thus, in order to meet the requirement of travellers, travel agencies/tour operators must maintain a strong linkage with the car rental companies.

Hotels/Alternative Kinds of Accommodation Providers

The packages offered by tour operators include accommodation arrangements for a traveller that maybe a hotel or any other similar accommodation. Thus, it is important for the travel company to maintain a healthy relationship with the accommodation providers.

Restaurants

The travel packages arranged by travel companies may sometimes include local food arranged in local restaurants of a destination. Thus, it is important to maintain a liaison with the local restaurateurs of a destination and to ensure that the guests are served hygienic and good quality food in the restaurants.

Cultural and Entertainment Organizations

Entertainment is an important part of the overall package offered by the tour companies for prospective travellers. Visiting museums, heritage walks, amusement parks, gaming zones, spa centres and so on are generally an integral part of the tour packages. Thus, maintaining linkage with the cultural and entertainment organizations is a must for the travel intermediaries.

Travel Insurance Companies

An important component of a tour package is the travel insurance for the travellers that acts as a safety valve in an unforeseen situation that may or may not happen. Thus, travel agents/tour operators must maintain a close liaison with insurance companies to get the timely insurance done for their clients with adequate coverage.

Banks

Day-to-day transactions take place between the travel companies and banks. Sometimes, banks also provide loans to the travel novices for new travel start-ups. Thus, maintaining a close linkage with banks is a must.

Government

The travel agents and tour operators in India work in close collaboration with MOT, Government of India. The MOT provides the list of approved travel agents/tour operators who are authorized by the Government of India which is very useful for the tourist to avoid falling into trap of any fake transactions or cheating faced by the foreign tourists. It acts as a regulatory body that monitors the compliance of these businesses according to the set of rules and regulations laid by them. The government also ensures their participation in international forums such as *World Travel Market (WTM), London, ITB, Berlin,* so as to promote the Incredible!ndia brand and increase the footfalls of tourists in the country. It also addresses their concerns affecting their travel businesses. It may also provide the necessary support to them by offering tax holidays, supporting them in their projects, providing them with financial funding or sometimes marketing these travel companies towards the travellers. Thus, it becomes important for the travel businesses to maintain a good relationship with the government officials of their area.

Trade Associations

It is very important for the travel intermediaries to be in touch with the tour operators' associations within their country that represents their common interests and concerns. These associations such as FAITH, IATO, TAAI and ADTOI are an important platform for the tour operators to discuss and resolve their issues that may be affecting them such as increased government taxes, delays in getting approvals from the government and many other travel-related challenges.

Embassies and Consulates

For outbound travel agents/tour operators who help in facilitating the visas of the travelling passengers who have booked their travel arrangements with the travel company, it is important to maintain a liaison with the embassies and consulates that reserve the right to grant the visa to the clients.

Tourism Educational Institutes/Universities

Travel companies need human resources to run the organization. Every year they require youngsters who can bring new ideas to the organization. Moreover, due to the high attrition rate in the tourism industry, people leave companies at a very fast pace. Moreover, a company needs more manpower in case it is diversifying or expanding its existing travel business. In all such cases, travel intermediaries have to maintain a liaison with the tourism educational institutes/universities that aid the travel companies in procuring with the fresh blood.

Ground Handling Agents (GHAs)

All the land arrangements (that include all transfers, accommodation and food arrangements, local sightseeing and services of a tour guide) are generally arranged by the local tour operators/FTO at the tourist receiving region. These may be referred to as GHAs. As all travel intermediaries may not have their branches in every destination of the world, they rely on GHAs who are responsible for the real execution of the travel arrangements of a traveller when he/she visits that destination. Ultimately, the reputation and business repetition of a travel organizer largely depend upon how well GHAs delivers the travel services to the client so that he/she returns satisfied. Thus, it becomes mandatory for the travel intermediaries at the ground level to maintain a close liaison with GHAs by ensuring their prompt payments, maintaining clear lines of communication with them and being fair and transparent in all the transactions with them.

SUMMARY

Travel intermediaries play a pivotal role in shaping the holiday plan of a traveller. Their invaluable advice and counselling, along with all the assistance in making the travel arrangements, make the travellers free their minds. They make travel hassle free and convenient for them. Although now many new-age travellers make arrangements on their own, the importance of these conventional travel intermediaries in creating memorable trip memories cannot be undermined. They are still the first choice for first-time travellers, especially for those who are travelling overseas, for groups and for all those who value comfort and relaxation.

ACTIVITIES

Activity 1

Identify any top five travel companies that promote MICE (business tourism) in your country. What are the challenges faced by the MICE operators according to you? You may also interview the MICE operators for more clarity.

Activity 2

Name the best 10 adventure tour operators along with the famous adventure associations that promote adventure tourism in your country. Discuss the kinds of threats and obstacles faced by the tour operators and tourists.

The Tour Leader

25

SEGWAY TOUR: A NEW WAY TO EXPLORE THE CITY WITH THE TOUR LEADERS!

- Segways are a great way to explore a destination!
- These tours are generally led by tour leaders who lead the tourists on Segways.
- The group size is generally small, and to ensure the safety of tourists, proper safety gears such as helmets, kneepads and elbow pads are provided for free.
- Many travel companies in Delhi organize 1–2 hours of Segway tours where visitors can enjoy gliding through some of the spectacular places in the heart of the capital city while also enjoying the company of a tour leader who gives live commentary while passing through different landmark attractions.
- In Delhi, some of the famous Segway tours are as follows:
  - **Lutyens' Delhi Tour** starts at the Secretariat and covers the Rashtrapati Bhavan, along with other famous government buildings and famous landmarks.

o **Delhi Art Segway Tour** covers the entire Lodhi art district (India's first open-air art district) and Lodhi colony filled with wall arts made by 30 artists from all over the world, which is a treat to the eyes, especially for the lovers of art.

INTRODUCTION

The tourism industry is growing exponentially, so is the need for tourism professionals to manage the tourists when they visit a destination. No matter what may have been promised to the client, but professionalism in the delivery of services makes all the difference. One person who bridges the gap between the planning of the tour and its real execution is the tour leader who acts as a representative of the travel company on the tour. He/she may be addressed differently by different names in various parts of the world as a 'tour leader', 'tour conductor', 'tour facilitator', 'tour director' or a 'tour escort'. He/she generally travels with *group inclusive tours (GITs)* to various destinations to take care of them and aids them in any kind of decision-making required during the tour. Many *free independent travellers (FITs)* who may be travelling on customized packaged tours may also hire the services of a tour leader. These kinds of tourists may make their arrangements through a travel company who may depute their tour leaders to take up these individual assignments. The particular assignment may just be a day tour or a tour for multiple days. A tour leader acts as a professional help on the tour by taking care of the guests and the logistics and making sense of the place that integrate together to make the tour successful. On day tours, the tour leader may pick up his/her guests at the airport and help them in checking in at the hotel. He/she may then take them around the city, sometimes maybe for food walks, heritage walks, shopping walks and so on. He/she may also hire the services of a local guide while visiting the monuments.

WHO IS A TOUR LEADER?

Now, let us understand who is a tour leader? In simple words, a tour leader acts as a constant companion of his/her guests. A tour leader accompanies his/her guests throughout the tour and helps them discover and explore the places being visited. He/she travels with them at every point of the trip, such as at the airport, hotel, restaurants, sightseeing attractions and local markets, on different modes of transportation such as coaches, airlines, trains, cruises, ferries and gondolas. He/she leads the group of holidaymakers from beginning to the completion of the visit to various domestic and international locations. He/she is responsible for the overall administration of the group during the tour. In other words, he/she helps in the real-time execution of an itinerary planned by the company that he/she works for.

Gradually, the tourists start living a destination through the eyes of the tour leaders. For this reason, they are also referred to as the 'brand ambassadors of a destination' as they promote and sell the destinations to their guests.

A tour leader does not need a licence to operate. He/she may be attached to various travel companies at the same time and work in the capacity of a freelancer.

IMPORTANCE OF A TOUR LEADER

Let us now discuss the importance of a tour leader both from the perspectives of a travel company and the guests.

For the Company

A tour leader has a very strategic role for a travel company. *He/she is the face of the company.* He/she is the *front-line staff* of a company who directly interacts with the tourists and delivers those travel promises that the company has made to its guests. He/she is a vital link between the company and his/her guests as he/she is responsible for the 'moments of truth.' Being the representative of his/her company, a tour leader has the onus of carrying the reputation of his/her company. His/her conduct with his/her guests can decide, to a great extent, the future business of his/her company. If guests return happy, they may like to travel with the same company in the future. The guests may also spread a positive word of mouth to others which may mean business for the tour operator/travel agent.

From a company's perspective, a tour leader is like a glue stick who keeps the group of guests together. *The objective of hiring tour leaders for travel companies is to ensure that guests have a fantastic holiday of their lifetime with the services of a tour leader available for the guests throughout the tour.* Through the services provided by the tour leader on the tour to his/her guests, the company ensures that everything on the trip goes pleasant and trouble-free for the guests as well as the company.

For the Guests

Some tourists are not comfortable venturing on their own. They do not favour wasting their precious time hunting for places, hotels, local restaurants and local markets. They do not want to bother themselves, at every point, struggling to figure out which sites to see, where to eat, where to shop, where to stay and so on. Therefore, *guided or escorted vacations are taken by such guests to have a hassle-free holiday as they have a person, that is, a tour leader who manages the whole show.* The logistics may have already been pre-arranged by the operations department of the company. However, *a tour leader ensures that there is no difference between the cup and the lip, that is, what has been precisely promised to the client initially while booking the tour is actually delivered during the trip.* This will allow the guests just to sit back and relax during their vacation and not unnecessarily get bothered in fixing arrangements for their travel.

Also, the guidebooks may not always be a great help for the guests. Sometimes, the tourists want to delve deep into the destination. The tourist is often interested to know about the local life at the destination. Beyond the gaze, they are genuinely interested in 'feeling' the life at that destination. However, they may not have direct access to the local community. For that, the services of a knowledgeable tour leader are required who has the local expertise with him/her. A tour leader is a *link pin* who connects the tourists to the life of locals. He/she introduces the guests to experience new things at a destination and helps them unfold new perspectives of a destination.

Besides, there is always a fear of the unknown when the tourist travels to a destination for the first time. The tourist needs a person who can help him/her conquer that fear. A tour leader bridges the gap between the unknown and known. The fear of being lost in a strange place is the driving force for tourists to take the services of a tour leader. They know that they are in the safe hands of an experienced person who can protect them from any difficulty that they may face on the tour.

A tour leader is a *caretaker* of his/her guests. He/she takes care of every need of his/her guests throughout the trip. Therefore, tourists feel more comfortable and secure in the presence of a tour leader.

CHARACTERISTICS OF TOUR LEADING PROFESSION

Now let us have a detailed discussion on the various features of this profession.

Freelancing

A tour leader may act as a freelancer. He/she may associate himself/herself with different travel companies and work on a contractual basis with them. Alternatively, he/she may commit to a particular company. He/she may work for various international corporations or special interest tour operators. Besides, working for travel companies, he/she may also take up individual assignments for the tourism authorities such as handling a group of delegates or FITs depending on his/her personal rapport with the tourism authorities.

A tour leader may also be self-employed. Many new start-ups/travel apps have been started by young travel enthusiasts who have knowledge of destinations. These tour leaders organize private tours for the groups on their own without attaching themselves to any company. They may liaison themselves with all the local suppliers of a destination and offer independent tour packages to the travellers. When travellers book their travel arrangements with the tour leader, he/she then may lead the group through the destinations. The package may be offered for short-haul destinations and multiple destinations.

Specialization

While choosing to join this profession, a tour leader may opt to work for outbound, inbound or domestic tour operators/travel agents. If he/she wants to serve his/her countrymen, then he/she may work for a domestic travel company. If he/she has an interest in his/her own culture and likes interacting with foreigners, he/she may become an inbound manager and contribute to the tourism in his/her own country's economy. If he/she has a lure for travelling overseas, he/she may choose to become an outbound tour leader.

Likewise, he/she may also choose his/her area of specialization in which he/she wants to lead the groups. *He/she may become a tour leader for leisure tours, MICE tours, nature-based tours, food tours, heritage tours, wine tours, wildlife tours, mountain excursions or any other special interest tours.*

You Are Your Own Boss!

Every tour operator/travel company has its own regulatory framework, protocols and its own reporting relationships within which a tour leader must operate. A tour leader is expected to follow the fixed itinerary assigned to him/her by the company. In case of any unforeseen situations, a tour leader may have to take deviations, that he/she must report to his/her company about the same and may also seek its opinion before proceeding for any corrective action when required.

Despite all the precincts mentioned above that constrain a tour leader's movement, he/she still enjoys autonomy in his/her job to a reasonable extent. Compared to any other profession, where one has to work under close supervision, this role promises the least intervention by the company unless and until it is really required. This profession allows a tour leader to be on his/her own. No one is continuously poking in his/her job or keeping a track of him/her. He/she does not have to work under any constant supervision or someone. With the passage of time, when he/she becomes a senior tour leader, his/her negotiation power may increase. He/she may dictate his/her own terms and conditions of working to an extent. This may be a significant advantage in this profession.

Thrilling Job

A tour leader can have some of the most intense, exciting, risky and remote experiences of his/her life in this job. Every day can be a bundle of joy for him/her. Every day has something to offer! Welcome to an Indiana Jones Adventure! You may be on a jungle safari, tasting the sumptuous local delicacy of a country on a cultural tour, visiting the snow-capped mountains of Switzerland, hiking the hills, visiting a vineyard in Melbourne, going on a Gondola ride at Venice, watching a whale show at SeaWorld, Los Angeles, or going for a cruise with your group members! That is how life would be for you—thrilling and exciting!

Seasonal Job

Seasonality of this occupation may be considered both as an advantage and a disadvantage. The peak season for any tour leader is when there are a maximum number of tourists visiting that destination. Generally, the peak season of a destination is when the weather is congenial for the tourists to travel to that destination. However, even if the temperatures of a destination are not welcoming, many destinations still position and sell themselves as round the year destination associating themselves with different tourism products during different seasons of the year. *Taking India as an example, the season for inbound tourists (foreigners) is generally from October to March when the outdoor temperatures are congenial for tourists.* Hence, October to March is the super busy time for inbound tour leaders in India when they may have to take up back-to-back trips due to the massive tourist traffic in the country. However, some foreign tourists also visit India during summers. The main reason for foreigners visiting India at this time is that it is an off-season time for the tourists. Therefore, the summer rates of the packages are quite cheap which may be affordable for backpackers who wish to visit India besides seeing the summers as they may not experience it in their country due to the kind of topography that exists there. However, inbound tour leaders may report the little volume of work during summers as compared to the season time. Likewise, for domestic tourism, the season for tour leaders is round the year though destinations may change depending upon the weather. Similarly, international and domestic business tours take place throughout the year that is a perennial source of business for the tour leaders working for MICE tour operators.

Therefore, a tour leader may work for only six months while some may choose to work for seven–nine months, and still, some work around the year depending on their personal choice and willingness to work. The good part about the seasonality is that a tour leader has to work only for a limited period. In other words, he/she has months of leisure time with him/her. He/she is, therefore, mentally relaxed to pursue other things during his/her free time.

Lucrative Job

Being a tour leader, one can earn a fortune of money. A smart tour leader may make money at every point. This profession is gratifying as far as the salaries and perks are concerned. The sources of earnings may be multiple. A tour leader gets paid on a daily basis for the number of days he/she operates a tour. *He/she receives the daily wages, also referred to as a tour leader's allowance, that may vary from company to company. Besides the tour leader allowance, he/she earns a significant portion of his/her income from the commissions.* He/she may charge a commission at different points of the tour. Generally, the tour leaders have a fixed commission structure with the local suppliers that they are in touch with that the company may not have arranged. A significant portion of a tour leader's income also comes from the shopping done by his/her guests at the shops he/she may take his/her guests to though this practice is not really encouraged by some countries. Besides the above sources, a tour leader may make money through *gratuities* too. In many countries of the world, it is a common practice to give tips to the tour leader. Some guests may be very generous in giving tips if they are happy with the services offered by the tour leader, which may mean a lot of income for the tour leader.

Besides, the monetary rewards, a tour leader may enjoy many *fringe benefits* from the company he/she works for. He/she may get mobile phones or *mobile bill reimbursements, laptops, daily allowance, bonuses, uniforms* and so on depending on the company's policy he/she is working for. *Everything from travelling, boarding and lodging to excursions and entrance to various attractions during the tour is complimentary for a tour leader.* Many travel companies also offer *discounted travel* to the tour leaders for different domestic and international destinations that can be a big motivation for them to travel on vacations.

Travelling Job

A tour leaders' job is not a desk job where his/her whole day is spent in front of the desktop from 9 to 5. It is a field job as it involves extensive travelling. It is more about staying outdoors and exploring the world. The tour leader lives a large part of his/her work life with a suitcase and a rucksack moving from one place to another. The world is his/her office as he/she is continuously on the move. He/she only has to visit his/her company's office, when the company calls him/her for a new assignment, a meeting, training, informal catch-up, a new product launch or for settlement of bills.

Flexibility

A tour leader has the liberty to decide when he/she wants to work. Although he/she is constrained by the peak season of work, this job allows him/her enough flexibility to determine the timings of his/her working. Since the tour leader enters into a contract with different companies, he/she has the choice to choose when he/she wishes to work. When he/she feels unwell or overstressed, he/she may decline the assignments. This liberty empowers him/her. There are hardly any such professions where you can afford to choose your timings of working. However, the disadvantage is that if you are not working, you are losing your money.

Glamour

This role promises extensive travel that may also include an overseas trip depending upon the kind of tours one chooses to conduct. While people spend a fortune on travel, the tour leader gets to travel the world on the company's money, that is, free of cost. The whole trip is taken care of and sponsored by the travel company that hires him/her.

Mostly, the tour leaders have the privilege of travelling in the best of the airlines or the other modes of transportation. They stay in some of the best hotels and other accommodations of the world, have some of the most exceptional dining experiences at the best restaurants in the world. They get to see the best of the attractions around the world and watch some of the best shows at the destinations. *It sounds glamorous to visit the most spectacular landscapes and built structures of the world!*

Long Hours

Before opting for this profession, one must understand that this is not like any other regular 9–5 job. This job demands a lot of one's time and energy. One may have to remain for long hours on duty. *A tour leader sometimes has to work 24 × 7, that is, round the clock during the trip. A tour leader, when on duty, does not have any weekends to relax.* He/she is even required to work on weekends. In fact, when the whole world is enjoying their vacations, for example, Christmas and New Year holidays, that may be the peak season of his/her work. Although travelling is the best part of this profession, the same travel can become an exhausting activity too for the tour leader if he/she has the pressure of handling back-to-back tours without appropriate breaks in between. A tour leader must also keep a check on his/her physical fitness to catch up with the hectic routine of this job.

Meeting New People

One of the most exciting parts of this profession is getting an opportunity to meet new people. On different journeys, a tour leader comes across hundreds of various kinds of tourists. He/she, thus, gets an opportunity to understand new cultures of different countries very closely. This is a rare opportunity of its sort.

Stressful Job

The job of a tour leader is very demanding and taxing. Sometimes, this task can become nerve-wracking for the tour leader. A tour leader is always under continuous pressure to meet deadlines. His/her job is timebound. He/she must do everything on time and ensure that the trip is moving in a timebound direction. In other words, a tour leader has to follow the set timetable given to him/her by his/her company. He/she is under continuous pressure to complete the day's itinerary. The tour leader at any point in time, during the tour, cannot afford to sit back and relax. He/she cannot have the laxity of delaying things. He/she must ensure that he/she does not skip any point mentioned in the itinerary. Otherwise, the guests may complain about him/her.

Challenging

On one hand, the job poses challenges because a tour leader is leading a group of unknown people who may be difficult to handle, while on the other hand, he/she may have to deal with unanticipated situations that may come up on the tour. Also, the pressure of being under a continuous scanner of his/her guests under observation makes his/her job more challenging. He/she may also have to manage multiple things at the same time. He/she may be required to do the coordination and liaison with the local suppliers and take care of his/her guests, and at the same time, he/she also manages to answer their questions besides keeping his/her office in the loop. This makes his/her job challenging too!

Away from Home

The most challenging part of a tour leader's job is to stay away from his/her family and friends. A tour leader has a difficult family time. He/she has to sacrifice his/her family life to be on his/her duty. The call of his/her duty is his/her first duty. There are months when he/she may have to remain away from his/her family. The client's commitment stands the supreme when he/she is on duty. When his/her family needs him/her, he/she may not be there to support them during his/her duty time. He/she may also miss out on important family occasions and friend get-togethers that may fall during the tour. As a result, his/her family life and social life may suffer.

ROLES OF A TOUR LEADER

A tour leader has the following roles to play.

Leader

A tour leader leads his/her group at every point. He/she guides and directs his/her guests at every point. He/she never leaves them alone. He/she also makes decisions for them.

Facilitator

A tour leader is basically a facilitator at a destination who ensures that travel arrangements go as smoothly and enjoyable as possible for his/her clients. He/she makes the stay of tourists at a destination more comfortable and hassle-free with his/her presence.

Caretaker

A tour leader takes care of the safety of his/her guests at all times. As a caretaker, he/she may ask his/her guests to look after their belongings all the time. He/she also ensures that the guests are taken to all places, they are fed on time, they get adequate rest during the tour and their individual requests, if any, are met on the trip.

Companion

A tour leader acts as a fellow companion of his/her guests during the trip. The only difference is that the guests have high expectations from this mate, unlike other fellow tourists on tour. The tour leader acts as a friend and a philosopher for his/her group. Like a friend, he/she accommodates his/her guests in every way he/she can.

Travel Consultant

A tour leader acts as a local consultant for a destination. He/she provides insights about the destination to the visiting guests. He/she advises his/her guests what activities to undertake at the destination during their free time, what special events to attend, what to see around, what to experience, what to eat and what to shop, that may also not be included in the itinerary. He/she acts as the local guy.

Liaison

A tour leader acts as a liaison officer among all service providers. The tour leader may liaison between:

- The company and the guests
- Local community and the guests
- Local service providers and his/her guests

Presenter

A tour leader provides instructions to his/her group members at every point in the destination. He/she helps in building a connection to the place with his/her guests. He/she provides commentary and instructs them about the dos and don'ts at a destination. He/she presents the exciting facts of a destination in the most informative, engaging and in a professional way.

Organizer

A tour leader organizes everything during the tour as per the timetable given to him/her. He/she ensures that every point, as promised, in the itinerary is covered. Although the things may have been pre-arranged by the company, a tour leader coordinates and reconfirms with the local service providers to organize the travel arrangements on time. He/she ensures that the rooms are ready for his/her guests, the guests are served meals on time, the guests are taken to places around, the guests are taken for activities and so on. *He/she knows the art of organizing time minute by minute as he/she has to adhere to the itinerary strictly.*

Moderator (of Expectations)

A tour leader must be able to handle the expectations of his/her guests gracefully. He/she should not shirk from his/her responsibilities. Instead, he/she must try to deliver more than expected so that the tourists go back home happy. He/she must understand the needs and wants of his/her guests and clearly inform them about what he/she can do for them and what he/she cannot do for them as per the guidelines of his/her company.

Entertainer

A tour leader should also take care of the entertainment of his/her guests. He/she should make the vacations of his/her guests more exciting with his/her presence. For the entertainment of his/her guests, he/she may organize games or recommend activities that they may like to pursue during their spare time, for example, adventure activities, nightlife, shopping and so on at a destination. He/she may also add humour to his/her commentaries to keep the tourists happy.

Accountant

A tour leader must be good at numbers. He/she may anticipate the expenditures that he/she may have to incur on the trip and accordingly plan the money required during the tour. He/she may carry cash or keep debit/credit cards with him/her for making the payments towards services and optional activities organized during the trip. He/she must also keep his/her documentation updated, that is, a proper record of all the bills and receipts received during the trip for the services taken for the clients. These bills and receipts are required to be submitted later to the travel company on the completion of his/her tour.

Troubleshooter/Grievance Handler

For the guests, a *tour leader acts as a single-window clearance* to all their problems. A tour leader is a troubleshooter for the guests on the tour who shall evade away all their worries by giving them solutions for the difficulties they may come across. For every grievance, they approach a tour leader. Apparently, for many guests, a tour leader is a crucial psychological support.

Salesperson

A tour leader may act as a salesperson for his/her company as he/she may promote the other travel-related products of his/her company such as related tours or other domestic and international packages through brochures and relevant literature. He/she may also sell the *optional excursions* on a tour to his/her guests that may not have been included in the package.

Crisis Manager

A tour leader may have to deal with unforeseen circumstances. He/she should, therefore, be prepared to deal with any kind of emergency situation that may come on the tour.

For any further information on tour leaders, you may refer to my book, *Tour Leadership and Management*.

SUMMARY

A tour leader is a *journey mentor* of the tour. For a traveller travelling to an unfamiliar place, a tour leader is a crucial omnipresent support available to him/her arranged by the tour company for the clients throughout the trip. He/she is the one who organizes everything on a tour at the right time and right place. *The job of a tour leader offers a world of opportunities. However, it is worth mentioning here that it is also not a cakewalk. It has its own share of highs and lows.* Although this profession promises goodies such as money, glamour, extensive travelling, thrill, flexibility, autonomy, meeting new people and a decent lifestyle, it can get very taxing and demanding for the tour leader. One must not forget to appreciate the hard work and dedication of this person that goes in making a tour successful for his/her guests.

To be able to do this, a tour leader must wear different hats at the same time—leader, facilitator, caretaker, companion, presenter of the place, organizer, liaison, moderator, accountant, consultant, entertainer, troubleshooter, crisis manager and so on.

ACTIVITIES

Activity 1

You are leading a group of women travellers to Thailand. One day, you take the group on a shopping tour as per the set itinerary given to you. While you are waiting for the group outside the shopping street, a shopkeeper calls you inside the shop. There is also a police cop inside. On enquiring, you get to know that one of your lady guests has shoplifted things from the shop and she was caught red-handed by the shopkeeper who then called the cop. Now, what would you do in such a situation as a leader of the group?

Activity 2

Interview any five outbound tour leaders and ask them to narrate any two emergencies that they faced while leading a group of tourists and the way they dealt with the situation. Also, take notes of the company they were representing during that incident, the kind of tour they were operating and any other detail, if required. Now document everything and submit a write-up of the same to your teacher. Also, share the same information with the class through a PowerPoint presentation. In the end, discuss your learning outcomes. The same exercise may be done with the inbound tour leaders also.

Activity 3

Would you like to be a tour leader? If yes, why, and if no, why? Be candid in your thoughts.

Activity 4

'Tour leaders are the convenient punching bags for the tourists.' Discuss.

The Tour Guide

LEARNING OBJECTIVES

The given chapter shall clarify the following:

- Who is a tour guide?
- What is the nature of a tour guide's job?
- What are the challenges of the tour guiding profession?

GUIDED TOURS

- Tour Guides are known to bring life to a city by introducing the tourists to the aromas, sounds, culture, religion and heritage of a city. He/she may involve his/her guests in *creative experiences* on the tour.
- The Kutch district of Gujarat in India offers very impressive guided tours of different kinds where the tour guides give very creative narrations, quote anecdotes and make these guided tours very engaging, interesting and creative for the guests. Some of these must-try guided tours include the following:
  o Textile tours at Bhujodi village in Kutch (famous for textile production with more than 1,200 inhabitants involved in textile handicraft production. The guided tour includes a visit to weavers, block printers, tie and dye artists and so on).
  o Cultural tour of Hodka village.
  o Photography tours at Mandvi.
- The capital of India, Delhi, equally mesmerizes the tourists with guided trips by travel companies such as *India City Walks* and *Thrilophilia* with some of the following creative guided experiences:
  o A cycle-rickshaw tour in Chandni Chowk.

o   Taking a guided food tour in Old Delhi, especially Paranthe Wali Gali and Jama Masjid area, which is a heaven for non-vegetarian gourmets.
o   A guided heritage walk in the Nizamuddin area.
o   A Segway tour in Rajpath.
o   A spiritual tour to Chandni Chowk with a visit to a temple, mosque, church and gurudwara in Chandni Chowk and making of rotis (bread) by the foreigners at the Gurudwara Shish Ganj Sahib in the *Langar* (the most extensive community kitchen in the world).
o   Guided cooking tours in traditional homes of Delhi.
o   Taking guided tours with experiences such as making pottery by the tourists and applying different designs of henna by the tourists.

INTRODUCTION

A key person who plays a major role in facilitating a holiday and making it worth remembering is the tour guide. He/she may be referred to as the 'experience facilitator' as his/her presence enhances the experience of a traveller during his/her holiday. Guides are specialists for the attractions being visited at a destination. *They are responsible for painting the picture of a destination or an attraction that they make their guests visit.*

A tour guide is a person who conducts the sightseeing tours for a limited duration of time. He/she may be hired by the tour operator for a half-day or full-day sightseeing tour. Thus, his/her role is site-specific as he/she interprets a site for his/her guests on guided tours or takes them around the city for sightseeing, unlike a tour leader who remains with his/her guests from beginning till the completion of the trip.

According to the *World Federation of Tour Guides Association (WFTGA)*, London, 'A tour guide is a person who guides the group of guests in the language of visitors' choice and interprets the natural and cultural heritage of a place to his guests.'

Thus, according to this definition, a tour guide must be well conversant in the language of the visitor. This means that he/she must have knowledge of other languages too besides his/her own language if he/she wants to deal with inbound tourists visiting his/her country. Another dimension to the definition is that his/her major role is of interpretation of sites that he/she accompanies and guides his/her guests to. It means that he/she helps his/her guests to make sense of a place by interpreting its heritage, cultural or natural appeal for their better understanding.

BENEFITS OF HIRING A TOUR GUIDE

A tour guide has a prime significance in conducting the itinerary of the tour. The following are the reasons why tourists hire the services of a tour guide.

Expertise

Guests hire tour guides to take advantage of their local knowledge that they may have by being a local person of the city. *The tour guide, being a local guy, is well aware of the social dynamics of the destination and the local sensitivities to be considered while visiting the destination.* Therefore, the guest has an opportunity to learn about the local sensitivities to be followed at the destination through a tour guide's expertise. For example, many tourists while visiting *Trinity College in Dublin* opt for guided tours.

Hassle-Free

With a tour guide, guests feel more comfortable as everything is being taken care of by the tour guide. The guests do not have to do any homework as to which place to visit and which not to. *Everything has already been filtered by a tour guide.*

Time-Saving

A tour guide knows how much time to spend at an attraction. *He/she expedites the purchase of entry tickets, pulls his/her guests through the attractions, briefs them at the attraction and makes sure that everyone in the group adheres to the time limit set for visiting another attraction. Everything is time-bound.* Hence, the guests get to see the maximum sites in the minimum period with a tour guide. Every minute and penny spent by the guests on their tour is optimized by the presence of a tour guide who knows how to make the most of the guest time.

To Feel Safe

Many guests feel safer in the presence of a tour guide. Especially when the guest is in a new country, they may feel jittery and lost. The presence of a tour guide gives them moral support that there is someone whom they can bank upon in case of any difficulty they may face.

CHALLENGES OF THE TOUR GUIDE'S PROFESSION

Every day is a new challenge for the tour guide. He/she may not know what kind of guests he/she may encounter, what temperament his/her guest may have, what expectations they may have come with, what questions they may ask from him/her, what emergencies he/she may encounter and so on. Therefore, on being given any assignment, preparation for a tour guide is a must while on tour. A tour guide must be mentally prepared to handle any kind of issue on a tour. Let us discuss some of the reasons in detail that make his/her job more challenging.

Delighting the Guests Is Not Easy

Holidays are both a financial as well as an emotional investment. It is not easy to please anyone entirely and that too all the tourists. The guests may have spent a good deal of money and spared their valuable time to be on the tour. They may have very high hopes from the trip as well as the tour guide. Satisfying the guests is not that easy. This entirely depends upon the performance of the tour guide how well he/she conducts the trip and takes care of his/her guests. So the pressure of performance and managing the multiple expectations of guests is not always easy for a tour guide. He/she must be able to live up to the expectations of his/her guests. Therefore, we may say that tour guiding is a challenging job.

Dealing with Different Types of Guests

On every tour, a tour guide is meeting a new set of tourists except in some circumstances where the guests may have placed a request to repeat the same tour guide. Every group may have a different composition of group members. Some guests may be of a different nationality while some may be from a different religion. Some groups may have expecting mothers, while some may have parents with infants who need adequate attention. Some may be women travellers, while some may be elderly citizens. Some may be allergic patients, while some may have a medical history. Yet some may be differently abled in the same group. Handling different types of such guests in the same group or even in different groups may be very challenging for a tour guide.

Always under a Scanner

A tour guide may feel that he/she is continuously being judged and monitored by the guests for his/her performance. As a result, he/she may feel pressurized and nervous. To perform under pressure may be challenging for many.

Adjusting to Weather Conditions

A tour guide may have to operate his/her tour under extreme weather circumstances for his/her scheduled assignments. He/she may have to guide his/her guests in the scorching heat, chilly winter or on a rainy day. Saying no to the assignment means loss of opportunity for earning money.

Working Time

A tour guide may have to work on weekends or even on public holidays. The festival time may be the peak season for a tour guide as the guest may be on holiday during that time. He/she may also have to work for months together during season time without any breaks in between. Sometimes, he/she may have to go on back-to-back tours. This may be personally quite taxing for him/her.

Handling Questions

The guests may have a series of questions to ask from the tour guide. On every tour, a tour guide may be asked different questions by different guests that he/she may not have even predicted. For them, the tour guide is an 'Encyclopaedia' who has all the answers to their queries. This makes his/her job quite challenging.

Handling Emergencies

The kind of conditions that a tour guide may have to face on the tour can never be predicted. While guiding his/her guests at a monument, someone may steal a phone of a guest or some-one may even tease a female traveller in a crowd. *The magnitude of situations faced by a tour guide may be myriad and entirely unpredictable.* Thus, we may say that a tour guide's job is quite challenging.

QUALITIES OF A TOUR GUIDE

Based on the challenges faced by a tour guide, a tour guide must possess the following qualities:

1. Overall knowledge of the destination such as its history, culture, geography and politics
2. Flair for travelling
3. People's person
4. Good communication skills
5. Well-groomed
6. Excellent management skills
7. Good orator
8. Cross-cultural competence
9. Bilingual
10. Calm and poised
11. Good decision-maker
12. Physical stamina

13. Proactive
14. Dynamic and energetic
15. Assertive
16. Amicable
17. Good listener
18. Positive attitude
19. Creative
20. Time efficient
21. Audible
22. Enthusiastic

WORKING OF TOUR GUIDES

Now let us understand how tour guides work:

- To practise tour guiding, a tour guide must carry a *valid licence* with them issued by the competent authority to guide individuals or groups.
- Tour guides generally work on *day tours* or *half-day tours*. Accordingly, they are paid per day or half-day tour wages.
- Tour guides may *work as freelancers* too. Some tour guides may work for a particular company whereas some tour guides may attach themselves to multiple companies taking assignments as and when they come. Alternatively, some tour guides may be chosen for handling the government assignments taking the delegates on sightseeing tours.
- Some assignments may be FIT based where individual guests may have booked the services of a tour guide whereas some assignments may be a big group of more than 10–30 travellers.
- Different types of guides may be *monument guides, full-time guides, part-time guides* or *linguistic guides.*
- Some tour guides are specialized in tours based on *inbound, outbound* or *domestic* tours. Within these areas, tour guides may specialize in leisure tours, nature-based tours, heritage walks, food walks, MICE tours, photography tours, wildlife tours, luxury tours, rural tours, wine tours and so on. The kind of tours a tour guide conducts depends upon his/her interests along with the type of tours that a travel company conducts that he/she works for.
- Many times, tourists book regular brochure-guided tours in which the itinerary is already fixed, whereas in some cases, tourists choose their own sightseeing points and request the company to customize the itinerary according to their interests. However, in many cases, the tourists are not clear as to what he/she wants to see. *In such situations, some tours may sometimes be at the discretion of a tour guide who may take his/her guests to places according to his/her own choice.*

TRAINING OF TOUR GUIDES

Tour guides undergo training at two levels. First, *at the fresher level*, when someone aspires to be a tour guide and second when the *experienced tour guides undergo refresher guide training* to keep themselves upbeat on the latest practices in the trade. At entry and refresher level, the following are the general mechanisms that tour guides are generally trained under.

Competent Authority

Having a valid licence is a prerequisite to becoming an authorized tour guide. Anyone who aspires to be a tour guide may acquire formal training from competent authorities of his/her domicile. Many government bodies in different countries may be the responsible authorities who provide the licence to the tour guide. In some countries, there are written examinations followed by practical examinations to evaluate the participants. Only after the aspirant has qualified the evaluation system of the competent authority, he/she may be granted the licence to work as a tour guide. *In India, we have guides at three different levels that include regional-level guides (being the highest level of guiding), state-level guides and the local-level guides.* For regional-level guides, it is the MOT, Government of India, that trains the *regional-level* guides through various *Indian Institute of Tourism and Travel Management (IITTM) centres* across India. In the case of state tourism guides, the state tourism departments are responsible for licencing them, and for being a local guide, local municipality bodies are responsible for licensing them.

Tour Operators

Working for different travel companies may be different for a tour guide as they may have different policies and regulations. Therefore, while working for a particular tour operator, tour guides may attend formal training sessions organized by them. Courses such as inputs on tourism, history, geography, architecture, trends in travel, needs of a tourist, cross-cultural differences, handling emergency situations, and techniques of guiding may be imparted to tour guides by the experts.

Novice tour guides may also be associated with experienced tour guides on tours to acquire hands-on training from the experienced tour guide.

Associations

Many associations may also organize training sessions/seminars for the tour guides to keep them updated about the upcoming trends taking place in the tourism industry, particularly in the field of guiding.

PERFORMANCE EVALUATION OF TOUR GUIDES

A lot depends upon the performance of a tour guide. If tour guides do not perform well, the tourists may ask for the refund of money as their holiday experience gets ruined. It may also affect the reputation of the company. Therefore, it is important for tour operators to have a mechanism to monitor the performance of tour guides continuously. Thus, tour companies may evaluate the performance of tour guides using different tools and techniques. The mechanism of motivating the tour guides may vary from company to company. Generally speaking, the guides are rated on the following parameters in travel companies:

- Number of positive feedbacks about the tour guide posted by tourists on travel review sites
- Positive feedback of the tour guide on feedback forms given by the company to the guests
- Number of optional tours sold by the tour guide
- Number of refunds of trips against each tour guide (in case the guests was not satisfied with the performance of tour guide and opted for return of his/her money)
- Demand raised by the tourist for repeating the same tour guide on another tour based on the tourist's previous experience or the positive feedbacks of others

To further motivate the tour guides, companies may also introduce various means of appreciating the tour guides, for example, *sending appreciation letters to the performers, giving a star performer award to the best tour guide, giving holidays packages, giving incentives, sending them for further trainings, giving them promotions* and so on.

ROLES OF A TOUR GUIDE

A tour guide may perform the following multiple roles during a tour.

Consultant

It is the tour guide who would be the local guy for the guests who has expertise in the city. He/she is expected to be a tank of the information who knows the intricacies of his/her city thoroughly. He/she is supposed to direct his/her guests to various sightseeing points depending upon the interest they may have. Therefore, he/she acts as a consultant for his/her guests.

Mediator

A tour guide connects the guests with the real life of his/her city. He/she may take his/her guests to places that have limited access and go out of his/her way to bring the local community closer to the tourists. Therefore, he/she may act as a mediator between his/her guests and the local community of the destination.

Creator

A tour guide is a creator of experiences for his/her guests. *Guiding is all about being as creative as possible.* It is not expected of a tour guide to be creative in distorting the information. However, creativity may be experimented with the delivery of information and to an extent with the content of the commentary. A tour guide may *make his/her commentary more creative by adding some voice modulation, fancy words, interesting facts, narrating stories and anecdotes, adding humour to his/her commentary* and so on.

A tour guide may experiment with his/her creativity in providing offbeat experiences for his/her clients that may not necessarily be included in the itinerary. He/she may introduce add-ons to his/her existing itineraries or customize his/her own itineraries to make them more interesting and engaging. The basic idea is to give an experience to the guests from an insider's perspective. Basically, through their narratives, the tour guides add life to the tours that the tourists otherwise may not be able to connect to a destination or make sense of things in their absence.

Caretaker

Tour guides *act as custodian of groups.* They are expected to take care of their guests during the sightseeing tours. Right from ensuring that all guests are together and no guest is missing to reminding them to take care of their valuables, a tour guide continuously acts as caretaker of his/her guests during the sightseeing tours.

Seller

Many tours are sold as optional tours. Generally, tour guides have a target of selling these optional tours to guests. Their incentives are linked to the number of optional excursions sold by them. Therefore, tour guides must have robust and convincing abilities and the art of selling optional tours to their guests.

Cashier

Many travel companies may take some booking amount of day tours and then later receive the pending balance from tourists after their day trip gets over. In such cases, it becomes the responsibility of a tour guide to collect money for the trip on behalf of his/her company. A tour guide must be aware as to how much money has to be received from the guests. They must also know the criteria for payment collection of their company. It may be cash or cashless. In case of cashless transactions, a tour guide may carry the payment machine with him/

her on the tour and swipe the equivalent amount to be collected from the guests or may ask their guests to transfer the amount online using apps such as Paytm, Bhim, etc. depending upon the policy of the company.

Link Pin

A tour guide ensures that all his/her members stay together. Through his/her commentary and organizing different games, he/she tries to bring all his/her members closer to each other.

DON'TS OF A TOUR GUIDE

There are certain things that a tour guide must avoid while guiding the group of guests. Here is the list of few don'ts.

No Use of Writing Notes

The mantra for a tour guide is to practice and only practice. A tour guide should know things verbatim. Use of notes should be totally avoided.

No Drinking and Smoking

A tour guide must not be drunk while reporting for his/her duties. Likewise, he/she must not smoke during his/her duty hours.

No Glares

Avoid wearing glares while guiding as it looks more casual. It is always good to maintain direct eye contact with the guests.

No Chewing

A tour guide must not chew anything, such as chewing gum and tobacco, while doing his/her duty.

Restrict Usage of Phone

Avoid taking any personal calls while guiding. It may distract the guests and agitate them too.

No Personal Relations during the Tour

A tour guide should not make any special advances towards any guest he/she may like on the tour. Indulgence in personal relationships should be totally avoided.

No Prescribing of Medications to the Tourists

There are chances that a guest may fall ill during the tour. *In such a case, a tour guide must not act as a doctor to his/her guest.* Even if he/she may know the remedies or the necessary medication to be taken for certain sickness, he/she may not suggest the same to his/her guests. The reason is that the tour guide may not know the medical history of the tourist, and he/she is not a medical expert. His/her guests may be allergic to certain salts in medicine that may further deteriorate the health of the traveller if he/she suggests medicine to them. Thus, a tour guide should not prescribe any medicine to his/her guests. Alternatively, he/she may request his/her guest to seek the opinion of a doctor.

SUMMARY

Guiding is a very responsible job. The roles of a tour guide are multiple. These involve taking care of guests and their safety and making their trip a memorable experience. Some guides with their conduct may spoil the whole tour, thereby affecting the reputation of the company they are representing, whereas some guides with their quick wit, emotional intellect, enthusiasm, knowledge and winsome nature may win the hearts of the tourists. It is a few practices and tips that clearly delineate a successful tour guide from an average tour guide. Being a good tour guide requires a lot of dedication, devotion and commitment on the part of a tour guide to handle this challenging profession. *A tour guide must know the art of handling people.* Sending the tour guides for training and evaluating their performances from time to time are equally important.

ACTIVITIES

Activity 1: Interview

Interview any three tour guides. Ask them their area of specialization and the nationalities that they deal with. Also, discuss their challenges in their profession and ways of dealing with them.

Activity 2: City Tour

Create a virtual city tour of your city and be a tour guide for your class. Now, making use of interesting anecdotes and narratives while also adding some humour, give a city tour to your friends.

27

The Cab Driver

BLACK TAXI POLITICAL AND MURAL TOURS

- The famous Black Taxi Political and Mural tours of Belfast, North Ireland, are very popular among tourists.
- Here, *the driver acts as a guide who shares interesting stories and real experiences and narrates anecdotes* on the history of troubled Belfast through his/her intimate knowledge of the conflicting history of the city between the Protestants and Catholics.
- The two-hour political tour, guided by the drivers, takes you through the interesting historical places such as one of the world's biggest outdoor art galleries depicting the pictures of conflicts of Irish history and also a visit to the peace walls.
- The drivers are very articulate in their explanations who also with their humour make the tours very interesting. They are also happy in answering any kinds of questions asked by the tourists!
- In all, this tour is truly a value-for-money experience!

The tourism industry is all about 'intangible takeaways' that may be in the form of *memories* and *experiences*. As the tourism industry is a combination of various industries put together, every service provider involved in the delivery of services has an important role to play in creating a positive impression for the tourists. In other words, we may say that in the process of seamless delivery of tourism services, *every touch point counts*. A pivotal role played by a service provider in creating positive experiences for the tourists is the cab driver whose role cannot be undermined. He/she is a key person in making the holiday of a tourist a memorable experience. It is high time that the tourism industry acknowledges the importance of drivers in creating pleasant memories for tourists.

INTRODUCTION

When tourists travel to a destination by road or travel within the destination for local sightseeing, they may travel by coaches, buses or cabs. Thus, they may utilize the services of the drivers. *Drivers may work for the private taxi transporters, tour operators, coach operators, car rental companies or the government.* As the tourists are mostly on sightseeing tours of destinations travelling from one point to another, they spend substantial time with the driver. If the tourists are on a group package tour arranged by the tour operator, they may be on the same coach from the beginning till the completion of the tour on a *Seat-in-coach (SIC)* basis. Mostly, the driver may remain the same in such cases. Also, in the case of FIT tourists who prefer to travel in personal cars that are chauffeur-driven and may be arranged through a tour operator (if they have taken a customized package on an individual basis) or through a car rental company, the driver may remain the same with them. Alternatively, on reaching a destination, if the tourists have not made arrangements either through the travel company/local transporter or a car rental company, they may hire private cabs such as *Uber* and *Ola* or the *government-approved taxis*. Some taxis may be especially tourist cabs such as *Black Taxi tours in Belfast, Dublin,* and *London Taxi tours* that are quite famous among tourists. Tourist buses like *HOHO buses* are also dedicated to providing services for tourist where the drivers act as *driver cum guide* giving live commentary about the important points of interest being passed by through the way while driving. In all the cases, the drivers spend the maximum time with the tourists. Thus, the drivers may also be referred to as 'companions' of the tourists.

IMPORTANCE OF DRIVERS

It is imperative for the tourism industry to understand the importance of drivers who have an important role in building and communicating the image of a country. Since these drivers are generally the initial point of interaction when tourists reach a destination, their behaviour and driving speak volumes of the priority that they are attached towards the safety of life and respect for the tourists. Their interactions with the tourists about a destination can make or mar their impression as they spend the maximum time with the tourists.

For this reason, they may be referred to as destination ambassadors of the country or may also be called as city ambassadors. They may also be addressed by the other name 'pilot' in other parts of the world.

It is equally important for the drivers to understand their role and their contribution to the image building process of their destination and country. The drivers must maintain the pride of the nation at all times by speaking in favour of their nation.

RESPONSIBILITIES OF THE DRIVERS

Although the job of a driver seems trivial, his/her scope of roles and responsibilities is quite broad. For the sake of our own clarity, we have divided the roles of a driver into two categories:

- Responsibility towards the tourists
- Responsibility towards the vehicle

Now, let us have a detailed discussion on each of these expected responsibilities.

Responsibilities towards Tourists

When tourists visit a destination, they entrust their lives in the hand of a driver. They expect a pleasant and comfortable journey along with the driver. For them, he/she is a companion and a guide who drives them through various places of interest at a destination. For the tourist, the driver is the *spokesperson of a destination*. Let us elaborate on some of the roles that are expected of a driver.

To Take Care of Safety of Guests

The most important of all roles is the *safe manoeuvring of tourists from one point to another*. The safety of guests should be the most important concern for the drivers. The guests must feel safe in the company of the driver. The driver must assess the road conditions and know the speed with which to drive safely along with the safe distance to be kept from the vehicle ahead while driving. The speed under which the cab drivers operate must be within their control and must not cross the speed limits set in the given area. He/she must incessantly follow the traffic rules. Bumpy rides should be avoided, and the driver must know to slow down on a speed breaker. The transporters must also ensure that the drivers are given adequate rest that does not make them sleepy while driving that may endanger the safety of the guests. They must be given enough time to cope with fatigue and stress. Thus, we may say that the drivers are entrusted with the responsibility of the safety of guests.

To Give Information about the Points of Interest

An important role that is expected of a driver is to satisfy the inquisitiveness of his/her guests. The driver may sometimes have to act as a *driver cum guide*.

Being a local guy of the destination, the tourists expect him/her to know everything about the destination that they are visiting. They, thus, expect the driver to share the local information of a destination with them. Therefore, the driver must have the up-to-date and relevant information of the city surroundings, tourist points or places of interest, and he/she must have the art of disseminating information to his/her guests when he/she passes by the important landmarks while driving through the destination with his/her guests. He/she must be competent enough to answer the questions and concerns raised by the tourists while visiting a destination. He/she should be able to share interesting anecdotes, use his/her sense of humour to make his/her running commentary interesting and smart enough to realize the exact interests of the tourists. Understanding the interest of the tourists may help him/her to customize his/her information and filter it according to the interests of the tourists. This may not make him/her sound dull and boring. It is also expected of him/her to share his/her knowledge about the city in a positive light without lying about the realities of the place.

All these ways help build up his/her personal rapport and credibility in the eyes of guests. Besides, it also gives an impetus to the goodwill of the travel company and also increases its chances of repeated business on behalf of whom the driver is representing.

To Sensitize the Tourists about Local Sensitivities

While visiting a destination, if time permits and the guests are genuinely interested, the driver must share the local sensitivities to be followed by the guests while driving from one place to another. This helps the tourists to appreciate and understand the importance of local culture and sensitivities of the place. Sharing the ethos of the country is a great way to start the conversation with the guests. The driver may discuss various developments taking place within the city or country, the reforms or campaigns, if any, introduced by the government. For example, when foreigners visit India, the driver may inform the tourists regarding the underlying philosophy of Indian hospitality where the *Atithi Devo Bhava*, that is, 'the guest is God' is at the heart of this industry.

To Sensitize the Tourists about Environment

Sharing with the guests as to how they could contribute to the environment responsibly while visiting a destination is equally an important role of a driver. The driver is expected to act as a spokesperson of a destination and its environment and remind his/her guests of the ways in which they can keep the environment clean by not littering around. For example, while driving with his/her foreign guests in India, the driver may educate his/her guests about the 'Swachhta Action Plan' (the largest cleanliness drive in the country) that has been successfully operational since October 2014 and is continuing till now.

To Take the Pictures of the Guests

The driver, while giving a sightseeing tour to his/her guests, may also allow his/her guests a photography opportunity to capture the scenic locations and famous attractions in their camera lens. He/she may also suggest different angels or points from where pictures may be best taken. Sometimes, he/she may also take photographs of his/her guests on their request.

Responsibilities towards the Vehicle

It is the prime duty of the driver to keep his/her vehicle in an orderly condition. As the driver spends maximum time in the vehicle, he/she is expected to know the lacunae that he/she may find while operating the vehicle. In other words, we may say that he/she is the 'caretaker' of his/her vehicle.

Now, let us discuss a few responsibilities of a driver towards his/her vehicle.

Vehicle Maintenance

Every vehicle demands maintenance after a certain run of kilometres. A cab driver must know when the vehicle needs to go for preventive maintenance. He/she must also inspect the vehicle daily and check the following:

- Braking and driving controls
- Hand brakes
- Gears if they are working properly
- Lubrication and gear oil
- Lighting control
- Headrest and correct head support
- Wheel alignment and wheel balancing

If a vehicle demands servicing, he/she needs to communicate the same to his/her company. If there seems to be *any wear and tear in the vehicle such as the seat covers need to be changed, the tyres need to be replaced or the car needs a change of the lubrication oil,* the same needs to be informed at the earliest by the driver to the company for which he/she is working. Any delays caused in the maintenance of the vehicle can cost a life that can eventually bring a very bad name to the company besides the risk of losing the job by the driver himself/herself or even sometimes leading to the cancellation of his/her licence. Besides, the regular maintenance, the driver must himself/herself be *aware of the regular and basic procedures to be followed in case of breakdown of machinery like the change of tyres in case the tyre deflates.*

Maintaining Vehicle Hygiene

As they say 'cleanliness is next to godliness', a cab driver must take care of his/her office space which is the vehicle itself. He/she must maintain the vehicle hygiene at all times. He/she must clean and dust the vehicle every day. Periodic washing of the vehicle is very important to maintain the hygiene of the vehicle. The driver may also additionally make use of the *car sprays/car perfumes* and so on to maintain a pleasant odour within the cab. He/she may keep a *garbage bin in case of a coach or garbage bags in small cabs for the guests to litter*, in case required, while travelling.

Defensive Driving

A driver must be well versed with defensive driving. He/she must also know how to drive in difficult situations like bad weather conditions such as heavy rain, fog and crosswind. Additional knowledge of driving in deserts, snow and ice or driving in crosswinds is equally important for professional cab drivers. Safely driving the vehicle at night is equally important for the driver.

QUALITIES TO BE A GOOD CAB DRIVER

A cab driver must be a thorough professional. His/her demeanour on duty must be maintained at all times. He/she must exhibit the highest level of etiquettes that make the tourists feel safe and comfortable. So what makes the cab driver professional? A good cab driver must have a set of requisite skills, knowledge and abilities to help him/her sail through this difficult profession. Some of the listed knowledge, skills and qualities that make him/her a professional driver are as follows.

Knowledge

Knowledge may be acquired by the driver in the following areas.

Knowledge of Driving

A cab driver must have the basic knowledge of driving as well as the vehicle that he/she is driving. He/she must have a thorough knowledge of the traffic rules. He/she must keep all the relevant documentation in order within the vehicle at all times. It is also expected of him/her to be well versed with the local routes. In these modern times, where the technology drives everyone, the driver must also know how to use the GPS technology that may help him/her to reach a point in the least of time. However, he/she must be familiar with the routes of a destination as the Internet may not always work. He/she must also know how to read the interstate route maps if he/she is licenced enough to travel long distances that may be interstate. He/she must know the local service centres for the car in case of its breakdown.

Technical Know-how

It is important for the cab driver to be well aware of the technical know-how of the vehicle that he/she is driving. This might be especially very useful when the vehicle breaks down while driving on a long trip. A cab driver must be well versed with the make of the vehicle that he/she is driving. He/she must know the general parts of the vehicle and their systems of maintenance. He/she must know how to repair the vehicle in case of an emergency. He/she must also know how to use the toolkit. *He/she must visually check the vehicle for the fire extinguishers, airbags, toolkit, windscreen, steering and the spare wheel.*

Knowledge of the Local Surroundings

It is always desirable for a cab driver to have knowledge of the destination in which he/she operates. It is quite natural that the tourists may be inquisitive to know about the city. They may have a number of questions in their mind that they might pose to the cab driver. Thus, a driver must know the basic history, geography, culture and lifestyle of people at a destination. He/she must not only be aware of the important tourist points but also be aware of the eating outlets, pubs, bars, pharmacy shops, hospitals, ATMs, authorized foreign exchange dealers, supermarkets, local markets, local police station and so on within the city. In short, he/she must be well aware of his/her city surroundings. Many tour operators/transporters expect the drivers to also act as driver cum tour guides.

Only if he/she has accurate knowledge, he/she can satisfy the appetite of the tourists. Not having enough knowledge of the destination may embarrass him/her and make him/her feel less confident about himself/herself.

Knowledge of First Aid

One can never predict any kind of accident that may happen during the journey. Thus, an important practical input for the drivers is to know how to deal during an emergency, if it arises, when they are driving. The drivers must, therefore, be well-trained in first-aid procedures to deal with any crisis such as an accident, a minor injury, a casualty during the journey and so on. He/she must always keep a first-aid box in the cab for his/her own safety and the safety of the passengers.

Qualities

Now, let us have a discussion on the qualities that a driver must possess and develop with his/her experience.

Amicable

A cab driver must try to strike a positive conversation with his/her guests. He/she must be friendly in his/her approach and must keep positive facial expressions so that the tourists feel pleasant in his/her company. He/she must be a good companion with whom travelling is a pleasure and fun for the tourists.

Good Communicator

A driver must be a good communicator. If the tourists ask him/her something, he/she should not shy away from answering. He/she must try to engage the tourists with his/her knowledge of the city provided they are interested in listening to him/her. He/she must introduce his/her city in the friendliest way to the guests by amusing them with the most interesting facts and anecdotes about the destination. Through his/her observation and experience, he/she must be able to judge whether the tourist is enjoying the conversation, or he/she does not want to continue the discussion. Accordingly, the driver should act as per the situation. He/she must also avoid listening to any personal conversations between the guests and rather focus on his/her job of driving.

Courtesy

A cab driver must be courteous by nature. The way he/she conducts himself/herself and the way he/she speaks shows his/her compassion towards the guests. He/she must be able to extend his/her basic courtesies towards his/her guests such as opening the door for the guests, keeping their luggage inside, asking if they are comfortable with the temperature inside the vehicle and if they wish to listen to any kind of music. These small courtesies go a long way in comforting the guests. In some cabs, there may be music facilities, a provision of drinking water inside the cab to extended facilities like a minibar cum refrigerator, especially in luxurious cabs like a limousine. A cab driver must be able to extend these facilities to his/her guests. In case there are magazines/newspapers for the tourists, the same may be offered to them.

Personal Hygiene

Being presentable is very important for a cab driver. A cab driver must be properly groomed and well presentable at all times while on his/her duty. In case there is a uniform code to be followed by the company, the drivers must wear their clean and ironed uniform and adhere to the set standards. He/she must take a daily bath, shave every day and smell good. Having a pleasant body and mouth odour is important while exchanging pleasantries.

Empathy

A cab driver must have empathy for fellow passengers. *He/she must show the utmost respect towards women, expecting mothers, senior citizens and people with special abilities.* He/she must go the extra mile to ensure their safety and security. For example, if an expecting mother is sitting in the cab, he/she must slow down his/her speed of driving and keep the travel comfortable for the expecting mother. Likewise, he/she may assist the senior citizens and anyone who is physically challenged to open the doors for them, help them get out of their seats and make them feel comfortable in every possible way.

Command over Language

It is important for the driver to be well conversant in the English language besides knowing his/her local language. As English is generally the most spoken by maximum tourists visiting the world, a cab driver must know the language in order to be well conversant with the guests.

A Good Observant

A driver must have *an eye for detail*. He/she must be able to understand the body language of his/her guests immediately if they are comfortable or not. He/she must also be aware of which areas and routes are safe to drive, the road conditions, any speed breakers or any pits coming on the road and so on that can help him/her have a safe trip for his/her guests. His/her continuous eyes set on the road along with his/her awareness of the surrounding environment may help him/her keep the passenger safe and protected during their journey.

A Law Observant

A cab driver must abide by the laws set by the government authorities. He/she must carry a valid driving licence with him/her at all times. He/she must also get his/her licence renewed before its expiry. He/she must also be aware of the other documentation such as *the car insurance, car registration papers and the driving licence* that must be carried by him/her at all times while on duty. Thus, he/she must always be in possession of these important documents whenever he/she drives the vehicle. He/she must also follow the traffic rules religiously.

Punctuality

It is important for drivers to respect time. The driver must observe punctuality at all times while on his/her duty. In fact, he/she must be ahead of time that maybe 15–30 minutes before the actual arrival of the tourists in the vehicle so that he/she has enough time to physically inspect the vehicle and check for anomalies, such as if the vehicle is in order or not and if it is clean or not. Being on time is the first sign of professionalism of a driver that makes his/her impression more favourable in front of the tourists.

Gender Sensitization

Maintaining sensitization towards gender is very important. It is imperative for male drivers to be wary of their gestures especially when they are accompanying female passengers. Any kind of inappropriate gesture may offend the women traveller. Touching one's hand with one's lips, seeing the passenger from the front mirror, playing of inappropriate indecent songs can make the tourists, especially female travellers, very uncomfortable. Utmost attention should be paid to respecting the opposite gender.

Personality Development

It is important for drivers to focus on their overall personality. The way they communicate with the tourists which includes both verbal and non-verbal communication, their facial expressions and body posture conveys a lot about them. The drivers must be trained in such a way that they use their body language and confidence to their advantage. They must be aware of their body postures at all times. In short, various aspects of one's personality that include *one's body language, way of speaking, gait* and a *smart dressing* sense are a must in a driver.

Physical Stamina

Reinforcing the physical, mental and emotional well-being of the drivers is very important for the safety of the guests. As this job is very taxing and may sometimes demand odd hours of working that may be quite strenuous for the driver, his/her physical stamina is very important to do justice to this profession. A driver must be in good health at all times. He/she must equally be mentally alert all the time while driving. Thus, he/she may practice Yoga and meditation to take care of his/her overall well-being. This may help him/her keeping his/her stress levels low too.

WORKING CONDITIONS OF DRIVERS

Drivers may work for tourist cabs, buses and tourist coaches. The tourist cabs may vary from small hatchbacks to sedans to SUVs. These may be high-end luxury cars or elementary cars. Tourist coaches may also vary depending upon their size and the number of passengers that they may carry.

The working conditions of the cab drivers may vary from country to country. The working conditions may not always be very pleasant. In a country like India, the drivers may find it difficult to operate as they are not paid well enough and also have strenuous working hours. Thus, giving them a decent remuneration is very important to keep them happy.

Also, sometimes, the cab drivers may have to drive back-to-back trips due to which they may not get adequate rest. This may get very strenuous for them. The tour operators and local transporters must understand that for the safety of the guest, adequate rest for the cab drivers is imperative. Thus, they must be given adequate resting hours. However, in countries like the USA and some European countries, there are fixed norms for the transporters and tour operators to be followed for the drivers. The drivers must be given enough rest breaks in between the trips that ensure their safety as well as that of guests. A *tachometer* is fitted inside the coach that tracks the number of kilometres driven by the drivers. Any driver driving beyond the stipulated kilometres may have to bear a heavy penalty for not following the rules. This may also lead to the cancellation of his/her driving licence as well as a strict action may be initiated against the transporter/travel company.

TRAINING OF DRIVERS

The drivers must be trained well before they take up their jobs. Thus, they must be sent on various training programmes from time to time to keep themselves upbeat of the latest things happening in the field of driving. The training programmes must be tailor-made, keeping in mind the capacity up to which the drivers can assimilate the classroom teaching in a day. While imparting training, there must be a lot of focus on building the communication and presentation skills of the drivers using activity-oriented pedagogy such as organizing ice-breaking sessions, role plays, storytelling, behavioural modelling, simulation exercises, narrating case studies, showing videos and using various other activity-oriented pedagogical techniques that help the drivers to get their hands-on with the practical aspects besides making the learning more interesting and engaging for them while also adding on to their confidence.

Various inputs may be added depending upon the duration of the training programmes or precisely for the total number of hours for which they need to be trained. However, *teaching them the importance of road safety and honing their soft skills should be the prime concern and fulcrum of the training programmes aimed at training the drivers.* The idea is to help them appreciate their roles in delivering and ensuring a positive experience of the tourists. Teaching them how to meet and greet the tourists, how to extend the basic courtesies to the guests such as the opening and closing of the door for the guests, keeping the luggage of the guests and being honest and punctual in duties are some of the pivotal roles for which drivers should be trained. Sessions on personality development and grooming may also be introduced along with instilling a sense of pride among themselves towards their profession and their country as a part of the programme. Imparting knowledge about the destination in which they drive is equally important as the tourists may ask questions about a destination from the tour guide. Sessions on how to disseminate information about a destination and make the commentary interesting while driving and guiding along with the ways of handling questions along with some inputs on first aid may also be kept as a part of the training programme. Along with all these inputs, sessions during training may also be arranged on various stress management techniques that may help them to cope with day-to-day stress as per the nature of their job. The basic idea of all these training programmes is to give a bigger picture to the drivers about their jobs, help them appreciate their jobs and reinstate their importance, inform them about the latest developments of their city and country where they drive and also keep them in the loop about the latest information regarding the technicalities of driving that are emerging from time to time besides testing the drivers' skills and attitude and also reinforcing better learning through peers who may share their ideal stories/incidents during training sessions.

DOS AND DON'TS OF THE DRIVER

Let us review the checklist of things that the drivers must know while on duty. The same may be ensured by their owners who may be the transporters or the travel companies on whose behalf the drivers may be working.

Dos

- Be respectful of the guests while on duty.
- Maintain a distance with the guests.
- Take adequate rest before taking up driving especially on long journeys.
- Make the guests comfortable in the vehicle.
- Only speak, when the guests show interest to know about the place.
- Be aware and mindful of the surroundings.
- Know your job well.
- Observe the speed breakers.
- Take care of the guests.

Don'ts

- Do not drink and drive.
- Do not overspeed. Always follow the speed limits of the surrounding area.
- Do not do rash driving.
- Do not make advances towards your guests. Never get personal with them.
- Do not chew tobacco while on duty.
- Do not see your guests from the rear mirror. It makes them feel uncomfortable and intrudes into their privacy.

SUMMARY

Drivers are one of the most important pillars of the tourism industry. Their role in creating a pleasant stay for tourists at a destination is equally important. They must be made aware of their roles towards the tourists as well as the vehicles. They must take pride in their job. They must be thorough professionals who with their presence add comfort to the overall tourist experience. They must possess the right knowledge and aptitude to perform better in their jobs. Working conditions may vary for drivers from country to country. Thus, drivers must be trained to take up the challenges of this profession. There are certain dos and don'ts that drivers must abide by. The industry must understand their issues and grievances and help in mitigating them.

ACTIVITIES

Activity 1: Roleplay

Divide the class into groups. Ask each group to conduct a roleplay in which two students may act like the tourists, one may act as the driver, and the other may act as a moderator. Roles may be added or reduced depending upon the need of the roleplay and the strength of the class. Now ask each group to present different situations in which the driver interacts with the tourists. For example, one group may enact the first scene where the driver receives the tourists and drops them to the hotel. The appropriate questions asked by the driver may also be emulated. Another group may show the driver taking the guests on a city tour and so on. Here, the tourists may pose questions to the driver. Likewise, in another situation, a driver may be shown misbehaving with the guests. Similar situations may be brainstormed and shown in the class for a better understanding of students. After that, the teacher may evaluate the best group.

Activity 2

Interview any two drivers and ask them to share their experiences and challenges that they may face on their job. Discuss the same with the class.

28

Role of Government in Promoting Tourism

LEARNING OBJECTIVES

The given chapter shall clarify the following:

- What is the role of government in promoting the tourism sector?
- What are the various schemes launched by the Government of India to increase tourism in the country?

MAYA BAY IN PHI PHI ISLANDS, THAILAND: BETTER LATE THAN NEVER

- A stunning bay located on Phi Phi islands in Phuket known for *sunbathing, snorkelling* and doing *photography* became famous after its appearance in the film *The Beach* in 1999.
- The sudden hike in the number of tourists caused severe damages to the ecosystem of the beach, leading to the death of corals in that region as more than 5,000 tourists were visiting Maya Bay every day.
- This forced the Government of Thailand to temporarily close the bay from 2018 to 2021 to make the beach sustainable for future generations.
- The authorities have maintained a strict ban on tourists so that Maya Bay's ecology can recover. Approximately, 10,000 corals have been replanted to sustain the ecology.
- The Department of National Parks (DNP) and Wildlife and Plant Conservation authorities are aiming for sustainable tourism by deciding to install floating docks, eco-focused boardwalks, electronic ticketing system to ensure limitations in a number of visitors per day and digital trackers for tour boat operators.

- Currently, people can still see the nature's wonder from a distance on boats as visiting outer limits of the bay are still permitted, along with snorkelling.

INTRODUCTION

With the tourism industry becoming a prime engine to the economies of the countries, it has become an evident barometer of a country's economic prosperity. The tourism sector has now become a top priority for the governments of different countries of the world. Realizing the contribution of tourism to the economic growth of the countries and the social benefits that it brings to the societies, tourism is being acknowledged as the yardstick for the world.

The government has a primary role in shaping the future of the tourism industry. It is important for the government to realize that the economic development must reach out to the communities in such a manner that it supports the inclusive and sustainable growth of a destination.

As the inclination of people towards tourism is increasing and the travellers are looking for novel options to travel, the role and scope of the government towards the tourism industry is equally increasing.

At the national level, we have the National Tourism Authority (NTA), a government body, which primarily deals with formulating a national tourism policy, strategies and master tourism plans; allocating budgets, developing tourism infrastructure, identifying tourism resources and products, developing tourism circuits, encouraging the private sector to invest in new tourism projects, training manpower for serving the tourism industry and tapping the tourists by aggressively marketing a country as a tourist destination so as to increase the tourist traffic in the country. For example, in India, we have MOT that is a government body responsible for executing all the national policies and plans related to the tourism sector. MOT acts as a nodal agency that works in coordination with various central government agencies, state governments/union territories (UTs) and the private sector to develop and promote tourism in the country.

Likewise, countries may have national tourism boards, like the *Singapore Tourism Board, or ministries, like MOT, Israel,* as NTAs.

At the state level, we have RTOs responsible for promoting tourism within the regions or states. In India, we have state tourism development corporations (STDCs) that execute all of the above-mentioned functions at the state level. They are basically responsible for increasing tourism in their respective states. Some of the examples of STDCs in India are *Kerala Tourism Development Corporation (KTDC), Tourism Corporation of Gujarat Limited (TCGL), Punjab Heritage* and *Tourism Promotion Board (PHTPB)* and so on.

At the local level, the government may have a local tourism authority that regulates and promotes tourism at the local level by involving the local stakeholders and the local community. For example, in India, *Jammu & Kashmir Tourism Development Corporation (JKTDC)* has various local tourism authorities such as *Patnitop Development Authority, Pahalgam Development Authority* and *Leh Development* Authority that operate at a local level to promote tourism through community participation and local stakeholders support.

The main fulcrum of all these governments bodies is the *destination itself around which the whole tourism activity revolves.*

FUNCTIONS OF GOVERNMENT

Having discussed the types of various government bodies engaged at different levels for promoting tourism, let us now have a detailed discussion on the functions of the government in promoting the tourism sector.

Developing Tourism Plans, Policies and Strategies

The role of government in developing policies, plans and strategies cannot be undermined. *Planning of tourism resources forms the edifice of a successful and competitive tourism destination. The ultimate objective of any tourism planning is to increase the number of tourist visits at a destination.* Short- and long-term planning is required for planning the future of the tourism industry. In other words, *strategic (long term)* and *tactical (short term) planning* is imperative for the tourism planners to put the things in a proper perspective. The master tourism and the state-wise tourism plans are formulated by the government bodies responsible for promoting tourism in the country. From deciding on the expected numbers of tourist who must visit a destination to identifying tourism resources, allocation of resources, creating new tourism products, allocating the tourism budgets, developing tourism circuits, etc. for promoting tourism within a destination are all the responsibilities of government bodies that come within the formulation of tourism plans. Thus, the government may be referred to as the *planner, regulator, legislator* and *custodian of destination interest.*

Exploring New Destinations

The role of government in the identification of a destination that has a tourism potential by virtue of its rich history, art and culture, natural landforms and so on is pivotal. From researching a tourist destination to getting it registered as a UNESCO site (if it has a competitive distinctive advantage) is the job of government bodies. Identification of new tourist circuits, creation of feasible itineraries, promoting rural and remote destinations, gaining the winning cooperation of local communities and so on come within the purview of the government sector.

Developing Infrastructure

The government authorities lay out the basic infrastructure for the growth of the tourism industry at a destination. Where the private sector may not be eager to invest in low-income return areas, the government plunges and takes the responsibility of developing the infrastructures in areas that may not promise very high yields. The government bridges the gap between the requirement of local communities and the demands of the tourists. Creation of basic infrastructure such as communication systems, water and electricity supply, fire protection systems and support systems like public facilities must be developed at a destination to sustain the visits of tourists at a destination. Besides the basic infrastructure, creation of airports, roads, highways, railways tracks, railway stations, hotels, guest houses, lodges, runways, museums, historical monuments and so on that require massive budgets are created and maintained through government bodies. In India, the regulatory body for the maintenance of historical bodies is the *ASI*.

Launching new tourism-related projects like developing tourism superstructures such as man-made attractions, spa centres, ecotourism-related projects, ropeways, resorts, amusement parks, business centres and other entertainment centres for tourists also comes within the purview of the government. Thus, the creation of world-class infrastructure for the tourists is the responsibility of government authorities.

Creating Tourism-friendly Destinations

It is the responsibility of the government to introduce amenities at a destination to make the destination more tourists friendly. It may introduce Wi-Fi facility, touchscreen kiosks, public conveniences, cafes and restaurants, signage and digital boards, foreign exchange counters, ATMs, first-aid facilities, availability of forex facility, charging points and so on at a destination to facilitate the tourists and make their stay comfortable and hassle-free.

Providing Information to the Tourists

The government bodies have an important responsibility of providing the right and authentic information to the tourists visiting a country. Any false information given to the tourists may create a negative impression of the country and its people. Creating *Visitor Information Centres* from where the tourists can seek information is a way of facilitating the tourists. The staff such as the tourist information officers posted at these centres may guide the tourists about the places to visit, best modes of transportation to visit them, where to stay, the precautions to be taken, the local sensitivities to be taken care of and so on while visiting a destination. They may also provide all the information to the tourists about the registered tour operators and registered tour guides to avoid any mishaps or false traps that tourists might get into.

Handling Complaints

The government also acts as a *troubleshooter* for the tourists (both domestic and inbound) if they encounter any mishappening or incident while visiting a destination. It may include cheating by the taxi operators, overcharging by the merchandisers, chasing of tourists by the unauthorized guides, making of false promises by the tour operators, crime at a destination such as an eve-teasing, a theft, rape and attacks on the tourists and so on. These complaints must be taken very seriously by the governments. There must be a proper government mechanism in place and redressal machinery of which the tourists are aware that immediately addresses the issues and challenges faced by the tourists. Dedicated tourist police and tourist police stations who know the rules of dealing with the tourists, especially foreigners, must be in place. The staff posted there must be trained and competent enough to address the issues and complaints of the tourists. Otherwise, unaddressed complaints may badly tarnish the image of a country that may eventually reduce the influx of tourists at a destination.

Protecting the Interests of Stakeholders

The government also has to ensure that while promoting tourism at a destination, the interests of various stakeholders associated with it are not jeopardized. Every stakeholder closely associated with the tourism industry must be consulted and made an integral part of tourism planning and development. Organizing the meetings of various stakeholders from time to time, listening to their grievances and challenges, having them as members on the advisory board and so on are some of the ways of collaborating with the stakeholders. In fact, the main stakeholders in the tourism industry are the local communities of a destination. Winning their willingness and their acceptance in promoting tourism at their destination is equally important for the holistic development of a destination.

Marketing New Destinations

Destinations are the main tourism products that need to be marketed by tourism marketers. Tourism marketers could be the tour operators/travel agents who sell a tour package of a destination, or it could be the government that is responsible for promoting tourism. *Destination Management Organizations (DMOs)* are primarily responsible for marketing and selling destinations. We have *NTOs or RTOs* that are the most reliable source of information for the tourists. *NTOs are responsible for marketing a country at the national level.* For example, in the case of India, MOT, Government of India, is the NTO that markets India on a global scale with the *Incredible!ndia* campaign. The *RTOs in India are the STDCs* that are responsible for the marketing of states. Some of the examples are *JKTDC, KTDC, Madhya Pradesh Tourism Development Corporation (MPSTDC)* and so on, as already discussed above. These organizations may use print, electronic and now mostly social media to promote tourism in their destinations. They may also participate in various international and national events such as *travel shows, travel exhibitions* and *roadshows* to publicize the destinations. Alternatively, *press conferences* may be organized on the launch of new tourism offerings to invite media attention. Various *familiarization (FAM) trips* may also be organized by the various tourism boards for professionals of the travel fraternity or the media personnel. Likewise, the printing of *new tourist literature*, being present on all social networking sites, publishing of right and updated information of a destination on the website are all the possible measures that may be adopted by the government authorities to market and promote the destinations in order to woo the tourists. Besides, the above-mentioned marketing tools, events such as *fairs* and *festivals*, *business events* and *sports events* may be organized by the tourism authorities at a destination in order to increase the influx of tourists.

Monitoring the Management of Existing Tourism Products

Once the tourism products have been identified and are being marketed for the tourists to consume, their management and maintenance are very important. Maintaining tourism attractions, introducing technology to make the attraction more attractive and interactive for the tourists, introducing new facilities, making the attractions accessible and tourist-friendly is the responsibility of government authorities if they are maintaining that tourism product. Many tourism products may also be operated by private players where the overall management and maintenance of the tourism products are in the hands of private organizations operating them. However, in some tourism products, their ownership and maintenance may be the responsibility of both government authorities and private players if they operate under a PPP model. Thus, in all kinds of arrangements, the government authorities must ensure the proper monitoring of the tourism products so that they may be used sustainably to ensure their usage not only for the present but also for future generations.

Capacity Building of Service Providers

Since the *tourism industry is primarily a people-based service industry*, there are chances of maximum human error. It is very difficult to keep a check on the quality of services due to the human element involved in the delivery of services. Thus, training of human resources involved in the delivery of tourism resources is a prime responsibility of the government. Training the tourism service providers to give an impeccable service to the tourists and behave politely and sensibly with them is very important to ensure the pleasant experience of a tourist at a destination.

The Capacity Building of Service Providers scheme allows for training the service providers and all the stakeholders involved in the tourism supply chain. This may include the travel agents/ tour operators, tourist information officers, linguistic guides, tour leaders, tour guides, cab drivers, airport representatives, porters, restaurateurs, immigration officers, tourist police and various other service providers involved in the delivery of services to the tourists.

Providing Incentives to the Private Players

The government may provide incentives to the private players to encourage them to invest money in tourism infrastructure. They may give tax waivers, reduce taxes and so on to increase the influx of investment in tourism infrastructures by the private sector. They may also encourage civil societies and NGOs to organize and promote tourism activities. The idea is to create a conducive environment for the private sector so that they are able to invest in the tourism sector, thus creating opportunities for local communities to benefit. Besides the above, the government may also fund various specialized tourism agencies working on tourism-related projects.

Issuing Travel Advisories

It is the responsibility of tourism authorities to issue travel advisories of countries that may not be safe to travel or the precautions that the tourists must adhere to if they are visiting those countries. In the case of India, the MEA issues the travel advisory.

Implementing the Code of Conduct

The government acts as a regulatory body for private tourism players in a country. It acts like a watchman that keeps a check on the various stakeholders of the tourism industry. It lays down the rules and regulations that must be followed by the stakeholders associated with the tourism industry. In other words, it provides a framework for the functioning of the tourism industry by creating the requisite legislation and controls for tourism. The framing of legislations and code of conduct is the core responsibility of government authorities of a country. For example, *there is a separate code of conduct for the tour guides in India.* Likewise, there are rules for all stakeholders not to indulge in unfair practices or cheat the tourists. For this, *MOT, Government of India, has a clear-cut code of conduct governed by a safe and honourable, responsible and sustainable tourism approach* that propagates an overall responsive approach of the service providers towards the tourists. It also talks about having a *code of conduct that may be followed by the tourists while visiting a destination* to maintain its pristine ecology and the social ethics of the local communities. The basic idea is to create a pleasant experience for the tourists that help in building the image of a country while also protecting its environment.

Promoting Sustainable Tourism

One of the most important roles of government organizations is to promote sustainable tourism. *The sustainability to be practised must be in consonance with the established 17 SDGs as suggested by UNWTO.* In simple words, tourism must be developed and marketed only to the extent of carrying capacity of the environment and the social carrying capacity of the local communities of a destination. The approach for overtourism by tourism planners should be discouraged. For example, *Botswana is a high-cost eco-tourism market that promotes tourism to classes and not masses.* The idea is to have a low volume of tourists visiting the destination but who are ready to spend more. Thus, the focus is on creating an exclusive experience for the tourists and doing away with the idea of mass tourism. This helps in saving the tourism resources for the coming future generations without compromising on the quality of the tourism experiences.

Implementing New Schemes

The government has a major role in creating and developing new tourism schemes to support tourists at a destination. Developing amenities at a destination, creating infrastructures to facilitate the tourists at a destination, identifying new destinations for tapping tourist and so on are the responsibilities of government authorities. Now, let us have a detailed discussion on some of the schemes launched by the Government of India for promoting tourism in the country.

PRASHAD

Pilgrimage tourism is very popular in India as India is home to many religions such as Hinduism, Buddhism, Jainism, Sikhism and Sufism. Religion and spirituality are very important motivations for travellers. Pulled by religious sentiments, this form of tourism contributes majorly to domestic tourism in India. Lakhs of domestic and international tourists visit these pilgrimage places to offer tribute to God.

Aiming to enrich the religious tourism experience of the pilgrims, a scheme was launched in 2014–2015 by MOT, Government of India. It refers to *Pilgrimage Rejuvenation and Spiritual Heritage Augmentation Drive (PRASHAD).* The objective of the scheme is to develop the pilgrimage and heritage destinations of India in a competitive and a sustainable way. In order, to enhance the religious experience of pilgrims visiting these destinations, the government initially launched the scheme with 12 sites, namely Ajmer, Amritsar, Amaravati, Dwarka, Gaya, Kedarnath, Kamakhya, Kanchipuram, Mathura, Puri, Varanasi and Velankanni. A total number of 28 projects have been sanctioned till 2019.

This scheme focuses on identifying deficiencies and providing amenities for developing religious tourism in the destinations. It calls for the holistic development of pilgrimage destinations by developing tourism infrastructure along with the beautification and facelift of the destinations by the government along with other stakeholders. It focuses on creating ATMs, foreign exchange counters, information/interpretation centres, first-aid centres, Wi-Fi hotspots, parking facilities, eco-friendly public transportation systems, street lights using green energy, drinking water, toilets, waiting rooms, cafeterias, telecom facilities, rain shelters, craft bazaars/haats/souvenir shops, green landscaping, creating walkways and so on in order to facilitate the tourists visiting the destination in every way. It also includes vocational training programmes that create tourism ecosystems.

The ultimate goal is to increase tourist footfalls in these places of faith, spirituality and religion that eventually gives a boost to the local economy by generating employment and economic development and also makes these places look more cleaner with a decrease in pollution as well as crime rates.

HRIDAY

The acronym of the scheme, HRIDAY, stands for *Heritage City Development and Augmentation Yojana. Launched in the year 2014 by the Ministry of Housing and Urban Affairs, the scheme was introduced in 12 cities of India to instil and preserve the heritage of these cities.* The objective of the scheme is to make the cities aesthetically appealing, accessible and more secure for the tourists. The other objective is also to develop the basic urban infrastructures such as roads, drainage, footpaths, electrical wiring, sanitation systems, streetlights, water supply, waste management, landscaping, tourist conveniences and security systems for these heritage sites. Installation of CCTV cameras, using modern ICT tools, building digital records of the heritage, developing roads and so on also comes within the purview of this scheme.

It also involves renovating and preserving the heritage sites and aims at creating a heritage asset inventory by classifying them as built, cultural, living and natural heritage sites. Developing a PPP model and skill development is also an important objective for the development of these heritage sites. *A lot of focus would also be on service delivery. Cleanliness and hygiene would also be the major considerations for the planners.* In collaboration with the state/local government bodies, private players, academic institutions and local community, the government will focus on the sustainable growth of these heritage cities. It is a central government's scheme where 100 per cent funding is provided by the central government.

The 12 cities include the following:

- Ajmer
- Amravati
- Badami
- Gaya
- Mathura
- Puri
- Varanasi
- Velankanni
- Warangal
- Dwarka
- Kanchipuram
- Amritsar

Swadesh Darshan Scheme

This flagship scheme was launched in 2014 by MOT, Government of India. It aims at developing thematic circuits across India to attract different segments of tourists. It primarily focuses on an integrated development approach of theme-based tourist circuits through providing engaging experiences to the tourists. *Seventy-seven projects have already been sanctioned to the 30 states and UTs till 2019.* The objective of this scheme is to provide quality infrastructure in the country for providing better facilities and a pleasant experience to the tourists. It is a 100 per cent centrally funded scheme. Various facilities such as public conveniences, Wi-Fi, cafeterias, last-mile connectivity, solid waste management, drinking water facility, tourist facilitation centres, haats and activities will be developed on these circuits.

The various thematic circuits identified under the scheme are as follows:

- North East India Circuit
- Buddhist Circuit
- Himalayan Circuit
- Coastal Circuit
- Tribal Circuit
- Eco Circuit
- Rural Circuit
- Krishna Circuit
- Desert Circuit
- Spiritual Circuit
- Ramayana Circuit
- Heritage Circuit
- Wildlife Circuit
- Gandhi Circuit
- Tirthankar Circuit
- Sufi Circuit

Visa on Arrival (VOA)

Being recognized as an instrument to the economic growth of the country in 2010, the Government of India introduced TVOA to increase the influx of foreign tourists in the country. It gave a huge boost to inbound tourism in India. The VOA may be applied from the respective countries by the citizens 3–5 days prior to their landing in India. The citizens may apply from nine selective international airports of India, that is, Delhi, Bengaluru, Chennai, Cochin, Goa, Hyderabad, Kolkata, Mumbai and Trivandrum. After applying for the visa online 3–5 days prior to visiting India, the citizen will receive ETA via email that can be printed and presented to the immigration officials on arrival to India on which they would be granted VOA.

The e-visa facility has been launched for citizens of 169 countries. The e-visa is presently given under four categories that include eTV, e-business visa, e-medical visa and e-medical attendant visa. In order to increase the tourism competitiveness of the country, the e-visa fee has also been reduced.

This kind of visa is valid for 30 days that cannot be extended, or even the visa cannot be converted. This visa is a single-entry visa. A citizen can apply maximum twice in a calendar year. It is for visiting India for sightseeing, recreation, meeting friends and relatives, attending a short-term Yoga programme, conferences/workshops, taking medical treatment for a short period or a casual business visit. However, certain terms and conditions apply for taking this kind of facility.

Adopt a Heritage: Apni Dharohar, Apni Pehchaan

This project aims at procuring the heritage sites/tourist sites with tourist amenities in order to make them tourist-friendly. The project is in collaboration with *MOT, the Ministry of Culture, state/UTs governments* and *ASI*.

Swachh Bharat Abhiyan

Sanitation has become a very important issue for our country. Taking a step forward in this direction, the Government of India launched the *largest cleanliness drive of India called as Swachh Bharat Abhiyan* in Hindi. Also referred to as Clean India campaign, this campaign was initiated in the year 2014 on 02 October on the eve of Gandhi Jayanti by the Prime Minister of India, Shri Narendra Modi. The campaign aimed at presenting India as a clean country to Mahatma Gandhi, the 'Father of the Nation' as a fitting tribute on his 150th anniversary in the year 2019. *It has two sub-missions: Swachh Bharat Mission (Grameen or Rural) which operates under the Ministry of Drinking Water and Sanitation and Swachh Bharat Mission (Urban) which operates under the Ministry of Urban and Housing Affairs.* It spans around 4,041 cities and towns.

It aims to sensitize the Indians to the idea of cleanliness and hygiene in their daily lives. It aims to bring them to consciousness to the idea of keeping their country clean not only for the betterment of themselves but also for the tourists visiting the country. The mission mainly aims to achieve two targets.

Clean India

The idea is to make the country clean by cleaning its streets, roads and infrastructures. It involves the active and engaging participation of all Indian citizens who aim at making Indian cities, towns and rural areas clean and litter-free.

Open Defecation Free

Usage of toilets by people residing in rural areas has always been a distant dream. One reason has been the resources which are not affordable for the construction of toilets and another has been the superstitious attitude of people for not constructing toilets inside the house. Eventually, this transformed into a habit for the villagers in defecating in open-free areas that have led to many health-related issues for the people besides the daily inconvenience caused to them. Thus, another very important objective of Swachh Bharat Abhiyan is to make India open defecation free by constructing *90 million house-owned and community-based toilets in rural areas* by 2nd October 2019 on Mahatma Gandhi's birth anniversary, the goal of which has been already achieved till now.

The volunteers involved in the campaign are called as *Swacchagrahis* or *ambassadors of cleanliness*. More than three million government employees and students are a part of this campaign besides the NGOs and the various private organizations that are contributing to this initiative as a part of their corporate social responsibility. Many educational institutes in the tourism sector like all centres of IITTM and Institute of Hotel Management (IHM) and have been instrumental in creating awareness among the various domains of the public to create an overall sensitivity. The programme is initiated at three levels that include visiting the schools and sensitizing them to the idea of hygiene, visiting tourist sites and creating awareness among the domestic tourists and organizing tourism stakeholders' meets who are involved in the delivery of services. The campaign has been a successful attempt by the government to sensitize the people of India about the importance of sanitation and hygiene.

Incredible !ndia

India's competitiveness lies in its diversity. With an eclectic fusion of modernity with the traditions, different cultures, religions and topography, India has an untapped tourism potential that charms the entire world. The *mysticism and magic of India* bring tourists to India. With the objective of luring international tourism markets, the *Incredible!ndia campaign* was launched in the year 2002 by MOT, Government of India, at a global level to capture the global appeal. The major focus of this international marketing campaign since then has been to increase the footfalls of foreigners in the country by creating and projecting tourism products that cater to the preferences of different international travellers while also focusing on the servicer delivery process of tourism services in order to create a pleasant experience for the tourists in the country. The services of *Ogilvy and Mather India*, an advertisement agency, were hired to create an integrated communication strategy that would promote India as a preferred tourism destination for foreigners for all the reasons around the year.

The various tourism products showcased throughout the campaign have been the Spirituality, Yoga, Ayurveda, Himalayas, festivals, monuments, medical tourism, business tourism besides the various niche tourism products such as rural tourism, golf tourism, tea tourism and many more. Many sub-campaigns have been a part of this umbrella brand that has continuously evolved over the years and has been successful enough in chasing the eyeballs of the tourists to visit India and be surprised by its innumerable facets that create a 'wow effect' and surprise the tourist creating incredible moments for the tourists capturing the real essence of this campaign. *The exclamation mark, '!', in Incredible!ndia campaign itself connotes that India is a land of surprises that are waiting for the tourists to be discovered.* One important objective of this campaign since 2009 has also been of *promoting domestic tourism*. As another part of the campaign, in 2008, MOT also launched the 'Atithi Devo Bhava' campaign that connotes that 'the guest is God'. The campaign focused on sensitizing the local population and the service providers involved in the delivery of services and their behaviour towards foreign tourists. However, the main focus of the Incredible !ndia campaign is to promote spirituality among both the domestic and international tourists. Few milestones that have been achieved under this campaign are as follows:

- A 24 × 7 free multilingual tourist information helpline was launched in 12 languages under this campaign to support the foreign tourists visiting India.
- Another Incredible!ndia 2.0 campaign was unveiled in the 2017–2018.
- In 2018, Incredible!ndia campaign also launched its Incredible!ndia mobile app to assist the travellers to plan their holiday and assist them in each phase of their journey to India.
- In 2019, MOT also changed the website by launching it in Hindi language and many other major international languages.

Further initiatives taken by the Government of India in 2019 to promote tourism are as follows:

- *Tax Refund for International Tourists (TRT)* scheme has been launched to encourage tourists to do more shopping and spend more money within the country, thereby increasing the foreign exchange within the country.
- It is proposed to develop *17 iconic tourist sites* into world-class destinations in India so as to encourage tourism.
- FDI up to 100 per cent has been allowed in the tourism and hospitality sector.
- A five-year tax holiday has been offered for two-, three- and four-star category hotels located around UNESCO World Heritage Sites (except Delhi and Mumbai).
- The government has also reduced GST on hotel rooms to increase the footfalls of tourists in the country.
- To support the new investors who have applied for hotel projects, a web-based public service delivery system (PSDS) has been launched that can assist the applicants in tracking their applications online on a real-time basis.

SUMMARY

It is important for the learners to appreciate the role of the government in framing the tourism policies and delivering a pleasant experience to the tourists. Without the necessary support and intervention of the government, it may not be possible for the private players to coordinate and synchronize their efforts in the delivery of seamless experiences for the tourists. The timely interventions and support extended by the government authorities plays a major role in developing new destinations, maintaining the old ones, creating new infrastructure, training the human resources and so on to support the tourists visiting a destination.

ACTIVITIES

Activity 1

Visit the official website of Incredible!ndia campaign. Discuss, whether it is tourist-friendly or not. Suggest if any further improvisations are required. You may also visit the website of Australia tourism board for a better comparison.

Activity 2

Visit the official website of MPTDC. Identify the various tourism products offered by the state in India. Also discuss the various tourism markets that they are keen to capture. Identify their tourism tag line and now evaluate the various marketing strategies adopted by them to attract tourists after visiting their website.

Case Studies

D.1. ARDHA KUMBH MELA 2019

The Ardha Kumbh Mela of 2019 organized in Triveni Sangam in Allahabad, Uttar Pradesh, India from 15 January to 4 March 2019 was the most successful event as compared to Maha Kumbh Mela celebrated in 2013. This event is considered as an important topic to study and discuss because of the following factors:

- This has been the most-well-planned, organized and well-executed largest religious conglomeration of people getting together to date.
- The number of visitors who attended this event was nearly 24.01 crore, including 10.30 lakh foreign tourists. This was a huge increase as compared to the Maha Kumbh Mela celebrated in 2013 with 7.86 crore visitors, out of which the number of foreign tourists was 3.50 lakh.
- The case study is an excellent example of a well-managed and well-organized successful event through proper visitor management.
- The Prayagraj Mela Authority (that organized the event) along with the UP government and the central government's initiative and dedicated hard work was remarkable.
- This year's Mela was much bigger and better. The area for the event was doubled.
- The Kumbh Mela was eco-friendly this time and encouraged the use of jute bags and terracotta utensils among the visitors during their stay.
- The government allocated approximately ₹4,200 crores for the Ardha Kumbh Mela 2019 which was more than thrice the budget of the Maha Kumbh in 2013.
- The Railways commissioned 41 projects at a cost of ₹700 crores for the Kumbh Mela.
- The crowd management was much more sophisticated and digital, which helped in the smooth functioning of the event.
- Prayagraj Kumbh was set up with modern amenities which helped the crowd to have a wonderful experience.
- The government put a lot of efforts in ensuring the security of the visitors. This resulted in a very controlled crowd movement throughout the event as compared to the last mela.
- The city infrastructure went under a major overhaul which in return helped in traffic control and smooth travels.

Kumbh Mela is one of the greatest peaceful gatherings and is recognized as the 'world's largest congregation of religious pilgrims.' It has been listed on the UNESCO's Representative List of Intangible Cultural Heritage of Humanity.

It is one of the oldest festivals which is celebrated four times every 12 years in the world. The first written description of this mela can be found in records of Chinese traveller Xuanzang (Hiuen Tsang) who visited India during the rule of King Harshavardhana. Those records are said to be around 2,000 years old!

Kumbh is a Sanskrit word for a *kalasha* (pitcher), and mela means a gathering or an event. The journey of this mega event began in Hindu mythology when Lord Vishnu dropped the drink of immortality (*amruta*) at four locations while carrying it in a *kumbha* (pot). These places are now recognized as special sites for celebrating Kumbh Mela, and the mela site keeps rotating among one of the four places on four sacred rivers as listed below:

- Haridwar on the Ganges in Uttarakhand
- Ujjain on the Shipra in Madhya Pradesh
- Nasik on the Godavari in Maharashtra
- Prayagraj at the convergence of the Ganges, the Yamuna and the Saraswati in Uttar Pradesh

Types of Kumbh Melas

- **Maha Kumbh Mela:** It is held only in Prayagraj. It is celebrated in every 144 years or after 12 Purna (Complete) Kumbh Melas.
- **Purna Kumbh Mela:** This comes after every 12 years. It is mainly held at 4 Kumbh Mela sites in India, that is, Prayagraj, Haridwar, Nashik and Ujjain. It rotates every 12 years at these 4 sacred places.
- **Ardha Kumbh Mela:** It means half Kumbh Mela which is held every 6 years in India only at two places, that is, Haridwar and Prayagraj.
- **Kumbh Mela:** It is held at four different places after every 4 years in 12 years and is organized by the state governments. Millions of people participate with spiritual enthusiasm and positive expectations.
- **Magh Kumbh Mela:** It is also known as mini Kumbh Mela which is held annually and only at Prayagraj. It is organized in the month of *Magh* according to the Hindu calendar.

The ceremony at each place is based on a definite set of astrological positions of the Sun, the Moon and Jupiter. The celebrations occur at the precise moment when these positions are fully engaged, as it is considered to be the most divine time in Hinduism.

A Brief Walkthrough

The mela attracts tens of millions of pilgrims over nearly 48 days to bathe at the sacred convergence of the Ganga, the Yamuna and the Sarasvati. Primarily, this gathering includes ascetics, saints, sadhus, *sadhvis*, *kalpvasis* and pilgrims from all paths of life.

The first holy bath at Kumbh Mela is led by a saint, which is famously known as the 'Shahi Snan of Kumbh' which starts at 3 AM. After the early morning custom, other devotees are allowed to enter the water for their holy bath. Hindus believe that bathing in the sacred water during the Kumbh Mela makes them eternally blessed by the divine. Also, bathing in the river cleanses away the sins, and you become one step closer to salvation.

During the Kumbh Mela, several ceremonies take place; the traditional parade of *akharas* called 'Peshwai' on elephant backs, horses and chariots, the gleaming swords and rituals of *naga* sadhus during 'Shahi Snaan', and many other cultural activities that captivate millions of pilgrims to attend the Kumbh Mela.

Prayagraj Ardha Kumbh Mela 2019

The Prayagraj Kumbh Mela is the oldest and the most famous among the rest of the melas. As it is the only mela organized at the convergence of three holy rivers—the Ganges, Yamuna and Saraswati. Thus, adding much to its ethical importance.

This particular event is considered as the most successful event because of the government's hard work in making this festival an unforgettable experience for the visitors.

The mela certainly was a grand show to enjoy with the beautiful and joyous evening '*aartis*' to the sight of bare body *naga* sadhus covered with ash to take the holy bath. Apart from dips and huge gatherings, the Ardha Kumbh Mela of 2019 offered a lot of activities and events to savour such as waterways, tourist walks, Kalagram, cultural events, laser light show, thematic gates, 360-degree virtual reality experience at Kumbh 2019 and Peshwai Yatra (A royal entry or a reception of an important guest) and so on.

Management and Organization of Ardha Kumbh Mela 2019

- The government of Uttar Pradesh made no compromise in making this historical event a huge success. Below are some of the grand initiatives taken by the government and Kumbh Mela authorities to ensure a safe and smooth experience for the devotees.
- Modern sustainable construction work was done. Construction of flyovers, railway under bridges, road widening in the city and beautification of major junctions are

few highlights of the huge construction and upgradation assignments
which were undertaken by the government to make Prayagraj fit for the
mega Kumbh event.

- All departments of the government
  carried out development works.
  These included important initiatives
  of upgradation of railway stations
  and the construction of the new
  Prayagraj Civil Airport to provide to
  the incoming pilgrims and visitors
  from all over the world. Further, the
  National Highways Authority of
  India took the initiative of repairing
  and upgrading major highways connecting Prayagraj to Pratapgarh, Raebareli and
  Varanasi.
- Many roads were constructed and stretched by the Public Works Department.
  Parking spots were built at short distances from the site.

Preparation and Wellness Management

- **Disease surveillance:** Inspection units were placed at Kumbh Mela to keep an eye
  on the pattern of diseases during the festival. Population density of the mela town
  would make it highly exposed to the spread of diseases. The government stationed
  'epidemic intelligence officers' who coordinated with the medical units to keep
  Kumbh safe from infections and diseases.
- **Disaster management:** Disaster Management Control Cell was set up for assisting
  and surveying the mela premises. To fight the diseases, fire hazard, flood, stampede
  and so on, a dedicated team was formed, and procedures were designed accordingly.
- **Waste management and cleanliness:** More than 115,000 toilets were placed, and
  more than 1,500 Swacchagrahis joined in the monitoring of the operations and
  usage of dustbins and toilet. To create awareness for the security of the biodiversity
  of the River Ganga, various roadshows, workshops and so on were organized and
  banners, hoardings and so on were distributed to advertise information regarding
  the importance of sanitation.

Crowd Control

- Over 1,000 CCTV cameras were used to monitor various movements across the
  mela which was spread over 3,200 hectares.
- More than 30,000 police and paramilitary personnel were deployed to deal with traffic and security ensuring the safety of every visitor.

- AI was used for a safe and smooth experience.
- Railways made use of the technology, including AI, in a huge way to tackle the enormous hustle of passengers to the holy city during the Kumbh Mela. IBM's Intelligent Video Analytics was used for crowd control at the stations and their connecting areas.
- Also, a new mobile app called 'Kumbh Rail Seva' was launched to broadcast important information to train users and others relating to Kumbh Mela. This made the Kumbh Mela 2019 as a digital Kumbh.
- Digital lost-and-found centres were set up. All centres were interconnected with a central server. The information of lost and found pilgrims was broadcasted with photos on LED screens at each centre.

Transportation

- 800 special trains: To help pilgrims who arrived in large numbers during Ardha Kumbh Mela, the railways initiated 800 special trains with extra coaches from multiple stations of Allahabad district. These trains were in addition to the regular trains run by the North Central Railway.
- Eighteen pontoon bridges were constructed using 1,537 pontoons.
- The Inland Waterways Authority of India worked hard towards aiding safe passenger journey for Kumbh Mela. The set-up had four floating terminals and deployed two vessels for pilgrim's journey.
- More than 524 shuttle buses and many CNG auto-rickshaws were used for transporting pilgrims. About 54 holding areas were developed which were used for waiting and resting of visitors at different areas in the city.

Public Accommodation

- Premium tents for tourists were built, and they were operated on a PPP basis.
- Luxury tents were set up in Prayagraj for VIP guests and for those who wanted to enjoy a luxurious stay. The facilities provided in those tents were high tech and very modern.
- Public camps and cottages with a capacity of 20,000 beds were allocated.
- Ganga Pandal, with a limit to accommodate 10,000 people, was used for organizing cultural, spiritual and official programmes with state-of-the-art facilities.
- Four convention halls, with functional and contemporary decor for each zone was built.
- A *Pravachan Pandal* with a capacity for 2,000 persons was built in the mela area for spiritual and religious programmes.

PRAYAGRAJ ARDH KUMBH MELA 2019 SET UP

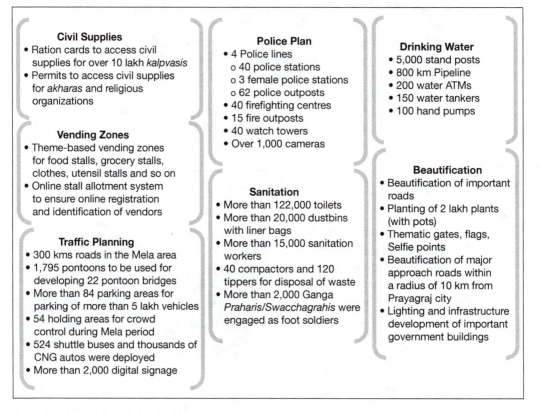

Civil Supplies
- Ration cards to access civil supplies for over 10 lakh *kalpvasis*
- Permits to access civil supplies for *akharas* and religious organizations

Vending Zones
- Theme-based vending zones for food stalls, grocery stalls, clothes, utensil stalls and so on
- Online stall allotment system to ensure online registration and identification of vendors

Traffic Planning
- 300 kms roads in the Mela area
- 1,795 pontoons to be used for developing 22 pontoon bridges
- More than 84 parking areas for parking of more than 5 lakh vehicles
- 54 holding areas for crowd control during Mela period
- 524 shuttle buses and thousands of CNG autos were deployed
- More than 2,000 digital signage

Police Plan
- 4 Police lines
  - o 40 police stations
  - o 3 female police stations
  - o 62 police outposts
- 40 firefighting centres
- 15 fire outposts
- 40 watch towers
- Over 1,000 cameras

Sanitation
- More than 122,000 toilets
- More than 20,000 dustbins with liner bags
- More than 15,000 sanitation workers
- 40 compactors and 120 tippers for disposal of waste
- More than 2,000 Ganga *Praharis/Swacchagrahis* were engaged as foot soldiers

Drinking Water
- 5,000 stand posts
- 800 km Pipeline
- 200 water ATMs
- 150 water tankers
- 100 hand pumps

Beautification
- Beautification of important roads
- Planting of 2 lakh plants (with pots)
- Thematic gates, flags, Selfie points
- Beautification of major approach roads within a radius of 10 km from Prayagraj city
- Lighting and infrastructure development of important government buildings

Source: http://kumbh.gov.in/en/making-of-kumbh (accessed on 31 July 2020).

Conclusion

Kumbh Mela is more than an event as its history, culture and various characteristics make every Kumbh Mela different from one another. Not only it is a grand gathering of the people from every corner in this world, but it is also a platform for MOT to promote its culture, history and tourism of India. The Ardha Kumbh Mela 2019 was a grand success. The government and organizing committees took a lot of initiatives to make this event memorable for everyone.

Learning Outcomes

- Events are a significant marketing tool for the tourism industry. Large-scale events and their popularity attract diverse communities from all corners of the world.
- Many countries have capitalized on their local event by not only promoting them within their own country but also internationally. If managed well, these local

events that showcase the local culture, history and traditions of a place have huge potential in becoming a mega-event globally.

- Governments are the most vital one as they are responsible for promoting and ensuring the functioning of an event in a proper way. They play a vital role in making such events a huge success.
- A lot of preparation at the grassroots level goes in to make an event a success story. It includes creating adequate infrastructure, superstructure, amenities, accommodation and making the destination accessible to attract the maximum people to a destination.
- For organizing the event, not only the government authorities should be at the forefront, but it also equally requires active engagement and cooperation of various other important stakeholders such as the private sector and local communities.

Points for Discussion

- Kumbh Mela is the biggest festive event not only for Indians but also for devotees all over the world. Discuss.
- Such large-scale events are very critical to organize as well as manage. How do you propose to improve the current standards of management and security by the government?
- Kumbh Mela has a mega impact on the people who attend. Debate on the positives and the negatives.

Bibliography

https://timesofindia.indiatimes.com/life-style/events/kumbh-mela-2019-meaning-symbolism-and-significance-of-the-religious-pilgrimage/articleshow/67525171.cms (accessed on 31 July 2020).
http://www.ijbmi.org/papers/Vol(8)4/Series-2/F0804024247.pdf (accessed on 31 July 2020).
https://www.djjs.org/kumbh (accessed on 31 July 2020).
https://www.haridwarrishikeshtourism.com/haridwar-kumbh-mela.html (accessed on 31 July 2020).
http://kumbh.gov.in/en/making-of-kumbh (accessed on 31 July 2020).
https://www.nativeplanet.com/travel-guide/ardh-kumbh-mela-2019-top-attractions-of-ardh-kumbh-mela-2019/articlecontent-pf26642-005434.html (accessed on 31 July 2020).
https://economictimes.indiatimes.com/industry/transportation/railways/railways-to-run-800-special-trains-for-kumbh-mela-pilgrims/articleshow/67112634.cms (accessed on 31 July 2020).
https://www.hindustantimes.com/india-news/a-record-over-24-crore-people-visited-kumbh-2019-more-than-total-tourists-in-up-in-2014-17/story-9uncpmhBPnBj11ClnTiYQP.html (accessed on 31 July 2020).

Picture Source

www.kumbhmela.com

D.2. THE REVIVAL OF KERALA TOURISM

Introduction

Kerala is a beautiful coastal state in India, which is listed as one of the 10 paradises in the world by *National Geographic Traveller*. It is famously known as 'God's Own Country'—a tagline initiated by Kerala Tourism. Kerala is a proud owner of beautiful palm trees, mountain ranges, backwaters, canals, spice plantations, wildlife, local culture, traditions and so much more! The top-most destinations in Kerala include Periyar, Bekal, Munroe Island, Illikkal Kallu and Munnar. Apart from being a beautiful state filled with local culture and traditions, the Department of Tourism, Government of Kerala, has introduced a few specialities to attract the tourists. Some of them include Ayurvedic treatments and massage centres, Kettuvallam (houseboat cruise), beach cottages and homestay facilities, elephant safaris and more. It is also famous for their approach towards ecotourism as it became the destination with Thenmala being the first eco-friendly destination in India. Tourists from all over the world travel to this destination to indulge in its local beauty and coastal charm. The tourism industry accounts for about 10–12 per cent GDP of Kerala's economy, and there are 15 lakh jobs created due to the tourism industry.

However, something disastrous was written in the fate of this destination. In 2018 and 2019, Kerala suffered through devastating floods which killed more than 400 people, devastated lakhs of people and hundreds of animals. Besides the loss of life and damage to the local resources, the complete tourism infrastructure was shattered such as airports, roads, railway lines, railway stations, major hotels, resorts, transit stations and transportation. As the economy of Kerala was thriving on inbound tourism as well as domestic tourism, due to the natural calamity, Kerala's economy was hit hard. The tourism industry faced a big blow when approximately ₹1,500 crore worth of loss happened due to the damage caused by flood and cancellation of bookings. Up to 90 per cent of the travel bookings were cancelled by the tourists after the flood happened. MICE bookings were cancelled due to the floods in August, which cost an estimated loss of ₹500 crore to the business sector.

This disaster put a lot of pressure on the tourism of Kerala, and the government had to take heavy measures to ensure the economic and social stability of this place. Aggressive marketing strategies and innovation were much needed for the revival plan of Kerala tourism to beat the highly competitive tourism marketplace.

Here's how Kerala government and tourism authorities managed to help Kerala stand back on its feet:

Re-establishing Connectivity

- **Roads:** After a few months, despite facing a huge amount of monetary loss, the Government of Kerala started funding for reconstruction and repairing of roads. Roads being a major path of travel for tourists, the revival of roadways was a priority to Kerala government. Majority of roads in all sectors of Kerala was done and thus, ready to receive the tourists again. Domestic tourists are a big fan of road trips and Kerala being their number one destination, the revival of roads was an important step taken by the government.

- **Rail lines:** Transportation is a major feature of the tourism sector and Kerala tourism understands that. Along with repairing of roads, the government also put a lot of efforts into putting railways back on track by repairing and remaking. After the inspection team gave a green light, the transit service was started again which helped the tourists to reach the destination without hassle.
- **Airports:** Repairing the condition of airports and starting the airlines again allowed people to travel internationally, which worked great for Kerala tourism.

  The addition of the fourth international airport in Kannur district made Kerala the only state in India with four international airports. This helped Kerala by strengthening the tourism sector and it also created a boost for business travellers too.
- **Building infrastructure:** To get back on track, the government dedicatedly put efforts in repairing the conditions of the massive infrastructure such as hotels, resorts and wellness centres so that the tourists can again have a pleasant stay in this 'God's Own Country'.

Launching Innovative Tourism Products and New Attractions in 2018–2019

- The Department of Tourism and Government of Kerala started concentrating on the two most popular and successful tourism products—adventure tourism and monsoon tourism. Efforts were also taken to promote Kerala as a MICE destination. For this, the tourism department partnered with Indian Conventions Promotion Bureau (ICPB) to attract business tourists even during off-peak season.
- A new attraction was launched known as Jatayu Earth's Centre (Hindu mythological bird) at Eco-park in Kerala, which also has a state-of-the-art ropeway and a virtual reality museum too.
- Another attraction known as Malabar river cruise project was also launched which created a new waterway by linking seven rivers.
- One of the most hit attractions among tourists was Neelakurinji (a beautiful blue flower which blooms once every 12 years). Luckily, this flower bloomed in 2019 when Kerala needed most of the tourists.
- Hop on the bus tours were also introduced by the tourism department.

Attractive Offers by Tourism Service Providers

Resorts, hotels, airlines and various other tourism and hospitality industries introduced amazing packages, discounts and offers for the tourists.

Image Makeover

After the devastating downfall of Kerala tourism, the tourism department started an aggressive marketing campaign approach to attract domestic and international tourists. Initiatives taken are as follows.

Image Makeover by Introducing New Marketing Campaigns

- Kerala's revival was promoted by advertising the marketing campaigns over various trade bodies and tour operators. Also, tour operators and other travel organizers started advertising about Kerala to the general public as being a safe place to travel again. The motive was to create maximum reach and invite domestic as well as international tourists back to God's own country.
- Many companies took an initiative to create advertisements and campaigns of their own to promote Kerala's revival. For example, the hashtag #Keralaisopen campaign initiated by a luggage company known as Samsonite was a huge hit. The locals such as auto-rickshaw drivers, fish vendors, homemakers and so on shown promoting this campaign by holding a sign saying, 'We Are Open'.
- Creative campaign videos were marketed by streaming them on various flights and airports. These videos were broadcasted on overseas flights before the start of a movie to create awareness about the revival status.
- Social media marketing became a huge success as the advertising campaigns got about 2.5 million views.
- As public figures and celebrities have a huge impact on the psyche of people, the tourism department of Kerala used celebrity marketing in order to promote the revival and attract more tourists in Kerala. For example, Indian cricket player, Virat Kohli, wrote a letter saying there is no other beauty than God's own country, and its energy is intoxicating.

Image Makeover by Participating in and Organizing Events

- The tourism of Kerala and government authorities took the maximum initiative by participating in trade fairs and tourism meets as the revival plan was set in action. For example, Kerala had participated in the Asia Tourism Fair to attract more Asian travellers and to promote the revival of Kerala. This alerted the market that Kerala is already back on its feet.
- Kerala tourism held many press conferences and marketing fairs in many destinations to inform people about Kerala being a safe place to visit again. They also took initiative in organizing a few events to accelerate the revival plans.
- Some of the events organized by tourism authorities and the Kerala government are as follows:

o India's largest contemporary art expo known as 'Kochi-Muziris Biennale' 2018–2019
o Kerala Travel Mart in 2018
o Champions Boat League in 2018
o Malabar Carnival 2019–2020
o Beach Carnival 2019
o International Arts and Crafts Festival 2019

Image Makeover through Fam Trips

- The government also took an initiative to invite the various tour operators from other parts of the country to visit Kerala and see the revival for themselves. These familiarization trips motivated the tour operators and travel agents to spread the positive word of mouth about Kerala once again.
- The government also organized familiarization trips for many travel bloggers and various media owners to experience the post-flood status of Kerala. With the help of blogger's and media's coverage, Kerala was able to promote their stability even better.

Aftermath

As a result of consistent efforts initiated by the Government of Kerala and the tourism authorities, Kerala witnessed the highest footfall of domestic and international tourists for the first time in the last 24 years. The foreign exchange earnings (FEE) in tourism sector received ₹10,271.06 crores, crossing ₹10,000 crores for the very first time.

In the tourism sector, Ernakulam ranked number one in earning total revenue of ₹12,816.54 crores. Although the harsh rains and floods of 2018 and 2019 caused great damage to Kerala tourism, it successfully managed to attract around 1.96 crore tourists, both domestic and foreigners, in 2019. It is said that the recent growth rate is highest since 1996. Tourism centres conveyed that majority of budget hotels and star hotels were booked in advance, including the flight tickets as well. Kerala tourism also received three Pacific Asia Travel Association (PATA) gold awards in 2019.

Conclusion

Natural calamities can cause a huge negative impact on the tourism of a destination. Kerala fell prey to such a catastrophic situation which caused an immense drop in tourism and caused damage to the local resources. The Government of Kerala and the tourism department worked extremely hard in reviving the 'God's Own Country' by creating impressive campaigns, introducing new marketing strategies and repairing the damage caused by flood in a short period. Kerala is now thriving with tourists, and its tourism is slowly going back to its former glory.

Learning Outcomes

- Natural calamities can put a complete stop to the tourism of a destination by causing discontinuation of transportation, accommodation, damage to the tourism products (natural and man-made), the spread of fear amongst tourists and thus leading to the cancellation of tourist bookings.
- Anything that is broken can be fixed. Reviving the tourism of a destination requires collective and coordinated efforts not only of the tourism government authorities but also the private tourism service providers and also of the locals' community.
- Social promotion using bloggers, media, celebrities and so on is a smart move to prove a campaign as they have a high number of followers which means a much wider reach.
- Transportation is the most important part of tourism. It is important to make sure that transit services are up and running smoothly to ensure a safe and enjoyable travel experience for the tourists.
- Trade fairs, tourism events, promotional meets and so on are the best source for advertising the tourism marketing campaign.

Points for Discussion

- Apart from the above-mentioned initiatives, what other methods can be used to promote the revival of Kerala tourism?
- In today's era, social media is the dominant platform for promoting campaigns. Comment.

Bibliography

https://www.keralatourism.org/ (accessed on 31 July 2020).

https://economictimes.indiatimes.com/industry/services/travel/kerala-tourism-bags-three-pata-gold-awards/articleshow/71219610.cms?from=mdr (accessed on 31 July 2020).

https://timesofindia.indiatimes.com/travel/destinations/kerala-is-back-on-track-after-floods-open-to-tourists-with-more-developments/as65935752.cms (accessed on 31 July 2020).

https://www.thehindu.com/news/national/kerala/malabar-river-cruise-project-to-take-local-people-on-board/article24243433.ece (accessed on 31 July 2020).

www.newindianexpress.com (accessed on 31 July 2020).

SECTION

CHALLENGES AND OPPORTUNITIES IN TOURISM INDUSTRY

This section has been introduced to impart knowledge to the students about the challenges faced by the tourists and the tourism industry along with the promising opportunities and avenues this industry holds for the future. The section begins with a discussion on emergencies faced by the tourists along with the possible ways to deal with the situations. This is followed by an elaborate discussion on threats and obstacles faced by the tourists/tourism industry today. As tourism is always evolving, there are always new trends in tourism markets that are flourishing. Therefore, it is important for the budding tourism professionals to be aware of the contemporary trends and at the same time be prepared to assume roles in this sector. Thus, the next chapters would focus on the contemporary trends that are evolving in the tourism industry along with a discussion on the career options that students may opt for after the completion of the courses in tourism. This section will both introduce the learners to new trends in tourism and at the same time prepare the youngsters to deal with the nuances of the trade. Overtourism is a matter of grave concern for many countries of the world, which has been discussed in a separate chapter (Chapter 33) followed by a discussion on how to practise sustainable and green travel by being a responsible tourist, which has also been discussed in this section.

At the end of each chapter, there are activities related to each chapter, which students may practise in their classrooms. Also, every chapter has interesting information for students to know, organized in the boxes that the students are advised to read to increase their knowledge of tourism. After the completion of chapters in the section, there are certain case studies related to the section for the students to read, comprehend and analyse, followed by questions to be answered.

After going through the section, the students would know the following:

- What are the possible emergencies in tourism, and how one should deal with them?
- What are the obstacles and threats to the tourism industry?
- What are the contemporary trends in tourism?
- What are the various career opportunities in the tourism industry?
- What is overtourism?
- How can a tourist behave as a responsible tourist?

Hope you continue to be on the journey of knowledge and enlightenment and contribute your talent and energies for the good of the tourism industry.

Wishing you a happy journey of learning, dear readers!

29

Handling Emergencies

LEARNING OBJECTIVES

The given chapter shall clarify the following:

- What are the kinds of emergencies that a tourist might face on a tour?
- What are the things that a tourist must take care of while dealing with emergencies?

BETTER BE SAFE THAN SORRY: TRAVEL SAFETY TIPS

- Be well-informed. Do your research well. Always be aware of the latest news about the destinations that you are visiting. Keep all your travel alerts active.
- Know the important contact numbers to reach out to in case of an emergency. Especially while travelling to a foreign country, learn about the important emergency numbers such as your country's embassy contact number, ambulance number and so on.
- Know, the basic emergency phrases in the local language of the place being visited.
- Be proactive. Seek the help of local service travel providers in case of an emergency.
- Always get a travel insurance done while travelling with a 24/7 assistance that may be handy in case of hospitalization, cancelled reservations, loss of luggage or any other mishap.
- Always keep the soft copies of all travel documents in your email.
- Share your itinerary with a trusted family member or a friend.

INTRODUCTION

Travelling may not always be a cakewalk. Sometimes, it can be a nerve-wracking experience for the tourist too. Every tourist wishes that he/she has an exciting experience on the tour. However, this may not always happen. Along with the good experiences come the stressful situations that a tourist may have to face. *Travelling may be a roller-coaster ride at times.* A tourist may have to encounter unforeseen circumstances or an emergency on a tour that he/she may not even have anticipated and thus may not be prepared to handle.

Emergencies may be defined as those situations that are uncalled for. These are undesirable situations that may happen to the tourists on a tour. Sometimes, not always, these circumstances may have an element of risk and danger involved with them.

However, with more experience of travelling, a traveller may learn to anticipate situations with the passage of time. He/she may be able to assess the possible risks and ways of dealing with them. However, he/she can never be 100 per cent sure of the unexpected things that he/she might have to deal with in an unpredictable future. 'Expect the unexpected' is the only mantra that he/she should think of while travelling.

TYPES OF EMERGENCIES

The emergencies faced by the tourist may be classified on the following bases.

Emergencies Created by a Tourist/Accidental Situations

These kinds of situations may arise from the tourist due to his/her negligence or sometimes due to his/her non-conformist/deliberate approach towards things. Some situations that may happen to him/her are as follows:

- Loss of passport due to negligence
- Loss of personal belongings and valuables at a destination
- Leaving things at a hotel, restaurant, sightseeing attraction and so on by mistake
- Shoplifting by a tourist and being caught red-handed
- Accident of a tourist due to his/her non-adherence to the safety procedures (e.g., a tourist may fall from the boat accidentally being on the verge of drowning if he/she refuses to follow the instructions of a tour guide of wearing the life jacket)
- Sudden ill health of a tourist such as an allergy, diarrhoea, stomach pain and vomiting
- Injury or accident of a tourist like an ankle twist
- Road accident of a tourist
- Heart attack of a tourist on a tour

- Death of a tourist on a trip
- Family issue of a tourist due to which he/she has to return home in an emergency

Emergencies Created by Nature

These are the actors that are beyond the control of a tourist. A tourist may face any of these situations when he/she visits a destination. These may be as follows:

- Natural calamities such as floods, earthquakes, tsunami and volcano at the destination
- Adverse weather conditions such as rain, heat and strong winds
- The outbreak of a pandemic such as Coronavirus (COVID-19) or an epidemic such as SARS, Swine flu, Ebola and so on

Emergencies Created at a Destination

Many emergencies may arise at a destination. These may be as follows:

- Outbreak of communal riots at the destination
- Terrorist attacks or blasts
- Political instability at a destination
- Sudden change of Government policy (e.g., demonetization in India that happened in November 2016)
- Theft with a tourist
- Molestation with a tourist

Emergencies Created by Various Service Providers

Some conditions may be created by the service providers that may make the tourist suffer. As the tourism industry is dependent on all the service providers, any service not offered appropriately or on time may create a bad experience for the tourist. Some of the emergencies created by the service providers may be as follows:

- Postponement or cancellation of flights/trains due to bad weather/technical fault by airlines/railways
- Overbooking by an airline
- Closure of an attraction such as a monument, museum and amusement park on account of a mishap/strike/procession

- Loss of luggage/damaged luggage by an airline carrier
- Embassy/consulate mistakes in visa issuance, for example, wrong name or passport number, visa validity and so on of the tourist mentioned on the visa
- Airlines issuing the ticket with the wrong spelling of the tourist
- Sudden breakdown of a coach
- Increase in taxes by airlines, hotels and so on
- An outbreak of a fire in a hotel
- Water scarcity in a hotel
- Food poisoning due to serving of contaminated food in a restaurant

DEALING WITH EMERGENCIES

Let us have a detailed discussion on the things that a tourist must take care of while dealing with emergencies on a tour.

Maintaining Cool

A tourist might face different challenges on the tour. Two things are critical while handling such cases. *First, the tourist must keep his/her cool and not panic when things go wrong. Second, a tourist must calmly evaluate all possible alternatives and think logically which solution can be the most suitable for handling a particular situation.* He/she must determine all possible pros and cons of the situation and then make a calculative move in the light of circumstances.

Whatever be the situation, a tourist must be guided by the principle that he/she has to be always ready to take things as they come on the tour. Under no circumstances, he/she should succumb or lose his/her heart. He/she must chivalrously face an odd situation that might come his/her way with his/her willpower and undeterred faith during the tour. He/she must be gracefully able to get hold of the situation he/she is likely to handle instead of panicking around. He/she must stay calm and poised.

Informing the Tour Operator

While dealing with unforeseen situations, a tourist must apprise his/her company about the situation and wait for the necessary instructions, in case he/she has made his/her arrangement through a travel company. This helps him/her to get guidance from them, and also, the company may be able to make some special arrangements for the tourist that may facilitate him/her in handling the whole situation in a much better way. However, this mechanism is only workable for a tourist if he/she has taken a package tour from a tour operator. For example, a tourist may have booked his/her package tour of Dubai through a travel company in which he/she has a reservation on a cruise on the same day when he/she reaches the destination. However, it may happen that the airlines on which he/she is flying may be delayed due to a technical glitch due to which he/she may reach his/her destination late and hence may miss his/her cruise. Thus, in such a case, the traveller must inform the tour operator about the complete scenario on time so that the company may make an alternative reservation or reschedule his/her reservation on the cruise, if possible.

Taking Decisions

A tourist must have the capability of making spontaneous decisions that may be the demand of the situation. His/her timely decisions and presence of mind can sometimes save his/her own life and other lives too. Weighing the pros and cons of each possible alternative is essential for arriving at the right decision by the tourist. Therefore, *spontaneity* and *timeliness* are two necessary qualities that a tourist must possess while handling emergencies. It might so happen that a tourist is about to visit another destination as per his/her planned itinerary, and he suddenly gets his ankle twisted in the city. Thus, he/she may have to take the decision that whether he/she wishes to continue his/her journey and proceed for the destination or needs to drop the destination and go back home.

Being Proactive

For taking better decisions, a tourist must be able to anticipate challenges. He/she must be proactive in his/her approach. He/she must have a nose for sensing the issues, and he/she must also find possible solutions in his/her mind in case, a particular situation happens. He/she must be able to anticipate situations and have workable solutions in his/her mind.

Preparation to Deal with a Situation

As they say that 'prevention is better than cure,' preparing for any kind of crisis is a must for the tourist to deal with them in a better way. For example, before boarding a coach, a tourist must know the course of action in case a fire breaks out in a coach. He/she must imagine such possible scenarios in his/her mind. Then, he/she should procure himself/herself with the right options in case any such unfortunate incident happens on the tour. For example, in this case, before he/she starts the trip on the coach, he/she must figure out the fire extinguisher, emergency door, emergency window, hammer and a first-aid box inside the coach. He/she should also carry with him/her the local numbers of the fire station and ambulance to deal with this emergency, in case it happens.

SUMMARY

Every trip comes bundled with different situations that a tourist may not be ready for or may have not even thought of. Travelling can be challenging too. However, the rule of the game is to take these situations as an opportunity for learning new aspects of life. Every situation handled by a traveller instils confidence within him/her and makes him/her better procured to deal with any situation in the future.

ACTIVITIES

Activity 1

You are travelling with a group of travellers for five days. There are five more days to go. You have made friends with almost everyone. You are thoroughly enjoying your Europe extravaganza package with all the luxury travel package comforts. On the 5th day, suddenly one of the old-age travellers comes drunk in the coach and starts abusing you in the coach. What would you do in such a situation?

Activity 2

You are travelling from Delhi to London through a reputed airline for the first time. On reaching your holiday destination, when you reach the conveyor belt to collect your check-in luggage, to your dismay, you realize that your luggage is missing. You then speak to the concerned airlines authorities who apprise you that due to some issue, your luggage will reach London after two days. Now, how would you manage the situation as a first-time overseas traveller?

Obstacles and Threats to Tourism

30

LEARNING OBJECTIVE

The given chapter shall clarify the following:

- What are the factors that stop a person from travelling to a destination?

CORONAVIRUS (COVID-19): A DISASTER FOR TOURISM

- The unprecedented challenge that the world is globally facing today is the outbreak of the dreaded disease Coronavirus.
- Having spread across approximately 216 countries and territories in the world, this disease has been declared as a pandemic by WHO.
- To contain the spread of this highly contagious disease and putting people first, travel restrictions have been imposed by almost all countries of the world since January 2020.
- Almost 96 per cent of the world's international and domestic airlines, railways and other modes of transportation have stopped their operations, hotels and other accommodations types, and all shopping establishments and cultural and entertainment organizations were shut down temporarily since January 2020.
- The residents of nations have been advised to stay home and practise social distancing, which has put the whole tourism industry to a standstill. The tourism sector is one of the most badly hit sectors of the economy, like no other event in history.

- It is expected that amid this pandemic that has taken a toll on unlimited lives across the world, more than 60 to 80 per cent tourists' arrivals have dropped as compared to tourists' arrivals in 2019. Millions of jobs are at risk as no one knows the duration of this crisis.
- UNWTO has called for urgent fiscal and monetary measures for the tourism sector to protect the jobs, especially of the vulnerable sections such as women, self-employed, SMEs and artisans and support the liquidity and operations of travel businesses.
- *#Travel Tomorrow* is the new campaign launched by UNWTO to deal with the COVID-19 pandemic in solidarity with other nations facing this.
- It aims at the tourism service providers to show resilience in this hour of crisis and stay united. The UNWTO is channelizing all the stakeholders of the tourism industry to come forward and cooperate and find ways to accelerate the recovery of the tourism sector by having strong mitigation and acceleration plans to bounce back again to its former glory.

INTRODUCTION

Many people may not travel to a destination, even if they may wish to travel. There are many factors that are not congenial for a person to travel. *Sometimes, these may be personal factors while sometimes these may be destination-based factors.* In both cases, the traveller, inspite of wanting to travel to a destination, may not be able to travel. Thus, the threats and obstacles to tourism may be referred to as the various factors that deter a tourist from travelling to a destination. *In other words, the threats and obstacles may collectively be referred to as barriers to travel.* However, there is a thin line between the threats and obstacles that must be clarified here before proceeding for further discussion. The threats refer to the various external factors that discourage the tourist from travelling to a destination. These are generally destination generated. Whereas, obstacles may be referred to as those factors that are generally personal in nature. When the situation of either the person or the destination changes, the person decides to travel. One thing that is common between both threats and obstacles are that these both affect the flow of tourists to a destination. Now, let us have a detailed discussion on each of the obstacles and threats to tourism.

FINANCIAL CONSTRAINT

A person may have the desire to travel, but he/she may not have enough funds to realize his/her travel goals. He/she may not be able to afford a holiday at an expensive destination, especially to an overseas/international destination. This may be due to the increased transportation cost to an overseas destination that is comparatively a more expensive component of the overall travel arrangements as compared to the other travel components. For example, a traveller residing in India may find travelling to Dubai much cheaper as compared to travelling to the USA or Canada as the only option to reach these destinations from India is the flight that is more expensive due to the distance required to reach the destination. Thus, a traveller may avoid travelling to those countries that are expensive as they are out of his/her budget. Therefore, in such cases, the state of one's own finances becomes an obstacle to travel.

LACK OF TIME

Many people may not be able to travel to a destination due to the paucity of time. The working professionals may not have enough holidays with them to spare and take a longer break. Likewise, the business class people may not have time to leave their businesses during their peak season and travel to a destination. Thus, they may plan their visit to only nearby destinations where they may spend the least time on travelling. Alternatively, they may not travel. Thus, the lack of time becomes an obstacle to travel in such cases.

COMFORT OF TRAVEL

Many travellers may not be comfortable travelling to certain places. This may be due to travel-related health issues. Some travellers during travel suffer from motion sickness while some suffer from seasickness, airsickness, backache, acidity, diarrhoea (due to erratic timing of travel) and so on. Thus, such travellers may avoid travelling. For example, a person who suffers from air sickness may avoid travel to far off destinations where the only medium to reach the destination is by air. Likewise, an asthmatic patient may avoid travelling to Ladakh, India, due to lack of oxygen in the high altitudes of the region. Similarly, some travellers, due to motion sickness or backache, may not prefer travelling to those hilly areas where road travel is quite curvy and bumpy as the traveller may feel nauseated and uneasy. In such cases, one's own comfort becomes an obstacle to travel.

STATE OF ONE'S HEALTH

One's health is a determining factor while planning a vacation. A person will only travel to a destination if he/she feels that he/she is fit enough to travel. If somebody has undergone a surgery and he/she is bedridden or is suffering from any disease, he/she would not think of visiting a destination. For example, a person who wants to go on an adventure trek would only be advised to travel if he/she is physically fit and has enough physical stamina. Thus, the ill health of a person becomes an obstacle to travel.

PROXIMITY

Another deterring factor to travel is the proximity of a destination to one's place of residence. Many travellers prefer to visit only nearby destinations due to the paucity of time in hand. They may be constrained not to choose a destination due to its long distance. For example, many tourists who avoid long air travel may avoid visiting long haul destinations. Thus, distance is a major factor that discourages a person to travel, especially if he/she has less time in hand.

GENDER

In certain countries of the world, where the society is driven by defined patriarchal structures, the outlook towards women is very conservative. Women are restricted from travelling alone due to the cultural limitations of society. They are only encouraged to travel with the family. Thus, gender in such countries becomes a limitation to tourism.

AGE

Age is one of the prime obstacles for tourists while visiting a destination. Mostly, the health of a person and his/her mobility deteriorates with the age though exceptions to this are always there. Also, with age, one's physical stamina may decrease, thus limiting him/her to fewer tourism options. For example, an old-age traveller of 60 years may not be able to do adventure activities at a destination. Thus, destinations that promote themselves as adventure destinations such as Ladakh or Uttarakhand in India would not be within the wish list of such a traveller.

Similarly, visiting caves (e.g., Batu Caves in Malaysia with 272 steps), temples with difficult steps, stepwells (such as Chand Baori, one of the largest stepwells of India in Abhaneri village that has 3,500 narrow steps or Agrasen ki Baoli in New Delhi with 108 steps), forts, castles and so on that may have difficult terrains and are at a height and involve a lot of walking, may not be very easy to tread. Thus, such tourists may avoid travelling to such attractions. However, they might visit those attractions that are made accessible for them through providing facilities for old-aged travellers such as wheelchairs, elevators, ramps, cable cars and golf carts. Old-aged travellers may prefer to visit those places/attractions that are easy to access and offer facilities for them. They may also not prefer visiting amusement parks as certain rides may be restricted for them due to their age factor. The travelling pattern of such travellers may also change. Thus, age, at times, becomes a barrier to travel.

FOOD

Conservative food habits of many people stop them from pursuing travel. Many people who are vegetarian, vegans, allergic to certain kinds of food like seafood or have conservative food habits by virtue of their religion such as Muslims (who only eat halal meat), Jains (Hindus who neither eat onion nor garlic) or followers of religious movements such as ISKCON (who also do not eat garlic nor onion) find it difficult to travel due to fewer food options available with them, especially while travelling overseas. Thus, in such cases, food becomes a deterring factor for people to undertake travel.

LANGUAGE BARRIER

Many people may not visit a destination due to the fear of facing the language barrier at that destination. Many nations of the world are not English speaking. Thus, travellers while planning their vacations may not consider such destinations, even if it is in their consideration choice. For example, as most of the population in China is Mandarin-speaking, with very few people who can speak English, most of the tourists would only prefer to visit China on package tours. Solo travellers who do not understand Mandarin may find it difficult to communicate with locals, thus the language in this case becomes a limiting factor for the traveller. Likewise, while visiting Mexico, if one does not understand Spanish, one may find it difficult to communicate during one's stay with the locals who preferably speak Spanish.

Although with the help of various language apps such as *google translator* or *language interpreters*, the language barrier can be taken care of to an extent, many people may not opt for these options. Instead, they may travel to those destinations where they can easily communicate with the locals, and they may not have to face any language barrier.

EXTENT OF TRAVEL DOCUMENTATION

Many people are spontaneous travellers who believe in instant travel plans. Sometimes, such travellers may plan an overseas trip. In such a case, travellers would only think of travelling to that country that has easy documentation procedures. With elaborate documentation required and the long time for visa processing by many countries, many destinations may simply be out of the consideration set for such visitors. On the contrary, destinations that have simple visa procedures or VOA becomes a pull factor that attracts the tourist to these destinations. Likewise, if special permits are required to visit a place, many people may avoid visiting that destination. For example, *for visiting the Nicobar Islands and certain states of Northeast India such as Sikkim in India, the tourists (even the domestic tourists) are required to have a special permit before travelling to these destinations.*

Thus, for destinations to be tourist-friendly, they must have VOA facility and easy documentation procedures. Otherwise, elaborate documentation and the time required for getting a visa processed become an obstacle to travel for the yearning traveller.

MARKETING BY TOURISM DESTINATIONS

Lack of awareness about a destination is an obstacle to travel. Many destinations of the world do not promote themselves and thus remain a hidden gem for the prospective traveller. They may have been in the consideration set of a traveller if they would have been marketed well. However, due to lack of publicity of the destinations by the tourism authorities, such destinations remain unexplored, and as a result, people do not travel to those destinations.

SEASONALITY OF A DESTINATION

Seasonality of a destination sometimes can be an obstacle to travel. A traveller wanting to visit *Ladakh* or *Manali* in India during monsoons or winters may not be able to travel due to closure of roads because of landslides or heavy snowfall there. Likewise, for a foreigner visiting *Mumbai* during monsoons may not be a very good time to explore the city. Similarly, visiting the *Scandinavian countries* or *Canada* during winters may not be a very good idea for travellers. Thus, seasonality in such cases affects the flow of tourists to a destination.

IMAGE OF A DESTINATION

Sometimes, the image of a destination poses a threat to the prospective traveller. Many destinations of the world are not considered safe to travel and are, thus, notorious and unsafe destinations. They may be seen in bad limelight due to the crime prevailing there such as theft, cheating, molestation and rape. Thus, travellers may avoid visiting such destinations, and thus, the image of the destination becomes a deterring factor in such a case.

Even many destinations of the world are considered unsafe to travel due to frequent terrorist attacks, bomb blasts, communal riots, civil unrest or agitation, strikes and so on. Sometimes, the outbreak of a disease at the destination also makes it unsafe to travel. The outbreak of Coronavirus in China in December 2019 has led to a major threat to the tourism industry as the disease is highly contagious. Not only China has been affected, but also the world's economy is completely affected. Likewise, a natural calamity such as an earthquake, volcanic eruption, tsunami, flash floods and so on may make the destination unsafe to travel for the prospective travellers. Thus, travellers may decide to avoid travel during such situations.

Also, many destinations, especially the Third-World countries like African countries, are portrayed as poor countries that lack in facilities. Thus, due to their poor image, many travellers may not be interested to travel to these destinations due to lack of amenities available there.

To ensure the safety of its citizens, sometimes government authorities issue *travel advisories* for them. If the travel advisory portrays the image of a country in bad limelight, the travellers may restrict themselves from visiting that destination.

SUMMARY

When people travel to a destination, they consider many factors. Certain aspects of an individual such as age, health, comfort of travel, time, financial constraints, proximity, food, language, the extent of documentation or sometimes threats to a destination like its image restrict a traveller from visiting that destination. Every destination may have its own specific threats while people may also face personal obstacles in travelling to a destination. It is important for the tourism industry to identify the various threats and obstacles of a destination as well as the obstacles that affect the travellers to undertake travel. The tourism industry must provide workable solutions to the threats and obstacles wherever possible in order to encourage tourists to travel to the destination and thus promote tourism at a destination.

ACTIVITIES

Activity 1

Think of a destination you wish to travel. Now, enlist and discuss the various threats and obstacles with the class that deter you from visiting that destination.

Activity 2

Take any destination of your choice that had faced any threat such as an outbreak of an epidemic, earthquake, floods and terrorist attacks in the past that had affected the tourists' arrivals in that destination in the past. Now, discuss the various successful measures taken by that destination to combat the negative image that helped it in bouncing back.

31

Emerging Trends in Tourism

LEARNING OBJECTIVES

The given chapter shall clarify the following:

- What are the emerging trends in the tourism industry?

A SMART CITY FOR SMART TOURISTS!

- One of the most visited cities in the world and also officially recognized as a smart city in Spain in 2014 is Barcelona.
- Until 1992, there were no beaches in Barcelona. The redevelopment took place when the Olympic games happened in Barcelona, and the city used the seashore line to make Barcelona a leisure-, entertainment- and activity-oriented spot for tourists as well as locals. Now, Barcelona has about nine beaches.
- One major early step for Barcelona was to establish a city-wide technological infrastructure to support and improve the city and make it smart.
- Some of the high-tech infrastructure development include smart waste bins, fab tabs, LED streetlights, city bike system and noise sensors.

INTRODUCTION

With the changing travel habits of new-age travellers and the effect of technology on tourism, the tourism industry is undergoing a radical transformation. To keep up with the changing travel trends and changing demands of new-age travellers, the destination marketers are continuously evolving new tourism products that are mostly experiential in nature, positioning and marketing themselves more aggressively to offset the competition of similar offerings by other destinations, revamping their existing tourism products and building upon new marketing strategies making heavy use of social media.

Also, with respect to the Indian tourism markets, the holiday patterns have dramatically changed. *The Indian market is one of the fastest-growing outbound tourism markets.* Taking an international holiday has become an annual ritual for the young Indian holidaymakers. In fact, *Indians are among the top spenders for the overseas trip.* Not only the outbound tourism market in India is growing, but domestic tourism is also increasing. Domestic tourism has also reached a new milestone. The young travellers have an appetite for exploring new tourist destinations within India. With its kaleidoscope of traditions, cultures and geographies, India is a *soul-stirring destination* for the travellers across the world. It is also considered as the *travel magnet* for the world.

Thus, with the burgeoning growth of the tourism sector, the tourism suppliers need to be upbeat to stay in their businesses and evolve new concepts and ideas that lure new-age travellers. Now, let us have a detailed discussion on the following emerging trends that are increasingly being adopted by today's travellers.

AIRBNB

Welcome Drinks Served by Hosts at AirBnB Apartment

One of the massive transformation in the tourism and hospitality sector brought by an American company is the AirBnB, *the leading accommodation leaders worldwide.* With their headquarters based in San Francisco, California, USA, the website was officially launched in 2008 as *airbedandbreakfast. com.* Later, the company rechristened its name to *AirBnB.com.*

Basically, AirBnB provides an online marketplace giving lodging solutions to the tourists. It connects people who want to rent out their properties or extra rooms with tourists by charging commission from both the hosts and the guests.

Through AirBnB arrangements, travellers can actually experience offbeat stay experiences by booking their stays in self-catering apartments, villas, private homes, castles, cottages, private rooms in apartments or any other similar properties listed on the site. Many tourists who have a keen interest to see the life of locals from a close may even share the spaces with the hosts by staying in one of the rooms let out by the hosts. Tourists may choose their accommodation using various filters such as the accommodation type that they want, their budget, the dates on which they want the accommodation, the amenities that they are looking for, parking space for vehicles, if required, the kind of area that the tourist wants to stay in whether a peaceful location or a touristic place with nightlife around, ease of access and proximity to public transportation, local markets nearby and so on.

A Type of Accommodation Provided by AirBnB

AirBnB provides value for money by providing a variety of accommodation choices at prime locations at fewer prices.

Staying through AirBnB arrangement is a unique experience unlike staying in a hotel as one gets to live in a city like a local and experience the local life of a destination instead of just gazing a destination from a distance. Tourists may interact with hosts if they wish to, visit the local markets, buy local stuff from supermarkets, make their own food and so on that gives them the local 'feel' of a destination.

For those looking for a luxury vacation, AirBnB has launched 'AirBnB Plus' in 2018 that offers quality designs and services in homes for travellers.

In short, it is one of the largest platforms that connects hosts who want to let out their accommodation on temporary basis to tourists.

COUCH SURFING

Accommodation accounts for a major portion of a traveller's expense. Many friendly people around the world who want to interact with other people from different cultures open their homes to travellers for their stay. *Couch surfing* is a website and an online community created to connect travellers sharing the same interest together. It is a new concept in travelling adopted by especially backpackers and budget travellers that allows them to travel around the world at a comparatively lower price. In couch surfing, the host provides the lodging to the couch surfer/traveller and does not charge any money from him/her. The couch surfers leverage on the hospitality extended by the host community. The host may provide the hospitality services such as providing meals to him/her, introducing the couch surfer to the local community, suggesting him/her the local events to attend, hidden hotspots to explore, things to avoid, local food to try and special tours to be taken that make the stay of a traveller more meaningful and comfortable. The traveller can get an insider recommendation like local's advice which can save a great amount of a traveller's money and his/her precious time. In turn, the couch surfers pay back their hosts with everlasting friendships and wonderful memories and experiences. The traveller may share stories about the life and culture of their country with the host and also may invite the host to his/her own country to stay with him/her. It is important for the travellers to keep interacting with the host so that he/she does not feel neglected.

Sharing and connecting is the main mantra of the couch surfing phenomenon. *Couch surfing is a great way to strike new connections, make friends locally and build up networks. Couch surfing is more about the human connection* where people from different parts of the world come together and connect at a common platform, thereby learning to respect each other's differences.

To access this facility, the couch surfer has to first create a verification account for couch surfing. Before making a *couch request,* it is important for the couch surfers to properly review the profiles of the hosts through the reviews of other couch surfers posted there. The couch surfers may choose their hosts by having a chat with them and finding out if they share similar interests or not.

However, every traveller may not find this option to be very feasible and a safe option to travel, especially for those who are travelling with their families who may prefer privacy.

WORKAWAY

It is a new concept that allows a traveller from different parts of the world who are workaway-ers to connect with the host and exchange each other's culture. It is also an opportunity to connect with local communities around the world and meet the other workawayers. This concept promotes home stays, farm stays and family exchanges. *The workawayers stay for free with free accommodation and meals in exchange for work for a few hours a day at the hosts' place of residence.* The traveller may stay at the host's accommodation either for days or a few months and con-tribute in different ways to the hosts by volunteering to do his/her different jobs. A traveller may aid in teaching the local kids, work in the farms staying in farmhouses, take care of ani-mals and pet sitting, work in the hostels or B&B businesses of the hosts, taking care of the household chores such as cleaning, ironing, teaching Yoga and meditation and babysitting. The workawayers must always be respectful of the agreed time schedules of work and the house rules as set by the hosts.

Besides involving themselves in the local work, the workawayers after the working hours can have great conversations with the hosts, learn about their food habits, pick up new skills like learning a local language, learn about their local delicacies, their traditions, their local music, attend music concerts and prepare their own local meals for a tasting of the hosts besides exploring the nearby places. This mutual exchange of cultures is the motivating and binding factor for both the host and the workawayer to practise this phenomenon. The work-awayers eventually become the members of the families of the hosts.

STAYCATION

Another new trend emerging in the tourism industry is that of a staycation also referred to as a *holistay.* For certain people who cannot afford to go on holiday vacation due to the paucity of time, lack of holidays, money, ill health or any other situation, the answer is a staycation.

During staycation, the traveller does not visit another destination but instead stays home and moves around his/her city. One may visit nearby attractions such as amusement parks, attend local events, bath in the backyard pool, take a Yoga retreat, listen to the music, watch movies, relax or bask in the sun in one's backyard, take a massage, indulge in a vacation-reading binge, take a camping trip in one's own backyard, get a spa or indulge in any similar leisure activities that relaxes oneself completely. The advantage of a staycation is that the traveller experiences a change of routine that refreshes his/her mind and body. Besides, the staycation is less stressful as it does not involve much planning. It provides a person with the time away for oneself by committing oneself to unplug.

SLEEPCATION

As sleep is a very important part of one's well-being, yet it is not the privilege for all, especially the new millennials who are suffering from insomnia. For those who are sleep deprived and wearied of the city life with its hullabaloo, a sleepcation is the panacea to all sleep-related disorders and fatigued bodies. Sleeping on a vacation in a resort or a hotel is the new trend now. Many travellers who want to be in deep slumber visit destinations with the objective of sleeping there. Thus, sleepcation as an antidote provides the sleepcationers with rooms that have dim lights, sleep massage, sleep spa, pillow menus (foods that increase sleep) and a sleep patrol officer that boosts sleep. After a sleepcation, the travellers feel more energetic, charged and more focused to deal with day-to-day pressures.

Many resorts of the world promote sleepcation. For example, the *Four Season Resort* in Bali gives the chances to travellers to sleep like a baby by giving them a spa treatment consisting of body massages, facials and an air nap where the traveller is made to lie in a silk hammock which is suspended in the air and is made to sleep in the background music of the river flowing and a Buddhist nun telling stories of lord Buddha making one sleep. Likewise, in the *Sivananda Ashram in Nassau, Bahamas,* one may enrol for Yoga of sleep programme that focuses on sleep and enlightens the travellers on various ways in which Yoga can be applied for sleep. The psychologist and sleep specialist help the travellers to deal with their sleep-related disorders. Likewise, in *Six Senses Yao Noi Hotel, Phang Nga Bay, Thailand,* the travellers are made to sleep with the help of technology. The villas in the hotel are designed as high-tech sleep sanctuaries where the machines have been placed under the mattresses that track the body movement and respiratory rates of the person sleeping. Along with that, organic beds, eucalyptus-scented organic cotton, bamboo pyjamas, down blankets, body pillow and so on are some of the exclusive bedroom accessories that are used to make the sleep-deprived individuals sleep.

HOUSE SITTING

For those who love to take care of pets, house sitting is a new way. It can take them to places. Basically, certain websites allow a platform for the homeowners and the house/pet sitters to come together around the globe and find each other. If a homeowner who owns pets is going on a vacation, he/she may need someone to take care of his/her pets in his/her absence. Such caretakers of pets may be referred to as house sitters. Thus, the house sitters get to have free holiday accommodation in turn for taking care of the pets of the house owners. This way house sitting allows the house sitters to travel around the world and explore new places by just taking care of a pet. It also gives an opportunity to the house sitter to stay in another country and experience life as a local in the company of the animal. At the same time, the pet owners can travel with a free mind that they have someone to take care of their pet as they may feel that their pet is in safe hands. This kind of arrangement also keeps the pets happy in their own home as their comfort is not disturbed while helping people to travel around the world. One may explore the world by registering oneself with websites such as *MindMyHouse, TrustedHousesitters* and so on by paying an annual membership fee for the sits across the globe.

EMERGING SEGMENT OF TRAVELLERS

Many new segments of travellers are emerging today that are being encashed by tourism marketers. Now, let us have a detailed discussion on each of these.

Solo Trips

Solo trips are increasingly trending. Wanderlust and spending time with oneself are the main driving forces for travellers obsessed with discovering new facets of destinations. In order to capture this segment of the emerging market and encourage solo travel, many travel companies are offering *value-added single tour packages* without even charging a single supplement for a room on the single basis from the solo travellers. In fact, now more and more women travellers have started travelling solo either for business or for leisure unlike earlier when only men used to be travelling solo. The tourism industry is highly sensitive to the needs and preferences of this gender. Hotels have recognized the need for these segments and devised various mechanisms to ensure the optimal safety of women travellers. For example, many hotels have dedicated women-only floors and rooms only for their female guests. The staff catering to this segment are also only the women. Videophones, rooms near the elevators and brightly-lit parts of the corridor, women-only bar, lady-only amenities, women chauffeurs and women guides for sightseeing and not sharing the room number details of the women travellers are some of the practices being adopted by the hospitality industry to stay sensitive to the needs of women solo travellers. Solo trips in India are also quite popular, especially amongst youngsters, who may visit *Himachal Pradesh* and *Ladakh* on bike trips or do solo treks in *Uttarakhand* or *Himachal Pradesh* and so on. Countries such as the USA, Canada, Bhutan and European countries are among the chosen destinations opted by many women solo travellers as they find these as safe destinations.

People with Special Abilities

Another important emerging segment is that of travellers who are differently-abled and have special needs. As a mandatory requirement by the law, hotels need to provide a minimum number of accessible rooms for such travellers. These rooms may be located on the ground floor, have wide doors to allow wheelchair access, a variety of grab rails, emergency pull cords, roll-in shower, low-level washbasins and bathtubs, lower vanity light, heating controls at a lower level to make it accessible through a wheelchair. Besides these particulars mentioned above in the hotel rooms, the hotel may have *entrance ramps, food and beverage facility situated on the ground floor,* that enables easy movement for the differently enabled.

Likewise, for promoting a country as an accessible destination for people with special abilities and old-age travellers, the attractions must have the following features:

- Ramps at entrance and public areas
- Facility for wheelchairs
- Accessible washrooms
- Elevators

LGBTQ

One of the important segments of tourists visiting various countries of the world is the LGBTQ community that stands for *lesbian, gay, bisexual, transgender and queer.* A term coined for such travellers going on vacation is *gaycation.* Realizing the need for this segment of travellers, many tour operators offer special packages to destinations that are sensitive and considerate to the need of such travellers. These are considered as very important segments now as they bring *pink dollars/pink pounds* to the economies of the world. Safety is a prime concern while planning a vacation for this segment of the tourism market as many destinations are not friendly and welcoming towards such travellers. Some LGBT-friendly countries are *Sweden, Canada, Norway, Portugal, the UK* and so on.

Bleisure Travellers

The new millennials are travelling both for business and leisure. When travelling for work, they may combine work with leisure while sometimes taking their families along. Thus, they may be referred to as bleisure travellers. Hence, it is important for tourism marketers to provide opportunities for leisure to business travellers who are primarily visiting a destination related to their work.

Young Adventurers

The millennials are core adventure seekers who want to try new experiments and engage in seeking new adventure experiences such as sky diving, caving, white-water rafting and mountain biking. They want to move out of their comfort zones and do things that they have not done before in any holiday that they take.

DINKS

DINKS refers to 'double income, no kids'. As mostly now there are *dual-career couples* with both the husband and wife working; and therefore, with enough discretionary income, travel is the best way to splurge their extra incomes. Luxury at every step of holiday and taking more and more frequent holidays, especially overseas holidays is the new trend among DINKS.

NEW TOURISM PRODUCTS

It is a well-established fact now that the preferences and consumption patterns of tourists are fast changing. The new-age traveller wants more variety and novelty. As a result, new trends in tourism products are emerging day by day. Some of the upcoming tourism holiday products are as follows.

Food Tourism

The gourmet travellers are on a rise. An upcoming trend is the rising interest of tourists in food-inspired travel. Taking culinary tours or food walks has become quite evident now. Tasting local cuisines in local markets, trying one's hands at learning regional cooking delicacies and visiting destinations during food festivals along with the wine pairing are some of the upcoming trends of food lovers. Some of the gourmet experiences that travellers may try in different countries are as follows:

- Spending an afternoon with a gourmet set brunch in Spain amidst the vineyards
- Taking cooking lessons from chefs of India
- Learning about local fresh produce of staple food during farm tours in Israel
- Taking a gastronomical tour of Paris
- Taking a tour of tasting dumplings in Nanjing, China

Wellness Holidays

Another upcoming trend is travelling to destinations to keep up with one's physical and emotional well-being. Destinations such as *India, Austria, Turkey, Thailand, Japan* and *Bali, Indonesia* are most visited for taking wellness retreats, detox programmes, stress-buster rejuvenation programmes, spa treatments, bathing in hot springs, mind and soul embracement, taking Ayurveda treatments, chakra balancing, weight loss, meditation, aquatic therapies such as balneotherapy, thalassotherapy and hydrothermal environments.

Let us take an example of *Turkey, one of the leading tourist destinations in the world, famous for spa tourism* where tourists can pamper themselves with luxurious spa treatments at hotels and wellness centres mostly in the coastal resorts of Mediterranean and Aegean region and spoil themselves in the traditional Turkish *hammams* or relax in thermal springs. *Anatolia, famous for approximately 1,300 geothermal resources* has a high density of minerals that cures people of various illnesses.

Wildlife Tourism

Wildlife tourism is highly picking up in various parts of the world. *Africa is the most visited destination among wildlife enthusiasts.* Most of the travellers interested in watching wildlife, especially to see the endangered species and taking safari trips to national parks and wildlife sanctuaries prefer to visit *Africa, especially Kenya, Tanzania, South Africa, Botswana, Namibia, Ethiopia* and so on. Among other countries in the world, most visited destinations for wildlife tourism are Brazil, India, New Zealand for marine reserves and so on.

Cruising

Cruising is also trending. The new-age travellers want to spend their holidays on a cruise while exploring destinations through sailing waters. For those seeking a luxurious experience, cruises are larger than life experience offering luxury at its best. The concept of having family celebrations on cruises is increasingly becoming a fad. Whether it may be a romantic getaway on one's honeymoon or celebrations such as anniversaries and birthdays, sailing in the water is one of the best ways of spending one's vacation.

Voluntarism with Purpose

Many people use travel as a tool for serving the society. More and more travellers are visiting destinations to offer voluntary services while visiting destinations. This gives them a sense of purpose. Participating with natives in community-driven projects such as participating in ecological conservation, educating poor children, teaching a language, promoting sustainability, assisting in animal conservation and bringing medical aid are some of the reasons and motivations for many travellers to visit a destination.

Many other similar new products are being demanded by travellers, especially the special interest tours. To catch up with the increasing demand of the market, the service providers must study the consumer patterns and evolve the new products from time to time.

NEW DESTINATIONS

The conventional destinations are fading over the offbeat experiential travel destinations. The new-age traveller wants to choose *exotic and less-travelled destinations* over the commercialized or most visited destinations. He/she wants to soak himself/herself into newer destination experiences. The lesser-known destinations are becoming more popular among tourists. There is also a paradigm shift in the travel destinations from North America and Canada to Southeast Asia, Middle East and Africa. Some of the upcoming popular offbeat destinations emerging among new-age travellers within Europe are *Iceland, Norway, Belfast in North Ireland along with Eastern Europe such as Czech Republic, Hungary, Croatia, Slovenia, Poland, Romania, Russia, Estonia, Lithuania and Latvia.*

To promote experiential travel, different countries are identifying their new tourism products, promoting and positioning themselves in different ways. For example, *Australia* and *New Zealand* are positioning themselves as self-drive holiday destinations and adventure destinations offering activities such as jet boating and bungee jumping. *Turkey* and *Israel* are promoting themselves as wellness tourism destinations. Likewise, South Africa is also promoting itself for wildlife safaris, wildlife photography and more than 3,000 adventure activities. Similarly, Seychelles and Maldives, along with Bahamas and Fiji, are promoting themselves as idyllic holiday island destinations for tourists. Yet countries such as Jordan and Mexico are also getting famous among tourists.

Among Indians, countries such as Dubai, Singapore, Thailand, Malaysia, Indonesia and Bhutan are getting more popular due to their proximity to the country and similar fusion of food and culture. Especially among first-time travellers who are travelling abroad, these destinations are more popular. India is also promoting its lesser-known destinations such as small rural villages such as *Pali and Chanoud Garh in Rajasthan* and *Lahaul and Spiti in Himachal Pradesh* and many more.

CUSTOMIZATION

It is an era of customization. The FIT travel is increasing against package tours where travellers choose their own travel arrangements to the destination that they may wish to visit. The new tourists do not want routine-based fixed itineraries or package tours. On the contrary, they want *cookie-cutter itineraries* that are different and customized to their own needs. In other words, they want personalized travel itineraries or customized tours such as special interest tours that may be cookery tours or stay in boutique hotels.

GROWTH OF LUXURY TRAVEL

Luxury travel is a new trend. The segment of tourists seeking luxury during travel is fuelling. The new-age traveller has more discretionary income and thus may not like to compromise on the quality of tourism services. He/she wants impeccable services at every step of his/her holiday. Thus, he/she is ready to pay for luxury. He/she does not mind paying extra as long as he/she is promised luxuries at every step of his/her holiday. He/she wants to be thoroughly pampered during his/her travel through availing the highest quality of services such as travelling by a premium airline, train, cruise liner, or chauffeur-driven luxurious car, stay in a luxurious camp or any other kind of luxurious accommodation while also taking personalized customer services. In fact, the adventure travellers staying in camps are also seeking off-site camping in luxurious settings. *This phenomenon of staying in deluxe camps is called as glamping.* Whether it may be a stay in *Maasai Mara forests* in safari lodges or a stay in the *floating cabins on the coast of Cambodia* or a stay in *igloos to see the Northern Lights,* the new-age traveller wants to stay in deluxe camps with the best of amenities.

EMERGING TECHNOLOGICAL TRENDS

Technology is a game-changer. The tourism industry, too, is driven by technology. Most of the tourism businesses have gone online now and now have their own portals or apps (applications). The presence of online travel portals 24 × 7 with customer service round the clock for the traveller and the facility of chatbots that aid the travellers in tour planning has made the travel bookings very easier for the traveller now. Not only the booking behaviour of the traveller has changed due to the technology, but also the new-age traveller regularly updates his/her travel secrets on social media, uses Instagram to share his/her every travel experience with others and writes his/her own blogs making full use of technology. *All bloggers, whether they are travel bloggers or food bloggers, have become destination ambassadors.* Use of AI in the tourism and hospitality sector is also being increasingly encouraged.

SUSTAINABILITY

The complete orientation within the tourism industry has transformed towards sustainability. *In fact, the year 2017 was declared as the International Year of Sustainable Tourism* for Development. Responsible travel is strongly being advocated where the travellers when they visit a destination are expected to remain conscious of the environment and help in minimizing carbon prints. Spreading eco-awareness among the holidaymakers, visiting eco-tourism destinations, taking care of waste management, promoting culture and heritage in local communities and so on are some of the goals of the destinations having a sustainable approach towards tourism. *Philippines, Costa Rica* and *Alonnisos in Greece* are among the most sustainable destinations in the world.

SUMMARY

The tourism industry is growing by leaps and bounds. New trends are emerging day by day to attract tourists. In fact, we have new-age travellers now with different needs and preferences who want more luxury as well as customization. Destinations are launching new tourism products to attract new-age tourists such as food tourism, wellness tourism, wildlife tourism and cruising. At the same time, a new segment of travellers is also emerging who were not travelling before such as women solo travellers, people with special abilities, LGBTQ, bleisure travellers, DINKS and adventurers. Technology is also a game-changer for the tourism industry. The new-age traveller wants to stay in more authentic locales, making use of technology through websites and apps such as AirBnB, couch surfing, workaway, staycation, sleepcation, house sitting and home stays. Increasingly, the tourism industry is much concerned about the sustainability of destinations.

ACTIVITIES

Activity 1

'Festivals are a trending tool for branding destinations.' Thus, think of any five major international festivals of the world that are being promoted to attract the tourists. Now, discuss in detail the profile of the festivals along with their history, significance, the kinds of tourists who come to attend the festival and the kind of activities that are performed there.

Activity 2

Interview any three tourists who have tried the AirBnB app. Ask them to share their experience. Discuss with the class the pros and cons shared by the travellers of making stay arrangements through AirBnB.

Activity 3

Go through the websites of couch surfing and house sitting. Share your inputs on the same with the class.

Activity 4

Share the domestic destinations within your country that are trending now along with the tourism products that they are offering.

Career Opportunities in Travel and Tourism

LEARNING OBJECTIVES

The given chapter shall clarify the following:

- What are the various career opportunities in tourism?
- What are the challenges of this profession?

DO YOU HAVE IT IN YOU?

- A travel bug
- A service-oriented attitude
- People's person
- Extrovert
- Good communication skills
- Good interpersonal skills
- Convincing skills
- A good personality
- Confidence
- English proficiency
- Knowledge of a foreign language
- Destination knowledge
- Knowledge of computer reservation system (CRS; e.g., Amadeus, Galileo and Sabre)
- Knowledge of the travel trade
- Ready to work for long hours

- Flexible
- Patience
- Calm and poised under pressure

If yes, the industry is eager to see you! Come and be part of the world's most glamorous industry!

It is a recognized fact that the tourism industry is the largest earner of foreign exchange across the world. It has secured bread and butter for millions of people around the world who are employed directly or indirectly through tourism. The sector has a high potential in both the private and public sectors as it is considered to be one of the world's largest economic sectors. In India too, the travel and tourism industry is growing tremendously by leaps and bounds, where 46 million jobs are expected to be created by 2025 directly and indirectly through the tourism industry. Considering the increasing growth of this industry, there is a dire need for tourism professionals to manage the industry. The tourism industry is basically a *labour-intensive industry where personal interaction with tourists* is still very important today. Skilled personnel are the need of the hour to manage and operate the tourism business.

INTRODUCTION

The travel and tourism sector promises a bright future for those who aspire to make a fulfilling career in this field. Tourism has a pool of career roles for various professionals. The opportunities are endless in the tourism sector if one has a true passion for this field.

Choosing the travel and tourism industry as a career option may be the first choice for many. They may be driven by various factors that make them choose this profession. Many students find this profession to be very attractive and glamorous. One of the important reasons for students in finding this job to be attractive is that travelling is a part of the job. *It is a job that takes you to places. This profession provides international travel opportunities due to which the students find it very glamorous.* Based on one's job profile in tourism, many roles such as being a tour leader, tour guide, salesperson, travel writers and travel journalists allow an opportunity for the professionals to travel, stay in the best of hotel properties, travel in best of the airlines, see the attractions of the world and enjoy many other similar benefits at the cost of the company that is sponsoring the entire travel of the tourism professional. *This makes it a thrilling and adventurous job to explore new places and meet new people from different parts of the world on every new assignment that the tourism professional may be sent on. Added perks for free travel or reduced rates for you and your family* bring bonuses and commissions to the tourism professionals who have been working for a long time in this profession.

Now, let us have a detailed discussion on the number of career options available for tourism aspirants in the travel and tourism sector.

TRAVEL COMPANIES

The most obvious and the safest choice made by most of the career aspirants of the tourism industry is to work for travel agencies and tour operators. Starting a career with a multinational travel company such as *Thomas Cook, SOTC Travel, Le Passage to India (LPTI), Carlson Wagonlit Travel* and *Balmer Lawrie Travel & Vacations* may be the dream of many. However, it is important for students of tourism to understand that the tourism industry is mostly dominated by SMEs. Thus, most of the new students may get an opportunity to work with small travel companies that may not be the first ideal choice for them. However, working for a small company gives them more exposure. They may be working from sales to operations departments and handling many more functions that may make them more familiarized with the working of the tourism industry, giving them more confidence and know-how of the travel trade. Students may work as holiday consultants, travel experts or travel advisors, booking consultants, supervisors, product managers, sales and marketing executives, operation managers, website designers and so on depending upon the profile that they are looking for and also subject to the vacancy in the travel company.

They may work in any department such as inbound, outbound, domestic, leisure travel, business travel, study tours, sales and marketing, operations, customer service, contracting, public relations, ticketing department, visa department, information technology (IT), HR and accounts depending upon the scale of operations of the travel company.

As the travel trade is mostly technology-driven now, where most of the travel companies have become online portals, students may opt for working for these travel portals such as *Expedia, Booking.com, MakeMyTrip, Travelocity, EaseMyTrip, Cleartrip* and *Yatra*.

AIRLINES AND AIRPORTS

A very glamorous and an impressive job that appears to many youngsters pursuing tourism is to work for reputed airlines (such as Emirates, British Airways and Singapore Airlines) or at an airport. The tourism aspirants may work for various international or domestic airlines either in their reservation offices or at the airports. They may further enhance their knowledge by doing recognized certified courses in the aviation sector from certified institutes that prepare, groom and educate them on inputs specifically related to this sector.

They may opt for becoming a ground handling staff of an airline, a ticketing assistant, a reservation manager, customer service assistant, an air hostess, a flight steward, a part of the security management team, working at the information or travel desk or working as a staff in duty-free shops and so on depending upon the varied profiles available with the respective airlines or the airport.

CRUISES/OCEAN LINERS

Cruising in the waters or selling the luxurious product of cruise liners is a choice of many tourism aspirants. Some of the career options for tourism students in cruise liners or travel agencies selling cruise liner packages are in sales and marketing, operations division of travel agencies or working as a manager of logistics in the cruises, F&B managers, fitness trainers and so on.

TRANSPORTATION SECTOR

Another interesting sector to work for is the transportation sector. The tourism professionals may work for either private transport operators or coach operators such as *Cosmos Tours* and *Globus* that sell coach tours to tourists or for government-approved tourist coaches, that is, HOHO buses such as HOHO buses in New Delhi that takes the tourists on fixed sightseeing tours. Students of tourism may alternatively operate their own transportation business and generate employment for others. The aspirants may also work for *car rental companies*, such as *Avis, Hertz* and *Budget*, as travel consultants or in sales and marketing department and so on if they wish to choose transportation as a career choice.

RAILWAYS

Railways are an important recruiter for tourism professionals. The students may work as reservation agents, sales and marketing executives, supervisors and so on in tourist trains. They may also work for semi-government corporations such as IRCTC in tourism-related projects or departments such as product development, sales and marketing, operations and customer service. They may sell tour packages offered by IRCTC and even travel as tour leaders on the rail tours that they operate.

ACCOMMODATION SECTOR

Travel and Tourism students may opt to work for the accommodation sector that may include hotels and other alternative accommodations such as youth hostels, B&B inns, guest houses, self-catering apartments and caravan parks. They may also work for accommodation-related apps or websites such as AirBnB, CouchSurfing, Workaway, Trivago and Tripadvisor. Alternatively, students who have entrepreneurial skills and are risk-taking may also plan to start their own ventures in the accommodation sector that may be opening of a resort, a hotel, B&B and so on.

FOREIGN EXCHANGE COMPANIES

Students may opt for working in the foreign exchange department of travel companies. They may also work for travel companies like American Express (AMEX) that primarily deal with travellers' cheques and credit cards.

TOURIST ATTRACTION MANAGERS

The tourism professionals can also work for various attraction authorities. They may work in monuments, national parks, amusement parks, theme parks like *Disneyworld*, man-made tourist attractions like gardens, iconic structures like *Burj Al Arab*, museums and so on.

They may work as information assistants, attraction managers or officers depending upon the post on which they join.

EMBASSIES AND CONSULATES

Tourism aspirants may also work for embassies/consulates/high commissions of various countries in their own country. Generally, the job of a visa counsellor may include consultancy, checking the travel documentation, grant of visas and so on.

TRAVEL APPS

Tourism students may also opt to work with various travel applications and may work as holiday consultants, reservation assistants, customer service executives, operations executives, sales and marketing executive, digital content writers, bloggers and so on. Alternatively, they may make their own travel application if they are technically sound and may initiate their own travel business on these apps.

GOVERNMENT TOURISM DEPARTMENTS

Many tourism students join the tourism industry with the aspiration to work for the government. They may work for MOT, directorates and departments of tourism, tourism boards, STDC, local tourism authorities, and Visitor Information Centres and so on. They may work in the capacity of *tourism information officers, regional directors* or any other related government posts depending upon the structure of the government organization that they join. They may also sometimes work temporarily on tourism-related projects/schemes for the government.

RESEARCH AND TEACHING

Many students may opt to choose academics as a career after completion of their postgraduation. They may further get into research and complete their PhD or work on tourism-related projects of the government. Projects may relate to deciding on the impacts of tourism policies, campaigns and schemes, visitor profiling, tourism products being offered by the government and so on. Students may further give various tests pertaining to teaching and lectureships in schools, colleges, institutes and universities depending upon the requirement of educational institutes and government norms being followed in a particular country. In India, at present University Grants Commission-National Eligibility Test (UGC-NET) is one of the criteria for taking up government jobs in teaching besides holding a doctorate for regular teaching positions.

CULTURAL AND ENTERTAINMENT ORGANIZATIONS

Tourism professionals may work in related cultural and entertainment organizations such as theme parks, amusement parks, water parks, casinos, sporting arenas, go-kart places, gaming zones, spa centres and shopping emporiums. They may also work for cultural organizations like NGOs promoting the culture and heritage of countries such as *UNESCO, Indian National Trust for Art and Culture Heritage (INTACH)* and *ICOMOS* that promotes culture and heritage through organizing workshops, heritage walks and so on.

Dolphin Show at SeaWorld, San Diego, California

ADVENTURE TOURISM EXPERT

Many tourism aspirants look forward to taking up the adventure as an exciting career. Although adventure may not be everyone's cup of tea, still it may appear to be one of the most thrilling opportunities to the adventure enthusiasts. Careers related to adventure may be working for adventure-based travel companies who organize holidays to adventure destinations that include doing adventure activities. Students may also work as adventure activity trainers provided that they do various certified adventure-related courses in reputed institutes. They may also travel as tour leaders on adventure treks with the tourists for various companies offering adventure activities such as trekking and river rafting. Alternatively, the students may also open their own adventure companies after gaining some work experience in an adventure travel company.

WELLNESS EXPERT

A very exciting career option for tourism professionals is to be a wellness expert. Wellness tourism is really picking up well in the tourism industry, so is the need for tourism professionals to manage the wellness centres. Doing specific additional courses related to wellness may be an added advantage for tourism professionals aspiring to be wellness experts. They may work in destination spas like *Ananda in Rishikesh, India,* or in wellness centres, Yoga and meditation centres, Ayurvedic centres and so on.

CARGO COMPANIES

Students may also work for cargo and logistics companies after pursuing tourism- and cargo-related courses. They may work as managers in operations or marketing division with various cargo companies.

EVENT MANAGER

Many tourism students also opt for a career in the events sector. As *MICE sector or in other words corporate travel* is one of the most important aspects of the tourism industry, professionals are required to manage these events such as meetings, conferences, exhibitions, conventions and trade fairs. From the complete conceptualization of travel packages for the corporate movement that may include travel, stay, transportation arrangements, food arrangements, venue arrangements, registration and other logistics involved in the complete process, the tourism professionals have complete responsibility of marketing and managing these events. Budding professionals may join as events assistants or managers, meeting managers, conference managers, sports and recreation managers and so on.

FREELANCERS

Students may also work as freelancers by attaching themselves to various companies based on contracts as tour leaders and tour guides that give them enough independence to work within stipulated hours. Let us have a discussion on each of these roles.

Tour Leader

Tour leaders are basically responsible for accompanying the groups of tourists from one destination to another. Taking care of the guests and the logistics during the entire duration of the trip is the complete responsibility of the tour leader. For this reason, we may also refer to them as companions of tourists, their caretakers, destination spokesperson and grievance handler.

Students who have good managerial skills and can work under the pressure without losing their calm may choose this profession. However, the most exciting part of this profession is that it promises a lucrative career, extensive travel (that may be domestic or international), autonomy, less supervision and a life full of exciting and thrilling experiences and experiments.

Tour Guide

Tour guides guide the groups or individuals at attractions that may be historical buildings, monuments, attractions and so on that have a natural, cultural or a heritage appeal.

Many tourism aspirants who have an interest in showcasing the culture of their country and who are good orators and want to exchange and share the culture of their country with others may wish to choose tour guiding as a profession. This is a very exciting career option for many as it is a freelancing profession that promises independence in one's job where the guide is his/her own boss.

ENTREPRENEURSHIP

After gaining some experience working for travel companies, tourism aspirants can also start their own businesses. They may open their travel company, a transport company, start a hotel or a B&B, a tourist cafe, an entertainment centre and so on.

TICKETING

Another profession opted by many students of tourism is working for ticketing division in airlines or travel companies. Students may begin as reservation executives after doing a certificate course in CRS such as *Amadeus, Galileo, Worldspan* and *Sabre* or studying this CRS module while pursuing their graduation or postgraduation.

TRAVEL WRITING

As generating content is the soul of any tourism business, travel writing can be a very interesting option for all those who have a flair for writing. The budding aspirants may work for various travel media-based organizations such as travel magazines, travel newsletters or give write-ups in various newspapers. Alternatively, they may also work for travel companies as content developers for their websites or developing any related digital marketing material such as pamphlets and brochures.

TRAVEL BLOGGER

A new trend that has recently emerged among the youngsters is to travel to destinations and then post their write-ups about the destination on their travel blogs. These are called as travel bloggers. Travel bloggers also create their own videos of the destination and post them on YouTube. They may be called as *vloggers*. The number of followers they are able to generate on their websites increases their credibility and thus improves their chances of increasing their business.

TRAVEL PHOTOGRAPHY

For all those who have a penchant for capturing the images in their camera lens, travel photography can be a good career option. Once a person turns from an amateur to a professional, he/she can work for various travel companies and tourism boards and sell these pieces of art to these clients and sometimes even to the public and earn very lucrative offers.

INTERPRETERS

An important essential for tourism professionals is to get their hands-on with a language. Knowledge of an additional language is value addition in tourism that can open additional avenues for students aspiring to take up a career in tourism. Learning a language and gradually becoming an expert in a language can help them choose the option of language interpreters. These kinds of jobs are highly in demand as there are a lot of international tourists coming to the country that may be coming for leisure or conducting business. These interpreters may be hired by foreign tourists to understand the local language of a place. Additionally, these language interpreters may be called for international assignments by the government of the country to interpret the documents or work with the delegates.

CHALLENGES OF THE TRAVEL AND TOURISM CAREER

Having discussed the various career options in this trade along with the various advantages of choosing tourism as a career, it is equally important to discuss the various issues affecting this industry. Many concerns discourage the new aspirants to take up this as a career option. *One of the major issues of this industry is the low salary offered to postgraduates vis-à-vis other industries. Due to the fewer remuneration structures prevailing in the industry,* the professionals leave their existing jobs at the drop of a hat even for a very less increase in the salary. Thus, it is important to set standard benchmarks for the salaries to be in place for the tourism aspirants that encourage them to choose this as a career. Another discouraging factor may be the *slow career progression time* that takes for a novice to reach a particular position in the travel trade over the traditional career choices that makes students think twice before choosing this profession. Also, the *issue of job security* and the *lack of work–life balance,* especially during the peak season, are some of the obvious reasons for youngsters to think twice before choosing this profession.

SUMMARY

The tourism industry offers a very promising career for all those who are ready to slog and have the patience to bear the fruit of their labour. The budding aspirants may choose various career options within this industry depending upon their interests and aptitude and the profiles available in the company. Students may choose to work either in the private or public sector. Although the public sector has limited openings, the private sector offers an array of choices for the students to choose from. They may work for travel companies, airlines, hotels, airports, railways, transport companies, cruise liners, freelancers or may start their own ventures, get into research and consultancy or opt for government jobs depending upon their interests. The new prevailing career trends in tourism are related to working as travel bloggers, travel writers, travel photographers, adventure trainers and so on. For all those who want to make travel a part of their lives and who want novelty and thrill in their profession, this is the right career move.

ACTIVITIES

Activity 1

Examine the various career opportunities in the tourism sector. Now discuss the career opportunity that you would opt for along with valid reasons and justifications.

Activity 2

Interview any three professionals working for the tourism sector in different domains such as airlines, hotels and travel agencies. Ask them the various merits and challenges associated with this profession. Now discuss and share your learnings with the class.

Overtourism 33

LEARNING OBJECTIVES

The given chapter shall clarify the following:

- What is overtourism?
- Which are the destinations in the world that have been affected by overtourism?
- What are the ways in which we may combat overtourism?

UNTOURIST GUIDE MOVEMENT IN AMSTERDAM!

- Amsterdam invites you to be a part of the 'Untourist Movement' and co-create the future of travel in the world by being more than a tourist to the city, which could be 'a changemaker' or a 'travel pioneer'.
- To cut the cord of mass tourism hitting the city, the movement aims at asking the tourists to contribute to the well-being of the local communities, by engaging in fun activities along with the locals while visiting Amsterdam.
- With the aim to disperse the high-tourist traffic visiting the most popular places of Amsterdam, which is causing harm to the environment and the local community, this movement encourages travellers to explore Amsterdam from a newer perspective by visiting lesser-known areas of Amsterdam, interacting with locals and indulging in off-beat tourist activities.
- The tourists transform themselves from a regular tourist to a changemaker by participating in tourist activities such as 'marrying an Amsterdammer', 'plastic fishing in the canals'

(finding trash in the canals and helping in cleaning the city), weed dating, making souvenirs from trash, cooking Dutch dishes with kids and growing trees.

- Creating lives for the betterment of localities of Amsterdam, this movement involves various social entrepreneurs, tour guides, hotels, hostels and all others who want to contribute to tourism in a better way in the city.

INTRODUCTION

The saying that 'tourism kills tourism' holds absolutely true in today's era. The extent of tourism development at the cost of the environment and local communities has caused unprecedented harm to some of the destinations of the world.

The tourist spots across the world are bearing the burden of overtourism. Many nations of the world are sick of tourism activities and are finding new ways to stop this activity. If tourism keeps growing at an uninterrupted pace, soon people would find it impossible to fulfil their travel fantasies. We are heading towards irreversible damage of earth if we do not take enough steps to balance tourism.

Since 2017, the travel industry and media began to talk about the negative impacts of tourism and coined the term 'overtourism' when there was a sudden backlash against mass tourism globally by the local communities. The local communities of many countries of the world no more want tourists. For them, enough is enough. They have become openly vocal about it. For them, tourism is not tourism, it is an invasion into their privacy. For them, tourism is a source of grief.

Since then, this issue has been a trending topic of discussion among researchers, academicians, environment authorities, the news industry and the general public too. The government is having debates and discussions about how many tourists should be allowed in a destination to safeguard the natural resources and attractions of that place.

The country of *Amsterdam* had 19 million visitors in 2018, and its local population is under 1 million. Likewise, *Prague* attracted 10.6 million tourists when they had only 1.4 million residents in 2018. Overcrowding is an understatement for *Barcelona* as they had more than 30 million visitors with just 1.6 million local population. This kind of overpopulation in a place puts a lot of strain on the local resources and the environment of that destination which causes a lot of negative effects. The uncontrolled growth of tourism without focusing on the impacts has led to overtourism. These impacts are more evident when the carrying capacity of a destination is overwhelmed. This carrying capacity is threatened when substantially a high number of people are visiting a destination. Overtourism has affected many places of the world today, including many cities of European countries such as *Barcelona, Venice, Iceland* and *Budapest.* Croatia, which became a famous tourist destination after the television series *Game of Thrones* was shot there, has become a victim of tourism too.

The advent of low-cost airlines, cheap accommodation options, aggressive marketing strategies adopted by various destination marketers of the world along with an improved economy has led to an upsurge in travel. Travelling to different parts of the world is almost within every one's reach now.

Many countries such as Spain and Venice that had over-commercialized themselves and had allowed mass tourism activity to flourish for decades due to the economic benefits that the tourism activity was contributing to them have now closed their doors for the tourists. Their uninterrupted approach of mass tourism has caused havoc to the environment as well as the local population of these countries. The chronic overcrowding of destinations with hordes of tourists visiting the towns and cities of Europe in summers has led to a backlash among the locals who are facing the rising prices and depletion of local resources. Many demonstrations and marches by locals in the cities of Europe along with the paintings on the walls saying, 'Enough is Enough', 'Tourist Go back Home' are visible all over Europe. Such has been the rage of the locals that *a group of tourists in a coach was attacked by locals in Barcelona, Spain in 2017*.

Venice Flood

On 12 November 2019, Venice experienced the worst flood since 1966.

Italy had declared a state of emergency in Venice after the Italian city was engulfed by 1.87 m (6 ft) high water levels.

Two people were dead.

Climate change is behind the highest tide in 50 years.

The famous saying, 'See Venice and Die', has gone against this country. The city on the sea has always been in the bucket list of many travellers. Approximately 25 million tourists visit this small city of Italy every year, out of which around 14 million tourists are daytrippers who spend hardly a day in Venice visiting the church and taking a gondola ride in canals. The total population of Venice now is around 50,000 people. The 'Eat and Run coaches' for daytrippers have become a menace for the locals. *In 2018, 594 ships entered the city of Venice* causing air and noise pollution. It is reported that one cruise ship emits air pollutants equivalent to one million cars. So we can well imagine the extent of environmental damage to this city.

In fact, AirBnB is killing the city as there are more than 8,000 registered properties (as in 2019) listed on the AirBnB as many locals of the city have converted their residential apartments to lucrative tourism rentals. This has resulted in squeezing the locals out of the homes as they cannot match their rent incomes to tourists' rents. Thousands of the angry residents of Venice have been found on the roads marching and displaying banners saying, 'My future is Venice'. They have been protesting to keep the cruise ships out of Italy's city lagoon. The *clash of a large ship with a riverboat in 2019* which killed a few tourists also added fuel to the fire for the locals. The last year floods are a testimony to this, and the rising sea levels are drowning Venice. *In fact, it is being considered in the 'World Heritage in Danger' list of UNESCO.*

In order to deal with overtourism suffered by Venice, various rules have been introduced for the tourists to abide by, the non-compliance of which may lead to punishments or even deportation of the tourists. Some of the rules to be observed by the tourists that are considered an offence in Venice are littering, drinking alcohol in public, swimming in canals, sunbathing, loitering, riding bikes or even sitting around and outside monuments and roaming around shirtless. Tourists are fined in Venice if caught in such acts.

Rome is also considering limiting tourists, and it has already started imposing rules on the tourists. The famous *Trevi Fountain*, which is a must-see in the itineraries of tourists visiting Rome, have the continuous patrolling by the police to ensure that nobody swims in the waters of the fountains.

Marry an Amsterdammer

- In 2019, to combat with overtourism and its negative effects, Amsterdam has come up with an innovative way called 'Marry an Amsterdammer for a Day'.
- This initiative is a part of 'Untourist Movement' that aims at making Amsterdam more liveable for both residents and tourists.
- This initiative aims to diversify the tourist traffic to less-crowded areas of the city that are equally beautiful. A fake wedding takes place between the tourist and the local in which they are dressed in the Dutch attire.
- The decorations are done in such a manner which gives the real feel of a wedding. After the mock vows, the couple leaves for honeymoon to lesser-known destinations and takes part in activities such as picking up plastic from the canals, laughter therapy with lonely locals and interacting with people about culture and so much more!

Taking another example of *Amsterdam, famous for its marijuana cafes, is a Mecca for bachelor parties*. It has become a playground for such unruly tourists who behave irresponsibly after drinking. Screaming on the roads late night and having a brawl with others is a common sight for the residents of Amsterdam who cannot even have a peaceful night sleep. To deal with overtourism, the city that receives more tourists than its own population has now taken it seriously to stop the mass tourism movement. It has taken various measures such as banning any new shop opening for the tourists, cracking down the AirBnB rentals, using technology embedded in travel cards to find out where the tourists are visiting and their timings of visits, live streaming of queues outside the attractions to make the tourists delay their visits, Amsterdam's council moratorium on new hotels besides the Untourist Movement to curb the numbers of tourists visiting the city.

Tourism has created a huge negative impact on the livelihood of the locals too. To explain it with an example, *Bloemenmarkt (iconic floating flowers market) in Amsterdam* has beautiful flower shops which are now closing due to overtourism as the local sellers are complaining that tourists block the locals from buying the flowers because they keep clicking pictures.

Another example is of the *train street in Hanoi, Vietnam,* which has become a famous tourist spot due to the single-train track that runs through the homes, cafes and shops. The place became an Instagram-famous street, as it became a hub for selfie-obsessed tourists standing or sitting on the train tracks or lining up dangerously on the side of tracks, waiting to take a picture of the passing train. Because of tourists coming in, many localities opened up cafes and shops near the tracks. As the number of tourists increased, the government had to shut down the cafes on the streets as it became a safety issue because of the irresponsible behaviour of the tourists visiting the place with the sole objective of clicking their pictures putting their own and other lives at risk.

Denmark also has realized that it is the end of tourism. It has removed the word tourist in favour of its residents.

In fact, many destinations of the world are shutting down their attractions temporarily to restore the harm done by the tourists to these attractions. For example, the world-famous tourist spot, *Boracay island in the Philippines* known for its white beaches had to be shut down by the government for six months in 2018 as it had turned into a cesspool and the only way to rehabilitate the island, restore its ecology and bring back its former glory was to restrict the movement of tourists completely to the island. Since then, there has been a restriction of tourists visiting the island. As was the similar case with *Maya Bay in Phi Phi Island, Thailand,* that has been closed since 2018 and is likely to open in 2021 to restore its ecology.

COMBATING OVERTOURISM

We need to understand that tourism is about the people-to-people connection that is the only key to increase the visits of tourists at a destination besides achieving sustainability of a destination. We need to be more mindful and respectful towards destinations. Instead of focusing on marketing the destinations, we need to shift our focus to managing destinations. We need to understand that benefits of tourism cannot just be measured in monetary terms, but it has an environmental, a cultural and social aspect too.

Thus, the government needs to control the tourist numbers. It needs to ensure that travellers visit in small numbers. It needs to sensitize itself towards the extent of harm that overtourism can cause to the environment as well as society. It may introduce the following measures in destinations to discourage the tourists from visiting them:

- Increase tourist taxes.
- Raise prices of services used by the tourist.
- Introduce permits for certain attractions restricting the number of visitors per day (e.g., China has put a capping to the number of tourists to 65,000 visitors per day visiting the Badaling section, the highest visited spot of the Great Wall of China in order to protect and restore it. Besides this, they have also made the reservation process stricter by making it possible for travellers to make the reservations online, that too a week prior to their visit to the site).
- Introducing the trekking permits to maintain the ecology of mountains.
- Banning cruise ships over a certain size.
- Charging cruise liners for docking.
- Educating tourists to behave as responsible tourists.
- Introducing strict rules for tourists to be followed.
- Sharing of responsibility and accountability by the tourists while visiting a destination.

> ## Barcelona
>
> - Barcelona is suffering from overtourism with more than 30 million visitors in the year 2018, and their total population is 1.62 million.
> - The local streets are always jam-packed with tourists which makes it hard for the locals to move around.
> - Due to the increase in tourism, the local shops are now replaced with rental bikes, souvenir shops and rental accommodation services.
> - The big group of tourists block subway validating ticket machines which cause trouble for the locals to do their daily jobs.

SUMMARY

Overtourism has been a big reason for causing negative impacts on the environment as well as society. Nature is connected to everything. Destroying it will bring nothing but doom to mankind. Crossing the limit of a destination's land capacity can cause huge damage to the nature and cultural heritage of a destination. The society is also facing several negative reflections of tourism, as the local communities are feeling that they are better off without tourism. Tourism can cause huge damage to the social values of the local communities. It is very important to understand the importance of such values, and tourists must behave respectfully. Such negative impacts can cause the destinations to shut down the entry of tourists for a while to repair the damage caused by overtourism. Stability and control on visits of tourists will maintain the balance between the environment and tourism. Every individual should try to bring some positive change in themselves by avoiding the actions which lead to the destruction of nature and the local resources of a destination.

ACTIVITIES

Activity 1

Nature is suffering too much. Give concrete solutions to help stabilize the damage from tourism's point of view. State various possible solutions which can help in solving overtourism in a destination.

Activity 2

List the names of places which have suffered because of overtourism. Discuss the issues that they are facing due to overtourism.

Activity 3

Did you visit any such place where the beauty of a destination is ruined because of overtourism? Discuss with the class.

BIBLIOGRAPHY

www.abc.net.au (accessed on 31 July 2020).
www.express.co.uk (accessed on 31 July 2020).
www.untouristguide.com (accessed on 31 July 2020).

Travel Green: Practise Responsible Travel

34

LEARNING OBJECTIVES

The given chapter shall clarify the following:

- What is responsible travel?
- What are the ways in which a tourist may practise responsible travel?

'TERA MERA BEACH' CAMPAIGN

- Beaches are a fragile ecosystem and are an important product that need to be protected and kept clean and hygienic in order to attract tourists at a destination.
- On the similar line of the Netherlands, a Goa lifeguard service agency, namely Drishti Marine, initiated a 150-day cleanliness campaign known as 'Tera Mera Beach' on Baga Beach in 2017, which aimed at sensitizing the people about coastal hygiene, waste segregation and spreading awareness about tourist responsibility.
- Pop-up waste bars were set up which offered free drinks in exchange for beach trash such as beer bottle caps, cigarette butts and bottles.
- Many other stakeholders supported the campaign such as the Department of Goa Tourism, Government of Goa, Museum of Goa and Nestle.

INTRODUCTION

When tourism is promoted beyond the carrying capacity of a destination, it brings destruction to the environment as well as to the local communities of a destination. It is very important for the leaders of the tourism industry to understand that in the rat race of increasing the number of tourists, we are forgetting the harm that tourism is doing to a destination. Thus, it is very important to promote eco-friendly ways to travel green. We need to promote responsible tourism that fixes the responsibility on tourists as well as the various stakeholders of the tourism industry to behave responsibly towards a destination.

When tourists visit a destination, they carry a lot of responsibility along with them. Behaving responsibly towards a destination while visiting it is one of the least expected courtesies that a traveller can extend to the local community and environment of a destination. Practising sustainability during vacations is the new trend.

Responsible tourism is an approach to tourism that advocates responsibility on the part of tourists as well as the various tourism service providers involved in the delivery of services. This approach aims at respecting the lives of the host community as well as the environment of a destination. It aims at leaving the destination in the same state, if not better. It focuses on contributing to the economic, social, cultural and environmental well-being of a destination while visiting it. Thus, we may say, the tourists may be referred to as the 'champions of promoting responsible tourism in a destination'.

Apparently, the new-age traveller is more conscious now about his/her carbon footprints. He/she knows that his/her irresponsible approach can devastate a destination that may eventually diminish tourism there. Now, let us have an understanding of the various ways in which the tourists may act as responsible tourists while paying a visit to a destination.

ACT RESPONSIBLY TOWARDS THE ECOSYSTEMS

Every destination has a fragile ecosystem that tourists visit. The flora, fauna and the environment of a place need not be disturbed when tourists visit a destination. The ecosystems of a destination need to be respected. The tourists, thus, may observe the following.

Avoid Visiting Areas That Are Restricted

Many places known for their natural beauty and which have a fragile ecology have a restriction for visiting them such as certain islands, forest areas, biosphere reserves, mountains, islands, rivers and beaches. Some tourists in order to explore the pristine nature try to disrupt the ecology of a place by visiting there and not following the regulations set by the concerned authorities there. Such irresponsible behaviour shown by the tourists can adversely put a strain on the environment and may affect the ecosystems which should be allowed to flourish in their natural settings with least human intervention. Thus, tourists should not visit areas that are restricted by the authorities.

Follow the Rules while Visiting Havens of Flora and Fauna

Many national parks and wildlife sanctuaries have well-defined rules to be followed by the tourists. These may be as follows:

- Follow the code of conduct.
- Do not remove flora.
- Respect wildlife.
- Avoid chasing animals.
- Maintain a safe distance from wildlife.
- Seek the assistance of a forest guard.
- Do not do photography/use flashlights or make videos of the animals while visiting these havens of wildlife that may put stress on the wildlife.
- Do not make noise while visiting these national parks that may disturb them. Shouting, talking loudly, honking in the jeep safaris, playing music and so on are all prohibited in these areas that must be taken care of by the tourists. The tourists must observe silence.
- Do not hand-feed animals wherever prohibited.
- Avoid wearing bright clothes and using perfumes while visiting these places that may attract wildlife. Browns and greens should be preferred while visiting such places.
- Avoid buying animal products as souvenirs.
- Try to move into small groups.
- Do not litter in the surroundings.
- While making travel bookings, opt for sustainable tour operators.

ACT RESPONSIBLY TOWARDS THE LOCAL COMMUNITY AT THE DESTINATION

Every destination has its own social fabric and its own local laws. Thus, while visiting a destination, tourists must observe the following things:

- Before visiting a destination, research, learn and know about the local sensitivities expected to be followed at a destination. Respect the local sensitivities.
- Respect the local laws. In many countries of the world, littering, chewing gum, smoking, drinking in public and spitting is illegal. There are penalties or punishments if the tourists break these laws. Thus, it is important to respect such rules laid out by the government authorities.

- Always respect the local culture and social customs of the place being visited.
- Dress according to the place. If dressing conservatively is the norm, follow it.
- Learn the basic dialects in the native language of a destination. The local community feels more connected with such tourists who show interest in their local language. It also makes them feel more important.
- Interact with the locals only if they like doing so.
- Respect their privacy at all times.
- Be open to cultural differences.
- Be polite to the native people. Ensure not to hurt them.
- Do not entertain the beggars.
- Shop local. As much as possible, try to buy local products of a destination to boost its local economy.
- Do not unnecessarily bargain with the local shopkeepers or artisans and so on while buying things from them.
- While visiting religious places of a local community, follow their norms. Respect the religious places and their code of conduct. If photography is prohibited, do not click. Remove footwear outside in religious places wherever required such as while visiting temples in India, tourists are expected to do the same. Dress conservatively. If one has to cover the body with appropriate clothing while visiting a worship place, that should be done without disobeying. Cover your head with a proper headgear if it is required. For example, while visiting the *Gurudwaras,* the worship place of the Sikh community, being in appropriate clothing with head covered with a scarf or a handkerchief or any other cloth is mandatory before going inside. Likewise, for travellers visiting *Jama Masjid in Old Delhi, India,* the holy place of Muslims, for tourists who are not properly covered with enough clothing are required to cover their body with a gown before entering inside the mosque. Thus, tourists must respect these religious norms and must observe the dress code wherever required.
- Tourists must also try to move to a city in fewer numbers so that they do not disrupt the local life of residents, such as creating traffic jams and disturbing the movement of locals on the street.
- Many tourists treat the locals as the tourist objects that they want to capture in their camera lens. Thus, it is always advisable for the tourists that before taking any pictures of natives of a country, the tourist must seek their permission. If they are not comfortable with it, the tourists must respect their decision and not force them.
- On coming back from the destination, promote the local culture of the visited destination to your family and friends.

ACT RESPONSIBLY TOWARDS THE ATTRACTIONS

Tourists travel to a destination generally with the purpose of seeing the attractions. Thus, being responsible at the attractions is very important. *Destruction of preserved ancient rock paintings at Karikiyoor in Tamil Nadu* by apathetic trekkers using whitener pens for writing religious and political messages *and carving of names on rocks by couples over the 5,000-years-old imagery of Irula tribe* is a leading example of how tourists can ruin and disrespect the resident tribes and communities of a destination. To ensure that such incidents do not happen in the future, the following things may be observed while visiting attractions.

- Every attraction may have different rules and regulations to be followed by the tourists. Be aware of the attractions' rules and regulations.
- It is also important not only to be aware but also respect the dos and don'ts as laid out by an attraction.
- Avoid photography and videography inside the attraction, wherever prohibited.
- Do not litter the surroundings of the attraction. Make use of garbage bins.
- Maintain discipline at all times.
- Always move in designated queues to avoid chaos at the attraction. Avoid standing in groups so as to not obstruct the views of other tourists.
- Many items may be prohibited from being taken inside an attraction. Respect that.
- Do not damage the walls of historical sites or artefacts by writing on them.
- Do not touch artefacts or any prohibited displays in an attraction such as artefacts in a museum or flowers in a garden.
- Do not smoke or drink at the attractions.
- There are many attractions in which one needs to maintain silence, especially worship places like *Lotus Temple in New Delhi* and memorials like the *War Memorial, India Gate in New Delhi*. Thus, tourists must maintain the sanctity of such places by observing silence there.
- Avoid printing tickets to save the paper and benefit the environment.

ACT RESPONSIBLY TOWARDS THE ADVENTURE TRAILS

While going for adventure treks, we need to ensure that campsites should always be left clean as they were before. Thus, we need to observe the following:

- Do not litter the surroundings.
- Avoid campfires and open fires in places.
- Reduce wood usage while camping.
- Avoid trampling.
- Plant saplings near the campsites on the trails.
- No cutting of trees or roots should be done on the treks.
- Keep a track of your waste.
- Take all non-biodegradable garbage back for proper disposal.
- Have the group size according to the carrying capacity of the place.

ACTING RESPONSIBLY TOWARDS THE HOTELS

While visiting hotels, tourists are expected to behave responsibly by following the set norms of a hotel. Some of these are as follows:

- Do not destroy the property of the hotel.
- Conserve energy while staying in the hotel by switching off the lights when going out of the room.
- Save water by using tap, mug and bucket. Chuck the showers.
- Avoid giving your linen such as towels and bedsheets for washing every day in order to conserve the water.
- Choose sustainable options for a stay like eco-lodges.
- Never leave your baggage unattended.
- Do not steal things from a hotel such as toiletries and towels.

Yet some other ways of being responsible towards the destination are as follows:

- Ride a cycle. Opt to cycle instead of driving wherever possible. It saves energy consumption and keeps the destination pollution-free.
- Rent hybrid cars and take eco-friendly trips.
- Use public transportation wherever possible.
- Buy organic produce from farmers of a destination.

Not only the tourists but also the tour operators should carry the equal onus of advocating this important cause of responsible tourism. Following are the ways in which the tour operators may practise responsible tourism:

- Educate the tourists about the importance of responsible travel through organizing interactive sessions, audio-visual presentations, printed material and so on.
- Train tour leaders about the importance of practising responsible tourism so that they may share the same information with the tourists.
- Organize campaigns to sensitize the tourists on a large scale. This may be done by organizing workshops on responsible tourism at tourists' attractions, organizing conferences/seminars involving other stakeholders of the tourism community, taking the responsibility to keep a monument clean and so on.
- Include sustainable accommodation such as eco-lodges and ecotels for tourists in travel packages to promote the cause.

SUMMARY

Travel is a very important responsibility that each one of us needs to understand. Almost everyone on the planet is a traveller now. This increases our responsibility and accountability towards the mother earth. Tourism is not only about leisure. We also need to understand the nuances involved in it. We need to practise it in such a way that we also leave the destinations the same way or even better for our future generations. Thus, tourists must act responsibly towards the ecosystems, local communities, attractions, adventure trails, hotels and so on. We also need to understand and appreciate the role of tour operators in promoting the cause of responsible tourism by educating the tourists. It is important that as new-age travellers, we leave footprints in the destinations that we visit.

ACTIVITIES

Activity 1

If you were a tour operator, how would you practise responsible travel?

Activity 2

Name any two destinations in the world which according to you are practising responsible tourism. Also, discuss the ways in which they are promoting responsible travel.

Case Studies

E.1. SRI LANKA EASTER SUNDAY TERROR

Introduction

Also referred to as the 'Pearl of the Indian Ocean', Sri Lanka is a beautiful island country in South Asia. With a stunning coastline and the marine national parks, the country is known for its pristine beaches, serene climate, ancient heritages (that include the UNESCO's eight world heritage sites), scenic wildlife, irresistible cuisine and, of course, the tea plantations. It is a dream destination for surfers, divers and snorkelers. The Sri Lanka Tourism Development Authority (SLTDA; the principal governing body of Sri Lanka, responsible for planning, developing and promoting tourism in Sri Lanka) offers many interesting tourism products which have become a magnet for tourists from all over the world. Tourists are mostly attracted to this country to experience beaches, nature-based tours, pilgrimage tours for Hindus such as Ramayana Yatra and pilgrimage tours for Buddhists, adventure activities such as hiking, underwater diving, scuba diving and hot air ballooning; traditional festivals, events, wellness tourism, wildlife expeditions, heritage tours and many more. In 2018, about 2 million foreign tourists visited the island which was an increase in the number as compared to 2017's data. *Sri Lanka has many accolades to its credit including the Best Travel Destination in 2019 by Lonely Planet, one of the top 15 best islands in the world by travel + leisure and many more!*

On 21 April 2019, Sri Lanka was celebrating the Easter. This auspicious occasion is celebrated as the holiest festival worldwide, especially amongst the Christian community. That day, many people were praying in the churches of Sri Lanka when a horrible incident happened. Right around 8:25 AM, a series of similar bombs went off in several churches and three five-star hotels in Sri Lanka killing more than 250 people (including about 42 foreigners) and injuring more than 500. It was the most traumatic terror attack targeting eight locations where many locals and tourists were present.

This incident had a heavy impact on the tourism of Sri Lanka as the death of tourists in the bombing scared people from travelling to the country for a long period. After the bombings, the tourism industry faced a huge economic crisis, and the high number of jobs were lost within the industry. All tourism service providers were devasted with the crises as the tourism industry was the main source of economy for them. As the after effect, the beaches in Sri Lanka which once used to be filled with tourists were now empty. People who provided transportation services, souvenir shopkeepers, water-sporting activities, beach resorts and so on faced great financial difficulties as tourism was their main source of bread and butter.

In 2018, Sri Lanka was one of the top destinations in the world for tourists, but the Easter bombings in April 2019 caused major downfall for tourism. Terrorism has a very negative impact on the tourism of a destination as the country loses a high number of tourists, sometimes even permanently.

Currently, tourism of Sri Lanka is gaining back their reputation and some number of tourists. The revival is slow, but the authorities are assuring that the percentage of tourist will be back on track very soon.

Conclusion

Terrorism is a major downfall for tourism of any destination as it not only causes a high loss in the number of tourists but also disturbs the local economy. Sri Lanka went through a tough time when the world started losing interest in travelling to the country which caused job loss in the tourism industry. Government authorities are taking initiative to revive tourism and make it stable, if not popular as before.

Learning Outcomes

- When tourists decide to travel to a destination, the first thing that they check is how safe it is. A destination having a history of unsafe environment creates a negative impact on the tourism of a destination. Travel advisories issued by the governments for their citizens further restrain and warn the travellers from visiting the unsafe destinations.
- Lack of tourist traffic in a destination adversely affects the tourism service providers as they suffer the most. Some of them are travel agents, tour operators, hoteliers, cab drivers, tour guides, merchandisers and so on.
- It is up to the dedication and initiative of the tourism development authority and the governing bodies to take collective measures for reviving the wounded tourism of a destination.

Points for Discussion

- Terrorism has caused the destruction of tourism in many destinations. Name a few of those destinations and discuss their impact.
- In the case of terrorism and tourism, what measures should be taken by the government? Discuss your opinions.

Bibliography

https://www.srilanka.travel/ (accessed on 31 July 2020).
https://www.sltda.gov.lk/ (accessed on 31 July 2020).

E.2. JOHN'S TRAVEL NIGHTMARE

Introduction

John who lives in Vancouver in Canada is a travel enthusiast. Being a backpacker, John has a huge appetite for travelling and likes to read a lot about new places that he can explore. He works hard for six months, saves money and travels for the next six months. John is very spontaneous when it comes to travelling. So the idea of making an itinerary is unnecessary for him. This time, he wanted to visit Mumbai city which is in the state of Maharashtra. He was very excited for his upcoming trip to India as he had read amazing things about Mumbai being the 'Bollywood hub' of India and also its beaches, architecture, history and people. Also, he saw beautiful tourism advertisements and campaigns of **Incredible!ndia** (an international tourism marketing campaign initiated by MOT, Government of India, since 2002), which further reinforced his resolve to visit the country.

In the month of June, he spent his last working days in his office sincerely and then went home to pack his bags for the trip. He is a very careful person when it comes to packing as his history in travelling has taught him enough. Little did he know, he was about to face his worst nightmare in the dream city of India.

The Gateway of India, Mumbai

After a long flight, he reached the Mumbai airport. Too excited to rest, he could not wait to see the Gateway of India as he had heard so much about that historic place. Before getting in the taxi, he withdrew his wallet from his bag for buying some water and kept it in the back pocket of his jeans. As an Indian, we are very much aware of the risks of such actions. After he sat inside a taxi, he saw a warning notice behind the seat of the driver which said, 'Keep your belongings safe.' The solo explorer was unconcerned about the severity of these warnings. He was unaware of the problems and dangers faced by tourists when they visit Mumbai city.

After a few minutes, John reached the Gateway of India. He was very happy to soak in the beautiful architecture and the gentle sea breeze. He had never seen so many people in one place, which added to his excitement. After roaming around for a while, he decided to try the local street food. When he reached for his wallet to pay for his food, he noticed that it was gone. He panicked and aimlessly looked around. He searched his bags for the 10th time but with no luck. He went to the local police station and asked for their aid, but nothing was going to bring his wallet back which had plenty of money, credit card, visa card and a few pieces of important paper.·

After a whole stressful day, he somehow visited a family friend who lives in Mumbai. He helped John in his distress situation. Because of this incident, he had to cut short his travel plans as his whole perspective about Mumbai changed. The thrill and energy he had before the incident was all gone. After a few days, he decided to go back to Canada, and since then he had never set foot in Mumbai again. This incident not only affected his trip but also his will to visit the destination again in the future. He truly felt Incredible !ndia.

Conclusion

Travelling is not always a pleasant experience and certainly not a cakewalk. Sometimes, it might become the most challenging experience for a person. Travelling can be very unpredictable, and therefore, one must be prepared for the challenges one might have to face during travel.

Learning Outcomes

- Whenever travelling to any new place, taking care of your belongings should be your prime responsibility.
- Travellers should be aware of what measures to take if and after they face any such problematic situation.
- The NTOs and RTOs make a lot of promises to woo the tourists through their tourism marketing campaigns. However, it is their job to enable those promises by providing visitors with positive experiences during their visit to the country.
- Every tourist attraction should have proper security systems and guards to ensure the safety of tourists there. The government must ensure to depute the tourist police at the important tourist attractions.
- It is the responsibility of destination authorities to ensure that tourists have a pleasant experience at a destination. Such negative incidents may affect the reputation and image of a destination, which may adversely affect the tourist traffic to a country. Thus, to avoid the negative publicity of a destination, the destination authorities must take proper steps to avoid such incidents during the visit of the tourists.
- One must pay attention to the travel advisories happening before travelling to a new destination. Ignoring such details can be fatal.

Points for Discussion

- Every place is distinct. What are the types of challenges a tourist might face while travelling to a destination, especially a foreign country?
- The Canadian solo traveller was unaware of the problems one might face in Mumbai. What are the different ways to tackle such situations?

E.3. THE STINGY STARFISH

Introduction

Sanchi had been planning for a long time to go on a trip to Goa with her friends. But every time some or the other problem had cropped up that had consequently led to the plan being cancelled. But this time, Sanchi was hell-bent on making this trip happen. So she convinced all her friends to take out time from their schedules and booked their tickets. When they reached Goa, the first thought, all of them had, was to go and visit a beach as they were very excited about visiting one for the first time. So they went to their hotel, hurriedly checked into their rooms, kept their luggage inside, freshened up and called up the person who was supposed to lend them his car which they had booked on a daily rental basis. They then decided that they would be visiting Cavelossim Beach in South Goa as it was very peaceful and not crowded like the beaches in North Goa and would be best for their first experience. So they drove around and reached the beach. Everyone was interested in getting pictures clicked and so was Sanchi. They decided to venture near the sea as the aesthetic backdrop would result in some amazing pictures. So everyone started moving towards the beach. Suddenly, Sanchi felt a sharp sting on her right foot. She looked down and was aghast to find out that a starfish had bitten her. She was overcome with dreadful pain and could not move even an inch. She gave a yelp, and all her friends looked towards her to see what had happened. They were shocked to see her writhing in pain. None of them had any knowledge about handling this situation. As the beach was very secluded there were no locals who could help them, only one other tourist couple who also did not know what to do. When her friends thought of looking up the hospital number on the internet, they were disappointed to find out that none of their phones was working, as there was no signal. They somehow managed to get Sanchi on the road and kept yelling for help. Suddenly a car that was passing by stopped and luckily the people inside were locals who knew exactly what to do and where to take her. They gave her immediate first aid and then took her to the nearby clinic. Sanchi was advised to take rest for some time. This incident ruined their holiday, which they otherwise had taken to relieve their stress, but instead, they were left traumatized seeing their friend in this condition.

Conclusion

This case is about the gang of girls whose holiday experience turned out to be a nightmare. Intending to visit a beach, they had never imagined that one of them would ever be bitten by a starfish thot would ruin their holiday at Goa.

Learning Outcomes

- While visiting beaches, one must be aware of the good time to visit it. At times, entry to the beaches is restricted which people must abide by.
- The tourist must also educate himself/herself about the possible dangers, if any, associated with an attraction.
- It is equally important for the tourist to abide by the rules and regulations laid for an attraction such as a beach.
- The attraction authorities must have the first-aid facility with trained staff readily available at an attraction (in this case, a beach) to assist the tourist in case of any medical exigency.

Points for Discussion

- Share any of the similar incidents that may have happened with you during the trip. Discuss the steps, if any, you took to overcome the situation.
- While travelling to a beach destination, what are the things that you would consider to ensure your safety and well-being?

INDEX

CPSIA information can be obtained
at www.ICGtesting.com
Printed in the USA
LVHW100456140721
692619LV00003B/5

9 789353 885106